Awakening *from* History

Books by Edmond Taylor

The Strategy of Terror (1940)

Richer by Asia (1947)

The Fall of the Dynasties (1963)

Awakening

from History

EDMOND TAYLOR

Gambit INCORPORATED
Boston
1969

To V, a durable myth.

ACKNOWLEDGMENTS

The strictly professional debt owed by a writer to his publisher is generally, and in most cases properly, reserved for private acknowledgment. I cannot, however, leave unmentioned the more personal one that I owe to Lovell Thompson, my present—and in his former capacity, original—publisher, and to Paul Brooks of Houghton Mifflin Company, with which firm I signed the first contract for this book, or what became this book, more than a quarter of a century ago. Without the patient, imaginative encouragement lavished by both of them over the years, I suspect that it might never have been finished. I am also grateful to Houghton Mifflin Company for permission to use several excerpts from my earlier books, *The Strategy of Terror* and *Richer by Asia,* as well as for helpful comments on numerous chapters of this one contributed by members of its editorial staff; I am particularly indebted to Mrs. Maria Wilhelm for hers. Those of my agent, Carol Brandt, were useful for their human insight no less than for their technical competence. Manès Sperber, from friendship, read a number of chapters and offered friendly criticism of exceptional value.

My thanks are due to Dr. Max Ascoli for permission to quote from articles originally written by me for *The Reporter* (my gratitude for the privilege of having been a staff correspondent of that magazine, and for the intellectual stimulation from my association with its editor over a period of years, is likewise too deep not to be recorded here). I owe similar thanks to the Washington *Post* for letting me make extensive use of citations from feature articles or columns I wrote on the war in Algeria (and for helping to make possible the travels on which they were based), and to Harcourt,

Brace & World, Inc., for authorization to quote from *The Collected Poems of Cavafy*. Finally, I am glad to have this occasion to express, if belatedly, my thanks to the Council on Foreign Relations for a year of study, stimulation, and reflection which both directly and indirectly nourished my undertaking in its early stages.

EDMOND TAYLOR

CONTENTS

Book Six: The Crisis of Maturity

Book Seven: A Late Gathering

Prologue

Crisis and Growth

The deepest and most secret workings of history are those that take place within ourselves. It is in the individual mind that the molecule of group decision is formed. It is here that private scruple grows into the conscience of an age, that accepted evil one day is found intolerable, or that the unthinkable at last gets thought. It is here, an often quoted contemporary document tells us, that wars begin; here that the national purpose falters or stands firm; here, therefore, that revolutions are made, and that ancient empires fall to ruin; here that civilizations flower or decay. Whenever the old order of the world gives way, the slow erosion of inherited codes and loyalties has long since prepared its passing. Whenever a new age dawns, subtle alterations in the pattern of our thoughts and feelings have long foretold its coming. Wasting or building, the winds and tides of mental change endlessly remodel the contours of society, and in so doing, like the forces of nature, they transform the earth.

Every autobiographical work that is at all thoughtful can be considered molecular history, in the sense suggested above. This book has no unique claim to the designation, but it does bear witness to some of the transformations that have taken place in the mind of my generation since it came of age forty-odd years ago. The period covered has been a time of extraordinary growth and turmoil which, in retrospect, I feel I was lucky to have lived in, and through. (Though it didn't always seem such luck.) Certain episodes that are related here may help the reader who is more or less my contemporary to recall, perhaps with a kind of doleful pride, his own participation in the same or similar struggles, while the younger one will be made aware that we, his elders, are at least more complex anachronisms than he had previously realized.

This role of catharsis and interpretation is not, however, the book's essential aim. To fulfill it comprehensively and systematically for my generation—or any other—would require an impossibly authoritative spokesman of that generation's aspirations, an encyclopedic student of its history; one's life would have to have been the epitome of its experience. I cannot qualify. My experience has been in many respects atypical. I have lived too many different lives in too many different places.

What this book does attempt is to knit the story of these outwardly disconnected lives into a single narrative—I try to emphasize not the beads but the chain on which they are strung. The intent is to present not a conventional autobiography but what for want of a better term might be called an objective introspection. The kind of personal experience that is recounted may or may not be typical of my generation, or any part of it, but it always alludes, however atypically, to our common predicament: that of living in an age of permanent crisis. The successive private searches around which the story hinges are facets or particularizations of a broader general quest and of a single but many-sided collective problem. They illustrate in some way the ceaseless, intense effort of adaptation and mental reeducation that living in our century imposes on us; they exemplify in some fashion the travail of adult growth that to me, at least, seems the most significant variety of twentieth-century experience.

Since I was born in 1908, my story spans the years of America's final emergence on the world scene—after our stumbling entrance during the Versailles peace conference—as a quasi-imperial superpower with global interests and involvements. No American of my age, I suspect, can look back on the mutation in our national destiny that has taken place during his lifetime without a kind of giddiness coming over him, especially if he casts his eyes all the way back to his childhood.

I was six years old when I heard my father, one Sunday morning at the breakfast table, read aloud the news under the black headlines, thickened with doom, in our local paper: GERMAN GUNS

SHELL BELGIAN FORTS. The Kaiser's howitzers have gone to the scrap heap, along with the empire over which he ruled, but those of other warlords have been thundering ever since. Annexations and liberations, uprisings and partitions, revolutions and restorations, treaties made and broken have relegated the maps I studied in grammar school to the walls of some historical museum; they were soon joined by the ones I saw hanging in high school and college classrooms, or those I consulted later as a cub correspondent in Europe. The political and social geography of our minds has had to be rewritten no less radically.

The sense of territorial vigilance that centuries of warfare had bred into the European psyche was only feebly developed in the American at the time of my birth. St. Louis, where I was born, then seemed about as implausible a target for enemy artillery as Mars; it no longer seems implausible today, and neither does Mars. During my infancy, America—despite Teddy Roosevelt, who occupied the White House at the time of my birth—still dozed in a quiet bayou, remote from the mainstream of twentieth-century world history. Today we head a planetary alliance, the greatest and most committed of all the powers; but a single rash decision or a fit of national indecision tomorrow could level all our greatness and even lead to the destruction of civilization itself everywhere on earth.

Whether the development of our perceptions and the growth of our personalities have kept pace with the expansion of the requirements that the age has laid upon us, the future will tell. What cannot be denied is that the American mind, responding to the challenge of our matriculation to power, in the last thirty or forty years has accomplished an immense feat of enlargement.

During several dramatic years, notably in the late 1930's, the way the challenge was met may conceivably have determined the nation's survival, for what that may be worth, and with it the freedom of all the Western peoples. (It was close enough as things were.)

I was a correspondent myself in Europe during the thirties, as I have been much of the time since. Perhaps there were among us in those years some farsighted men who saw the picture whole and

saw it from the beginning—as we always contrived to see it in hindsight—but for most of us, learning to practice a quite different kind
of journalism from that for which we had been trained, and to
cover a world radically different in many ways from the one we
had imagined it to be, proved a strenuous experience. We liked to
romanticize ourselves in our own minds as scouts blazing the trail
ahead of the main body of American opinion ("Watchdogs of the
truth on the frontiers of the news" was the formula preferred by
one of my employers, who loved dogs, but not progress, and had
mixed feelings about his correspondents), and from certain viewpoints that is actually what we were, but much of the time we had
to grope and stumble our own way forward. That is precisely why
the story of our sometimes uncertain scouting seems worth retelling
today. Our flounderings epitomize those of the national mind during the years when America was deciding whether to grow or not
to grow, and even whether to be or not to be.

The story of the American people's self-education for world
leadership is an important one, but it is only one chapter in the
broader chronicle of our age. Twentieth-century man everywhere
has had to adapt himself to transformations in his social environment
so numerous and drastic as to constitute almost an evolutionary
ordeal. His plight is not entirely new, but the ever-accelerating pace
of historic change and the mental lag accumulated in earlier times
make the challenge harder to meet than ever before.

All over the world, more and more persons have been obliged
century after century to adjust themselves more quickly to greater
change. Revolutions—ideological, social, technological—from Lu-
ther to Lenin, and from Copernicus to Einstein, have transformed
nearly everything in our conscious universe from the order of the
heavens to that of society. Generation by generation, the impact of
these revolutions has spread in ever widening shock waves across
the surface of the earth, and at the same time the intervals between
the shocks have been getting shorter. Learning to unlearn has become an increasingly essential aspect of education.

We have been faced repeatedly with the need for revising not only our ideas and our beliefs, but also our deepest values. Our dreams and our ideals—not to mention our standards of morality and our canons of taste—have tended to grow obsolete almost as fast as our weapons systems and our geographies. Anachronism in our feelings is as much a problem as anachronism in our political or economic thinking. We keep trying to live with flat emotions in a world that our reasoning minds have long since admitted to be round—except, of course, when it is our dreams which in some wild, futuristic skip leave the world of fact and reason far behind.

Most members of my generation, I suppose, experienced the same mixed sense of awe and horror, the same almost instantaneous realization of a kind of quantum skip in human history, that came to me in a thatched bamboo hut in Southeast Asia on a certain morning in August 1945, when I read from an army information-service teleprinter that a bomb like no other bomb had been dropped by us on a Japanese city called Hiroshima. Yet how many of us—apart from the handful of specialists who have mastered both the strategic and the ecological implications of the nuclear age—can truthfully say that their minds have never wavered since 1945 between science-fiction nightmares of planetary disintegration and the urge to brandish the hydrogen bomb in the face of a potential adversary as if it were merely a huge, bronze-tipped javelin?

A reporter, and particularly a correspondent, is even more exposed than most men to the emotional buffetings of history. For any journalist who takes seriously the social and moral implications of his professional role, having to discard a simple working hypothesis about the shape of political reality in a given area at a given time may involve an intimate upheaval. To change one's mind about such questions as whether a certain foreign leader honestly seeks better understanding with one's country or whether he is merely trying to lull vigilance while he completes his plans for some deadly assault; whether an ally that one trusts or admires has ceased to be admirable or trustworthy; whether a diplomatic pact that one has looked upon as the chief bulwark of peace is not in fact more likely to provoke a nuclear holocaust—these, of course, are more than

xvii

purely intellectual issues for everyone in a politicized society like ours. For the present-day reporter they may—and often do—mean changing the habits, hopes, and friendships around which he had built a considerable part of his life.

Our inability to adjust our outlook and attitudes to the quickening tempo of modern history tends to undermine our faith in civilization and in ourselves as civilized men; at times it fills our minds with streamlined versions of the collective nightmares inherited from a barbarian past. More than once in my life, and especially in recent years, I have seen the buoyant New World, new century optimism on which I was suckled give place to a generalized despair, to a guild-laden foreboding of imminent doom . . . For this waning of man's hope—and for the inhumanities and horrors that have brought it about—I bear my share of responsibility, along with all men now living; but none of us, it seems to me, should blame ourselves too harshly.

The need of the day is less for self-criticism than for self-understanding and self-forgiveness in order to understand and thus forgive our brothers. It is through learning to admit without bitterness our personal failures and defeats that we become reconciled to history, the story of man, that chronic but indomitable failure.

It is not my intent in this book to offer an apologia, whether for my own life, or for my generation, or for America, or for mankind in general, but to call attention to certain aspects of the contemporary ordeal that are perhaps less sterile than we realize. One in particular has hopeful as well as painful implications.

The mature person has become one of the social ideals of our time, comparable to the knight-without-fear-and-without-reproach of the Middle Ages or to the universal man of the Renaissance, and the modern concept of psychological maturity from which the ideal has been derived marks an almost revolutionary development in human thought. Up to our day men have taken it for granted that the mind and the emotions grew as the body did; we are the first generation in history to look upon maturation as a problem—in some respects a lifelong problem—instead of merely as a process.

If growing up in our century necessitates reliving in adult life the peculiar ordeal of childhood, it also implies re-enjoying its unique privilege, that of experiencing one's own enhancement. In prolonging the need for growth to the end of our lives, the revolutionary period in which we live condemns us, perhaps, never to attain full maturity, but, providing we meet its successive challenges as they arise, permits us never to stop growing. Our predicament is thus an uncomfortable—and sometimes tragic—one, but it is neither ignoble nor desperate.

That, no doubt, is why some of the grimmest moments in the history of the West through which my generation had to pass stand out in my private memory almost as festivals of hope: why, for example, it is the larks singing in the sky of France, rather than the Stukas' drone, that I remember most clearly from June 1940; or why, again, one of the most lighthearted days I have ever known was spent rolling across the plains of western Hungary in November 1956, the month and year that Hungary's freedom was reborn, and strangled in infancy anew. All these ordeals—and others that come to mind—for me were growth ordeals that in some way helped me to achieve a great or little increment of maturity.

There are, of course, different forms, as well as different levels of maturity. The kind this book chiefly deals with is that involved in becoming full citizens of our century, or to put it more simply, in adjusting our minds and our emotions to the world of incessant social change in which we have to live. Learning and unlearning are both requisites of it, and both must be repeatedly renewed throughout life. This permanent education is not the whole story, however. The training—and retraining—of judgment and the development or correction of perspective in assessing various aspects of contemporary reality is essential, but educating—above all, reeducating—our moral and emotional attitudes in relation to it is even more important. Maturity in the sense intended here means not merely learning to know the world as it is, but learning to love it more as we know it better, even when—as in my case—the knowing concerns what are probably its least lovable features.

For an American of my generation, brought up in the cultural climate that shaped my childhood, the pursuit of such maturity is almost synonymous with the quest for adult hope—that is, for reasons acceptable to an adult mind for believing in man's future. I cannot pretend that in my case the search has so far been wholly successful, but neither, as the reader will see, has it ever been completely abandoned. In fact, it seems to me if anything more promising as it nears its end than it looked at its beginnings. That is my main motive for attempting to trace its progress.

To avoid possible misunderstandings later on, a point about the scheme and method of this book should probably be mentioned here.

In the case of a reporter like myself concerned with the recording of events, the process of adjustment or nonadjustment to the times can be clearly seen simply by reference to his writings. Of necessity he keeps a diary—whether literally or by virtue of the reports and notes he files—for a living. The diary reveals the extent of progression or regression in the maturing view. For this reason, it has seemed useful to intersperse throughout the narrative brief excerpts from my earlier writings of various sorts, published or unpublished, that reflect both the workings of history on my mind and the workings of the individual mind—as the ultimate unit of measurable change—in history. Some of the excerpts are from earlier drafts of the book itself—for more than twenty years it has served as a tool, no less than a record, of attempted growth.

This examination, however, must begin not with the written record but with the personal history that preceded it: the foundation experience of childhood. In detail each such experience is unique, but its general significance is the common property of a generation—a generation in which in America a secure and happy childhood was perhaps as universal as it has ever been or may be for many years to come.

Joyce's young protagonist, Stephen Dedalus, found history "a nightmare from which I am trying to awake." His words, first read some forty years ago, have stamped themselves indelibly upon my memory; they are the only ones in *Ulysses* that I recall today.

Here in this book it is the history nightmare, or dream, of my generation that I seek to record along with what I hope is at least a partial awakening from it. If tomorrow a reign of peace and justice should descend on earth, my story would seem little more than a personal footnote to the chronicle of distant wars and tumults, and other old, unhappy, best-forgotten things. If, however, the age remains one of crisis and upheaval—as seems all too likely—perhaps it will sometimes help the reader to recognize his own history nightmares for what they are, and thus to awake from them.

Book One

Heritage
and
Disinheritance

1

Dissolving Clouds of Glory

*R*emote *at first and muted like the dove, then near and poignant, a long-forgotten cry floats up from freshly sprinkled streets to some cobwebbed attic chamber of the mind, its plangency spreading in slow, dissolvent rings through the blue cup of morning. It is the symbol and recall of childhood summer's most fleeting perfections: dew on the purple morning glory, the prickly after-taste of breakfast cantaloupe, the last savored coolness before the soggy, poultice press of noon, all the lovingly tended sloth of August, grown tall and ripe on its stalk, doomed by September's impending diligence. Again the cry rises, grave, then piercing-sweet, then furled in sudden silence, leaving like the twinge of an old wound the memory of its haunting melodic phrase and the spoken wonder of its cabala: Iron, old iron, any old iron today?*

I don't know whether the itinerant junkman's cry still rings on calm, hot, summer mornings, or any mornings at all, through the leafy residential streets of St. Louis, where I was born and spent my childhood, but it etched itself so vividly on my memory—somewhere between 1908 and 1915—that his calling must have been a rather profitable one. The city—like all of America and much of the rest of the world—was then as now in a state of rapid social and technological flux; no doubt the attics of my fellow townsmen were as encumbered with metallic anachronisms as their lives were with every other kind.

Had air travel been developed at the time so that a foreign visitor could have flown nonstop from the Eastern Seaboard without seeing Cleveland, Chicago, or any other cities of the interior, he would probably have considered that St. Louis typified midwest America —its generosity, its breezy democracy, its spaciousness, its rawness, and its vitality. If he had voiced this opinion the mythical tourist would have realized his gaffe even before he reached Kansas City. The natives would have made it clear that they were not flattered.

They might have been less offended, but certainly no less startled, if the traveler, having arrived straight from Europe and having somehow missed the skyline of Manhattan, had told them that their city was the symbol of urban America in the twentieth century, the expression and prototype of a new technological civilization.

On the whole he would have been more right than wrong. St. Louis did not typify the Middle West, but it was midwestern, culturally as well as geographically. The high, rolling bluffs above the restless Mississippi; the corn rising tall, mile after mile, on the Illinois flats; the deep beautiful sky; the harsh light; the violent, continental climate, with its cold winters and scorching summers, its cloudbursts and blizzards and tornadoes—these were more than symbols. Along with gaudy memories of the frontier and the intoxicating vista of an ever expanding future, they were common elements of consciousness in the minds of all midwesterners.

As a twentieth-century metropolis, though already a city of more than half a million, St. Louis hardly compared with New York or Chicago. It was cast, however, in essentially the same mold. The difference was merely of scale. Seen from the low Illinois shore, or from a boat on the river, the city's business district with its paleo-skyscrapers, divided by deep, narrow canyons of stone, presented a typical modern urban silhouette.

4

Mile-long steel bridges, early triumphs of engineering, already spanned the Mississippi. Streetcars clanged and automobiles honked in the bustling streets. Enormous factories, apartment houses, schools, and hospitals were springing up. A pall of smoke, almost as substantial as Pittsburgh's, hung over the city. Electric lighting was rapidly replacing gas mantel-burners—somewhat to the concern of my family, which had a hereditary interest in the local gas plant. Telephones were in every office and in well-to-do homes. Often there were two of them, since the city at that time was served by competing local systems, the industry not having yet reached the stage of feudal consolidation.

Thus, my unsophisticated tourist, surveying all these wonders, breathing in this heady, heart-of-the-New-World air, could reasonably congratulate himself on having seen one of the century's outposts of progress. He would soon have begun to develop doubts—at least about the uniformity of progress—if some early student of urban ecology had taken him on a comprehensive tour of the city and pointed out its curious patterns of growth and decay, of social blending and curdling. At some distance north and south of the business center he would have discovered the unpretentious, usually decent, sometimes prosperous, middle-class residential districts, each with a dominant ethnic tone: north the Irish, south the Germans with their breweries and their shaded beer gardens.

Inward from these two poles, along the dying waterfront and loosely ringing the center in a wide zone of decay, the explorer would have found the slums with their tenements or cheap rooming houses and their brothels or saloons, run-down, shabby, and forlorn. Here the pattern of cohabitation by race, color, religion, income-bracket, profession, and lawlessness or respectable poverty would have been too intricate for anyone but an expert to discern. Here he would have found misery, degradation, crime, prostitution, illiteracy, and an appalling absence of sanitation. Here he would have often discovered—as I discovered myself twenty years later—hovels lighted with kerosene lamps, shanties with outdoor privies, and well-drawn drinking water. He would have come across odd rem-

5

nants of a dozen or more European cultures that had not yet been squeezed into the straitjacket of twentieth-century Americanism, and seen traces of primitive mores imported from the hagridden Tatras or the jungles of the Congo.

The tourist would have gotten his real surprise—and realized where he had gone wrong in thinking that St. Louis was typically midwestern, American, or even modern—when he followed the march of fashion and the curve of real estate values west from the business district. Moving out of the zone of decay through a purgatory of rooming and boarding houses that a decade or two earlier had been the homes of leading citizens, the visitor would have found them getting progressively larger and less slatternly as he neared the spacious, tree-lined avenues, the substantial private houses, and the smart apartment buildings of the West End.

At a certain point he would have come upon a confused borderland where the homes of some of the community's wealthiest and proudest citizens adjoined boarding houses for office workers, or sometimes survived as enclaves of aristocracy in a block closed in on all sides by brothels and the cheaper rooming houses. In this border region, or close to it, lived many old families of the city whose collective minds included contrasts of value and tradition as flagrant and as bewildering as the sociological paradoxes of the neighborhood in which they dwelt. Here one was psychologically nearer to Mark Twain's America than to that of Sinclair Lewis, and nearer still, perhaps, to the America of Edgar Allan Poe. Indeed, one was sometimes nearer to the stagnant backwaters of provincial France than to any America, nearer to the eighteenth century than to the twentieth. This was the offbeat neighborhood, queerly compounded of past and present, of progress and regression, in which I was born and spent the early years of my life.

The house where my maternal grandmother lived lay in the curious borderland I have described, and a year or two after my birth my parents moved into the same block of Delmar Boulevard, one of the city's principal east-west arteries. Only three or four of the families who had settled in it during its heyday continued to live there, and one of them was under the blight of some ancient scandal which in my childish imagination cast a sort of House-of-Usher pall of doom over their dwelling. The next blocks west on Delmar were if anything less fashionable, while the intersection at the eastern, or downtown, end of our block marked the irrevocable frontier between the socially dubious and the totally unacceptable. I suppose some children lived below that line, but I was never allowed to play with them.

A faint whiff of gentility rotting on the vine, more reminiscent of the South than of the Midwest—not too surprisingly, since St. Louis had been a hotbed of Confederate sentiment during the Civil War—overhung the whole neighborhood and for that matter my own family. Years ago we had been rich and prominent in the city; various accidents and the changing patterns of the American economy were steadily eroding our status. My father, who had been obliged to quit school at an early age to support his mother, held a modest bureaucratic job at the City Hall; Mother tried with a measure of luck to breast the tides of social history by launching a succession of tearooms, bridge clubs, and similar ventures. Perhaps a little oddly, in view of this background, my parents were politically liberal, by the standards of the time. Both, particularly my mother, were, for example, staunch Wilsonian internationalists.

My grandmother's home, a turreted, brick, pseudo-Renaissance structure across the street from us, was both the cultural and the emotional pole around which my childhood revolved. It was a kind of family museum stuffed with relics or mementos of ancestral splendors that were already worm-eaten or faded long before I was born; to my childish eyes they were evidence not so much of vanished glory as of a systematic malevolence on the part of man and nature that I supposed somewhat uneasily had by now yielded to the gentling trend of progress. There was the spacious Creole plantation house on the island of Martinique, razed by a hurricane in the 1830's, where Grandmother had been born; its ghostly aquarelle tints foretold its doom. There, even more dimmed by time

7

and disaster, was the chateau that had belonged to my grandfather's family near La Rochelle, burned in the French Revolution. There, painted in oil, were the gruesomely disembodied hands of Grandmother's Italian aunt, reputed by family legend to have possessed at some unremembered epoch the most beautiful ones in some forgotten town, or perhaps province, of Italy; the explanation never seemed completely reassuring, not in a family that boasted of so many calamities.

There, behind the velvet curtains of the never-used drawing room, an airless sanctuary of somber awe, hushed save for the faint writhing of walnut and mahogany, hung a cracked, darkened oil portrait of Mother's great-grandmother, born of French pioneer stock in 1780 in what was the Fort St. Louis, who had married a Royalist *émigré* from the south of France, and produced an immense brood. No special cataclysms were linked with her memory, but in the portrait the old lady wore a kind of Mona Lisa half-smile that I always found a trifle disquieting. Thanks to her fertility we were related to a number of St. Louis families who all traced their lineage back to pre-Louisiana Purchase days, were immensely proud of their French cultural heritage—one particularly spirited old aunt or cousin who died about the time of my birth had all her life refused to learn English on the grounds that it was a barbarous tongue—and in many ways lived according to a pattern that was more French than American. The female, elderly, and poorer members of this tight-knit clan particularly tended to revert to French ways. They were uniformly and ostentatiously pious—we were all Catholics, of course —wore deep mourning most of their lives, lived in small, stuffy overcrowded flats or apartments, and in general looked and behaved like the proud, dowdy old spinsters and widows that one sees peering from behind lace curtains or scurrying into cathedrals in French provincial towns.

On another wall of the same sanctum was a nearly life-size photographic portrait of my grandfather Socrates, struck down in his pride shortly before I was born. The rigid, stocky figure, the patriarchal beard, the predatory nose, and the piercing eye of my mother's father made his image a formidable and living presence. He was said to have once terrorized a barber in Punta Gorda, Florida, into shaving him on the veranda of the barbershop during a hurricane; in his picture he looked as if he had just detected the first premonitory tremor of an earthquake, and was about to make it clear to the photographer where his duty lay. Though I never knew him in the flesh, Grandfather Socrates was one of the vital influences of my childhood; I suspect it is at least in part due to him that several crises of growth in my later life have been such stormy ones.

Both because he was a symbol of bygone splendor, and because he had been an unforgettably vivid human personality whose boundless egoisms and flaming irascibilities only endeared him to those who suffered the most from them, Grandfather Socrates was a popular subject of conversation in my mother's family. Very early in childhood I discovered that questions about him were never discouraged, and I exploited this license at every opportunity, begging my mother, my grandmother, and my aunt to tell, to retell, and to elaborate upon the vast body of folklore that had grown around his memory. At the time I had not yet developed the skepticism about all human evidence that I was to learn as a reporter, and this firsthand testimony from unimpeachable witnesses, reinforced by the penetrating magic of the big house on Delmar Boulevard, had the impact of immediacy as well as the ring of authenticity. From it I did not merely learn about Grandfather Socrates; I lived him. In so doing I vicariously relived in the twentieth century what had been my mother's childhood in the nineteenth.

Mother had been Grandfather Socrates's youngest and favorite child. During his later years his chief concern was bringing her up —that is, making her into a feminine replica of himself—and he had given it his full attention. By present-day standards he was neither a model parent nor husband. In all, he fathered ten legitimate children, and it was his invariable custom when my grandmother was in her eighth month of pregnancy to bid her a tender farewell and

9

leave for the country, or for France, remaining away until the boring business of childbirth was finished. As far as possible he timed things so that his departures would fit in with the tarpon-fishing season at Naples, Florida, where he maintained a hunting and fishing lodge.

After my mother's birth, these ritual disappearances were no longer necessary but he still visited Florida every year. Almost as soon as Mother was able to walk, he began taking her with him to Naples. She accompanied him on fishing trips in the Gulf, and on long hunting trips through the Everglades in a screened and mule-drawn wagon he had invented for the purpose. At the age of six he taught her to play whist, which he considered the foundation of a liberal education; she could already shoot a rifle and handle a fishing rod.

To polish up the more genteel side of Mother's education, he introduced her to oysters at an early age, paying her five dollars for each one she ate. The money thus earned helped her to improve herself in other fields of study, for Grandfather was an inveterate gambler, and as soon as Mother had mastered whist, he initiated her into the mysteries of the race track, roulette, and poker.

Mother grew up in every way a credit to this inspired system of education. Mounted on a pony of legendary viciousness, her thick auburn hair flying in the wind, she would spread terror and rebellion throughout the respectable residential quarters of Victorian St. Louis, when she could spare time, that is, from accompanying her father on some hunting or fishing expedition, sitting up until after midnight playing whist with his male cronies, or plunging her saved-up luncheon money on some outsider at the Kentucky Derby.

The legend of her disreputable girlhood exploits helped me both to understand my mother and, through her, to reconstruct Grandfather Socrates in my mind. He had been as domineering biologically as he was in other ways. My own genes confirmed the evidence of anecdotes that he had been high-strung and somewhat unstable emotionally, with a pronounced manic-depressive temperament. He had a quick, violent temper and was equally quick to forgive. He was a man of strong emotions, and the cultural influence of southern France was still sufficiently alive in him to make him feel that strong emotions needed emphatic expression. My mother inherited this trait, along with several of the others, and it horrified my father, who came from a family in which deep feelings were deeply buried and public exposure of private emotion was considered indecent.

Mother was also energetic, shrewd in business matters—when not too influenced by superstition or emotion—inclined to be extravagant, gregarious, and generous. Grandfather had displayed all these traits on a fabulous scale. He had been a successful businessman—though when he had found time for his business was not clear—and through his enthusiasm and his readiness to take chances with his money he had helped develop a number of local industries.

Highly sensitive to the weather—as my mother is, and as I am myself—he would often come down to breakfast on a rainy morning, look around the table filled with children, houseguests, and poor relations who had sometimes come for a week's visit years before and never left, bury his head in his hands, and start talking about the poorhouse with every appearance of conviction. A few hours later, a change in the weather, a good meal, or a happy speculation would set his spirits soaring again. At such moments he had been known to hire a whole railway car, fill it with champagne and friends, and set out for Florida or Louisville or New Orleans.

A stubborn impulsiveness and the complete absence of any sense of self-ridicule seem to have been among his strongest traits. Once on a trip to France he insisted on taking a favorite Jersey cow along with him because he said it was the only way to get a decent glass of milk in that country. This anecdote particularly delighted me as a child, not only because it revealed my grandfather as a man of sound, independent judgment, but because it appealed to my puerile American nationalism, which was already reacting against the idolatrous cult of France in the family. It reassured me to know that Grandfather Socrates had done his bit to make cultural exchange between the Old World and the New a two-way traffic.

Grandfather probably attained his high-water mark in self-expression when he bought a decrepit shanty along with several hundred acres of worthless hill land in the Ozark Mountains of southern Missouri. He tore down the old shack and in its place built a large frame dwelling shaped like a steamboat with a covered veranda running its length, so that he could stroll up and down and take the air on rainy days. Next, he dammed a stream and improved his new estate with a big artificial lake, complete with an island.

Looking over the lake and the island, he felt that something was missing and concluded, as any reasonable man might have, that it was an alligator. No alligators had ever been found as far north as the Ozarks, but Grandfather felt progress would have no meaning unless it was capable of rectifying such flagrant injustices on the part of nature. Accordingly, Grandfather Socrates sent to Florida for a vigorous twelve-foot specimen, built a summer house for it on the island, and on the shore constructed an elaborate glass-walled structure with a coal-heating plant to keep the reptile snug on frosty winter nights. The alligator survived the trip and was a popular success from the first. When winter came difficulties set in, however. The farmhands were not fond of the creature, although Grandfather had explained that it was completely inoffensive, as well as educational, and they were inclined to be careless about keeping up the fire in the winter house.

On several occasions Grandfather Socrates, awakened by a premonition, had jumped out of bed and rushed down to the lake shore to find the furnace cold and the alligator lying in a frozen coma. Rousing up his staff, he would oblige them to massage the patient with hot bricks. When the reviving brute began to thrash its tail, the farmhands would scatter, but Grandfather Socrates, brandishing his cane, with his nightdress flapping around his calves, would drive them back to their task. Eventually, of course, his premonitions failed him, and the alligator fell into a final lethargy from which no amount of hot massage could rally him.

The caricatural elements in the saga of Grandfather Socrates were acknowledged by the family minstrels who perpetuated it. His memory was not worshiped with hushed reverence, but treasured rather as a tender satire on the male principle. From earliest childhood, I understood that he was not in all respects a model for latter-day imitation; yet at certain stages of my growth, I have had to pit my own will-to-mature against his venerable childishness, harden the purposes of my heart against the heritage of his implacable whimsy. Remorselessly I have forced myself to drive a stake into the grave of my unsleeping dream that somewhere beyond the far horizon, or the next, or the next, lay cupped in the hollow of the hills a secret lake where the magic alligator waited my coming to waken from his Ozark thrall. It has been all the harder because Grandfather Socrates was not merely the personal symbol of childhood's lost paradise; he also expressed—with a few exotic trimmings —the collective American nostalgia for the zest and fullness of living that had been our grandfathers' birthright, for the freedom, self-reliance, and buoyancy that were par excellence the traits of a frontier society, but characteristic as well of the rising nineteenth-century European bourgeoisie in an age when the frontiers of man himself were everywhere expanding.

There could hardly be a greater human contrast than between Grandfather Socrates and my grandmother, the sage and benign matriarch whom nearly everyone in the family called by the French diminutive, Mamou.

As a young girl teaching in the French school that her mother had founded in Carondelet, the old southern suburb of St. Louis high above the Mississippi, she had been called by her friends "La Petite Fleur d'Abnégation." In her serene old age, after a lifetime of self-effacing devotion to her flamboyant husband, bearing and rearing his turbulent breed, the name suited her more than ever. Her Catholicism was Franciscan to the verge of heterodoxy. I doubt, though, that my grandmother would ever have thought of preaching sermons to the birds of the air or the beasts of the wood. She might possibly have read to them—as she used to read to me—tales from Greek and Hindu mythology, weaving with the gentle magic of her voice a mantle of Christian Grace over the shady deeds of pagan gods and goddesses.

Next to my mother, I loved her more than anyone else in the world. Perhaps I loved her more, or at least with a more untroubled love, for her own selflessness radiated an invisible power that in her presence stilled all jealousy, all base possessiveness, that invariably ennobled the recipient of her bounties through the act of his receiving. Because of this, which I remember so well, it is hard to remember other things about her. The contentments of the heart, like happy nations, have no history.

I knew Mamou for fourteen years, and especially in my early and middle childhood saw her nearly every day. She was more than seventy when I was born, and eighty-seven, I think, when she died. In my earliest childhood she must have been still able to move about, for I have a memory of sitting with her in the backyard of her house, gazing at the miracle of a castor bean plant that from a lifeless pod, planted for my special wonder, had sprung up tall and leafy and tropical, looking nothing at all like castor oil, and smelling only faintly of that dreaded brew.

Later, she was bedridden with heart trouble, but cheerful and alert. Later still, as she was dying of cancer, I saw her lying only slightly raised in bed, her aged face ashen and deeply lined, never complaining, still managing a faint smile from time to time, but locked away in an inaccessible inner world of pain. Last of all, a waxen mask in an open casket, serene again, no longer drawn and etched with suffering, but completely unreal, incredibly absent to the heart, incredibly cold to the lips.

It is only with difficulty that I can separate these successive phases of her image in my mind's eye. Memory has promulgated the middle period as official, disowning the earlier and later versions as counterfeits of time, and it is as of then that I chiefly recall her, when she was between seventy-eight and eighty, and I was between five and seven.

She was then confined to her bed, or at least to her bedroom, on the second floor of the house overlooking the street, but save for having to avoid exertion and excitement, she showed no signs of invalidism. She was small and inclined to be stout. Her cheeks were wrinkled and sagging, but her forehead was smooth and very beautiful, and her hair, which she wore parted in the middle and coiled in a knot at the back of her head, was still a faded brown.

Though she devoted long periods every day to prayer and meditation, and rarely received visitors outside the family circle—after all, most of her friends were dead—she took a keen interest in the world, read many new books, particularly in French, and discussed public affairs of the day with shrewd understanding.

With gentle, invisible hands she guided the lives of her children and her numerous grandchildren. She appeased their frequent quarrels, solved their problems, consoled them in their sorrows. How she did it, I never discovered. She seldom volunteered advice and never admonished. A member of the family, fuming over some quarrel or misunderstanding, would come to her, and before he had finished reciting his grievances was ashamed of them and would go away to seek a reconciliation without Mamou even suggesting it. A difficult problem would somehow dissolve in the light of her strong common sense, and the person who had come to consult her would leave convinced that she had given him sagacious advice, when in reality she had said nothing remarkable.

It was the same thing with her wit. Everyone in the family was convinced that her conversation was brilliantly witty. There is no reason why it should not have been—she was an intelligent, polished, widely read old lady who had lived and learned a great deal. Yet I suspect that she was above all a catalyst of wit whose appreciation of her guests' conversation made them feel inspired. Certainly, no one in the family could remember any of her witticisms. Unlike Grandfather Socrates, she begot few anecdotes. Everyone felt that she was marvelous and unique, but she really accomplished only one miracle —her presence.

One of Mamou's rare failures, and the deep sorrow of her old age, was a black-sheep son whom I shall call Uncle Frank, though it was not his name. He lived only a few blocks away, but in a hotel of dismal repute, and nobody in the family spoke to him. Nobody but my grandmother, that is. About three or four times a year he would come to her for help, announcing his visit in advance by telephone. It was Mamou's order that her door should never be closed to Uncle Frank, and much as the rest of the family disapproved, she was nonetheless obeyed.

To my inexperienced eye Uncle Frank was a remarkably sedate and respectable-looking middle-aged gentleman, somewhat old-fashioned in his dress, and yet he always seemed to me a bit nervous and defiant as he was ushered into the front hall of the big brick house on Delmar Boulevard. Sometimes my widowed aunt, who ran the household for Grandmother, would meet him outside Mamou's door and unbend to the extent of hissing a warning to remember her bad heart. More often, he was taken up by a maid.

An hour or two later, Uncle Frank would come down. As I spied on him from some inconspicuous corner of the big hall it seemed to me that his expression had undergone a subtle change. His face looked more mellow, his eyes looked brighter, and not with a prodigal's tears. On the contrary, he seemed highly pleased with himself, and his walk was almost jaunty. Of course, the generous check folded in his waistcoat pocket had something to do with the transformation, but Uncle Frank, in addition to his other faults, was a sentimental old rip, and with any other benefactor would have poured out tears of repentance and gratitude by the bucketful. What Mamou did for him, besides saving him from jail or the poorhouse, was temporarily to restore his self-respect. This was Mamou's secret, insofar as it could be dissected at all: to bring out in each human being the awareness of his own worth.

Though intensely pious herself, Mamou almost never spoke about religion, any more than she spoke about her numerous and lavish charities. Her tolerance of others' beliefs or unbelief was founded upon an unshakable conviction of God's mercy and an equally unshakable respect for the dignity and integrity of the creatures made in His image. She listened without sorrow or reproof to the salty irreverences of my agnostic scientist cousin, and was venerated by my Freemason, vaguely deistic father.

Like her tolerance, her serenity was almost Buddhist in its perfection. It shed its absolution upon all who came near her. Neither the small nor the great upheavals of worldly life could disturb it. Only once, for a few seconds, did I see her discomposed. That was when I exploded a live .22 cartridge as I sat on the foot of her bed trying to extract the bullet from its case with a nail file. Though the powder burned my hand the bullet only grazed my thumb; and as soon as she realized that I was not seriously hurt her panic subsided. Though her heart must have had a dangerous shock, she applied the iodine to my open wound with gentle, unflinching hands.

Allied to her serenity, in a paradoxical amalgam that only another mystic could explain, were a deep compassion for all human woes and a typically Franciscan reverence of delight in God's creation. She loved sunlight, and my cousin's ferocious bull terrier and sparrows hopping on her windowsill and all green and growing things. The big bay window of her room was a miniature hothouse filled with ferns and geraniums and other plants that she tended herself.

Her influence on the formation of my character was immense. Undoubtedly, it was a deliberate influence. It is a tribute to her talents as a teacher that I did not realize for years that I was being taught, and taught, moreover, with a moral goal in mind.

I learned from her, for example, that in Martinique oranges cut in half were used to polish floors, and that a favorite relaxation of Creole planters was having the soles of their feet tickled by a slave. I was shown small, exotic red seeds, exactly like the seed that had lodged in Mamou's nose when she was a child on the trip from Martinique to New Orleans and thus saved the ship from a pirate attack (her distress had kept her parents awake, so that between her cries they heard the muffled oars of the pirates and gave the alarm in time). I heard about Grandfather Socrates and his varied exploits, about the giant devilfish that had towed my mother far out in the Gulf of Mexico, about her vicious pony and her convent pranks, about the house like a steamboat near Arcadia, Missouri, and about the twelve-foot alligator.

From all these teachings I learned what my grandmother mainly intended I should learn: the exoticism of goodness; the infinite mercy of God, who gave little boys grandmothers cunning as serpents; the infinite variety of His blessings, including alligators and pirates and Grandfather Socrates; the adventures and perils of the spiritual life; and finally, on a more practical plane, the marvelousness of reality, and the rare, whimsical charm of simple good sense.

I once had a neo-Albigensian friend in Paris who insisted that the biblical story of the Fall has been completely misread. It was Satan, he maintained, who tried to preserve the innocence of Adam and Eve, and God, through the serpent, who tempted them to the knowledge of good and evil. That was very much like Mamou's strategy of education.

It resulted, among other things, in endowing me at an early age with a purely inward-looking sense of sin. I have never been able to rid myself of it, since it was not founded on the dread of hellfire, which one can sometimes outgrow, but on a childhood glimpse of moral beauty, of virtue cunningly embellished to look as alluring as vice, on an observed masterpiece of ethical style as compelling in its way as a great artist's mastery of his brush, or a great athlete's of his body.

Even today, I do not always find this inheritance from my grandmother a light one to carry with me; I suspect that she realized perfectly well the risks of bestowing a sense of sin upon a twentieth-century grandson. For all her gentleness and compassion, she did not flinch when she poured the iodine on my torn thumb, and she was no more likely to flinch in applying the iodine of the soul. I do not hold it against her. Like Grandfather Socrates's extra-rugged individualism her ethical influence was a heritage that I have had to learn to adapt, but could never bring myself to disown.

Besides planting in my soul the germ of that "metaphysical need" which Nietzsche struggled against so violently—and so futilely—all his life, Mamou sought to stimulate my imagination by methods that a number of contemporary educators and psychiatrists look upon as no less deplorably retrograde than the notions of sin and spirituality. I was read—or encouraged to read for myself—the myths and fairy tales of the whole world: the legend of King Arthur and his knights, the *Jungle Books* of Kipling, the *Wizard of Oz,* the stories of the livelier saints, and countless other classic examples from all ages of man's inveterate flight from reality. The consequences—aggravated by a three-year period of ill health that intensified my native bent toward introspection—rapidly became apparent: I developed a morbid and unquenchable thirst for science. Between my tenth and twelfth years my favorite reading for a considerable time was an old-fashioned textbook of inorganic chemistry which had somehow fallen into my hands, and I even managed to extract some implausible emotional nourishment from the dessicated prose of Herbert Spencer, whose *Principles of Biology* I read—or at least reveried over—curled up on the foot of Mamou's bed, blissfully unaware that the author's nineteenth-century mystique of evolution was already a bit outdated.

Along with my passion for science there awoke in me at about the same time a no less passionate interest in the literature of travel and discovery. These aberrations apparently caused Mamou no concern or disappointment, either on theological or esthetic grounds; the blessing of her approval fell impartially on Spencer and on *Beowulf;* Stanley's travels were as warmly endorsed as those of Nils Holgerson. She manifested none of the symptoms of a jealous deity when I set up a secondary, quasi-idolatrous cult in veneration of the family's scientific member, my cousin Newman. By the time of my middle childhood, Cousin Newman was already respectably established as the staff pathologist of one of the local hospitals, but there had been an earlier, less reputable phase of his career when he had practiced as a veterinary surgeon. He still looked after some of his old four-footed patients for sentimental reasons, and acted as veterinary consultant to the St. Louis Zoo. The vocabulary and anecdotal range of the dissecting room, enriched with the ripe flavor of the livery stable and the wild-animal cage, lent an indescribable charm to his dinner table conversation.

As a magic intermediary between the human and animal kingdoms, between the living and the dead, with access to the mysteries of these several worlds, Cousin Newman had enormous prestige in my eyes. A little frightened by his Promethean impieties, I nonetheless regarded him with unbounded admiration and spent many rapturous hours in the evil-smelling laboratory he maintained in my grandmother's house, peering through his microscope at sinister, minute presences, occasionally allowed to participate in some macabre chore. Thus, with Mamou's blessing, he took his incongruous place alongside Grandfather Socrates in the pluralistic pantheon of the imagination over which she presided with more than Olympian serenity.

My father, a quiet man who lived, and eventually died, very quietly, seldom talked much about his family. In the main it does not seem to have been a particularly colorful one, at least by the standard of my mother's. There was, however, one notable exception: my father's own father, Theodore, more usually known as Tom—or among his male friends, Talking Tom—whose legend was even more glamorous in its way, if somewhat cloudier, than that of Grandfather Socrates. Grandfather Tom, according to my father's rare divulgations and to the fuller, if sometimes slightly contradictory, accounts I obtained from his sister, my Aunt Mary, was originally a land surveyor, before ideological passion and the spirit of adventure distracted him. He appears to have been a man of modest but genteel social status, since he had married a rich banker's daughter —my grandmother—and owned a house slave, a middle-aged Negro, who likewise happened to be named Tom. My grandfather served as a captain in the Mexican War, and I suspect enjoyed that experience more than home life.

When the Civil War broke out, Grandfather Tom naturally enlisted in the Confederate Army. (Grandfather Socrates was also a Rebel sympathizer, but apparently less of an activist, though he did get himself into some kind of trouble with what the family thought of as the Yankee occupation authorities in St. Louis.) Before leaving home, so the legend went, Grandfather offered to set his slave, Tom, free, but the latter indignantly rejected the offer and the two Toms, the white, talking one, and the black, presumably listening one, rode off together to uphold the southern cause.

As a boy, I remember a mild feeling of pride every time I heard the anecdote retold—it never occurred to me to doubt its authenticity—and I appreciated its romantic flavor. (It was not until several decades later that I thought of wondering whether the black Tom's grandchildren, if he had any, and if he had told them the story from his viewpoint, would have found it equally romantic.) The really glorious phase of Grandfather Tom's military career, however, did not begin as far as I was concerned until after the defeat of the Confederacy, when he refused to take the oath of allegiance to the Union demanded by Missouri law. Unable, because of that, to return or remain home, he buckled on his cavalry officer's sword once again and took part in the vain attempt of Prince John Magruder's freebooters to set up a new slave empire in Mexico. Throughout my childhood I remained firmly and proudly convinced that Grandfather Tom had eventually been killed in a gun battle in a Juárez saloon, though certain members of our family, including my mother, claimed to have seen him, or his ghost, years later, living as a pacific, if embittered, recluse on a floor of his own house in St. Louis, but refusing because of some ancient quarrel to speak to his wife. The one certainty about his end is that, wherever and however he died, the old Rebel bequeathed nothing to his children except his sword and the legend of his magnificently misguided idealism, or obdurateness.

The dreams of an all-too-romantic ancestral past that enthralled my imagination as a child were overlaid with a body of more typically native, but no less anachronistic, American folklore when shortly after my eleventh birthday my parents moved—chiefly because of my health—to an old farm in St. Louis County that had been the country home of my father's grandfather, a pioneer St.

Louis banker. The farmhouse itself was a handsome, two-story frame building with a touch of pillared elegance, but without electricity, central heating, or indoor plumbing.

Litigation among the old gentleman's heirs had kept the property, called Lackland Farm, intact as an enclave of nineteenth-century rural America in what was rapidly becoming a twentieth-century suburbia; it covered several hundred acres, partly in tangled woodland, partly in tillable fields that the executors leased to neighboring farmers.

The softly rolling countryside had a kind of slattern loveliness. It had suffered a bit from neglect, but not from overexploitation; several inches of good, though slightly acid, loam still covered the red Missouri clay. The spring winds smoothed out the long turquoise-blue swells of the wheat fields; the pelting rains of summer turned into sturdy green javelins of corn almost before they struck the earth; they were no sooner harvested than row after row of topaz stubble, cruel and hard as dragons' teeth, sprouted in their place. The fences were unkempt with honeysuckle and trumpet vine; coveys of quail exploded from the ragged hedgerows, scattering their fluff to the winds, and rabbits were so plentiful that they could be hunted on frosty mornings with a broomstick—at least they could if like the son of one of our neighbors you had the gift of clairvoyance and could see them from afar in your mind's eye, huddled under the matted tufts of perception.

Like the lands, the empty barn and outbuildings were somewhat run-down; the master's house, surrounded by a large, grassy yard shaded by tall locust and maple trees, overrun with lilac and honeysuckle, was itself in need of some repair. It was still filled with the furniture and knicknacks of half a century earlier. Once, raiding an old trunk in the hornet-haunted attic, my brother and I discovered a pair of high leather boots belonging to some great-uncle who long before we were born had walked the earth with vast, ancestral strides; with several pairs of wool socks and enough paper stuffed in the toes they proved excellent for hunting. The same trunk yielded a primitive .44 rim-fire revolver that would actually fire, at least two or three times out of five; it was a comfortable thing to have handy in the drafty, creaky old house, lit only by kerosene lamps, while waiting for our parents to return from the city on winter evenings, or lying in bed out on my sleeping porch under an arctic moon when the wind whistled down all night from the plains of Canada, and the owls of February hooted in the bony, gnashing maples.

During this period my brother and I were alone much of the time. He was two years younger, and the only other child in the family. Our parents continued to work in the city, making the long drive every morning and evening in the recently acquired family Ford.

For nearly four years, I lived a kind of studied revival of a classic American boyhood in this artificially preserved period setting. Both our servitudes and our delights, with only a few exceptions, were contemporaneous with those of Tom Sawyer. Most of the wood we burned in our stoves and fireplaces—the only heating we had—was sawed or chopped by my brother and myself; we carried it into the house and tended the fires, besides daily cleaning and filling the lamps, and drawing the sweet-tasting well-water. It was a little more than a mile to our school, and except in blizzards or downpours we rode our bicycles there and back, or walked. All summer long we went barefoot. In the cool of the morning my brother and I practiced pitching curves on the lawn; on hot afternoons we fished for crappy in the farm pond or stretched out naked, and slowly evolving with the tadpoles in the tepid, ancestral ooze of its shore, listened in uneasy wonder while the sons of the neighboring tenant farmers bemused us with talk of the almost supernaturally unnatural copulations of men and beasts. In fall and winter we hunted after school or on weekends, or combed the dark woods for walnuts and persimmons and the pennons of flaming bittersweet prized by Sunday motorists from the city. In spring we would decipher the wavering cuneiform script that the wild ducks wrote across the sky, and leaping upon our bicycles, pedal furiously half a morning to the banks of the Missouri River to gape at the annual widening of the waters.

23

Those years of old-fashioned country boyhood seem almost incredibly rich and unbounded, when I think back on them, but they were sometimes clouded with loneliness and even—like all human experience—with pain or sorrow. For some reason, what must have been one of the briefer and more trivial of my woes remains extraordinarily vivid in my mind. I was about twelve at the time, and no doubt like most of my age-peers in rural America dreamed of becoming an explorer when I grew up. Then came that bleak Sunday morning at Lackland Farm—it was March, and some snowdrops, the flowers of false hope, had sprung up in the lawn—when my dream was shattered by an illustrated feature in the weekly supplement of our local newspaper.

After tracing the history of exploration throughout the ages, the article concluded with a pessimistic summary of the current situation: Discovery was doomed as a career for American youth because there was virtually nothing left to discover. At the very end the author, undoubtedly a sadist, raised a vague hope of interplanetary explorations, but killed it almost immediately—a bit prematurely as things are turning out—by affirming that spaceships were still generations, if not centuries, in the future, and that long before they came into being the last remaining blank spots on the map of the world would have been filled in. An accompanying map featuring the few uncharted patches of the earth's surface drove home the point with brutal clarity.

Whether or not such childhood traumas have warped many adult American lives, the explorer-fantasy expressed in my case an authentic requirement, a deep-rooted urge, an unappeasable curiosity. I needed to travel and to look upon unfamiliar sights, to breathe strange air and to think alien thoughts, to accumulate new experience and to wonder upon it. Becoming a foreign correspondent eventually provided at least a partial fulfillment of my boyhood ambition; the political and social wastelands of the age that I came to know, along with the beasts of prey that haunted them, though less beautiful, were certainly as wild and strange as anything I had imagined in Africa.

We are not always so fortunate in discovering relatively feasible and acceptable contemporary fulfillments for ancestral dreams. The final disappearance of the American frontier in the early years of this century was not merely an emotional bereavement for little boys who had dreamed of growing up to be Davy Crockett; a certain freshness of the American imagination, a certain vitality in American culture, disappeared with the frontier, and nothing has yet been found to replace them. The dramatic finis that our generation has seen written to the epic of colonialism has undoubtedly inflicted a much graver cultural trauma upon the Western mind. Perhaps the conquest of space will provide a substitute for the dream of distant glory that has enthralled our imagination since the age of the Conquistadors. It has not done so yet. If the American is more sensitive to such invisible wounds of history than some of his contemporaries, it may be because his childhood, by its very richness, left him with so much to unlearn.

2

Classic Initiation

*L*ong, solitary, leisurely Sunday stroll this afternoon, a kind of rumination with the legs, through medieval Rome to the Tiber embankment and then up on the Capitoline. Little park that overlooks the Forum: a lonely peak studded with broken columns and outcroppings of ancient basalt wall. Swallows skimming and twittering against gray watered silk of sky, seen through branches of twisted pine and flowering oleander. Soft and tropic air, honeyed by June; angelus bells: slow sworls of sound that drift from hill to hill. Darkening moraine-rubble of history at my feet, splendor and litter of all high places. Surrealist magic of the Colosseum's ragged silhouette and the shattered basilica of Constantine. O cunning bite of time. Perhaps even something to be said for Romans themselves.

How lucky to have found Rome so young. And lucky that I have come back so often to learn how many Romes there were to find. Widening sediment-rings of old attachment in the mind that project themselves on stone—a private key to the archeology of growth. Earliest layers, of course, night-hued, Byron-tinted: cat-scamperings, nocturnal sewer smell of narrow, twisting streets; the verdict of midnight upon the Cenci Palace, implacable loom of St. Peter's under a baroque inquisitor's moon; mean streets beside the Termini Station in the hangman's light of a November dawn, and the purifying reek of a macedonia in sinful young nostrils. One morning-

memory, though, perhaps the first of all: the Spanish Steps pumiced by rain, fresh in the early sun, Keats's house—for Bob was along and this was a pilgrimage—banked flower stalls at the foot of the stairs; riot of the South.

Strange gaps and curious discoveries. The Campidoglio for instance: Acropolis of the Renaissance, its high noon in stone. How many times, how many years, I looked, yet never saw until today. Adolescent passion for pre-Raphaelites and lingering disapproval of Renaissance no doubt in part to blame. Deceptively enclosed Florentine harmony with unexpected openings upon the domes and roof-tops of eternity: transposed ideals of the city-state in a dawning world-consciousness. Great bronze equestrian statue of Marcus Aurelius on Michelangelo's pedestal in center of the square, rider and steed streaked with the green sweat of ages, a luminous footnote that interprets the architect's intent. Emperor with his blank eyes and stiff legs looks the bore he doubtless was in life, but tranquil power in curve of horse's neck and magnanimity in forefoot poised over now-vanished and decolonized barbarian (perhaps idealized horse stands for imperial bureaucracy in the Roman sculptor's vision) makes the essential statement. Ideal balance between grandeur and humanity, justice and authority, conscience and power.

Understand better now why all these years I passed so disregarding by this hardly inconspicuous jewel in the Western diadem. More than slow education of taste involved, more than changing fashions in appreciation of the past, or classic aging of romantic impulse. First time I looked on Campidoglio it was not only with the Gothic eye of adolescence but in the perspective of America's age of innocence; in a sense it was veiled for me by the Monroe Doctrine as well as dimmed by greater radiance of Assisi.

Similar evolution with regard to Romans. Ruins of Forum or Palatine rarely produced romantic frisson or elegiac pathos that with little help from poets came to me so easily in presence of feudal Rome.

27

Find them more moving today, thanks to neo-barbarian incursions witnessed since. Suspect what really put my generation off was Roman sense of decorum, Roman concept of civilization as discipline. Judging from own experience, idea of civilization itself had little glamor for us; lapping up Spengler, for instance: culture si, civilization no. Simultaneously cause and symptom of twentieth-century collapse.

"Generation" is a tricky unit of history, especially in times of rapid change. No one, for example, who was going to high school in 1914 belongs psychologically to the same generation that I do—even if there are only eight years between us—for he lived through the world cataclysm that began then, or through part of it at least, as a young adult, while I slept through it all in the latency of childhood. No one, on the other hand, born later than 1914 fully belongs to it either; he falls a trauma short.

One of the keys to the mind history of my age group in the West is that the caesura of the Great War falls across our lives between infancy and puberty. This is perhaps our clearest psychological caste mark, recognizable both in our strivings and in our betrayals. It helps explain why adolescence for us was often a singularly labored, if not always tragic, experience. We had opened the eyes of childhood upon one kind of world; we underwent the ordeals and initiations of apprentice-adulthood in what—though we did not realize it—was a quite different one. After the tempests that had raged from 1914 to 1920, the skies seemed to be getting steadily brighter—but we were only approaching the quiet eye of the hurricane, and wreckage and menace still lay about us, especially when we tried to look within. The second twentieth-century crisis of civilization was already gathering; the first had never truly been resolved. To the most sensitive minds of the older generation it seemed, in fact, that the Great War, with its aftermath of revolutionary turmoil, had virtually destroyed civilization, ushering in a new age of darkness, a "barbarism lit by neon," in the expressive phrase (coined even before the war broke out) of the Viennese writer Karl Krauss. It manifested itself not only in the often turbid art and literature of the period, but in the language itself: the vulgarisms and underworld slang creeping in, the grand abstractions that lay dead on the battlefields, the maimed or shell-shocked value words, and the propaganda clichés that already were beginning to anticipate Orwell.

Properly speaking, it was not—especially in prosperous, unscarred America—a time of despair, merely one of blurred and somewhat squalid optimisms: the euphoric stage of a spreading moral ataxia. The faceless, mechanized inhumanity of the battlefield that had patterned the century's first nightmare was a horror of the past; the horror of the present—and of the future—was the growing, faceless, mechanized inhumanity of twentieth-century industrial society.

Such was the springtime of our generation. I do not believe I have made its colors too dark. Where, save in an age of murk, could we expect to find the psychological roots of Auschwitz and Hiroshima and Vorkuta, the currents of opinion that helped shape the character of a Heydrich and an Eichmann?

It would be fascinating if memory could distinguish the elements in the juvenile malaise of my generation that stemmed directly from the traumas of history. In those European countries where the breakdown of society had driven a considerable portion of disoriented youth into the most delusive forms of political extremism, the connections were fairly apparent. Among the sons and daughters of the affluent midwest bourgeoisie with whom I grew up, they were much less so. We did feel, in a confused, shadowy way, that the time was out of joint; but if we identified ourselves with Hamlet at all, it was in estrangement rather than revolt. We were, perhaps, conscious at moments of a kind of usurpation that was somehow disinheriting us of an expected birthright, but nobody—nobody we trusted—seemed to know exactly who or what was the usurper. Our alienation was both less extreme and more diffuse than that of many young Americans today.

I do not remember that in the midwest America of my day, many of us, even in the stormiest moments of adolescence, were deeply or chronically disturbed; we were not deeply anything. We were unoriented, rather than disoriented; not a lost generation, but one that took an abnormally long time, despite the shock therapy of the next quarter century, to find itself. We were sick, in a way, but our illness was of the kind whose gravity becomes apparent only in convalescence. In my own case, at least, the converse was likewise true: Convalescence began as I gradually learned the gravity of those seemingly minor absences in the food of the mind and heart that were causing me to waste. The turning point was the trip that I made to Europe in my seventeenth and eighteenth years.

We sailed, if I can trust my memory, in the late summer of 1925, the high Coolidge era in America and one of Europe's years of remission (the Locarno security pact was signed in October). Like many things in my early life, the background of the trip reflected a curious mixture of epochs and mores. Its basic inspiration, no doubt, was the classic *grand tour* handed down from the eighteenth century, but the pattern had been modified in accordance with the Victorian ideal of cultural self-improvement so successfully exploited by Messrs. Thomas Cook and Karl Baedeker, and a few special New World touches had been added, unwittingly borrowed, I imagine, from Mark Twain.

In terms of twentieth-century social history the trip mirrored, among other things, the reviving market in gentility that accompanied the postwar economic boom: Mother had been doing well giving bridge lessons to the newly affluent and exploiting the tips on interesting stock speculations she picked up from her pupils. She was thus able to pounce with her usual energy and generosity upon a unique opportunity to round out my somewhat disjointed secondary education. Mr. Judson, a retired St. Louis schoolmaster of considerable local repute, was planning an economical trip to Europe and had announced his willingness to take with him some young gentleman who wished to be intensively prepared for college, providing the candidate was adequately qualified to profit by the in-

struction in the humanities that would be imparted *in situ* as it were.
Mr. Judson agreed to stretch a point as to my qualifications; we
were old antagonists who knew each other's mettle.

Somewhere in his late sixties or early seventies at the time, Mr.
Judson had an impressive silver mane, the forehead and nose of a
Roman senator, slightly bulbous eyes of a deep, childlike blue behind rimless pince-nez glasses, and a small, military moustache of
tobacco-stained white. His cheeks were startlingly puckered by the
scar from an operation for cancer of the mouth, and a lifetime spent
on the rough seas of learning had given him a rolling sailor's walk.
Probably he suspected, even before we left, that his malignancy had
come back and that no further reprieve could be hoped for through
the surgeon's knife. I know that I sensed from the start a kind of
tragic urgency lurking behind the caricatural mask. For Mr. Judson
the trip was unmistakably something more than an old man's sentimental pilgrimage to scenes visited in youth; it had an element of
final quest. Perhaps this accounted for the trace of metaphysical
anguish evident in Mr. Judson's impatience with my all-too-fre-
quently latitudinarian approach to Latin syntax.

Mr. Judson was a pedagogue of the old school. Apart from his
irascibility, he was a charming period piece, and in his naïvely
pedantic way he could be quite entertaining. Despite his obsessive
Latinizing, he seldom neglected the more worldly aspects of my
education. It is well when traveling, he frequently explained, to
drink the wine of the country: We started at Naples with Lacrima
Cristi, product of a volcanic soil ("not blasphemous to an Italian,
you understand"), and worked north to the chateaux of the Loire
with its Touraine blanc en carafe, not blasphemous to anyone.
Like my parents and most of our friends in St. Louis, Mr. Judson
was no sympathizer with the puritan seizure that a few years earlier
had brought an otherwise tolerably sane nation to adopt a constitutional amendment prohibiting alcohol, thereby ushering in the
era of the speakeasy, the bootleggers' wars and the juvenile hip flask.
He was curiously broadminded in other ways too. During our visit
to the glorious museum of Greek antiquities in Naples, he accepted

with a dignified leer the guide's offer to show us the marble and mosaic exuberances of the so-called reserved section, the red-light district of art. After all, they formed part of a classical education.

The fourteen-day sea voyage to Naples, stopping in the Azores and at Palermo, was filled with multiple, if simple, wonders: the sea dwelt upon, land descried, the thereness of Europe, the southness of the South, friendship disclosed. The last was of course the greatest, for it included the others shared; it was both experience and a strong amplifier of experience.

The friend was named Bob, and he was a year older than myself. He had been to art school and he was going alone to Rome for a year to paint, perhaps also to experiment with stained glass, for Bob was a great admirer of the medieval craftsmen. That would have sufficed; I knew little about medieval craftsmen, but they sounded right. In addition to showing himself a connoisseur of historical epochs and having the glamor of a full-fledged, independent painter, soon to possess a Roman studio—no doubt complete with model—Bob was an engaging youth from every viewpoint. Artists were looked upon in the United States with even more suspicion then than now, but Bob was manly, with an honest middlewestern voice, a wholesome smile, and a native bent for seeing the good side of everything—except, of course, academic painting.

Though dedicated to the graphic arts himself, Bob shared my love for the poets; our admirations and detestations in the matter were remarkably alike. Shades of fervor in our respective reactions to the approved poets naturally came to light from time to time, but nothing that a few hours' earnest talk could not clear up. Shelley was the more sustained, I forced Bob to agree, but, my friend wondered, wasn't he perhaps just a little too classical to scale the final heights? I was not quite convinced. Yet, I admitted, Keats had undoubtedly written:

> *"Beauty is truth, truth beauty,"—that is all*
> *Ye know on earth, and all ye need to know*

and as Bob pointed out, you couldn't very well top that. Privately I thought that Shakespeare could and had, but Shakespeare was distant, as remote in time and maturity as the nocturnal firmament, while Keats seemed incredibly near, as we lay on deck in the mild Tyrrhenian night looking up at the ghostly scud of cloud that intermittently blurred the stars, while Bob in his rich baritone intoned:

> *"When I behold, upon the night's starr'd face,*
> *Huge cloudy symbols of a high romance . . ."*

Here, it seemed to me, was friendship at last, such as I had read about in childhood books of chivalry and adventure but had never yet encountered in the casual sociability, based on propinquity rather than affinity, of American daily life. Unwittingly, I had discovered one of those missing vitamins of the spirit that the moral climate of the New World often seems to leach out of our soil, or did, at least, in those muggy years between the thunder and the sun. In due course I revealed my secret to Bob. I was a poet myself, in a modest way, though on the purely worldly plane I was aiming at a career as a scientific forester. I had done a number of sonnets, some short lyrics, a few experiments in free verse. I was thinking of starting on an epic poem in blank verse, as soon as I could decide on the theme. I recited two or three of the sonnets. "Good, oh very good," Bob commented in the consumptive tones the situation called for.

On the whole, I think I learned more from Bob than I did from Mr. Judson. To the latter I owe the rudiments of a grammatical conscience that has survived, a trifle weatherbeaten in spots, forty years of journalism or worse; perhaps he gave me an embryonic sense of order as the paramount sorcery. Bob taught me something of even greater, or at least more immediate, importance. The initial step toward healing is to give a name to one's disease, and since this step leads on to others, it hardly matters much if the first designation is a loose one. The name that Bob gave to the malady of our age—

that curious affliction I had noted, and felt, at home in St. Louis, whose symptoms to the uninstructed eye often appeared a mere surfeit of health—was loose enough. The war, or perhaps just progress, he explained, had brought down a plague of Philistines. I understood at last why my enthusiasms had grown so listless, my nostalgias so febrile; why the trueness of things had turned so pallid and their shadows so opaque.

Philistine, of course, was a multitudinous and complex name. Its connotations were social, and even political, as much as aesthetic. Our Philistine, though we thought of him as a bourgeois with rounded paunch, had several traits in common with the present-day square. He was conformist and a vulgarian by definition, but not necessarily a lowbrow; indeed the educated and intellectualizing strain was one of the most virulent. He might be unimaginatively earnest—whether orthodox believer or doctrinaire atheist—or a brittle sophisticate; a stuffed-shirt conservative, or the dessicated type of liberal. There were, naturally, gradations in Philistinism. Poor Mr. Judson was a patent example—after all, he doted on the Romans, worshiped Raphael, and agreed with Hawthorne that of all painters Murillo was the truest and tenderest—but a relatively innocuous one.

If we had been trained in the new Communist polemical technique of putting all one's rotten eggs in a single basket, we might have characterized the enemy as a materialist-conformist-vulgarian-ultrarationalist-authoritarian-academic-atomistic-plutocratic Philistine, and left him for dead. Whether his spiritual homeland was the nascent mass culture of Henry Ford's America, the dark, Satanic capitalism of nineteenth-century England, or the arid, frivolous enlightenment of Diderot's France, we would have been hard put to decide. The contours of the ideal anti-Philistine landscape that we carried in our minds were equally difficult to localize in time and space. Sometimes, fleetingly, one seemed to catch a glimpse of the woods around Walden Pond, or the cobbled squares of Rousseau's virtuous, true-hearted, imaginary Republic of Geneva; more often one recognized the tidy craftsmen's cottages and maypoles of William Morris's regreened and pleasant Britain. The lowing heifers the youths and maids of pre-Periclean Athens were always with us, of course; so was the clear and high-colored bustle of fifteenth-century Florence. All these were but the suburbs of utopia, however. Its citadel enclosed the spires, the cloisters, ar.d the fraternal workbenches of what Bob and I thought of as the Middle Ages, the time of Chartres and Giotto, the lost age of faith—not ours, of course— when men worked with glad hearts for God and guild and Our Gracious Lady. (Like other archaizers, we failed to realize how un-medieval—in the sense of being urban, bourgeois, and even skeptical—the later Middle Ages often were.)

There are familiar patterns, traces of a half-dozen recurrent modern heresies—apart from the perennial heresy of youth itself— in this adolescent world view that some mature minds of our age do not seem to have completely outgrown. As an interpretation of history, its underlying premises range from the questionable to the grotesque, but as an implicit critique of contemporary American society, and of postwar civilization generally, it had its uses. A diffuse, wordless alienation was transformed into conscious dissent, and dissent, through its own exaggerations, by slow stages grew into a kind of wary reconciliation.

Poking retrospectively into these long-buried compost heaps of the mind, I am more and more struck by the extreme complexity of the fermentation that has taken place—and is still taking place— within them. Does the intellectual retreat from the machine age into the supposedly more integrated society of the late Middle Ages represent a reaction to the atomized loneliness of twentieth-century life, or is it an oblique attempt to come to terms with the present behind history's back, like Mussolini's fascism, that reflects our increasingly collectivist trend? Did the anti-rationalism implicit in my adolescent infatuation with the romantic poets seek to free the pure soul, or to unseat the free mind? Was it a healthy response to the dessication of contemporary thought, or a symptom that within one brain contemporary civilization was breaking down?

There is a warning in such unanswerable questions against oversimplifying the subtle chemistry of historic process. To me, at least, the lesson becomes progressively more pointed as I retrace my steps in memory, side by side with my two guides, the old Mr. Judson, the young Bob, a shade accompanied by shades, through the echoing ruins and museums of the Mediterranean past, the imperishable netherworld of our civilization where the great spirits eternally live for us and live not, where the great voices reverberate forever in the booming caverns, endlessly deformed by their own reverberations, endlessly transfigured.

One of those voices is sounding in my ears as I write, Bob's again, but Shelley's words, the opening epode of his *Ode to Naples,* one of those majestic, musical fountains of rhetoric that I admired particularly.

> *"I stood within the city disinterred;*
> *And heard the autumnal leaves like light footfalls . . ."*

The screen of memory lights up and I see the three of us standing in the ruins of Pompeii: Bob, his head thrown back, his chest thrown out, declaiming; myself—a more intense and slender self—Mr. Judson—though he did not approve very highly of Bob, or for that matter, Shelley—wagging his head to mark the beat of the lines in the same emphatic way that he did to encourage Virgil. In a moment he will put in a word for Cicero and the rule of law as the cornerstone of liberty.

Abruptly, as in a Fellini film, the image changes. The ruins are still there, but now they are those of Naples itself. It is almost twenty years later and I am standing alone on the bombed-out waterfront of the old town. The same voice is in my ears, and though the poem too now lies in fragments, half-buried in the mental rubble of a generation, a few lines stand like the shattered columns of some antique temple.

> *. . . Heart of men, which ever pantest*
> *Naked, beneath the lidless eye of heaven! . . .*
> *Metropolis of a ruined Paradise*
> *Long lost, late won, and yet but half regained!*

36

I doubt whether even in my poetry-drugged youth I ever quite thought of Naples as a heart of men—some alimentary or genital metaphor would have seemed more apt—but its naked humanity, neither flaunted nor held abashed, had captivated my own heart from the moment I stepped off the ship with Bob and Mr. Judson, and suddenly, thanks to them, to Pompeii and to Shelley, it was as if the sordes of war had been wiped away, and the mutilated, half-regained city glowed once more with a refracted Grecian splendor that I carried away with me to the other side of the world.

The decisive influence of the Mediterrean past on my adolescent mind was unquestionably that of its sculptors and painters, especially the latter. It was Bob, of course, who first opened my eyes to the firmament of art. Besides showing me what to look at, he taught me the rudiments of how to look at painting or sculpture. Above all, he communicated to me some of the passion and reverence he himself felt for the works of the masters he admired. The gift of appreciation thus conferred—the new syntax of the eye and the heart thereby imparted—would have been valuable at any time. As it was, this was the time when eye and heart alike were freshest, mind most eager, and when the richest nourishment for them was close to hand, in the greatest abundance. Thanks to this sorcery of circumstance, the endless hours I spent in the museums or churches of Italy and France (above all those in Assisi and in Florence) count among the most luminous of my youth.

The lessons of the early Renaissance painters were sharpened and corrected for me by humbler, more contemporary Italian influences. We grow up to be human beings, as Boris Pasternak has said, in the degree that we have loved other humans, and no doubt our humanity is never full-grown until we have learned to love all truly human things, both great and small. Like many travelers before me, I found Italy an incomparable school of humanity, for it made accessible many essentially human things that at home had seemed either too great or too small for loving, too near or too far. Even the very small, very active and in those days omnipresent Italian flea had a certain educational value. I still remember Bob's naïve shout of joy during our first ride in a Neapolitan *carrozza* when he plucked at his ankle and came up with a minuscule black speck between thumb and forefinger. Mr. Judson himself chuckled: Fleas were recognized, if not quite approved, by Baedeker as a form of local color. Mayakovsky's anti-ideological Soviet bedbug had not yet crawled over the Western literary horizon, but I suspect that to us, in any case, our first Italian flea had much the same symbolic significance. Man, in the old full sense, must already have begun to seem scarce in his North American, no less than in his Russian, habitat, if the discovery of one of the body parasites that had kept him faithful company through the ages was felt by us to be such a reassuring indication of his continued survival on the Italian Peninsula.

Whenever barbarians identify civilization with plumbing, counter-barbarians will tend to equate dirt with culture; where Philistines deny humanity to the seedy, romantics are prone to cherish seediness as an essential attribute of the human condition. No doubt the cult of the flea that Bob and I practiced in our Italian youth was an illustration of this law; at least it facilitated our exploration of the living, teeming city, hygienically primitive but rich in sophisticated simplicities, that lay beyond the invisible pale of Baedeker's Rome.

Our favorite haunt was the old, once elegant Trastevere quarter, not quite a slum area, but a poor and populous one, in those days innocent of nightclubs or fashionable little restaurants. The *trattorie* where Bob and I consumed heroic quantities of Roman noodles, fried, rubbery octopus, and harsh, new Frascati wine were definitely not fashionable, and tourists were then sufficiently rare in such surroundings for us to establish a degree of human contact with the workmen or artisans who made up their normal clientele. The Italian we picked up was never quite enough to sustain our end of a free-ranging conversation with these highly articulate heirs of an ancient civilization—together with a handful of aristocratic facilies, the Trastevere plebs claim to be the most Roman Romans of them all—but in time it enabled us, if nothing else, to appreciate the quality of our interlocutors.

All of our Trastevere friends, it seemed, were outspoken, if not particularly militant, critics of the Mussolinian dictatorship (whose authentically totalitarian phase still lay ahead), and they denounced the old-fashioned iniquities of Italian bourgeois society in terms of a revolutionary doctrine more libertarian than socialist that a young Shelley-lover could easily assimilate. I had encountered victims of oppression and injustice before—every time, in fact, that I crossed the two Negro blocks from the streetcar stop to my grandmother's house in St. Louis—but these were the first who appealed to the romantic imagination, and through it bypassed the lamentable snobbery of the heart's defenses. It was Rome, and more particularly Trastevere, that planted in my mind the seedlings of that climax-growth of middle twentieth-century civilization: a social conscience.

A banal travel incident, which at the same time was an adventure as full of marvel as the Homeric explorations of early childhood, helped to fertilize the planting. For some reason that I no longer remember, Bob and I had decided to hike to Marina di Ostia, a depressing beach resort on the flat coast at the mouth of the Tiber, in order to visit the nearby ruins of the old Roman port of Ostia. Mr. Judson considered the project sufficiently worthy to give me an afternoon off, and we set out from the Porta San Paolo, then quite at the edge of the city, after a hasty *pasta* in a neighboring *trattoria*.

The distance to Ostia, we calculated, was only about fifteen miles, so we would have plenty of time to look at the ruins before taking the train back to Rome. It hardly seemed worthwhile to burden ourselves with topcoats or raincoats, though the sky was lowering and a wet-smelling wind whistled across the Campagna. The Campagna in those days was a lonely, often marshy waste almost from the gates of Rome, dotted with the ruined tombs of antiquity and at long intervals with dark, twisted parasol pines that looked as if they already had been there when Aeneas landed. On this late November afternoon it made a fine, forlorn landscape in the early nineteenth-century manner—as I recall it, we did not see a single automobile on the whole walk—and at the first tomb, shaded by the first pine, we simultaneously remembered Ozymandias, King of Kings, and looking on him in the might of youth, began to rejoice. Altogether, the hike turned out even more agreeable than we had expected, but, possibly because of our unsuitable town shoes, not quite so fast. Dusk was falling and a premonitory drizzle had set in by the time we reached the outskirts of Ostia.

We had time to eat a copious meal—accompanied by rather too many of those wide-mouthed, clinical-looking glass beakers of Frascati—and to get to the station before the last train of the evening pulled out for Rome. Dinner used up nearly all our money, but we had had the foresight to buy our tickets first. We were still fumbling for them when the conductor reached our compartment. His manner was nasty, and he looked the cool-executioner type of black-shirted bully straight out of Hemingway, which is exactly what he proved to be. When at last we were forced to admit that the tickets had somehow been lost, he listened to our explanations, our pleas, our entreaties, our reasonable offer to be put under arrest and turned over to the station police in Rome, just long enough to savor our helplessness and our knowledge of our helplessness; then with the stern flourish of an officer commanding a firing squad, pulled the alarm signal, flung open the door when the train jerked to a halt, and ordered us out into the night.

For a few minutes, as we watched the lights of the train dim out in the rainy blackness, we were sustained by the adrenal warmth of our sense of outrage at fascist tyranny, with its trains pompously running on time, and its black-hooded class justice. The bitterness of hate in our throats was intensified by the realization that we were pseudo-martyrs, objectively not weak and poor at all, but highborn young *signorini* with passports and a fat book of traveler's checks back at the hotel.

Such thoughts and feelings are red meat to the lion heart of youth, but it was no night for lions. The rain had turned into an autumnal storm driving in from the Mediterranean with a brute weight of wind and water that at moments felt like the jet from a hose. We were several miles out of Ostia and several times several miles from Rome. Our feet were blistered and we were beginning to feel chilled. It was painful stumbling along the railroad track, but in the dark with the rain squirting in our eyes, and with our minds still a little befogged, we were no longer quite sure where the highway ran.

I suppose we had been walking for only a few minutes when we came upon a small stone hut, hardly more than a tool shed, beside the track. Eventually, after long pounding, sleepy, startled voices answered us, and someone opened the door a crack. Bob took command of the situation, and in an unprecedented fluency of Italian that I could scarcely follow, launched into a detailed, dramatic recital of our trials and woes, starting from when we left Rome, laboring on foot across the waste. Bob's voice, the misfortunes themselves, in fact our very presence at this foresaken spot in the rain and night were more than enough to awaken the strong succoring instinct that inhabits most Italians—the very instinct of protective gentleness toward the defenseless that the gendarme-ethos of fascism was systematically trying to pervert.

A rush torch was lit, the door was opened wide, and we stepped into the hut, a low-ceilinged cubicle with a dirt floor, partly covered with straw, upon which three men had been lying. They smelled rank and looked villainous in the smoky light, but they made room for us in the straw, gave us a scrap of muddy rag for a towel, started a smoldering fire of brushwood in a corner of the hut, hung our dripping pants and coats on a rope above it, and insisted on covering us with the burlap sacks they had been using themselves as blankets. Above all, they warmed us with their articulate Mediterranean compassion for our distress, while their implicit recognition of our bourgeois status restored the sense of social identity that we had begun to lose as waifs in the night. "*Ah, poveri,*" they kept exclaiming, "*poveri signorini.*" Our being *signorini* evidently lent an almost Shakespearean pathos to our misadventure; they knew that *signorini* have tender feet and souls that wilt in the rain. Our hosts—three brothers from the poor, backward province of Apulia who had been without work for a long time until they found jobs as day laborers on the railroad track—shared our indignation as generously as they shared our self-pity.

This fortuitous encounter in the night with the three succoring brothers had an archetypal quality that could hardly fail to stamp itself deeply upon the imagination of youth, and as I lay sleepless on my soggy straw, listening to their snores, assailed by such swarms of fleas that it was like a continuous peppering with fine shot, half choking in the smoke and stink of the hut, I had ample opportunity throughout the night to reflect on its significance. The physical discomfort of my surroundings, following upon the humiliation and despair of our ejection from the train, gave me a new, more concrete realization of the kind of life led by the poor and the humble. At the same time, the experience somehow tempered the revolutionary enthusiasm that generous drafts of Shelley and Frascati were apt to induce in me. The brothers' humanity was so unconquerable that it made even their oppressors and the oppressive social system of which they were apart seem a bit less inhuman. These men, victimized by their society, were men first, victims only secondarily. It proved a useful thought to remember.

Another useful point of view which it seems to me was planted in my mind during that night in the hut on the Campagna related more directly to my contemporary, somewhat precious obsession with poetry and art. Our hosts, I realized, were only primitives in a technological sense, and something more elaborate than the pastoral tradition of the ancient Mediterranean, something more refined than natural kindness of heart had patterned their behavior toward their guests. There was a psychological delicacy in their attitude, a kind of educated chivalry, that bespoke the influences of a complex civilization. Above all there was the spontaneous charity reflecting the centuries of laborious ethical and emotional discipline that had made theirs a Christian civilization. It was—among other things— to teach men such unthinking reflexes of Christian civility, such almost somatic embodiments of the Christian faith, that the generations of Martins and Francises had preached by example, that the

Giottos and Fra Angelicos had painted their exegesis in fresco. The supreme measure of their achievement was not the cathedrals that their fervor had caused to rise, nor the masterpieces of color and design that their piety had bequeathed us, but the social attitudes, including those of railroad workers, that they had ultimately helped to form. Saints and artists, poets and philosophers, embelish civilization to the degree that they enrich human relations.

At the time these thoughts must have been more shadowy. In an inchoate form, however, they were gestating in my mind that night. Like a word at the tip of one's tongue, they were close to full consciousness when night at last came to its end in a faint, gray light in the chinks of the door, and the brothers rose to begin their long day's work, and Bob and I struggled into our damp, sooty clothes.

The brothers apologized for having no food to offer us. Their canteen was more than a mile away, in the wrong direction, they said, and probably we would not be allowed to eat there if they brought us along. There was an *osteria*, a country inn, nearer at hand and on the highway to Rome; with the three lire left in our pockets, we would be able to get some bread and coffee. Our hosts put us on the road and said good-by. We thanked them, and turned and started limping toward the distant city, stiff and itchy and a little queasy. It was a clear morning.

At the *osteria* we bought a half loaf of coarse peasant bread, then hesitated between a bowl of coffee with goat's milk in it and a morning cigarette apiece. Finally, we decide to spend our last *centesimi* on the cigarettes. It was probably a wise choice, judging by the bread, which like most sophisticated returns to the simple life proved to be a disillusionment. It was too hard and sour, and after conscientiously munching a few mouthfuls as we trudged along, we threw the rest into a ditch and lit up our cigarettes. They were rank but strong, and our stomachs contracted gratefully at the shock of the familiar poison. Then the sun, a huge disk of tranished copper, began to lift above the Alban hills, and Bob as usual found the right authority for its presence, Browning this time:

43

> *"Round the cape of a sudden came the sea,*
> *And the sun looked over the mountain's rim;*
> *And straight was the path of gold for him,*
> *And the need of a world of men for me."*

Without realizing it, I had changed professions in the night. It was a world of men that I, too, needed, rather than a world of poems or of trees.

From the Traveler's Log (1963):

Evening drink with V. at the Piazza del Popolo, and final reconciliation with Roman baroque (Central European variety of course an old love). Flowering weeds sprouting from domes of two matched seventeenth-century churches flanking Corso, Santa Maria in Monte Santo and Santa Maria de' Miracoli, gave needed touch. V. entranced because, she says, this is exactly Piranesi's Rome. Agree with her, but feel obliged to point out dangers of esthetic inflation in this approach. Praise Piranesi for discovering weeds flowering in crevices of Counter-Reformation—lurking existentialist doubts behind splendors and prisons of triumphant orthodoxy—but more praise to baroque architects who anticipated the weeds and a Piranesi to see them. Praise Rainaldi and the subtle Bernini, embellishing with decay. Marvelous, distraught Madeleines and Mary's outlined against the paling sky, ravaged by time and rain like corpses stripped of flesh beneath the flowing robes: twisted wraiths of stone. To St. Peter's in the last light, admiring Bernini's saints again, and awesome sweep of his colonnade: universe wheeling in infinity, ultimate curvature of time. Lighted window high up in Vatican where John XXIII lies dying, and small crowd already beginning to gather in square, pocket-transistors turned low and held close to heads in

spontaneous respect for occasion. Politicians I have been interview-
ing denounce Pope for betraying Italy to Communists, but I wonder
whether John's political errors—assuming they were errors—weren't
outweighed by his service in helping an euphemized age rediscover
dignity of death. Sudden, tremendous boom of nearby church bells,
tolling for all.

3

The City and the City Room

There is a certain bell sound that even today sets my heart leaping: the vibrant, insistent clangor produced by one of those electrically-operated signal devices, like the buzzer of an oversized alarm clock, that are often installed in schools, orphanages, and similar institutions. The one I remember most vividly had a particularly sharp and nickeled timbre. It rang in the emergency receiving room of the St. Louis City Hospital whenever an ambulance drew up under the covered portico. At the warning, stretcher-bearers, nurses, and doctors would spring into action with more or less alacrity—somehow they seemed to be able to tell from the very tone of the alarm when seconds were precious and when they were less important or no longer mattered—and I would come out of the cubicle allotted for the alien needs of my profession to try to get the facts from the victim, his distraught relatives, or the policeman who had picked up his corpse: who-including-middle-initial, please, when; where—and-do-you-mind-repeating-that-street-address; how; what hit him; or why did you do it?

When all these essentials, or as many of them as I could get, had been jotted down on copy paper—folded lengthwise as the old hands carried it—I would call up the city desk and report what I had learned. With luck, I might be switched over to a rewrite man to give a paragraph, providing the emergency had been sufficiently gory and the victim belonged to the right race (in the normal course of things Negroes had their own black emergencies and were taken to their own black hospital, where they rarely produced even a paragraph).

My paper, the St. Louis *Globe Democrat,* was a morning one, and my hours on duty at the hospital were from eight P.M. to midnight, except Saturdays, when I had to check in earlier. It was the *Globe*'s policy in those days, or at least the policy of the *Globe*'s publisher, to take on several young men each summer as temporary cub reporters. Usually they were students from some university school of journalism, older and considerably better prepared for such employment than I. The publisher, however, happened to be one of mother's friends. So it came about that shortly after my return from Europe with Mr. Judson, I joined the *Globe*'s staff as one of the neophytes.

I had better luck than the others, who spent the greater part of the summer relabeling old folders full of clippings and photographs from the *Globe*'s reference library, or morgue. Three days after I reported for work in the morgue, its head stormed into the city room and delivered an ultimatum. Either I would be pulled off the job, or I was going to be thrown out; my handwriting was totally illegible. The city editor, Francis Douglas, an easygoing but competent newspaperman of the old school, sighed, scratched the back of his large, sagacious head, and finally thought of the City Hospital assignment. At least it would keep me out of the office much of the time, and the experienced *Globe* reporter on the police headquarters beat could be counted upon to field any really important news that might slip past me.

I was delighted, of course, as I was by nearly everything in the enchanted new world that was opening before me: the adult and male society of shirt sleeves and gaudy hangovers and terrifying bawls of "Copy, boy!" in which I timidly took my eighteen-year-old place; the thrill of the weekly pay envelope—three crisp five-dollar bills; the easy camaraderie of the city room with its naïvely shamefaced idealisms and its even more naïvely flaunted cynicisms, its fascinating blend of tradition and today-ness; the pervasive smell of ink; the indefinable smell of the hot, crowded, downtown streets in the empty, nearly cool, blue evening—the true odor of youth; the almost audible sigh of the great, fevered city settling down to ease after its workday; the long, still canyons of reverie opening on the pale sky; the furtive shapes of the city's night-fauna beginning to stir in the shadowy side streets, its scavengers, its predators, and its predestined victims. All these blessings, and to cap them the City Hospital, with its receiving room and the clanging bell.

What the croupier's *"Rien ne va plus!"* is to the compulsive gambler, the sudden whirr of wings from the brambles to the inveterate hunter, the chatter of the ticker tape to the Wall Street speculator, the click of high heels on asphalt pavement to the incorrigible Don Juan, the clang of the receiving room bell speedily became to me. From the first premonitory rattle of its clapper I was lost. All the poisons of journalism entered my bloodstream in a quintessential, main-line solution, making me for the rest of my life the irreclaimable slave of event, a foredoomed addict of the randomness of human destiny.

The passion that tightened my throat every time the bell rang was not entirely base, however. Besides the constantly renewed bondage to chance—including, of course, my own chances for professional glory or disaster—that it signified, the bell also implied for me the almost limitless diversity of human misfortune, the never-staling variety of the human comedy. There was tragedy in its most elemental form: the couple dulled by shock or hysterical with grief, looking down at the small, crushed form under the blankets on the stretcher; the teen-age husband with the baffled eyes holding in his arms the limp body with the cyanosed face, found—but not quite soon enough—in the kitchen with the windows closed. There was ribald farce: the Chinese child with the chamber pot over his head, and the high-pitched glee of his parents when a resourceful intern liberated the prisoner with a deft hammer tap; the terrified fifteen-year-old girl with the milk bottle whose parents had neglected to teach her the basic laws of physics; the shriveled, grinning old faun who had to be hosed down outside the receiving room after police

48

had found him lurking under the seat of an outdoor privy, frightening his female neighbors. There was the Elizabethan tragedy of violence: the stab wounds or razor slashes inflicted by jealous lovers, the faithless wife with the battered-in face, the neighborhood vendettas. There was the more ominous, because faceless or mindless, violence typical of contemporary big-city life in America: the frothy blood bubbling out over tailored silk shirts—the gang wars in St. Louis, though less spectacular than those in New York or Chicago, were just as merciless; the whisky-crazed adolescents dragged from under their overturned cars with splintered thoraxes or gray matter oozing from crunched skulls. Some Saturday nights, when there had been multiple collisions, there might not be enough stretchers or operating tables or medical staff to cope with the flood of disaster, and the less urgent or the hopeless cases would be laid in rows on the floor as in some medieval charnel house; I would have to step over them, dodging the slippery spots on the linoleum, as I tried to keep the city room abreast of catastrophe.

The City Hospital was an education in human nature. It confronted me nightly, in the most inescapably concrete form, with the basic unit of history, all too often dehumanized by abstraction or buried in the ant heap of some collective designation: not Man, nor The Common Man, nor suffering or wayward mankind, but suffering—and usually wayward—men and women.

Though I soon developed the hardboiled manner in the presence of woe or pain that was *de rigueur* in the circles I frequented, I do not think that either the shallow cynicism of the city room or the verbal callousness of the receiving room hardened me very much inwardly. Perhaps the *Globe*'s old-fashioned decency—shared on the whole by the other St. Louis papers—helped to counteract such influences. Once, when I was misled by juvenile zeal to break into an empty tenement flat, after some rather daring acrobatics on the fire escape, in order to borrow a snapshot of a five-year-old motor casualty from his absent parents, Francis Douglas gave me a moderate but explicit lecture on the difference between aggressive reporting and burglary (a semantic frontier not always closely patrolled in some metropolitan city rooms) and ordered me to return the photo, uncopied, within the hour.

The hospital beat was an education in other ways, too. Many types of emergency, I discovered, had their peculiar social background and their own sometimes mysterious astrology that made them, however random from the victim's viewpoint, statistically predictable. August was the month of family or neighborhood quarrels, it seemed, July of drownings. Saturday night, of course, was propitious to undertakers and ambulance-chasers—it was the peak time for both automobile accidents and crimes of violence—while more children were run over on weekday afternoons. Monday was for suicides, but it was also good for industrial accidents. Greeks and Italians favored knives—as Negroes preferred the razor—except for the more or less formalized vendettas, when firearms were likely to be used; the Polish neighborhoods, along with the more turbulent Irish ones, seemingly produced more victims of the blunt instrument. The children of Syrian immigrants were run over by trucks while playing in front of their tenements; Sicilian ones fell off fire escapes.

Most of the attempted suicides, at least the poison cases, occurred in the lower-middle-class boarding or rooming houses that had finally taken over the midtown neighborhood where my grandmother's old home was situated (it, too, was a boardinghouse now). The victims were mainly young women working in offices or stores, and they usually survived. I would see them hustled into the stomach-pump room, their faces set in bravado and self-pity and the pride of imminent death; then, after ghastly moans and gurglings, emerge wan and limp, but smiling up at the harsh overhead lighting, purged of despair, along with the mouthful of iodine or domestic disinfectant they had swallowed. I remember, however, interviewing one exceptionally pretty girl who smiled at me and said, "Be sure and tell everyone what a little fool I was," while the intern who had washed out her stomach looked away and said nothing; she was one of the bichloride cases.

Looking back at it, it seems to me I should have realized, or realized more clearly than I did, from what I saw at the City Hospital—from the rooming-house suicides no less than from the gang massacres and from the weekly holocaust caused by drunken and irresponsible driving—that American urban civilization was entering a particularly acute crisis of adaptation, one comparable in its effects, perhaps, to some of the worst horrors of the early industrial revolution.

Thanks to Prohibition, law enforcement had fallen behind in the struggle to keep pace with organized crime. In a similar way, municipal sanity was unable to restrain the capacity of twentieth-century technology to clog the streets with quantities of automobiles which they had not been built to accommodate.

High salaries were uprooting young girls from their families and their communities to case them adrift in a wasteland of filing cabinets, cafeterias, and rented rooms that had once been homes. In this inhuman habitat, the most banal disappointments of daily life—a broken date, a minor quarrel with the only friend, a lost job or a failure to meet the weekly installment on a fur coat or a portable phonograph—were sometimes enough to bring down the bottle with the red death's-head from the washstand cupboard, to knot the slender length of clothesline where the silk stockings and nice underthings dried, to open the cock on the gas ring that warmed the midnight cocoa.

The late 1920's in America were already the age of David Riesman's lonely crowd. Our cities—and the whole technological civilization that had spawned them—were failing then as now to provide civilized environment for many of their inhabitants.

Even the clear-eyed, plain-speaking captains of industry whose momentously empty utterances I sometimes recorded for posterity at a later stage of my career seemed to be having difficulty at the controls—though their self-confidence was brasher than ever. Already the national fever of speculation was rising, and installment-buying was approaching a dangerous exuberance. The price of farm produce declined and the sharecroppers and homesteaders of the Ozark hills were driven from their submarginal land into the city slums. The older refugees were the human scarecrows I used to see

drifting between the flophouses and infamous speakeasies of the river-
front. They supplied most of our wood-alcohol cases at the hospital.
Their sons accounted for many of the amateur holdups that ended
in the receiving room. Their daughters could be found on the fringe
of the wholesale district in the rooming houses that served as clandestine brothels; some of them, full-bodied, straw-haired, schooled in
the secret depravities of a patriarchal family life, were extraordinarily desirable, if one did not mind the slightly sour smell.

Much of the degradation I witnessed as a cub reporter reflected a
kind of perennial social dross, a self-renewing reservoir of almost
irreducible human suffering, common to all cities and all civilizations. More of it, however, resulted from the gathering crisis of
twentieth-century civilization of which the two world wars were
probably as much a symptom as a cause.

Failure to realize the historic dimension of the drama I was learning to observe rendered its impact on young emotions more traumatic than it need have been. We can never share too much, or even
enough, the sufferings of our brothers, but it is a weakness of the
soul to let oneself be infected with their despair. Like many of the
sensitive-minded in my generation, I was tempted at times to deny
the successes of modern civilization generally, because of its failures;
to mistake a phase for a fate.

Two influences in my case tempered this pessimism. One was the
gradual discovery of the city as a social oragnism.

It was the City Hospital that opened my eyes. An institution
supported by the taxpayers of the community and supervised by
political appointees of the dominant City Hall machine could not
be expected to coddle the underprivileged; not in those pre-welfare
days when the Darwinian ethos ruled the social attitudes of the
nation's elite. The emergency treatment given in the receiving room,
for example, sometimes struck me as a bit more rough than ready.

But in the great majority of cases, when the receiving room bell
sounded it was to raise the curtain on a drama of human solidarity as
well as of human suffering. Policemen or firemen, ambulance drivers,
orderlies, nurses, and doctors were all actors in it. When the emer-

gency was acute they worked with unflagging dedication; more than once I saw lives saved at the critical moment by the professional conscience and discipline displayed by these human phagocytes of the urban bloodstream. Even at the time, I felt a kind of exhilaration whenever I saw the city triumph over its own chaos; later, when I had occasion to live where civilization had not secured such benefits or where war had destroyed them, it seemed that I had been the witness of miracle. To the degree that paradox implies miracle, it was one. The social jungle that I was beginning to explore with a mixture of fascination and horror and sheer youthful excitement was at the same time a jungle society. Its denizens collaborated no less than they competed for survival.

Like my fellow citizens I too was a jungle paradox. Exposure to the human wastage of an acquisitive and competitive society might deal a shock to young emotions, but the possibilities for journalistic advancement arising out of the exposure were meat to a hungry young competitor. That was the second antidote to pessimism. When I went to work for the *Globe Democrat* I was making a reconnaissance rather than embarking upon a career. On returning from Europe I had taken college entrance examinations and enrolled in an eastern university. However, my father was slowly dying of cancer, like poor Mr. Judson, and the spell of the city room, or that of the receiving room, had taken hold upon me. For a while I attempted a compromise: working for the *Globe* in the evening while attending courses at nearby Washington University. The experiment did not prove successful. As time went by the world of formal learning seemed increasingly pallid, while the journalistic world of seeing and doing became more bright-hued.

As a budding newspaperman I had luck. After a few months my pay at the *Globe* was raised to eighteen dollars a week. I was taken off the City Hospital beat—except for occasional Saturday nights— to be given more varied and responsible assignments. Less than eighteen months after I had started labeling envelopes in the *Globe* morgue, I was a rewrite man and by-lined feature writer, earning thirty-five a week, on the St. Louis *Times*. It was a dying and rather sleazy afternoon sheet, since defunct. Nonetheless, for a nineteen-year-old I felt I had scored a major professional break-through and I was beginning to think of journalism as some kind of stepping-stone. Dostoevski had for the moment superseded the romantic poets in my pantheon of the emotions, but somehow local misery and degradation lacked the appeal of the exotic varieties. I could not manage to feel quite as bleak about them as I thought I ought to. Perhaps because journalistic success was taking me farther from its original sources in the City Hospital receiving room, my imagination was beginning to feel confined. The traditional remedy for this state was Paris. In the summer of 1928 I decided to try it.

4

The Village of Dissent

Outwardly changeless but each year subtly different in mood, summer has come back to Saint-Germain-des-Prés, the meandering seventeenth-century village embedded in the flank of modern Paris that has become the haunt and symbol of contemporary intellectual torment. Once again the swallows twitter in the shallow evening sky, as they have these last ten hundred summers, around the weathered belfry of the abbey founded by Childeric, from which the quarter takes its name. Built foursquare in the sturdy Norman-Romanesque style to rise above hedgerows and human folly, the old cloud-gray tower has a country grace of its own. It is pleasant to look up at it in the warm, dawdling twilight of recovered June; and sadly pleasant to revisit the familiar landmarks charged with nearly forty years of memories.

The last revolutionary tumult—the fourth I have covered in Paris in my career as a reporter—appears to have subsided, and the *terrasse* of the Deux Magots is almost normal. The more sophisticated tourists are rubbing shoulders with the more prosperous native intelligentsia or with visiting patrons of the gray arts from across the river. On the next corner, at the Café de Flore, which has successively harbored Charles Maurras, Picasso, and Jean-Paul Sartre, bearded and seasonal young existentialists from Omahia or Appenzell with a sprinkling of shaggy, gaudy, pseudo-hippies loll under the trees and gape back at the busloads of conducted tourists, vainly craning their

55

necks for a glimpse of Sartre or of Simone de Beauvoir, who probably have not set foot in the Flore since central heating came back around 1947. Across the boulevard at Lipp's, haunted by the gray ghost of Joyce and the beery enthusiasms of bygone literary rebellions, intellectuals of a crisp new generation gesticulate over their beer mugs, dissecting some contemporary counterfeit or resurrecting some forgotten creed, perhaps the Druid cults of ancient Gaul, perhaps the Marcuse philosophy of revolution in the light of the new Structuralist revelation. In my day it was more likely to be Gide, and the Albigensian heresy or the technocratic utopia of the Synarchists.

I am thinking, of course, of the late 1920's, when I first settled on the Left Bank. Though my memories of the quarter sometimes get confused, half, I suppose, of my twenty-odd years in Paris were lived within a 1,000-yard radius of Saint-Germain-des-Prés, and though I have seldom been one of its true habitués, it is closely linked in my mind with several phases of my life. In the mid-1930's, for example, I lived for nearly a year in a little attic apartment in the Rue Bonaparte next to the École des Beaux Arts. Again, when I came back to Europe after the last war, I stayed at a small hotel between the Luxembourg Gardens and the Boulevard St. Germain, and for weeks spent most of my evenings in the cafés or bars that were already beginning to give the area its postwar reputation.

At that time the inhabitants of this resuscitated Bohemia—a blend of Pigalle and the old Montparnasse, with only traces of the original Saint-Germain-des-Prés—formed a strangely heterogeneous community, with its ruling caste of hyperalienated intellectual mandarins, its blue-jeaned cultists of world government and revivalists of nuclear doom, and its turbulent proletariat of frustrated jazz artists, juvenile delinquents, nostalgic saboteurs left over from the wartime resistance, small-time black-marketeers, G.I. deserters, prostitutes, pimps, press agents and miscellaneous misfits from all over. We had been a mixed lot, too, twenty years earlier, but not, it seemed to me, quite that mixed. The new generation was also unquestionably more picturesque, with its turtleneck sweaters, skin-tight black slacks for the girls and blue jeans or tight corduroy trousers for the boys, duffel coats in winter, and for warm-weather wear, the open-necked black shirt, redolent of anarchy, fascism, poets accursed, and laundry bills economized.

I remember sitting one evening in the Montana Bar, the old expatriates' home away from home in the Rue St. Benoit, talking with a doll-like little blonde of seventeen or eighteen who wore greasy blue overalls and a hairdo that suggested Ophelia after the muskrats had been at her. Originally a native of my own St. Louis, she was a refugee from some Swiss finishing school who had eloped with a surrealist photographer. The couple now had a baby and the young mother seemed happy, though she complained that it was nuisance not to have a room of their own.

"Where do you keep the baby?" I asked.

"Why, in a garage," she answered. "He sleeps on the front seats."

The girl reminded me of certain female waifs I had known in my young days on the Left Bank, but babies had not been in vogue then, even when parked in garages. I am not sure whether we were more responsible, or more estranged from the life force. Perhaps we were simply less adjusted to the machine age.

In any case, it is comforting as I continue my stroll—I am almost a tourist myself, these days—admiring the gracious seventeenth- or eighteenth-century facades behind which so many generations of artists and thinkers have kept their lonely rendezvous with truth, to reflect on the marvelous capacity of the human mind when left in freedom to think itself out of the bogs it has previously thought itself into. I have floundered myself in and out of more than one, in my time.

> *need we be bound by any chains at all*
> *surely by none not any chains*
> *especially Keats's golden ones*
> *gold are the worst*

and let us above all begin our lines modestly
capitals make everything seem too important
when nothing is surely not hunger
not thirst

we shall make the lines long or short
just as we like or just as they come
sometimes saying too much or too little
never enough
never anything whole or wholly avowed
or quite real or really unreal
only things that comfort a little or hurt a little
not enough

ODDS AND BITS   1928–1934

I had no thought of becoming an expatriate when I arrived in Paris in the summer of 1928, and it was not the lure of Bohemian life on the Left Bank that drew me there. The trammels of a puritan society had not seemed to me to lie heavily on the skeptical world of the city room, even in St. Louis; the disordered social landscape that I had observed from the City Hospital, if nightmarish at moments, was not driving me to seek refuge in an alien disorder. The natural restlessness of youth was an element in my decision to leave home, but ambition was a greater one; Paris, I had often heard, offered more journalistic opportunity, as well as more food for the imagination, than I was likely to find in America. If the expectation proved unrealistic, I could always return.

Scores, if not hundreds, of young Americans with similarly vague but normal dreams of a career as a foreign correspondent, writer, or painter turned up every summer in Paris. Those who lacked enough money to settle down, or who were unable to find work, went home after a few months, no worse for the experience. The smaller number who could afford to stay abroad, or who, like myself, stumbled into a regular job, soon found themselves absorbed into an expatriate society almost defiantly antithetical to the one they had known, yet in certain ways extraordinarily like it. The elite of this loose-jointed community, our pilgrim fathers and our first families, were the already famous Lost Generation, whose epigones in my day could still be seen nursing the traumas of war at the Dome, the Select, and other Left Bank haunts immortalized by Ernest Hemingway. Hemingway himself, though no longer a permanent resident, counted among the foremost patricians, and to be seen exchanging monosyllables with him in a bar significantly raised one's social standing.

The Left Bank expatriate ethos was mainly one of protest and negation, but there was a ritual uniformity in its expression that at times recalled a Rotary lunch in a midwestern town; essentially we were boosters in reverse, and being self-consciously anti-conformist made us instinctively no less gregarious. It was not enough to be expatriates: We had to be red-blooded, one-hundred-percent ones.

Many characteristic American attitudes and folkways could indeed be found, only slightly distorted, among the cultural rebels who thought they had discovered the new shores of freedom between the Pont du Louvre and Notre Dame. In St. Louis, for example, it had been considered essential to have a "good" address; in Paris, I discovered, it was just as important. The Seine was as much a social frontier as the railroad tracks in the average American town. The shantytown on the Right Bank, clustered around such centers of intellectual squalor as the American Cathedral on the Avenue Georges V, the American Club in the Faubourg St. Honoré, and Morgan's Bank on the Place Vendôme, was patently uninhabitable; the more elegant reaches of the Faubourg St. Germain, with its money-writers like Louis Bromfield, were little better. The desirable residential areas were Montparnasse, Saint-Germain-des-Prés, and the Latin Quarter, especially the warren of medieval alleyways winding down to the river. I had the good luck to find a room in the Rue Vaugirard, between the Luxembourg Gardens and the Boulevard St. Michel. The eighteenth-century facade of my hotel, the Lisbonne, had a disturbing list even then—it has settled a bit more since—but the building had once sheltered Baudelaire, the landlord was a colorfully truculent Auvergnat who used the only bathtub in the establishment as a coal bin, and the hot-water tap in my wash-stand ran for half an hour on Sundays, so you could shave. The Hotel de Lisbonne was occupied at the time solely by expatriate Americans, mostly temporary or part-time bachelors. Its atmosphere was a blend of that of an intellectuals' phalanstery and that of a rowdy fraternity house back home. With quarters like that, I never had to blush when people asked my address.

I was equally lucky in finding a job. Honest work, practiced in moderation and purely to sustain life, was not looked down upon in my Left Bank days, as it came to be later. Only certain activities were socially acceptable, however; others were quite out of the question. It was all right to be a tourist guide—if one had the panache to carry off such a preposterous role—but not a clerk at the American Express. Newspaper work was countenanced, except in the most arcane intellectual circles, and besides the bureaus of the chief American dailies or agencies there were three American news-papers published in Paris: the Paris *Herald* (later *Herald Tribune*), the Paris *Times* and the *European Edition* of the Chicago *Tribune*. The *Herald* had a professional standing that to some extent com-pensated for its identification with the Right Bank American colony, the Establishment of Club and Embassy and Cathedral, but the local Chicago *Tribune* was viewed across the river as having more glamor. I happened to try it first, and the day I turned up at the ramshackle offices which the *Tribune* shared with a French paper in a grimy building at the foot of Montmartre was one of the numerous oc-casions when a sudden vacancy had developed in the editorial staff.

The Chicago *Tribune*, I soon realized, might conceivably be a shortcut to journalistic success, but it was a highly uncertain one. Several brilliant young men—William Shirer, Jay Allen, Waverley Root, Vincent Sheean—with no more previous experience than I had myself had gotten jobs as reporters or rewrite men on the local paper. After a short period of training under Henry Wales, the chief correspondent of the home edition, they had been launched on the international scene as full-fledged correspondents of the Chicago *Tribune* Press Service, with world-copyright by-lines. There was, however, a long list of candidates, several better qualified than I, waiting for the legendary summons to Wales's sanctum and the casual announcement that his latest assistant had just been ordered to Manchuria. My chances seemed dim. Still it cost nothing to wait around for a while—or cost very little, since my franc salary was the equivalent of eighty dollars a month—and in the meantime I could improve my French, deepen my sketchy knowledge of the journalist's craft, advertise my talents by writing by-lined feature stories for the Paris *Tribune*, and enjoy the company of picturesque colleagues.

The *Tribune* was the expatriates' sheet par excellence; its staff was as heterogeneous as its readers. There were ambitious young men like myself—go-getters at heart, all of us, though we would not have dared admit it. There was a small nucleus of uncomplicated craftsmen who would have been happy anywhere, as long as they were getting out a paper; R. J. (Jules) Frantz, who rose to be managing editor of the local edition before it went under in the Great Depression, was the best of them.

There were stranded veterans of General Pershing's long-departed AEF, notable chiefly for their unquenchable thirst or their incomparable single-mindedness in the pursuit of sexual adventure; journalism could only be a minor avocation to such dedicated souls. There were the chronic drifters: the vagrant copyreaders and rewrite men who like the itinerant printer had once been classic features of the American journalistic scene. Most of them were erratic but highly trained professionals, good workers when sober, and usually able to turn out passable copy or headlines that counted up as long as their eyes focused, sometimes with a little help, well after they had ceased to. There were the pseudo-Bohemians and adventurers: a free-lance promoter resting up from some shady entrepreneurial feat who had managed to pass himself off as a veteran reporter; an advertising executive who had hypnotized himself into thinking that he was a newspaperman; a mysterious Central European who looked so much like a gentleman spy that even in the war he never managed to get a job as one.

Finally, there were the artists and the intellectuals, the *Tribune's* specialty. Some of the purer spirits worked as proofreaders in the composing room. They were inclined to be contemptuous of the overpaid bourgeois upstairs: I recall a tiresome, inconclusive argument, which took place after I had become night editor, with the head *guru* of the proofreaders' bench, Henry Miller, a gray, mousy man who looked even less like his books than most writers do. The issue, as I remember it, was a point of style in some late copy I had passed; Miller was technically right, but the Paris *Tribune* was noted among collectors the world over for its typographical howlers, and the press-room deadline was only a few minutes away. I was astonished by so much fuss about a minor linguistic refinement.

The editorial department itself, though it harbored some crypto-bourgeois go-getters and some secret money-writers, contributed conspicuously to the expatriate literary life of the day. The city editor who gave me my first assignments as a reporter in Paris was Eugene Jolas, a warmhearted Alsatian-American poet whose brain was so congested with metaphors in three languages that he seemed at times to be afflicted with verbal hay fever. Jolas was the founder and co-editor of the quartery *transition,* (later *Transition*), a cosmopolitan organ of literary revolt and linguistic experiment, strongly influenced by the surrealist and dadaist movements, which was then publishing in installments Joyce's new, unfinished masterpiece, *Work in Progress* (*Finnegan's Wake* in its final version). *Transition's* other co-editor at the time, the impish Elliot Paul, had only recently transferred from the *Tribune* to the *Herald;* its editing editor—and staff—was then the scholarly Robert Sage (alas, the late Robert Sage, a man of infinitely discreet jest, wondrously sober in his folly), who was a *Tribune* rewrite man in his spare moments and the leading contender for the next vacancy in the *Tribune* Press Service.

It was Sage to whom there fell such laborious chores as sorting out the original word-sequence in a contribution from Gertrude Stein which Paul had deliberately scrambled in type, and drafting a dignified apology to *transition*'s readers for the mishap. Altogether, it might be said that the avant-garde quarterly—and with it something of the subsequent expatriate vogue in American letters—owed a substantial, if indirect, debt to Colonel Robert R. McCormick, the Chicago *Tribune*'s eccentrically traditionalist publisher. (Now many years deceased himself; what lateness in the air!)

The *transition* group symbolized the literary wave of the future. The splendor of the past was represented on the *Tribune* staff by Harold Stearns, perhaps the most magnificently lost embodiment of the Lost Generation in the American diaspora. Stearns, a squat, puffy man with the eyes of a disillusioned mystic, wrote a racing column for the local edition—his only contribution to journalism or literature in those years—but he had once been a favored disciple of H. L. Mencken, and in his youth had written a study of American civilization which the Baltimore sage was rumored to have praised.

Though enlivened by occasional flashes of cosmic scorn, Stearn's conversation usually was not stimulating; it had the laconic and dejected cadence of the shorter dialogue bits in *The Sun Also Rises*, where there is a masterly barroom sketch of Stearns himself. To those of us who had read the novel—and few of us had not—it was always worth the predawn visit to Montparnasse to hear Stearns being monosyllabically insulting to some awestricken tourist who was paying for his drinks, or simply to watch him sitting like a smudged Buddha on a stool at the bar of the Select, aloof and motionless in some ultimate *nirvana* of despair. The sight has undoubtedly inspired other writers besides Hemingway, among them, I suspect, Samuel Beckett, for whose Godot Stearns may unconsciously have been waiting. He held out as long as he could, but in the 30's he finally went home, to settle down in suburbia and write a couple of best-selling books on the rediscovered wholesomeness of American life—a bad shock to many of his former admirers.

63

Montparnasse, rather than Saint-Germain-des-Prés, was the Left
Bank center of Bohemian life in those days, but the younger generation of expatriates, especially those who worked on the Paris
Tribune, spent little time there. It was too expensive for us. The
female tourists who could be picked up ordered too many and too
costly drinks, the spare-time artists' models were inclined to be firm
about their *petits cadeaux*, and relations with the lady expatriates one
encountered tended to have an incestuous quality.

For these and other reasons our amorous lives wherever conducted were tamer than might have been expected. The cause of
sexual freedom was sacred, of course, and from time to time one
was expected to accomplish some gesture of ritual waywardness—
to have one's little *accès* of madness, as the French romantically put
it—but in the main men and women on the Left Bank lived as they
live everywhere, in couples, no less and no more faithfully or last-
ingly than in other big cities of the West. We were not only faithful
in our fashions; we were sober much of the time as well. Even our
drinking bouts were less Homeric than they sounded when we talked
about them.

The most prized intoxicant on the Left Bank in the Flaming
Twenties was neither sex nor alcohol, but talk. Every famous café
had a resident philosopher—the larger establishments usually had
several rival ones—whose nightly symposia were attended by coteries
of faithful disciples. Stearns's academy—an unusually taciturn one—
was at the Select. Henry Miller likewise conducted his discussion
group in Montparnasse; I no longer remember where. Jolas and his
fellow conspirators in the revolution of the word held table, though
more sporadically, at Lipp's.

These informal conversation clubs, gathered spontaneously around
some commanding personality, represented a slightly blurred imprint of the traditional European intellectual café life upon American expatriate society. I frequented a number of them; my favorite
one drifted in a semi-peripatetic way between the Brasserie Balzar,
in the heart of the Latin Quarter, and Lipp's, with an occasional late
sitting somewhere in Montparnasse, but at all times it was authori-

tatively directed by one of my older *Tribune* colleagues, Alec Small (the late A. K. Small).

Small, then in his late thirties I suppose, had the features—and sometimes the inspired imprecation—of a Savonarola; the resemblance was heightened by an incipient bald patch, like a monk's tonsure, on the top of his head. His hair was thin generally, with a dark forelock that often sprang free in the heat of discussion, exceeding orthodoxy. Though he was a notable landmark of the Lost Generation, Small was atypical in several respects. He was one of the few Left Bank expatriates who knew French life and was deeply imbued with French culture. He was also a self-confessed reactionary who believed in paying his debts, who kept his covenants, and who even took a kind of somber interest in his work.

Eventually, Small abandoned his Left Bank clientele to concentrate on being a foreign correspondent for the *Tribune*. When the new days of wrath were upon us, he handled with credit to himself and to his paper some of the nastiest and most dangerous assignments of the epoch. In my early Paris time, however, Small's only job was to write a biweekly column of personal comment for the *Tribune*'s Paris edition. The paper's literary standards—when the copyreaders were sober—were considerably higher than its journalistic ones, but few things in it matched Small's column, either in brilliance of style or in irrelevance to the mainstream of twentieth-century life. His annual autumnal essay, inspired by the falling leaves in the Avenue Foch—with some bleak insights dredged from the depths of a seasonal hangover—was an unfailing masterpiece. Small's conversation was even richer than his prose style: an indefinable blend of Samuel Johnson, Brooks Adams, Rabelais, and Xenophon, with traces of Thomas Hardy and perhaps Ambrose Bierce. His chief contemporary masters were Mencken and Santayana, but as the evening wore on he would gradually work his way back through the eighteenth- and seventeenth-century classics to where his heart eternally lay, in violet-crowned Athens, dominated by the great statue of Pallas Athena on the Acropolis with the sun flashing from its gold-tipped spear. Even the clients of rival sophists would often drop into Lipp's about twenty minutes before closing time and join our table in the hope of rehearing this majestic finale.

The conversational level, of course, was not always that high. At all the Left Bank café-salons, including Small's, a good deal of time was taken up gossiping about celebrities, friends and acquaintances (who was on Vichy water this week, for instance, and why); after all, as an expatriate community we were hardly more than a big village, and gossip is everywhere the staple of village social life. Then came the ancient gossip resurrected as folklore, the oft-told, half-legendary epics of early settler life: the saga of the chronically nonwinning racehorse presented to Harold Stearns by one of his rich admirers; the pathetic love affair between one of the Lost Generation's most noted cynics and its most notorious literary lesbian; the upheavals produced at the Hotel de Lisbonne by the falsely chaste allurements of Yolande, the Rubber-Tired Virgin. When fresh, these ribald or sardonic anecdotes had enormous charm, but they staled fairly quickly.

I tired almost as fast of the repetitious expatriate embroidery upon such basic Menckenesque themes as the horrors of American puritanism, the boobishness of the American boobocracy—particularly evident in its tourists abroad—and the general uncouthness of a civilization without either *bidets* or *sauce béchamel*. Much of the indictment was valid at the time, and some perhaps remains so, but Bob and I had dealt with the question exhaustively three years earlier in our Roman disquisitions upon the Philistine. Those I heard —and sometimes still hear—in Paris were more sophisticated, but scarcely more mature. (I cannot recall any American *autocritique* quite so close to the mark as the hip-shot fired by one of my French friends: "It is not true that Americans lack taste; what you need to develop is more distastes.")

As a kind of probationary expatriate and as a member of the generation that had yet to find itself, I took more interest in the nightly autopsies which Small performed on the cadaver of Western civilization. It was not the lingering traces of a log-cabin culture in American life that he deplored, but the patterns of twentieth-century mass culture that were remolding and, in Small's eyes, degrading it. In reality, it was the machine age itself that he abhorred, and though the burden of the indictment was familiar, his viewpoint was in certain respects novel to me. In contrast to the adolescent romanticism that had suffused my talks with Bob, or to the metaphysical bent of such cultural dissenters as Aldous Huxley and T. S. Eliot, Small was hardminded, classic and rationalist: a twentieth-century Gibbon who traced the decline and impending fall of the West to the enervating religion of progress. The social philosophy of John Dewey and the political utopianism of Woodrow Wilson were perhaps Small's favorite ideological butts. Neither his own experiences in the war to end war, nor his close-up if low-level view of the Paris Peace Conference, had left him with much faith in the possibilities of establishing the rule of reason on this planet.

Pessimism, when systematized, can be a dangerous social depressant, but in reasonably spaced doses it is a good tonic for young minds, especially American ones. Listening to such corrosively articulate voices of the Lost Generation as Small's did not infect me. I was ambitious, if somewhat deviant in my ambitions, and one never wholly despairs of the society or civilization whose prizes one hopes to win.

Youth and the American cult of success were not my only protections against the miasmas of negation that hung over Saint-Germain-des-Prés and Montparnasse in the 20's. Knowing men like Small and Stearns made me realize what a moral cataclysm the war—including the fiasco of the peacemaking—had been. It had darkened the outlook of those who had experienced the ordeal, and seeped into the minds of many who had not. I could see how the most humane and cultivated spirits among the survivors would be tempted to disown the sullied present and retreat into some idealized past. I was not prepared to follow, not all the way. I agreed with my expatriate friends that not all change was progress. I shared their love for the quiet streets and placid tree-lined squares of the Left Bank and its old stones that evoked the invisible presence of history; I enjoyed the sane tempo of French life, its old-fashioned attachment to the human and the personal. Living here was definitely more pleasant than living in contemporary America—partly because in many respects it was like living in an earlier, more human America. I wanted to go on living in France but not to retreat into it, as into a bastion against the forces of change. I did not want to become an expatriate from my century. I had discovered in Italy the dangers of the archaistic temptation; yielding to it, I could now see even more clearly, was unhealthy as well as futile.

I had greater difficulty in recognizing and resisting the temptation of futurism. The literary and artistic life of Paris in the 1920's bubbled with avant-garde movements. Painters, writers, and musicians vied with one another in the boldness of their innovations, whether of form or theme. Elaborate doctrines, sometimes whole philosophies, of art and living were developed to justify and advertise these experiments: André Breton, the founder of surrealism and the apostle of the gratuitous act, was probably the most noted theoretician of the new Babel. Joyce and Picasso were its foremost builders.

A copy of the tenth-anniversary issue of *Transition*, published in the spring of 1938, with a cover in blue, red, and white by Kandinsky, was one of the few papers from my Paris flat, abandoned in June 1940, that I found again after the war. As I flip over the coarse, yellowed pages, a card drops out: an invitation to have drinks on Wednesday with somebody's father who is visiting Paris. The glossy vellum and the bright greenish ink look so fresh that I have a guilty start. Then I look at the name, and memory returns: that was a Wednesday before the war, and the friend with whom my wife and I were invited to drink has been dead since 1940.

Rereading the magazine gives me the same mixed feeling of freshness and staleness, of presence and remoteness. Many of the young word rebels whose names appear in the table of contents—Saroyan, Kay Boyle, Philippe Soupault, Max Brod, Samuel Beckett—are now respectable, sometimes eminent figures in the twentieth-century bourgeois republic of letters. Some of the causes that *Transition* championed were good and have since gained acceptance; the need for an incessant "de-banalization of creative language," as Jolas put it in his anniversary editorial, is felt by a number of contemporary writers both in English and French. To me, at least, *Transition*'s critique of early twentieth-century naturalism and ultrarationalism remains as cogent as ever.

On the other hand, it is now impossible to read Henry Miller on the "cosmological eye," or Jolas himself about *Transition*'s creation of "a new narrative in magic realism (paramyth) and a new form of dream poetry (hypnologue)," or its encouragement of the "phantasmatic metaphor," and its laboriously syncretistic quest for the "Euramerican language of the future." Such gobbledegook is always the language of futurism, and induces today the same blend of nausea and nostalgia as does the modernistic style of interior decoration sponsored by the Salon des Arts Décoratifs of 1925.

What I remember chiefly about my phase as a straggler behind the expatriate avant-garde was the curious mixture of excitement and dejection that contact with it produced in me. I am not a revolutionary by temperament. I might applaud Jolas whether at Lipp's or between the covers of *Transition*, but I despaired of developing the "absolute indifference to the sociological habit of thought" that Jolas explained was one of the secrets of Joyce's creativity.

Joyce himself was a turmoil in the breast, as well as in the brain. When I first read *Ulysses* I felt like Keats discovering Homer. Gradually the elation faded, particularly when I took up the *Work in Progress* as it appeared in *Transition*. The presence of genius was unmistakable, but it was the kind of genius, like Picasso's, that devours its children in its own revolutions. I would not have dared to utter, or even to think, this Philistine thought at the time; in aesthetic matters Saint-Germain-des-Prés had already adopted the slogan it was later to adopt in the political field—*pas d'enemis à gauche*—and speaking out against revolution, any intellectual revolution, would have been like speaking up for motherhood.

It took it for granted that with Joyce a gulf had opened in the history of literature: all writers who stood with him were on the side of the future; the rest of us already belonged to the past. The feeling of hopelessness this thought induced resembled that caused by my childhood discovery that there were no more unexplored lands left to discover, but of course it was deeper.

Looking back on it, it seems to me that in my youthful despair at ever becoming what I supposed a writer had to be, one can observe in a single brain, as if on a slide in a micoscope, the end result of a morbid process that in every field from art to politics has significantly contribtued to the disorder of our age.

It was not the old-fashioned techniques of expression that had to be unlearned—that was not really difficult—but the old ways of feeling. And sometimes it was not so much unlearning as relearning that was required. This lag between mind and heart was not, of course, the only thing that discouraged me. I evidently lacked the gift of obsession, if nothing else. Moreover, I was becoming too fascinated by the collective dramas of humanity to feel the jealous concern with private experience that a novelist or a poet must have. It was reading Joyce—or Vico through Joyce—oddly enough, that aroused my interest in history. Spengler had whetted it. But I was soon to find in the dynamics of events themselves a more formidable master than either of them. Surrealism, it became increasingly apparent, had its adepts in finance and diplomacy no less than in the arts; the masses as well as the intellectuals were casting off the "sociological habit of thought" and reattuning their ears to the ancient voices of the night. Paramyth had escaped from the literary cafés and was stalking the streets. The West's brief holiday from history was nearly over.

My own rather lengthy, and by no means uninstructive, vacation as a Left Bank habitué and as a reporter for the Paris *Tribune* was also coming to an end. The worldwide chain reaction of economic and political disasters set off by the Wall Street crash of October 1929 created a need for more coverage of foreign news in the American press, and therefore for more foreign correspondents. My chances of being drafted into the *Tribune*'s foreign service began to seem less problematic. At the same time, the American colony in Paris started feeling the pinch of the depression; the expatriate Bohemian life, at least in the gaudy phase I had known in 1928, was finished forever. In the editorial room of the Paris *Tribune*, I am proud to say, the era died not with a whimper but with a quite satisfying bang.

The day after Wall Street's Black Thursday—or perhaps it was just after the Black Monday and second Black Tuesday that followed —was payday at the newspaper, and that night we celebrated with a wild party, occasionally pausing in our carouse long enough to cheer some fresh bulletin of doom just off the agency tickers or to pound out a breezy eyewitness account of panic-stricken, sometimes penniless, American tourists whose credit had been wiped out in the disaster besieging the embassy and the local tourist office of the American Express Company. As the evening wore on the orgy grew more and more hysterical. Big firecrackers improvised from flashlight powder tightly rolled in copy paper and fused with an old shoestring were set off under the copyreaders' chairs, or fired down a tube into the composing room. Several times some maniac set fire to the knee-high drift of old newspapers that littered the floor in places and a bona fide Götterdämmerung was narrowly averted. It was a good wake, if a little eerie.

Book Two

Apprenticeship
to
Havoc

5

The Recession from Hope

The dream of becoming a "writer" had helped lure me to Paris. The hope of becoming a foreign correspondent held me there. One day early in 1930 hope crystallized into golden opportunity. The latest assistant to Henry (generally known as Hank) Wales, the Chicago *Tribune*'s chief correspondent in Paris, had just been assigned to distant glory, and Wales, a squat, barrel-chested man with the face of a harassed bulldog, offered me the vacant job.

A former war correspondent on the Western Front and a well-known figure in Paris sporting circles, Hank was reputed to be a harsh boss, suspicious, and ungenerous—though personally I never found him so—as well as exacting. His voice had a built-in rasp even when he tried to be ingratiating, and he had a legendary talent for invective, which he kept well honed on his staff. Naturally I jumped at the chance to work for him.

My duties, for a long time, were humble and unglamorous: They consisted mainly of sitting out the dead hours of the night in the drafty offices of the *Tribune* Press Service tucked behind the editorial room of the Paris *Tribune* and reading the early editions of the French morning papers, rushed up to us fresh off the presses by the cyclist-messenger boy of one of them, specially bribed for the purpose. (Later I discovered he was actually the chief of a syndicate of such messenger-spies who stole advance copies of every paper in town for every other paper, a system that for years operated to general satisfaction.) If there was any news of real importance in the papers I was supposed to call Wales at his favorite nightclub. If not, I went home or—at the risk of withering sarcasm the next morning in case I had guessed wrong—wrote a short cabled dispatch on some human interest feature or minor news item and sent it off on my own responsibility, though always signed with my chief's name. (Wales was even more sensitive than other American correspondents at the time to such punctilios of office etiquette.)

Being an apprentice foreign correspondent, I discovered, was rather like going back to being a cub reporter, but the discovery failed to tarnish the splendor of the job in my eyes. I knew my feet were now on the lowest rung of a ladder that with luck and nerve could be used to scale the summits. Foreign news was much less important to American newspapers in those days than it is now, yet I believe that foreign correspondents had greater prestige—even in the eyes of their editors—than they do today. To most young American newspapermen the life of a foreign correspondent, as they imagined it, seemed incomparably romantic—a reflection no doubt of America's dawning and still naïve world-awareness. Covering the news in a foreign country was somehow felt to be not so much a specialized reportorial assignment as a higher dimension of journalism. Foreign news was of a different essence from any other: It was not mere news, in fact, but living history. The distinction was completely fallacious, of course, but from the correspondents' viewpoint, it was a useful misconception quite apart from its evident contribution to bolstering their status. Thinking of foreign news as history unfortunately did not always inspire us to treat it with a historian's care, but at times it helped us inject at least a trace of historical perspective into our messages.

In the early 30's, moreover, there were no TV cameras—and very little on-the-spot radio reporting—to give the public the impression of history being brought live and raw, sometimes all too live, too raw, into the family living room. Consequently the less stodgy American papers, among them the Chicago *Tribune*, liked their correspondents' cables to be peppered with colorful detail and—up to a point—with exciting or homely personal impressions that helped give the reader the illusion of being present at the event reported. A correspondent was therefore expected to be not merely an instant historian, but an impresario of history—a function since taken over and sometimes monstrously overdeveloped by the stars of the electronic screen. This I-Was-There type of reporting, at which I regret to say I eventually became proficient, produced some painfully unsophisticated, and at times plain bad, journalism, but it may have helped give the American newspaper reader of the day a greater sense of participation in the travails of the age. I am certain that it helped the correspondents to feel more deeply concerned in the affairs upon which we reported. Indeed, the kind of lively, personalized reporting the *Tribune* expected from its European correspondents almost inevitably led us into the emotional involvement in the messy politics of the Old World that the paper's editorial columns ceaselessly anathematized.

Fortunately, our chiefs back in Chicago usually failed to realize what was happening until it was too late. SUGGEST YOU JOIN FOREIGN LEGION OR TAKE REST CURE IN NEUTRAL SANITARIUM, Col. McCormick finally advised me in a cable criticizing the more and more unneutral and anti-isolationist tenor of my dispatches. That, however, was in the fall of 1939, after war had broken out in Europe. By then I had been living with and through the century's second crisis of civilization for almost ten years. I had not merely watched it develop (much of the time, it is true, without realizing clearly what I was watching), but in covering it for my paper had become personally and deeply involved in it.

Maybe it was the girl they shot outside my hotel room window while I was eating breakfast, maybe it's the painful bruise on my instep from a horse's hoof when the Civil Guards rode into a crowd where I was standing, or maybe it's the way the airtight censorship is clamped down on telegrams and telephones.

77

At any rate, I have learned that a nightmare sometimes occurs in real life and it is hard to keep this from being an extremely biased story of what Spain looks like with the lid on.

The yellow and frayed clipping, one of the few from my *Tribune* days that I have kept—after all it was my first revolution—is date-lined Barcelona, by courier to Perpignan, France (the courier having been myself), and dated December 17. This was 1930. The events that a few days earlier had inspired a cable from Chicago instructing me to proceed soonest to northern Spain—Col. McCormick's correspondents in accordance with military tradition always "proceeded" on their assignments, and usually "soonest"—do not loom large in most modern histories of the peninsula. A rather amateurish conspiracy to overthrow the monarchy of Alfonso XIII and set up a democratic republic had been aborted when part of the garrison at Jaca near the French border in northern Aragon revolted prematurely. The leaders of the pathetic insurrection, Captains Firmín Galán and García Hernández, had been taken prisoner trying to march on Zaragoza and after a hasty court-martial had been shot. Their execution touched off a general strike and other demonstrations of popular indignation, particularly in the region around Zaragoza and at Huesca to the north, whose harsh repression I arrived in time to witness.

The story that appeared in the *Tribune* is a reasonably accurate account of what I saw and heard, but subjectively it was not quite honest. I had, it is true, been shocked by the nakedness of civic hatred I had seen displayed. My indignation at the police brutality, worse than any fascist bullying I had seen in Italy, was sincere. But as far as I was concerned, the discovery of such evils hardly amounted to nightmare. On the contrary, that first assignment in Spain looms in memory as one of the most splendid adventures of youth, and I never thought of it otherwise. The thrill of racing for the Sud Express and making it at the last moment; the sudden leap back in time on the other side of the border; the harsh steely light; the vengeful snow flurries and the endless hours driving across the high, bare, whistling plains of Aragon; the feel of an undiscovered, perhaps undiscoverable land seizing and wounding the heart; the Goyaesque vignettes of strife and passion under a sky Goya might have painted; the surrealist tumult in ancient streets; the momentary fright and retrospective glow of thinking oneself under fire; the Mediterranean swagger and rhythm of Barcelona; the gypsy dives where I roistered in with a local colleague; the cunning attempt to foil the censors with a private wire in hyperesoteric American slang (calamitously mistranslated in Paris by our French office boy, Robert); the dash by rented car to the French border; the imagined ambushes and pursuits—what incomparable delights for a twenty-two-year-old cub correspondent, ex-would-be-novelist-poet-explorer.

Despite the inadvertent hypocrisy, I cannot bring myself to blush at the clipping that lies on my work table with its naïve report from another age and another self, with its blend of youthful zest and slightly synthetic horror. There is no need to invoke the vast collective nightmares we are all familiar with; I can think of some relatively modest and quasi-private ones, including several I encountered a few years later in Spain, that give a kind of nostalgic charm to those homely 1930 outrages, or at least to the thought that a great paper was prepared to send a correspondent hundreds of miles and spend thousands of dollars to report them.

As spot news, my story was almost valueless, and the *Tribune*'s editors had not tried to pretend otherwise:

SPAIN—A STORY OF IRON RULE AT POINT OF GUN
Situation Described by Tribune Man.

For some reason, such a story, sentimental and moralistic, at most an oblique footnote to the situation in Spain, seemed—at least to the Chicago *Tribune*—a useful journalistic contribution. In that far-off age of innocence readers were not spoiled.

The *Tribune* usually disapproved of outright "editorializing" in

79

the news columns, but it had no inhibitions about presenting the facts in a way that left little doubt where its—that is to say, Col. Mc-Cormick's—editorial sympathies lay. And in retrospect, the most admirable thing about the Colonel's sympathies—or antipathies—was their inconsistency. A regal and autocratic figure around the Tribune Tower in Chicago, Col. McCormick had nothing but contempt for Old World tyrants, crowned or uncrowned, arrogant upstarts or degenerate scions.

An American diplomat once described McCormick as the most brilliant mind of the fourteenth century. The Colonel was indeed anachronistic in many of his social and political attitudes; he was nonetheless an early, outspoken critic of the nascent totalitarianism that was seeking to put the clock back in Europe. When Mussolini, resenting this criticism, expelled first one, then another *Tribune* correspondent, Col. McCormick retaliated by declaring Italy henceforth out of bounds to all members of his foreign service. In 1930 my uncomplicated American sense of outrage at regimes that depend upon murder, however judiciously practiced, to remain in power, and my implicit Wilsonian assumption that the alternative to an oppressive monarchy must no doubt be an enlightened democracy, were evidently compatible with the *Tribune* ethos.

It is pleasant, in any case, to look back on a time when Americans could indulge in the luxury of indignation at foreign misbehavior without having to worry lest its expression endanger a vital American base, alienate a valued ally, favor the triumph of communism in a key area, threaten goodwill, discredit the United Nations, or simply foster chaos.

Spain in 1930 could have been—and to some extent was—an instructive experience, for it was one of the first Western societies where the worldwide economic crisis was clearly revealed to be something even graver and more fundamental than that. What I, and most other observers, failed to realize was that Spain under its Gothic and sometimes African facade was an authentically Western society afflicted with the most contemporary of all social ills: the malady of anachronism.

Several months before my Spanish assignment one quiet weekend in the latter part of July 1930, I cabled an article from Paris which mirrors a different facet of the generalized Western breakdown. It was a "think-piece": not news properly speaking but a kind of interpretative essay stitched together out of scattered comment or bits of information in the French press. Like everything that went out of the office when my chief was officially at his post, the cable was signed "Wales," but Hank himself was unofficially weekending somewhere in the country. I had been particularly struck by a lead editorial in *Le Temps*, calling attention to the rather disturbing evidences of strength displayed in the recent electoral campaign by the German National Socialists, up to then regarded as the lunatic fringe of German nationalism. *Le Temps* had analyzed at some length the militarist and ultranationalist doctrines of the Nazis' leader, "the Austrian, Hitler," and concluded that a victory for his movement in the forthcoming parliamentary elections would mark a dangerous setback to the cause of European reconciliation. Several more right-wing French editorialists had commented in less restrained tones on the threat of resurgent German militarism, and had called for increases in the already huge French military establishment. It looked to me as if militarism was reviving on both banks of the Rhine. The more I thought about the situation, the more ominous it appeared, and I hung my think-piece on the grim theme: war clouds build up again over Europe.

The first thing Wales read when he returned to the office after his country weekend was the daily cable from Chicago notifying the overseas bureaus what items in the world news had been judged sufficiently important or readable to win a bit of the *Tribune*'s exceptionally limited frontpage space. "Frontpaging Hoover Gangsters Accidents Wales Warscare," the message read (as I remember it).

"Say, what have you been up to?" Hank asked in his rasping voice. Making front page on a newless Sunday was good, but not if there were witchcraft in it. As Hank started to read the carbon copy of my dispatch I saw him glance involuntarily at the open window, through which the sun was streaming; undoubtedly I had been the only American correspondent in Europe to notice those war clouds. When he finished, he emitted a muffled growl that apparently signified approbation, but I could see that on another level he did not quite approve. Hank was oddly straitlaced. A pillar of the Presbyterian Church—as well as of several Montmartre nightclubs—who would tolerate no profanity around his office (obscenity was another matter), he had a code of journalistic ethics as eccentrically rigid as his private standards of nighttime and daytime Christian behavior. His dispatches on European politics were sometimes masterpieces of irrelevance, but he frowned on sheer fantasy. Evidently he found my think-piece a trifle lurid.

My own conscience was a bit uneasy. In the eyes of most sound observers, foreign or native, the prospects for lasting peace in Europe had seldom looked brighter than they did in this summer of 1930. Only a few weeks ago—on June 30—the last French soldier had been withdrawn from the Rhineland—five years ahead of the schedule fixed by the Treaty of Versailles—a milestone in the policy of Franco-German reconciliation fostered by both the French Foreign Minister, Aristide Briand, and the recently deceased German Chancellor, Gustav Stresemann. In September Briand, already haloed as the "Pilgrim of Peace" for his role in various international conferences, was scheduled to present his audacious plan for a European federation to the League of Nations Assembly in Geneva. The text had been published the previous May, and even the *Tribune*'s editors, equally suspicious of Europe and of internationalism, had been impressed by this apparent evidence of the Old World's ability to rise above the futile and murderous quarrels of the past, in the last of which the United States had so unwisely allowed itself to become entangled. Writing about war clouds in such an atmosphere might well appear a bit farfetched.

Actually, though my knowledge of European politics might as easily have misled me, it had not, and Col. McCormick's dour historical perspective, which I had made my own, for once proved sound. The tenuous wraiths of suspicion I had detected in the summer sky became unmistakable, if not yet very black, clouds by September when Adolf Hitler's National Socialists, who had based their electoral campaign largely on repudiation of the 1919 peace settlements, polled some 6,500,000 votes and won 107 seats in the new Reichstag, as against 12 in the old one. The spreading economic depression, born of the Wall Street crash the previous October, was thought to be the main reason for this alarming resurgence of the most extreme and irredentist German nationalism, but there were more complex factors involved.

Looking back on the period, it seems to me that there is a curious analogy between the boom-and-bust economic pattern of the late 20's and early 30's and the trend of European diplomacy during roughly the same years. In the euphoric or inflationary, phase of inter-European relations, from 1924 to 1930, democratic leadership in postwar Europe had succeeded in modifying the bitter psychological climate generated by the conflict itself, and perhaps even more by the harsh peace conditions imposed on the vanquished. Though the Treaty of Versailles, which had solemnly affirmed imperial Germany's responsibility for the World War, continued to impose galling sanctions on the empire's successor, the Weimar Republic, the vindictiveness that had inspired it had gradually yielded to the confident and pacific spirit created by the Locarno Pact of 1925. Locarno had led to Germany's admission into the League of Nations, to the agreement on ending the Allied occupation of the Rhineland ahead of schedule, and to other constructive accords in Europe. For the first time in modern history, it had linked the continent's two greatest—and traditionally rival—powers, France and Germany, as partners in a mutual security pact, underwritten by two Allied nations—Britain and Italy—which had previously been leagued with France alone. Since no major war could break out in Europe again so long as the four partners respected their obligations, the "spirit of Locarno" had presumably ushered in a reign of eternal peace.

Though Briand's personal role in the Locarno negotiations had not been particularly flashy, the public—and not only in France—seemed to feel that he more than any other European statesman personified the Locarno spirit. A short, stooped, almost dwarfish man with a great, graying, Bohemian-looking mane, droopy moustaches, dreamy Breton eyes, delicate, violinist's hands and a rather slack mouth from which a half-smoked cigarette always seemed to be dangling, Briand was a curious, rather than an imposing figure. In fact, he looked— and was—a little seedy, politically and otherwise. Even his deep, sonorous voice, his greatest physical asset, was a bit equivocal; there was undoubtedly a hint of the patent-medicine spieler in it at moments, but when the authenticity of his emotions matched the cunning of his vocal cords, he was a great orator in the somewhat orotund French parliamentary style of the day. To hear him thundering, "Away with cannons, away with machine guns!" in the Assembly of the League of Nations was a memorable experience.

Unquestionably, Briand believed sincerely in the cause of peace, with which he identified the last phase of his political career. Though intellectually lazy and by no means a technician of diplomacy, Briand had an instinctive sense of the future and a gift of empathy that touched him with greatness. His failure lay in his inability to see that talking about peace does not automatically achieve it.

With his German counterpart, Stresemann, Briand had succeeded in superficially improving Franco-German relations, but a lasting reconciliation between the two nations—the precondition to the smooth functioning of the League of Nations, and to durable peace in Europe—would have required bolder concessions than either was prepared to make. Briand would not or could not offer either revision of the territorial clauses of the Versailles Treaty—Danzig, the Polish Corridor, that isolated East Prussia, the 3,500,000 so-called Sudeten Germans in Czechoslovakia—or further reduction in the too-heavy reparations payments which provided the Nazis with much effective propaganda. He could not make good the stipulation in the League Covenant that the wartime victors would gradually disarm down to the level imposed on the vanquished.

Stresemann (who died in 1929) was likewise holding something back. He was a thick-necked, bullet-headed Prussian type with an

84

unexpectedly quick and subtle mind—and like Briand a sincere believer in peace and cooperation. He was also a shrewd German patriot, who considered that patient negotiation was for the time being the best way of freeing Germany from the shackles of Versailles; various German documents now lead us to believe that during the post-Locarno period he was aware of the large-scale clandestine rearmament programs, including the fateful training accords with the Soviet Army, organized by the Reichswehr in cynical violation of the treaties.

The diplomacy of the big European powers, especially France and Germany, in the years from 1924 to 1930, thus involved elements of deception, along with the strong strain of wishful thinking. These flaws might have been less deadly if the diplomats had maintained the traditional circumspection of their trade. But various influences, of which the most significant was probably the existence of the League of Nations as a new kind of world forum, led to a wild inflationary spiral of rhetorical and largely disembodied internationalist idealism. The morale of the Western peoples was artificially sustained with token justice and verbal fraternity, symbolic cooperation and paper security. Progress toward building a new European order to avert the new anarchy in international relations that threatened as the victorious wartime coalition fell apart amounted at best to a nominal down payment on the millennium. Few of Europe's leaders appeared in a hurry to meet the next installment. The gap between ideal and performance in the political area became as outrageous as the gap between speculative prosperity and real wealth in the economic field. When history finally sent out its margin calls, Western leadership proved bankrupt for the second time in less than a generation.

The phase of diplomatic liquidation and deflation was just beginning when I took my neophyte's seat in the European press gallery. Like its economic analogue, the slump in international relations soon turned into a vast and seemingly uncheckable recession from hope. Covering the successive stages of this political recession became my chief assignment for the Chicago *Tribune*, especially after Wales fell out with the Colonel following a trip to Soviet Russia and I took his place at the sessions of the League in Geneva, as well as in Paris.

One of the first really big events on the international stage that I reported under my own by-line was the French presidential elections of May 13, 1931. Under the Third Republic, presidents were elected by the consolidated vote of senators and deputies, sitting together for greater solemnity at the Palace of Versailles. The whole ceremony had a characteristic bourgeois and anachronistic air that took one back in spirit to *La Belle Époque*. Political *Tout-Paris*, accompanied by wives or mistresses—sometimes both—the diplomatic corps, the press, and miscellaneous distinguished onlookers journeyed to Versailles for the occasion. The bright sunshine, the chestnut trees in bloom, the white waggish beards of the senators, the burgeoning buttonhole of the men's jackets, the gay dresses of the ladies made it seem like a gala day at Longchamps. Briand, despite a vicious nationalist press campaign against him, was the odds-on favorite. The outcome was all the more stunning.

"They broke Aristide Briand this afternoon," I began my dispatch to the *Tribune* that night, "broke him as a man and as a captain of state, and they figuratively tossed into the wastebasket the rampart of paper which for ten years he has been building up in the cause of peace."

I was right, I think, in saying that defeat hit Briand very heavily, and perhaps in implying that it was a fatal blow to the policies—or politically yea-saying mood—that might be termed Briandism, but my report was out of focus in one respect. From what I later gathered in talking with veteran French political reporters and with politicians themselves, it is doubtful whether the French nationalists' suspicion of Germany, and hence of Briand's policy of conciliating Germany, played as big a part in keeping him out of the Elysée as I first supposed. The voting at Versailles had not been so much against Briandism as simply in favor of politics as usual, and the friends of the successful candidate—the respectable, undistinguished, seventy-four-year-old president of the Senate, Paul Doumer—had joined forces with the personal or ideological enemies of Briand as a matter of routine.

Some French politicians undoubtedly had not yet mastered the most basic lesson of twentieth-century history—that modern technology had made war too destructive to be considered any longer a normal and acceptable means for achieving national objectives or settling national differences. Others, influenced by their personal experiences in the last war or by the swelling peace sentiment of the masses throughout the West, approved the policy of reconciliation with Germany, but failed to recognize any elements of emergency in the German domestic situation that necessitated exceptional measures on France's part to save the policy. Somewhat like President Hoover in dealing with the American economic crisis, these French politicians suffered from the delusion or fallacy of normality in an increasingly abnormal world. The same affliction of the spirit—perhaps more than anything else it is a sclerosis of the imagination—had brought low countless dynasties and empires throughout the ages, and my generation was later destined to witness some particularly striking examples of it.

Briand himself was not free from the weakness. For all his Celtic sensitivity and his lazy man's intuitive feel for the deep currents of history, he apparently failed to realize that a grave crisis was developing in Central Europe. A few weeks earlier, in March, the Catholic Centrist government of Chancellor Heinrich Bruening—the last German leader who seriously believed in European cooperation—desperately casting about for some triumph of foreign policy that would deflate the Nazis' propaganda, had hit on the idea of a German customs union with Austria. The scheme was warmly received in Vienna, where even the Socialists longed for the *Anschluss* (political union) with their brother democrats to the north that the peace treaties forbade them. To anyone familiar with German history, the proposed customs union might, in fact, appear to be a significant step on the road to total unification. For that reason, of course, the French opposed it.

87

In terms of the classic diplomatic and strategic chess game, the French were entirely right. Though Germany was theoretically disarmed, and the French army—in Anglo-Saxon eyes at least—almost scandalously strong, France was a nation of 41,000,000 with a falling birthrate, and Germany an industrial giant with a growing population of 65,000,000. To risk further tipping the economic and demographic scales in Germany's favor through the eventual absorption of Austrian industrial capacity and manpower was to imperil not only the postwar French hegemony in Europe, but also the long-range security of France itself. Moreover, the immediate economic benefits of the proposed customs union to either Germany or Austria were dubious, and the political effects potentially double-edged; they might just as well stimulate as appease the appetite of German nationalism. Briand had therefore said no. He had not pounded the table or threatened mobilization as almost any French government might have done a few years earlier, but he had effectively mobilized all France's diplomatic weight to block the project.

A responsible French foreign minister could hardly have done otherwise, especially one with his eye on the presidency. Even the British, normally inclined by sporting instinct and Foreign Office tradition to side with the Continental underdog, backed up the French position in this case. Yet scotching the Austro-German customs union turned out to have far-reaching and disastrous consequences.

The financial pressures that the French brought to bear upon Austria were at least partly responsible for the crash of the largest Vienna bank, the Credit Anstalt, which was obliged to suspend payments on May 13—the same day that Briand's presidential ambitions were dashed at Versailles. The Credit Anstalt was one of the most important credit institutions in all Central Europe; its downfall started a series of bank and business failures which rapidly spread from Austria to Germany. On June 6, Chancellor Bruening, without warning, publicly announced that Germany could no longer meet the already drastically reduced reparations payments its government had pledged itself to honor at the Hague Conference two years before.

88

It was one more cruel blow to Briand—who at The Hague had accepted premature evacuation of the Rhineland in return for Stresemann's word that the reparations settlement was final this time—and to Briandism. When President Hoover in July proposed a year's moratorium on both reparations and inter-Allied debt payments, France reluctantly and conditionally agreed to it. If the moratorium had been proclaimed six months earlier, and if it had emerged from frank and loyal consultations between France and Germany, it might have saved Europe. In July 1931, it failed even to avert a generalized bank collapse in Germany. In September the British pound, since the day of Victoria the symbol of bourgeois probity and the world's chief medium of international exchange, was forced off the gold standard—in part, at least, as a result of the complex forces set in motion by the abortive customs union between Germany and Austria.

Another victim of the diplomatic storm over Austria was Briand's own somewhat futuristic proposal for a European federation, which had been coolly received at Geneva the previous autumn. The only hope of making even a modest start toward realization of the European dream lay in convincing the nations of the Continent that organized, institutionalized cooperation would help solve the economic problems besetting them. A detailed French plan for the economic organization of Europe, on which the experts of the Quai d'Orsay had been toiling for months, was accordingly presented by Briand to a League-sponsored Pan-European Commission sitting in Geneva concurrently with the Spring Session of the League Council. The meeting took place on May 15, two days after the electoral disaster at Versailles; it had originally been planned as a sort of international apotheosis for Briand, but events turned it into something more like a wake.

The sessions of the Pan-European Commission, which I spent most of the day covering, were held in the same stuffy little conference room where the Council met, on the ground floor of the rambling Victorian edifice, overlooking Lake Geneva, that housed the League's permanent secretariat. The really decisive episode of the debate occurred before the French plan was even presented. Dr. Julius

Curtius, the German Foreign Minister, a cold-looking, hawk-faced man, and Dino Grandi, his handsome, black-bearded Italian colleague, jointly sponsored a substitute proposal based on the idea that organizing Europe should begin with customs accords between any two or more states desirous of entering into them—an obvious, if oblique, maneuver to refloat the scuttled Austro-German project. Briand woke up from the semi-somnolence into which he now drifted more and more frequently during long meetings, and protested strenuously. Curtius delivered what I termed in my cable to the *Tribune* a scorching reply. The spirit of Locarno had plainly ceased to exist, and that day's proceedings by the lakeside made it more unlikely than before that it could ever be revived. Above all, a chance was lost, the last, I think, to enmesh the less irresponsible German nationalists in the skein of European cooperation by accepting the principle of a limited Austro-German customs union integrated into a broader, all-European economic framework.

It was one of those days—there were several of them in the early 30's—when history slipped past on silent wings. I, at any rate, scarcely noticed their beat. I mentioned the Briand-Curtius duel in my cable, but most of it was devoted to a summary and analysis of the French plan almost conscientious enough to have satisfied the *New York Times*—a sad waste of cable tolls. I worked late on the story, as I remember, and ate a snack at the Bavaria, a favorite after-dinner meeting place for journalists and diplomats, before finishing the night at the Moulin Rouge, a dogged provincial imitation of a Pigalle nightclub whose hostesses usually sympathized with the problems of out-of-town newspapermen, including their expense account problems.

During the fall of 1931 I spent several weeks living or traveling in Central Europe on various assignments for the Chicago *Tribune*. It was an interesting experience, for both the lands and the peoples appealed to some hitherto dormant center of my imagination, but it was also a disturbing one. The shock waves from the Credit Anstalt disaster were still spreading throughout the whole region when I arrived at their epicenter in Vienna. Their impact in terms of human misery was apparent to the most casual visitor.

Thanks to the welfare state in miniature that the Social-Democrat municipal government of Vienna had managed to establish during the years of relative prosperity, the victims of the crisis suffered less cruelly than in some other countries where the economic machinery was almost as completely paralyzed as in Austria. Quite possibly, fewer Viennese suffered from cold or hunger in that depression year, 1931, than in the halcyon days of Francis Joseph's reign. There were some, all the same, who did—especially among the ruined middle classes and in various marginal groups that did not quite fit into the official welfare pattern—and coming upon them was a shock to me. I had not been back to America since the economic slump began, and France up to that time had scarcely been touched by it. My knowledge of breadlines and soup kitchens and apples sold on the sidewalks was all secondhand. Vienna was my first personal contact with the social havoc that depression was wreaking throughout much of the West, and not having been hardened to it by seeing it worsen imperceptibly under my eyes, day after day, I was horrified to discover it all at once.

It was not so much the scale of depression-pauperism in Vienna that wrung the heart—though it was vast enough to do so—as the unexpected and unsettling ways in which it revealed itself. At the back doors of fashionable restaurants and hotels, the crowds lining up for handouts of scraps and leftovers sometimes looked so well-dressed in a slightly shabby way that one wondered for a moment whether they had not simply mistaken the entrance. The genteel-looking old ladies whom one saw poking in dustbins seemed no less incongruous. There were also the diffident old gentlemen wearing spats and carrying brief cases who sidled up to one in the streets, asking in a discreet whisper for a few groschen. The saddest and most numerous beggars, though, were the young men, not decayed *rentiers*, but unemployed workers and office employees, hatless and coatless in every weather, with long, ragged, blond hair, and wearing the most forlorn of misery's uniforms: the blue or brown or gray lounge suit intended for Saturday dances and Sunday movies, but worn by necessity in rain and slush and to sleep in at night, until it was rumpled out of any shape, and frayed and spotted and often patched.

The misery of the street scene in Vienna was striking enough, but to me, at least, the atmosphere of gentle yet incurable despair that hung over the city was even more tragic. Pauperism was alleviated somewhat in the following years after French loans stimulated a partial revival of the Austrian economy, but hope failed to return. "Hopeless, but not serious," was the first thing every visitor learned about the Austrian situation from Viennese acquaintants who repeated the wintry little quip, inherited from the twilight of the Empire, with mournful pride. Later history suggests the epigram was not completely accurate on either count, but at the time it furnished the newcomer a good introduction to the study of a problem that Western statesmanship seemed to be treating too hopefully and not seriously enough.

Kind and well-informed local colleagues helped me fill in some of the more gaping holes in my background knowledge of contemporary Europe. One of them was John Gunther, then the Central European bureau chief of the Chicago *Daily News* and an outstanding example of the type of correspondent who made that paper's foreign service the most distinguished in America. A still more important factor in my Central European education was Marcel (Mike) Fodor, the veteran correspondent of the *Manchester Guardian*. Fodor, an owlish, moon-faced man with a toothbrush moustache, was a Hungarian by birth and had originally been trained as an engineer. He had guided the early footsteps of nearly every contemporary or earlier American correspondent in Vienna, including Dorothy Thompson and Gunther himself.

A Viennese through and through, Fodor presided nightly over a *stammtisch* (a permanently reserved table) at the Café Louvre, a journalists' gathering-place near the Bourse and the cable office, assisted by his charming Hungarian wife, Martha. A number of Austrian and Anglo-Saxon newsmen could be counted on to turn up during the course of the evening; one of the most regular attendants at Fodor's table, as I remember it, was Robert Best, then the local bureau chief of the United Press, a dark, moody Southerner whose love affair with Vienna ultimately turned into a tragic obsession that made him a traitor to his country's cause during the Second World War.

For a visiting correspondent on assignment in Vienna there could be no more useful or pleasant way of topping off a working day than with a glass of beer at Fodor's table in the Louvre. It was a miniature news exchange where the latest developments and rumors were related and commented on from different viewpoints by lively, informed minds. And it was a trivial piece of news, or a singularly vapid rumor, that did not launch Fodor into a long, erudite, colorful lecture on its historic background and implications. What made these discourses so valuable to a beginner like myself was that besides containing a wealth of accurate, factual information, they reflected the viewpoint of an enlightened Central European mind that had known Vienna when it was the capital of the Habsburg Empire.

Unlike many Viennese, Fodor was not bemused by nostalgia for the vanished glitter and ease of life under the Dual Monarchy. He was a British-style liberal, and therefore a Wilsonian, by conviction as well as profession, but he understood how Vienna had tied the Habsburg lands of the Danubian basin together, culturally and economically, when it was their political capital, and he recognized the havoc that had been wreaked when the peace treaties formalized the rupture of those ties.

Listening to Fodor, I understood why Vienna was such a tragic city and why Austria's plight seemed so hopeless. Neither the city, a metropolis of some 2,000,000 inhabitants, nor the country, a small, largely agricultural state with a population of 6,500,000, could ever prosper unless they were integrated, if only loosely, into some greater economic unit. The *Anschluss* with Germany was one solution, but it was expressly forbidden by the Treaty of Saint-Germain which the Allies had imposed on Austria. An economic organization of Europe along the lines of Briand's Geneva proposals was probably a better solution, but it had been put forward in a still vaguely thought out form, more as inspirational propaganda than as a practical blueprint, and had been doomed from the start by the Franco-German clash over the proposed customs union with Austria. Western statesmanship, it was all too evident, would continue treating the Austrian problem as it had been treated since the Peace Conference: by ignoring it, except in moments of particularly acute crisis, when alms, disguised as an international loan, would be offered as an economic palliative.

In the meantime, conditions were getting steadily worse, both in Austria and throughout the whole Danubian area. Political tension was rising ominously between the top-heavy capital with its Socialist majority and the clerical, conservative Austrian hinterland. Among the successor states of the Habsburg Empire the general depression, aggravated by the Kreditanstalt crisis, was accentuating their already strong inclination toward economic nationalism. This economic Balkanization of Central Europe, as Fodor remarked, was accompanied by an increasingly Balkan pattern of political life, marked by brutal dictatorships and fanaticized minorities, which was particularly disturbing to anyone who remembered 1914. A brief visit to Yugoslavia helped underscore some of Fodor's lessons in my mind.

Nominally a constitutional monarchy, Yugoslavia at the time was actually a military dictatorship in which autocratic power was exercised, with the army's backing, by King Alexander I. Alexander ruled through his prime minister and lifelong crony, General Pera Živković, an unusually perfect specimen of the Balkan professional conspirator in uniform, and a ruthless subtyrant. The police state that Živković had set up for Alexander lacked the systematic thought-control and other totalitarian features of Mussolini's Italy; it was content to cow every form of opposition by arresting, flogging, torturing, and imprisoning its active opponents. Whenever these classic Balkan techniques of oppression seemed ineffective, or were awkward to apply, the regime fell back on simple murder. Despite such practices the monarchy had authentic national roots, and the political atmosphere of Yugoslavia remained strangely breathable as long as one remained in the Serbian part of the kingdom. At the time, however, Yugoslavia was an empire in miniature in which the Serbs exercised a de facto racial dictatorship over Croats, Slovenes, Macedonians, and other minorities. In the non-Serbian parts of the kingdom, therefore, and especially in Croatia, the climate was more sinister.

A number of Croatian spokesmen I talked with seemed to feel that the Croats were hardly less oppressed by their Slav brothers than they had been by their Magyar overlords when they were part of the Habsburg Empire; a few extremists even maintained that there had been greater freedom in Croatia under Hungarian rule. I was warned, prophetically as later events proved, that in Croatia as elsewhere in the kingdom there were underground oppositionists who in their growing bitterness dreamed of splintering Yugoslavia into its component parts, and were prepared to use any means, or accept help from any allies, to achieve their aim. One heard little of all this in Paris, but then, the French counted heavily on the Yugoslav Army—allied with the Czechoslovak and Rumanian armies in the so-called Little Entente—to help maintain the post-Versailles status quo in Europe.

Instructive as my visits to Austria and Yugoslavia had been, the climax of my Central European travels was a brief assignment to Germany in mid-October of 1931 to back up the *Tribune*'s Berlin correspondent, Sigrid Schulz, by covering some political rallies in the provinces. The economic situation was graver than ever, and the German people were still in a state of shock from the bank crisis of the previous summer. With the support of President von Hindenburg and the glum acquiescence of the Social-Democrats, Bruening, the thin-lipped, ascetically pious Chancellor, had obtained emergency powers of almost dictatorial scope; he was using them to defend the mark by pursuing a rigidly orthodox policy of deflation, which inevitably intensified the sufferings of the underprivileged. Unemployment had risen alarmingly, and there was a suppressed violence in the atmosphere that I had not sensed in Austria.

On October 11, at the little resort town of Bad Harzburg in the Harz mountains, I had my first glimpse of Adolf Hitler, the Austrian-born ex-corporal and leader of the National Socialists, whom observers outside Germany still tended to look upon as the symptom of some morbid tumult in the depths of the Teutonic soul, rather than as a serious political menace. ("Hitler is henceforth excluded . . . even from the hope of power," the French Socialist chief, Léon Blum, normally a more percipient analyst of European affairs, wrote as late as November 1932, after the Nazis had suffered a minor electoral setback.) Hitler himself was not in good form at Bad Harzburg. The purpose of the meeting was to solemnize a tactical alliance between the Nazis and the traditionalist elements of the German Right; no doubt the Führer felt ill at ease in such bourgeois company. He was disgruntled, too, because the Stalhelm—the right-wing veterans' private militia organization controlled by the millionaire publisher Alfred Hugenberg—had turned out in greater numbers than his own Brown Shirts, and looked smarter, better disciplined, and more military.

While the Chaplinesque figure with the jerky, robot gestures, reading a more than usually turgid speech too fast and in a monotonously hoarse voice, aroused no premonitions of doom, I felt the hysterical tension in the air when he spoke, and I was impressed despite myself by the release of barbaric energies that Hitler's presence seemingly induced in every German crowd. Marginal brawls kept breaking out during the day between Storm Troopers and Steel Helmets, not so much, it appeared, because the members of these private armies had any uncontrollable hostility toward one another, but through a sheer overcharge of diffuse aggressiveness. To me as a fresh and groundling spectator of the German tragedy, the real shock in the day's performance was the speech by Dr Hjalmar Schacht, the former president of the Reichsbank. Accusing the Bruening government of deliberately falsifying Germany's financial position, Schacht proceeded to make what were evidently meant as sensational revelations regarding the depletion of the gold reserves and the resultant insecurity of the mark. The intent to foment a monetary crisis seemed flagrant. Naturally, the audience of Steel Helmets and fanatical Hitlerites gave him the loudest, longest ovation of the day; even Hitler could not vie with such incendiary demagoguery. I returned to Paris with many forebodings about the future of German democracy; a republic so topsy-turvy that its foremost banker could give lessons in rabble-rousing to its chief gutter-revolutionary was clearly headed for trouble.

The somber or disturbing impressions I had brought back with me from Central Europe, together with others, earlier or later, garnered in Geneva and in Paris itself, were present in my mind one afternoon early in March 1932 when I rang the bell of Briand's unpretentious bachelor apartment near the Place de l'Étoile. The Pilgrim of Peace had died in his sleep early that morning. His elderly valet opened the door, and when I identified myself as an American correspondent, led me without a word into the bedroom where his master's body still lay. There was only one living presence in the room when I entered: Alexis Léger, Briand's most faithful lieutenant, soon to be named secretary general of the Quai d'Orsay and already famous in avant-garde literary circles as the poet, St. John Perse. Léger's expressive Creole eyes were glittering with tears and his whole attitude was so unmistakably one of personal mourning that I automatically mumbled some words of condolence as I shook hands with him.

Briand lay on the simple brass bed in which he had died. Death had erased the lines of bitterness and despondency from his features; he might have been any old man gone to his rest. The scene was all the more poignant. Though only sixty-nine, Briand had lived at least several months too long. The collapse of his European dream— for his generation at least—could no longer be disguised. The state visit he had paid to Germany the previous autumn with Pierre Laval, his premier and eventual successor as the dominant influence in French foreign policy, had conspicuously failed to restore the spirit of the Stresemann era; German ultranationalism was waxing every day and the moderate Bruening was clearly losing his hold on the chancellorship. The Japanese aggression in Manchuria of September

97

1931, which soon developed into a methodical war of conquest, had shown up the weakness of the League. The bogging-down of a long-heralded Disarmament Conference almost immediately after it opened in Geneva on February 2, 1932, had further tarnished the internationalist ideal and dimmed the world's hopes for lasting peace. Briand had lived on, it seemed, only to see his life's work lying in ruins.

I felt my throat tighten as I looked down on the shrunken body, on the once familiar features, now subtly estranged in death. I had not had enough direct contact with the man to feel the affection for him that many of my older colleagues entertained—Briand's unique mixture of seediness and idealism, along with his personal charm, made him a natural favorite of the press corps—and I had come to have reservations about his statesmanship, but in that instant I felt a sense of affliction almost sharp enough to be a private bereavement. The grand cause with which Briand's name was identified in the public mind seemed to me more precious than ever before, and more irretrievably lost.

Being a foreign correspondent, I suddenly realized, involved a graver responsibility than I had thought: It was not enough to present the "facts" accurately as possible; one must try to find the underlying truth they ultimately expressed. How one went about this search I could not quite say—I am not sure that I can even now —but simply recognizing the need marked a change in my outlook. Perhaps it also marked the secret beginnings of my long decline as a witness of doom in the noninvolved *Tribune* manner. Nothing I had observed in the two years I had been helping to cover Europe for Col. McCormick gave me any basis for rejecting his doctrine of Europe's essential unregenerateness, but I no longer felt the same zest in proving the Colonel right, and I more often questioned the adequacy of the conclusions he drew from the apparent verification of his assumption.

Out of a kind of necessity I began to consider an alternative to the McCormick interpretation of modern history, one that applied as forcibly to America as to Europe. We should not blame our difficulties on the littleness of men, Montesquieu writes, but on the greatness of human problems. Certainly, the fearful discrepancy between the scale of Europe's problems and the caliber of European leadership in the two years I had been observing the affairs of the Continent could be accounted for more plausibly as well as more charitably in Montesquieu's somewhat fatalistic perspective. Yet the wise Frenchman's aphorism, like many others, is only a half-truth. Political and social problems are not always greater than the capacities of the men who have to solve them; they merely tend to grow faster, particularly when the solutions require institutional reform.

Perhaps at the time of Locarno, European leadership had been equal, or nearly equal, to the demands upon it, but it had not kept pace with the monstrous proliferation of these demands. The men —some of them at any rate—were not smaller; but the problems were appallingly greater. That was why leadership seemed so wizened, why so many European leaders appeared to behave like moral and intellectual runts. American leadership had failed no less dismally to grow with its problems. Europe's somber historical heritage was not entirely to blame.

A Banquet of Ghosts (1)

Chicago, February 17, 1936

Dear Taylor:

At what place or places in France is the poem "I Have a Rendezvous with Death" prominently displayed? One place should be our office.

If you can buy a decorative card with this poem on it, do so. Otherwise frame this.

Sincerely,

The penciled initials "McC" scrawled at the bottom of the page have become dim with the years, but even if they had faded out completely, there would be no problem in identifying the letter's author. Only Colonel McCormick could have drafted that characteristically abrupt communication with its enigmatic command and the attached text of Alan Seeger's famous lines, clipped from the Sunday edition of the Chicago *Tribune*. (The Sunday *Tribune* at that time was running a series of Favorite Poems, intended for readers' scrapbooks.)

Such messages, by mail or cable, were familiar features in the life of every *Tribune* correspondent in Europe. It was rare that Colonel McCormick employed the paper's normal executive channels in transmitting to us his instructions, criticisms, commendations, or mere reflections on life. We were his private army. During the seven or eight years I functioned as a *Tribune* bureau chief I suppose I heard directly from the Colonel on an average of twice a month, sometimes, of course, much more often. Most of the time his letters or cables, especially the latter, had a self-evident operational context. The difficulty, if any, lay in the implementation. Thus, when I reported in May 1937 that the only American correspondents who would be allowed to attend the forthcoming wedding of the Duke of Windsor and Mrs. Wallis Simpson near Tours were the representatives of the three big press associations, I received a reply saying: TAYLOR REPRESENT STRONGLY CHICAGO TRIBUNE FOREIGN NEWS SERVICE MORE IMPORTANT THAN UP OR INTERNATIONAL. The one question in my mind was why the Colonel had thus implicitly conceded the superior claims of the Associated Press. Even when I was awakened one night at my hotel in Tours during the same assignment by a cable informing me that AMERICAN PUBLIC OPINION OUTRAGED UNSPORTSMANSHIP BRITISH GOVERNMENT, I wasted no psychic energy looking for explanations. The Colonel might or might not be objective in his summary of the national reaction to the snubs suffered by the royal lovers; the fact that he himself evidently felt outraged was not without interest for a *Tribune* correspondent covering the

story. There were other occasions, however, when Colonel Mc-
Cormick's communications seemed to possess a kind of cosmic irrelevance that suggested the indecipherable cliff-writings of some
vanished civilization. The instruction to frame Alan Seeger's poem
was one of them.

Personal contact with the Colonel, judging from my own limited
experience, did not necessarily make his thought processes easier to
follow. He was, of course, already a legend in my mind before I
encountered him in the flesh, and I doubtless expected to be baffled
by him, as I was. Later in my career I had occasion to serve employers or chiefs more colorful or more distinguished than Colonel
McCormick—General William J. Donovan, Lord Mountbatten of
Burma, Sir Julian Huxley, Max Ascoli, for one brief moment; Lord
Beaverbrook—but none of them so captured, or at least so teased,
my imagination. They were heroic, brilliant, picturesque; the Colonel was Cyclopian.

I met him for the first time in the summer of 1931 during one of
his rare visits to Europe. Wales was away from Paris—I think he
was already in Russia—and I was covering the office in his absence.
The low voice, like a two-wheeled cart rumbling on cobblestones,
that roused me by telephone early one morning was unfamiliar, yet
I knew it instantly. "Taylor, do you get sick when you fly?" it asked
as I lifted the receiver off the hook. "No, Colonel," I answered in
my waking dream. "Meet me at the Ritz at eleven o'clock then," the
voice said. "I want you to fly to London with me."

Americans in those days needed visas for Britain, and it being
some French legal holiday, His Majesty's consulate general in Paris
was closed. That was a detail, since the Colonel had given his orders,
but details may take time. It was 11:20 A.M. when I rushed into the
lobby of the Ritz and recognized the towering, Lincolnesque frame,
the legendary Chaplinesque moustache, the calm look of a secret
possession. "Ha," the Colonel said as we shook hands, "you're twenty
minutes late." I started a hasty explanation about the British consul

and his golf game, but the Colonel was already striding toward the door, and in any case I realized no explanation was necessary. There had been indulgence, almost a hint of admiration, in his voice. I had thought my merit was in getting there at all; he seemed pleasantly surprised that I had managed to make him wait.

Colonel McCormick had chartered a small private plane for our flight, and a few minutes out of Le Bourget he ordered the pilot to circle low over the bluish swells of ripening wheat so that he could locate the farmhouse that had served as his headquarters during the battle of Cantigny, one of the first independent American actions of the world war. Alternately checking the map spread on his knees and peering out of the window, the Colonel at last pointed down at a blur of gray stone and said confidently, but I thought a bit vaguely, "That's it."

There was no further conversation until we landed at Croydon, where we were met by John Steele, the *Tribune*'s London correspondent, a British journalist of the white-moustache school. We all drove to the Ritz for a late lunch, washed down with ginger beer which the Colonel had remembered with nostalgia from his schoolboy days in England. The Colonel talked chiefly of Roman military operations and problems in ancient Britain. Steele had a number of more contemporary matters to discuss with his chief, but perhaps unwisely as things turned out, decided it was not yet the moment to raise them. Instead he spoke with such enthusiasm about the Roman ruins at St. Albans that the Colonel decided we would drive there immediately after coffee, rather than go to the office.

It proved a fairly long trip and the Colonel dozed, or brooded, most of the way. When we finally reached our destination he gazed absentmindedly for a few moments at a fragment of Roman wall, then declined Steele's offer of a personally conducted tour. He had just remembered, he said, that his old school was near St. Albans, and he wanted to see it again. After wandering around the English countryside for some time, we located the establishment and were received by the headmaster with puzzled civility. Eventually, the Colonel even managed to find the classroom bench in which he had once carved his initials with a penknife. They were still there, looking much the same to my eyes as those at the bottom of his letters.

En route back to London, we noticed a cricket game in progress on the outskirts of a village and the Colonel called a halt to watch it. We stood looking at the ballet of white-flanneled figures floating like somewhat jerky swans over the green English turf, while the shadows of an English summer evening grew longer, and the Colonel analyzed the fine points of the game for us. Knowing the *Tribune*'s often expressed contempt for colonial-minded American worshipers of foreign, particularly British, ways, I was a bit startled to hear the Colonel proclaim his freshly taken decision to introduce cricket into Chicagoland.

Back at the Ritz, the Colonel turned to Steele and me and said, "I know you two boys will want to go out on the town tonight, so I'll let you off now."

Late the next morning we were summoned to the hotel for a conference on a new British color camera the Colonel thought might be useful for the Sunday edition. The demonstrators were amazed by the Colonel's technical grasp of the subject, but after he had questioned them for an hour or so he got bored, and we went down for lunch, this time without ginger beer.

On the way to the airfield after lunch Steele managed to get in a few questions about office matters, and the Colonel offhandedly answered most of them. When Steele asked him, for example, what he proposed to do about the Vienna bureau—William L. Shirer, then the *Tribune*'s Vienna correspondent, was on assignment in India at the time—the Colonel jerked his head in my direction and said, "I think I'll send this fellow."

Unlike Steele, I had no pressing office problems to be settled, and I was always pleased to learn that I was being sent anywhere, but I remained a little curious all the same as to why Colonel McCormick had brought me along to England. I was enlightened on the way home, finally, as our little plane pitched and bucketed in the midst of a sudden rainsquall over the Channel.

"Taylor," the Colonel roared in my ear above the shriek of the wind, "I've noticed that when you translate from the French you sometimes follow the original sentence structure too closely. You should break it up into shorter English sentences."

Like many of the Colonel's nonpolitical criticisms, insights or hunches, the comment was as valid as it was unexpected, and in the thirty-five years since it was made I have often recalled it with profit. That was by no means Colonel McCormick's only contribution to my education as a journalist or as a human being during the years I worked for him, but without offense to the memory of an honest— if sometimes greatly misguided—American patriot, I am afraid the most important ones were negative. Forcing oneself to see the contemporary world in its real depth of complexity, rather than in the Colonel's authoritatively foreshortened perspective, was useful practice for a professional observer learning to resist the tyranny of his own prejudices. Striving to affirm one's existence as a real person rather than as a symbol of vicarious adventure in the Colonel's mind was helpful in outgrowing one's own boyhood fantasies of adventure and command.

6

The Rot in the Walls

C overing French internal affairs in the early 1930's was no less
educational than observing the darkening international scene;
sometimes it proved an even greater challenge to the growth
of understanding.

At the period I refer to—in fact right up to the war—France
offered an illustration of Montesquieu's dictum so striking as to be
almost paradoxical. From the viewpoint of intellectual vigor, talents
of persuasion, knowledge of men and affairs, the French political
elite compared favorably with that of most other countries. The
top French leaders, whatever their faults, were often men of considerable stature. Briand was the biggest of them, but ·even after his
death the Third Republic possessed such parliamentary stars of the
first magnitude as André Tardieu, the most forceful spokesman for
big business and sophisticated nationalism, Édouard Herriot, the
gross-looking but highly lettered mayor of Lyons and the golden
voice of classic French liberalism, Léon Blum, the subtle, cultivated,
profoundly humane chief of the democratic Socialists, and Pierre
Laval, whose early years in power by no means foretold his ignominious end. In the second row were a dozen or more figures from
each house of parliament—aging veterans of more spacious times or
rising survivors of the war generation—who in a public debate could
have made the best minds of the United States Senate look like
yokels.

In time I got to know most of the prominent French politicians, to the limited extent possible for the young correspondent of an American paper suspected of having little sympathy with French foreign policy. I managed to obtain formal interviews with several, chatted in more casual circumstances with others, attended their press conferences, cultivated their young aides, and above all studied them in action from the press gallery of the Chamber of Deputies or in its lobbies. Laval was my favorite; his unvarying white tie, invariably flecked with cigarette ash, his controlled professional gambler's gestures, and instinctive knowledge of human perfidy lurking behind his smoky eyes appealed to my sense of color. I also thought of him at first as a disenchanted yet authentic disciple of Briand, stubbornly dedicated to the Master's policy of Franco-German *rapprochement*. (Later, I discovered his motivation was more complex, though it seems to have included a genuine horror of war, perhaps because of the fevered herd-idealisms that war generates.) While none of the other front-rank French leaders interested me as keenly as Laval, I had a certain respect for most of them. They were professionals who had style and knew their jobs.

Yet, as I could not help noticing, these professionals of power often messed things up as badly as the rankest amateur. Tardieu, unable to convince even his own followers of the patent need for constitutional reform, finally walked off the political stage into bitter and sterile semi-retirement; Herriot, seemingly unnerved by the growing burden of responsibility, promoted himself before his time into the role of elder-statesman; poor Blum eventually was compelled by the inertia of events, the dire *force des choses*, to carry out policies he loathed and to abjure positions around whose defense he had built his whole career. Laval, for all his cynical opportunism, fared no better: Over the years I watched him writhing like a serpent in the eagle claws of circumstance, foiled, largely by Bruening himself, in trying to save Bruening, forced to woo Hitler when he wanted to wed Mussolini, trapped into concluding a military alliance with Soviet Russia instead of the alliance against Russia that he really sought. As for solving the nation's deeper problems, the brilliant and highly educated men who usually held power in France had no more luck than the hacks who governed in many other lands.

The most glaring weaknesses in the French political system were the instability of governments and the lack of a strong executive. The Third Republic, despite its ultimately dismal record, probably suffered less from these ills than its successor, but both Tardieu in his day and General de Gaulle later were undoubtedly right in calling for drastic reform. In the early 1930's I was not myself as conscious of the problem as events subsequently made me, but like most Americans, I felt that parliamentary democracy on the French model, if it had ever had any merits, was an outdated system in the modern world.

Gradually, I came to see that the machinery of government was not the only thing that needed overhauling in France. Bureaucratic or other corporate traditions, administrative doctrine, professional codes of behavior, in short, all the invisible institutions that shape the public mind, all the unwritten folkways that regulate the body politic, were corroded with anachronisms.

The whole structure and the ethos of French capitalism were likewise nearly half a century out of date; this backwardness helped spare France the runaway American boom of the late 1920's, and for a while it cushioned the impact of the worldwide depression, but the archaic gold cult of the French bankers forced on a succession of governments a fiscal policy so savagely deflationary that it eventually brought the nation to the brink of revolution.

It was not until much later I became aware of two particularly important fountainheads of French backwardness: the educational system, which in final analysis was responsible for most of the anachronistic patterns of thought in the public mind, and the military mandarinate crowned by the army's General Staff. If I read Colonel Charles de Gaulle's critiques of French strategic and tactical orthodoxy when they first appeared in print, they made little impression on me. The basic contradiction between a foreign policy based on alliances with the Little Entente and Poland and a military strategy based on holing up in the Maginot Line, which in retrospect looks so glaring to present-day historians, did not strike me before 1937 or 1938; I doubt that many French policy-makers were much struck by it.

The obsolescence of so many French institutions and the anachronistic nature of so many French attitudes often gave the foreign observer an impression that France as a nation was hopelessly decadent. This impression was misleading—the more I see of the world or study its history, the more wary I become of applying words like "decadence" to civilizations, nations or broad social groups of any kind—but certain sectors of French society in the 1930's could legitimately be termed decadent. Unfortunately, these sectors of decay—morally, as well as socially or ideologically, corrupt—included some groups from which the country's political and administrative leadership was recruited.

There was an endemic, attenuated form of corruption arising from the quasi-oligarchical, behind-the-scenes power and influence of certain wealthy families—what the historian Beau de Loménie termed the "bourgeois dynasties." Paradoxically, the general twentieth-century revolt against bourgeois values aggravated rather than diminished this evil: As "society" in the old sense lost its prestige, café society acquired new glamor, and café society, especially in Paris, is almost by definition tolerant of scandal. By the early 30's in France, or at least in Paris, social ostracism had largely lost its effectiveness as a sanction against scandalous behavior.

André Tardieu, during his years of power in the twenties and early thirties, had exemplified the unwholesome blend of the new personal freedom with the old dynastic manipulation: his private life was almost defiantly free from cant, his professional reputation was by no means irreproachable; as Minister of the Interior, one of his favorite posts, he had made no bones about using the police power of the state to serve his own political interests, and he had doled out secret government funds with a lavishness probably unequaled in France in time of peace. Laval, who favored the Ministry of the Interior no less than Tardieu did, had been somewhat stingier but just as unscrupulous.

Some of my most respected French newspaper colleagues could hardly have kept up their normal scale of living without their periodic "little envelopes" from the Interior or from the Quai d'Orsay. French diplomatic correspondents who faithfully hewed to the policy line of the government in power were allowed, if not encouraged, to supplement their incomes by accepting similar subsidies from friendly foreign governments; even when certain of these spare-time earners began stretching the concept of friendliness to include Fascist Italy, and ultimately Hitlerite Germany, no action was taken against them.

Parliamentary mores were no less easygoing than journalistic ones. The Chamber of Deputies under the Third Republic was not quite the "house without windows" an American social scientist termed it under the Fourth, but its atmosphere already suggested that of a private club operated for the comfort of its members more than that of a responsible parliament legislating on behalf of the nation. To the degree that parliamentary debate served the political ambitions of the parliamentarians, or simply provided them with wholesome sport, its proceedings sometimes had a measure of validity; that is to say, the life of the nation was actually affected by the debate, somewhat as the lives of nineteenth-century Russian serfs were affected when their masters lost or won them at the gambling table.

More often, however, especially when important economic interests were at stake, the issue had already been decided elsewhere; parliamentary debate merely served to ritualize the decision. Lobbies and pressure groups of all kinds flourished in France, as they did in other democracies; one of the most notorious and influential was the *Comité des Forges*, the professional organism of the highly cartelized steel industry. In the old-fashioned, idealized, and purely abstract French concept of parliamentary democracy, however, there was no legitimate role for lobbies; they could only exist underground, where their activities, since they were not officially recognized, eluded regulation or control. Conspiracy and corruption were thereby encouraged.

To make matters worse, the agents of the lobbies, many of them unscrupulous adventurers and some of them plain crooks, devoted only part of their attention to influencing legislation. The executive branch of government was often a more interesting target. France at the time was—and to some extent still is—a queer mixture of eighteenth-century rhetoric and Napoleonic absolutism: liberty, equality, fraternity and bureaucracy. It was a commonplace of political observers that underneath its ministerial instability the country had the most stable government in the West because it was really governed by its permanent civil servants. This was largely true, but it was not officially acknowledged, so that bureaucrats wielded power without responsibility; and irresponsible power corrupts more absolutely than any other kind. Thanks to an almost Balzac-ian adventure in the French political underworld in which I once became involved, this basic law of politics and history was indelibly stamped on my memory.

For all the impression that the affair made on me, some details have inevitably become a little hazy with time. I am not sure exactly when it started: toward the end of 1931, I think, sometime after my return from Germany. Of the man himself, I remember that he was short, snub-nosed, blue-eyed, with thinning blond hair; that he was shabbily dressed and not very well shaved. I cannot recall any particular mannerisms or tricks of speech. What I remember above all is his cheerfulness, or more properly, the inexhaustible well of gaiety that kept bubbling up in his eyes and his voice. There was nothing frightening about this gaiety; it was simply infectious. I have encountered the same curious trait, or hints of it, several times since; the men—or in one or two cases women—who displayed it did not strike me as being moral monsters, yet they seemed to experience a kind of moral joy in the constantly repeated verification of human corruptibility. Perhaps they all belonged to some sect.

I remember my visitor's name—the name he gave me—of course, but out of some inner reluctance that I cannot rationally explain, I shall call him Nikho. He was an Ukrainian refugee who, he said, had done underground work for the French Army during the brief

Allied occupation of the Ukraine after the Russian collapse in 1917. The end of the wars and the triumph of Lenin had not ended Nikho's private crusade against Bolshevism, he explained, nor had it broken off his collaboration with certain French—and even American—intelligence services; he had continued to fight the good fight in Berlin, and in fact was still fighting it here in Paris, side by side with his loyal allies. The Chicago *Tribune* was known to Nikho and his friends as a staunch foe of Bolshevism; it was for this reason he had come to me rather than to any of my colleagues with a story that might well prove the journalistic sensation of the decade.

Nikho was not exaggerating in one respect. What he was offering to sell me was evidence of a formidable Communist conspiracy in the United States headed by Senator William E. Borah of Idaho, Chairman of the Senate Foreign Relations Committee, and Senator Hiram W. Johnson of California. At the time, these two were among the most prominent members of the United States Senate; both were Republicans and noted isolationists. The "evidence" included alleged photosatic copies of typed and signed receipts for large sums— $25,000 apiece if my memory is correct—paid each senator as a secret yearly salary by the Soviet government.

Nikho answered my first objection before I could utter it. As a responsible journalist I could not publish a story of such explosive nature merely on the evidence of photostatic copies; he, Nikho, was fully aware of that. Unfortunately, for reasons I would soon appreciate, the originals of the receipts could not be delivered to me. They could, however, be shown to me. When I had examined the originals and satisfied myself there was no forgery, would my paper than be prepared to buy the photostats?

I doubted it, I told Nikho. I was not a handwriting expert; how would I know the signatures on the originals were authentic? Ah, replied Nikho with one of his happy smiles, that was easy: Did I think the French Sûreté Générale (the national criminal and political police) could be fooled by even the cleverest forgery, or would keep fake documents in its files? For that was where the originals of the receipts were: in the files of the Sûreté Générale. How could I get to look at them then, I countered, or how would Nikho be able to prove that he had taken them out of the files to show me? Ah, he answered again, it was not he, Nikho, who would show them to me, but a good friend of his, a very high official of the Sûreté, who would open the Borah-Johnson dossier for me on his desk and let me inspect it to my heart's content, right there in his office.

This was getting interesting. Why, I asked, were the French state police so anxious to have the Chicago *Tribune* expose the treasonable relations of two American senators with the Soviet government? It wasn't exactly the police as such, Nikho replied; it was just his friend in the Sûreté, a man of very high ideals who wanted to go on fighting Bolshevism in the only way that remained possible, but a very human sort of man, too, with his family to think about. You mean, I asked, your friend in the Sûreté would get half the money if we buy the receipts? No, Nikho said, putting on a mournful look, but with pure merriment dancing in his eyes, not half; nearly all; I just collect a sort of commission. The asking price was substantial—$50,000 if I remember correctly—but not excessive, if those incredible photostats were authentic.

I could not believe that they were, but the alternative seemed equally improbable, unless Nikho was a lunatic or a very crude sort of *agent provocateur*. I began, accordingly, by looking up the character references he had given me. The main one was a retired American army colonel, a former military attaché in the Paris Embassy, married to a French woman and settled down in Passy. He received me cordially and answered all my questions without reticence.

Though the Colonel had not heard from Nikho in several years, he acknowledged that as an intelligence officer he once made considerable use of him; Nikho had proved an exceptionally reliable informant. The Colonel believed in his sincerity and, up to a point, in his honesty. (One look at the old soldier's blue, candid eyes, dispelled whatever doubts I had entertained about his own.) He knew Nikho's friend at the Sûreté, and knew about the famous dossier in the Sûreté's files; he had personally satisfied himself as to the authenticity of the receipts. For years he had tried to get the War Department in Washington to undertake a full-scale investigation of the case. Later he had written about it to several influential friends in private life at home. Nothing had ever come of these efforts; if I could get the shameful story broken, good luck to me.

I had, of course, immediately reported Nikho's offer to Chicago. Col. McCormick and the managing editor shared my skepticism about the documents; in those innocent days the thought that two respected United States Senators (and sound Republican isolationists, at that) might be on the secret payroll of the Soviet government would have seemed preposterous to almost any normal American. At the same time my chiefs agreed that the whole affair was too grave and too mysterious to be brushed aside; I was authorized to keep in contact with Nikho and to make every reasonable effort to prove or disprove his alleged evidence. No bona fide American newspaperman with real ink in his veins could have taken a different position. I was warned, however, to act with the greatest prudence.

The warning was unnecessary—especially after I had called on Nikho's friend at his office in the Sûreté. Nikho had not exaggerated his importance in the police hierarchy. If the Sûreté had been organized like a present-day government department in Washington, he would probably have been called an assistant director; his echelon in any case was higher than that of division head. Let us follow Nikho's practice and simply refer to him as *le Patron*, the Chief. He looked the typical French bureaucrat: sad, sallow, dusty of word and mind. Under the dust, however, I quickly discovered an intelligence of steel. He answered all my questions, directly, explicitly, a little bureaucratically; then he asked a few of his own. What, for example, was the exact sum that Nikho had mentioned to me? I told him. Nikho, he said, was a reliable person; I could have full confidence in him. The receipts were authentic and they were in the files. I could see them for myself when we finally came to terms. (When I reported the conversation to Nikho, his first question was, Did the Chief mention the same price for the documents I quoted you?)

At first there was a lingering question of identity in my mind, but the Chief's rank made it easy to settle. Discreet questioning of French colleagues satisfied me that the room in which I had been received was truly the Chief's and that the person who had received me there corresponded to his description.

The weeks dragged by, slow but fascinating. In those days it took a fortnight on the average to write Chicago and get an answer; the subject matter was too delicate for cabling. Besides, I was in no hurry; I wanted to keep Nikho and his chief dangling as long as possible. Meanwhile I kept in touch with the old Colonel in Passy and had several meetings with Nikho. Our favorite rendezvous, fixed by Nikho, was a sordid but legal gambling club near the Gare St. Lazare, patronized mainly by Russian taxi chauffeurs; we could talk there securely, he explained. The security aspect did not seem quite self-evident to me, but I enjoyed the Dostoevskian atmosphere. I never saw Nikho gamble and he made no overt attempt to induce me to.

Gradually, by piecing together scraps of information supplied by Nikho and the Colonel, I obtained a sufficiently detailed statement of the case against the two senators to provide a basis for some serious cross-checking. The results, both in Chicago and in Paris, were what I had expected. The deeper I delved, the more certain I became that the receipts were forgeries. Internal evidence linked them conclusively to a set of similar documents circulating around Berlin in the early 20's that had been officially exposed by the German police as forgeries. Error, like truth, seems immortal; crushed to earth, it rises again and again.

Once I had convinced myself—and my editors in Chicago—that Nikho was trying to perpetuate a vicious lie, it seemed an almost elementary civic duty to foil his efforts, the more so because he had warned me that in view of the *Tribune*'s dilatory attitude he had decided to approach one of my competitors. Accordingly, I called on one of my friends at the United States Embassy and told him the whole story. The ambassador, at that time Walter E. Edge, was informed, and discreet representations were made to the Quai d'Orsay, where Laval had just settled down as Foreign Minister. (Previous to that he had been Minister of the Interior and thus the chief of the Chief's chief.)

The result was somewhat more than I had bargained for. One afternoon I received a peremptory telephone call to report immediately to the Director of the Sûreté. In his anteroom I found the colleague whom Nikho had approached: a British subject with a wartime background in intelligence work whose paper, of all American papers, was the one least likely to consider that Nikho's story, even if it was believed, was quite fit to print. The colleague, who was also waiting to see *M. le Directeur*, gave me a British grin, and I grinned back.

The Director, M. Julien, a recent and only semi-professional appointee, received me affably. He asked me how I liked living in France and whether I planned to continue living there. I answered in the same spirit. Then he got down to business. He had heard that an unscrupulous swindler had been trying to sell me certain documents, and he wanted to warn me that they were forgeries. The matter was all the graver because it appeared that the swindler in question had been falsely claiming that the forgeries—which were of a nature to perturb Franco-American relations—came from the files of the Sûreté itself. At this moment Nikho's friend, the Chief, entered the room in response to the Director's summons. He expressed the deepest indignation when informed of the situation. He was all the more distressed, he said, because he had made occasional use of Nikho in the past as a low-grade tipster and had pitied him for his difficult life as a refugee in Paris. Evidently the fellow had abused his confidence in the basest way. He could assure me on his personal word of honor there was not a scrap of truth in Nikho's claim that the receipts in question, true or false, existed, or ever had existed, in the files of the Sûreté.

Though I knew much less about France at the time than I came to know later, I realized as I turned and met the Chief's cool, level stare—his eyes reminded me of Laval's—that I was standing on very thin ice and that the waters running underneath were very deep, very cold. From the bottom of my heart I thanked *M. le Directeur* and *M. le Patron* (the title seemed more apt than ever in the presence of his obviously flustered superior). I was particularly grateful for their unequivocal assurance about the receipts, the more so, I said, because it confirmed my own suspicions. In fact, I continued, matching frankness with frankness, it was only a question of journalistic scruple that had caused me to waste any time investigating Nikho's preposterous tale; I had been convinced from the start that he was a crook. The Chief looked a little startled, but the Director seemed relieved. Excellent, he replied, then I would certainly perceive the wisdom of breaking off relations with such an undesirable personage; indeed, I would find no difficulty in doing so, because within twenty-four hours Nikho would be expelled from France as an undesirable alien. Everyone thanked everyone again, and I left after exchanging warm handshakes with the Director and the Chief.

A few minutes after I got back to my office the telephone rang. It was Nikho and he was furious. "How dared you tell my friend the Chief I was a crook?" he said. "Don't you realize that kind of loose talk can be very dangerous—dangerous for you? As for that ridiculous story of my being expelled from France, just wait and see."

Nikho was right. He was still around nearly a year later, at the time of the Stavisky scandal—concerning which we shall shortly hear more—and thanks to his continued friendship with the Chief, he had some inside information I might want to buy, quite reasonably. One of the Chief's associates at the Sûreté, Inspector Bony, knew more about the background of the famous scandal than anyone alive (though not perhaps quite so much as one or two persons dead). This time I believed Nikho. The Chief's name had been discreetly mentioned by the press in connection with the affair, and Bony's was prominently, though by no means favorably, linked with it. This was the same Bony who under the Occupation acquired a sinister notoriety as the principal agent of the Gestapo in France; he was shot after the Liberation. I never learned what happened to the Chief.

As for Nikho, I kept on hearing from him occasionally; apparently he bore me no grudge. Sometime in 1937 or 1938, he suggested an exclusive feature story on the *"Cagoulard"* conspiracy. I was not very well informed about this right-wing terrorist organization— which we now know was subsidized by Mussolini's secret service while covertly sponsored by a Marshal of France—but from one of my French sources I had picked up just enough about it to realize that I did not want to know any more. The last time I heard Nikho's voice, except in dreams, was early one morning toward the end of April 1940, when he called me at my flat, waking me out of a deep sleep, to propose a little talk. Some very interesting developments were impending, he said.

In the real world with which we are concerned, human affairs cannot be properly understood, much less regulated, by merely tracing them back to simple, impersonal factors similar to those with which the natural scientist is accustomed to deal. The wayward human factor must always be taken into account, for though men may be shaped by many forces, in final analysis, human events are shaped by men. In explaining history, as in making it, there is no substitute for the toils and vigils of leadership . . . Democracy does not decline because the democratic idea has lost its vitality. It declines because democratic leadership has lost its vigor.

LEADERSHIP IN THE FREE WORLD

(UNPUBLISHED MSS. 1950–1951)

In all my years as a newspaperman, or as a watcher of living history in any capacity, I cannot recall an experience that has done more to shape my notions of political reality—and with them my own political attitudes—than covering the crisis of French democracy of January-February 1934. I am thinking, of course, of the bloody riots in Paris on February 6 and the following days—they could hardly fail to make a vivid impression on the mind of a young man hitherto little exposed to really large-scale violence—but not only of them.

117

The origin, or at least the detonator, of the crisis was the Stavisky scandal, which broke in December 1933. The affair is worth studying for the light it throws on the political and social history of the Third Republic, but it would take a long chapter, if not a whole book, to do it justice. Stavisky was a notorious but petty thief and embezzler who was found out almost at the beginning of his career; yet he went on to become a great adventurer of finance and a master corrupter of French public life.

Joseph, usually known as Alexander, Stavisky was the Russian-born son of respectable middle-class Jewish parents who had emigrated to France before the war; he was a naturalized French citizen. Starting out as a gigolo and small-time confidence man, he was arrested for the first time in 1909. In 1923 he was arrested and eventually sentenced to prison for check forgery. In the following years the sentence was commuted to a form of release on parole no less than nineteen times; new charges brought against him were repeatedly dismissed in court or by the public prosecutor's office. Banned from Paris by a court order, he kept on living unmolested in the capital. Changing his name to Serge Alexandre, Stavisky launched a series of acrobatic and sometimes quasi-legitimate financial operations. He made a fortune and spent most of it entertaining politicians, journalists, and high officials of the state. *Le beau Serge* and his beautiful wife, Arlette, a former mannequin, became ornaments of Paris café society, constantly seen at galas and first nights, in fashionable restaurants and nightclubs, and above all around the gambling tables of the best-known casinos.

Naturally, as Stavisky's wealth, prestige, and generosity increased, the mysterious behind-the-scenes protectors who from the start had tempered the rigors of the law for him became more numerous and powerful. The Paris Prefect of Police, Jean Chiappe, an important figure in French right-wing politics, issued him the rare, white *coupe-file,* a sort of badge similar to the ones issued newspapermen for passing through police lines but endowed with more magic virtues, since it was usually reserved for ambassadors and other notables.

One can easily imagine how its possession helped Stavisky obtain various favors from the lower echelons of the Prefecture, where he already had a number of useful friends. At the Sûreté Nationale Stavisky had some vigilant adversaries, but they were neutralized by high-level political influence. In March 1932 the head of the Sûreté's Criminal Investigation Division, Louis Ducloux, managed to obtain an administrative order barring Stavisky from all gambling rooms in France. On July 2 of the same year the order was rescinded by a ministerial decision, taken with the concurrence of the Sûreté's Director.

My own adventure at the Sûrcté with Nikho and his Chief helped me understand how such things happened, but as I followed the unfolding of the scandal day after day in the French press or in the gossip around the press bar at the Chamber, I realized that my education in the seamy side of French political life had not been complete. To understand why, it is necessary to recall briefly the denouement of the Stavisky drama.

With the help of one of his political friends, the Radical Socialist deputy and mayor of Bayonne, Stavisky had promoted the establishment of a municipal pawnshop in that town and had floated a sizable issue of its bonds, theoretically guaranteed by the pledges in its keeping. Many of these pledged articles turned out to be fake or stolen pieces of jewelry planted by Stavisky himself. Not content with fraudulently pyramiding the assets of the Bayonne establishment, Stavisky eventually took to outright forging of its bonds on a vast scale. The fraud was discovered in December 1933, shortly before some of the bonds fell due. Stavisky went into hiding, with the police, including Nikho's friend, Inspector Bony, hot on his traces. He was eventually run to earth in a rented villa near Chamonix, where, according to the official version, he shot himself as his pursuers were breaking in. As far as I am aware, no material evidence worthy of consideration has ever been unearthed to suggest that his death was anything but suicide. It was an extraordinarily convenient one, however, for a number of important persons, some of them in the police, and it was understandable that the French public at the time was not completely convinced by what the pro-government or conformist press related.

The public likewise had some reason, especially in the early stages of the investigation, to suspect that it was not being told the whole truth about Stavisky's high-level accomplices and connections. What was revealed was shocking enough: Two deputies, two publishers, the head of an insurance company, and the director of the Bayonne pawnshop were charged with witting participation in the dead adventurer's fraudulent schemes; a cabinet minister in the government then in power, which was headed by the Radical Socialist, Camille Chautemps, was gravely implicated and had to resign; the Director of the Sûreté, Thomé, and the Paris Prefect of Police, Chiappe, were seriously enough involved to be considered guilty at least of neglect of duty; so were either the government prosecutor—who happened to be Chautemps's brother-in-law, Pressard—or one of his subordinates, Judge Prince, or both of them (each put the blame on the other). A number of politicians, some of them well known, were revealed to have been on terms of casual fellowship with Stavisky, to have accepted lavish hospitality from him, and to have done him minor favors. The scandal took on a more lurid hue than ever— fortunately after the riots had ended—when the mangled body of Judge Prince was found on a railroad track near Dijon; the autopsy revealed traces of chloroform or some other narcotic in the respiratory track. The official verdict was suicide, but it was widely believed at the time that Prince had been murdered to shut his mouth, and sober present-day historians of the epoch consider it the likeliest hypothesis. Who instigated the murder, if it was one, is unknown, though some sketchy, indirect evidence points toward Chiappe.

Basically, I suppose, French public life in the last years of the Third Republic was only a little more corrupt than it is in most modern societies, democratic or not; the trouble was that parliamentary democracy as it operated in France at the time failed to produce the kind of leadership capable of meeting the periodic need of all societies for reform in public life. Indeed, democratic leadership in

France proved itself incapable of adapting itself to meet effectively any of history's challenges.

Even the defects of French leadership, or more fundamentally, the inability of the social machinery to produce sound leaders, were less deep-rooted than they seem at first glance. Hannah Arendt has written eloquently of the "banality of evil"; one can speak similarly of the triviality of doom. The differences between a healthy society and a fatally sick one, between a political system adapted to the challenge of its environment and one that has ceased to be, seem incredibly slight, almost trifling at times. The response of French political leadership to the challenge of corruption revealed by the Stavisky scandal, and even more its response to the revolutionary threat generated by the scandal, furnished an unforgettable illustration of this disquieting law of historic perspective.

It was the Republic's bad luck that one of its least impressive and rather substandard politicians happened to be in power when the Stavisky storm broke. A man of petty ambitions and routine mind, Camille Chautemps misunderstood the nature of the threat that confronted him. He correctly diagnosed a kind of plot by the leaders of the right—and the money interests they represented—to exploit the Stavisky affair in order to dislocate the center-left parliamentary majority that had emerged from the elections of 1932. It was an almost classic maneuver in French politics, and insofar as the moving spirits behind it were professional politicians like himself—Tardieu and Laval, for example—he felt he could cope with them. Chautemps failed to discern in time the Catilinesque figure of Chiappe in the background, and bemused by what I have called the delusion of normality, he underrated the revolutionary intent of a substantial part of the opposition.

To an outside observer, the developing conspiratorial pattern seemed unmistakable, and public indignation over the "thieves" in parliament made it extremely dangerous. The political leagues and press organs of the nationalist right launched a well-orchestrated propaganda campaign against the government; the guilt-by-association technique for which the American demagogue, McCarthy, later became notorious, was used to create the impression that the state was riddled with corruption. The more extreme rightist publications exploited Stavisky's Jewish background to whip up anti-Semitism and xenophobia, and attacked with insurrectionary violence not only parliament, but the democratic regime itself, "that bloody manure-machine," as Léon Daudet, the Royalist agitator, called it in *l'Action Française*. The mounting toll of Stavisky's frauds—some $60,000,000 altogether—the almost daily disclosure of new connivances and turpitudes—late in January, for example, it was revealed that the thick file of the late adventurer's brushes with the law had somehow vanished from the court records—would have sufficed to infuriate the French taxpayer. Popular fury, however, might have eventually burned itself out if it had not been systematically channeled toward insurrection by right-wing activist groups and cadres utilizing methods of psychological conditioning similar to those Hitler's Nazis had so successfully employed in Germany. Thus, the editor of the bulletin published by an association of war veterans, a right-wing Paris municipal councillor, covered his front page with a drawing showing the Chamber of Deputies in flames and its members hanging from lampposts on the bridge across the Seine leading to the Place de la Concorde. The legend beneath read, "Must we come to this?" The same suggestion—burn the Chamber, lynch the deputies—was repeated over and over in the same insidious fashion wherever a susceptible audience could be effectively reached. Toward the end of January the extremist organizations began launching their storm troopers in street demonstrations intended to feel out the government's defensive dispositions, and above all, to create the necessary atmosphere of revolutionary violence.

On January 27 Chautemps resigned, completely demoralized by the revelation that his Minister of Justice was implicated in a new financial scandal. Three days later another government was set up under Édouard Daladier, who had already held the premiership for a few months the year before. Daladier, a former history professor from Provence, was one of the hopes of the Radical Socialist party. He was surrounded by a small brain trust whose members were believed to favor a somewhat radical economic and social program modeled on the American New Deal. Daladier had a clean reputation and a good war record; he looked tough and vigorous, worthy of his nickname, the "Bull of the Camargue." Unfortunately, he soon turned out to be, as the wits remarked, a bull with snail's horns; all the errors of judgment, all the weaknesses of character that marked Daladier's leadership throughout the Munich crisis of 1938 and in the early months of the Second World War were foreshadowed by his actions during the week he held office in 1934.

Daladier appointed a special high-level commission to investigate all the possible complicities or derelictions of duty in the Stavisky scandal and promised that it would set to work without losing a minute—after the impending midwinter recess of parliament was over. (As a historian Daladier had seemingly never heard of Louis XVI.) He removed Chautemps's brother-in-law, the public prosecutor, and the Director of the Sûreté Générale from their respective posts, but gave them new, only slightly less honorific appointments. He sacked the Prefect of Police, Chiappe, on the grounds of his personal involvement with Stavisky, then promoted him to be French High Commissioner, the Republic's proconsul, in Morocco. Chiappe, an ambitious, hot-blooded Corsican, who may have been even more closely associated with Stavisky than he was accused of being, first accepted, then on advice from right-wing friends turned down the splendid offer. "In that case, I'll be out in the streets [i.e., on the barricades]," Chiappe replied, or is quoted as having replied, to Daladier when the premier ordered him by telephone to quit the Prefecture immediately. After that nothing could have averted a showdown with the Paris mob.

Like most of my colleagues, French or foreign, I awaited the inevitable explosion with mixed feelings; it would undoubtedly make an exciting story to cover—perhaps a bit too exciting. "Altogether it is a unique situation," I cabled the *Tribune* on February 5. "Thousands of Frenchmen are convinced a formidable revolutionary movement is on foot to overthrow the Republic. But nobody knows exactly what the movement is, where it came from, or who is back of it."

The Republic was unquestionably in danger, yet it is highly doubtful that there was any large-scale plot against it, mainly because the
would-be plotters failed to realize in time how vulnerable it had
become. What did exist was a kind of open conspiracy among the
leaders of a half-dozen or more political or para-revolutionary organizations with widely divergent aims to mobilize varying degrees
of mob pressure against the Daladier government by means of loosely
concerted street demonstrations. The eventual scope and violence of
the demonstrations surprised everyone, including their organizers;
they demonstrated the hitherto little understood capability of a few
trained agitators to detonate a formidable insurrectionary explosion,
once a certain critical mass of public resentment or irritation exists.
Daladier and his Minister of the Interior, Eugene Frot, misjudged
the police problem that confronted them: They suspected a revolutionary conspiracy of classic type, aiming at a coup d'état. To foil it
they decided to hold strongly a few vital centers in the capital and
to concentrate large forces of cavalry and motorized infantry on the
outskirts in readiness to deliver a crushing counterattack, wherever
it might be needed. In so doing, they virtually abandoned the vast,
open Place de la Concorde and the Champs Élysées to the mob, a
fatal mistake.

Daladier's adversaries chose February 6 as their D-day because the
Premier was due to present his cabinet to parliament on that date.
"The thieves have barricaded themselves in their cavern," screamed
the headlines in *l'Action Française* on the morning of February 6.
"Against the abject regime, general mobilization tonight in front of
the Chamber!"

The debate that afternoon on the Daladier government's investi-
ture was the most tumultous I ever witnessed. The deputies were
jittery at the thought of the mobs converging on the Chamber from
all over Paris; they vented their fear in hysterical outbreaks of hostility toward the government or toward their own political adversaries on the floor of the house.

"Adventurer," yelled Maurice Thorez, brandishing his fist at
Tardieu, "provocator." Learning forward in his seat Tardieu shook

his first back at the Communist chief. "I put you in jail before," he shouted, "and I'll do it again." Wild cheers from the right, animal bellows of fury from the left greeted the exchange; all over the house deputies banged their desktops up and down like maddened schoolboys. Daladier, standing in the speaker's rostrum with his burly shoulders hunched and his head thrust forward, looked more than ever like a stubborn and exasperated bull as he tried to make himself heard above the din.

Shortly after 6 P.M. another, more ominous sound could be heard: the muffled roar of the crowd surging against the police lines. I slipped out of the press box and walked through the heavily guarded police barricade across the bridge facing the Chamber, out into the Place de la Concorde. It was nearly packed with demonstrators, and reinforcements for the mob were constantly fighting their way into the vast square from the Rue de Rivoli and the direction of the Opéra. Coming over the bridge I had caught the distant war cries of other crowds trying to march on the Chamber from the Left Bank, chiefly along Boulevard St. Germain. It was plain that the Paris police, disaffected by the firing of Chiappe, were making only a halfhearted effort to control the riots. Moreover, the new Prefect had committed a strategic blunder in allowing the several veterans' organizations to mass their followers at the Concorde for a "peaceful and dignified" march of protest up the Champs Élysées to the Arc de Triomphe.

Many of the thousands in the Place de la Concorde were indeed, war veterans, but instead of marching in dignity they were battling with the forces of the law to get at the Chamber. Egging on the veterans and the more or less responsible right-wing groups were little bands of fascist or ultranationalist students; a column of Communist counterdemonstrators, massed around a red flag, added to the general confusion. More than half of the huge crowd probably consisted of curious bystanders who had originally turned out merely to watch the demonstrations; the first scuffles with the police had awakened their atavistic hatred of authority, and the mounting frenzy of the combat had sucked them into its vortex. "Down with the thieves," the mob chanted as it surged against the barriers; "assassins," it howled when the police countercharged with truncheons and weighted raincapes. From time to time the *Marseillaise* burst out in the distance to roll like thunder over the square as more and more voices took it up.

I was caught in the front ranks of the crowd, and found myself repeatedly swept forward against the police lines by the irresistible mass thrust from the rear. Except for the scale of the action and the special excitement that any large, angry crowd generates merely by its existence, there was little at first to distinguish this riot from others I had seen in Paris. Soon, however, the pattern of violence underwent a change. A group of rioters in front of the Hotel Crillon, next door to the newly finished United States Embassy, halted an autobus, forced the passengers to dismount, and set it on fire, while they performed a sort of war dance around it. The flames, fed with gasoline, leaped high in the air and were reflected back from the low-hanging clouds—it had been a dull, mild, winter day with passing squalls of rain. Suddenly a squadron of mounted *Gardes Républicains* swept down from the bridge and charged across the square, their polished brass cuirasses gleaming in the lamplight, the horsehair streaming from their helmets. Behind the horsemen followed black-helmeted *Gardes Mobiles*, charging on foot, swinging their rifle butts as they came on. Running with the crowd to escape them, I saw an improvised barricade on our flank, near the entrance to the Tuileries Gardens. From behind it a paving stone floated up, landing a few feet from me; a hail of smaller missiles, apparently aimed at the *Gardes*, whistled above my head. The *Gardes* broke ranks, halted momentarily to pick up the stones, and hurled them back at the rioters as they ran.

Several of the visual splinters from the scene are still bright in my memory after thirty years: the horses of the *Gardes Républicains* plunging and floundering on the steel ball bearings that the rioters scattered under their hooves; the sabers flailing and slashing above the tossing sea of human heads; the barricade of paving stones, surmounted with the tricolor flag, and silhouetted against leaping flames like a vignette out of some revolutionary picture book.

Just before the climax of the riot I managed to get on the terrace of the Tuileries Gardens, overlooking the Place de la Concorde, where for a while I had a panoramic view of the battlefield, now illuminated by several fires. Massed along the parapet under a tricolor flag was a phalanx of young *Camelots du Roi* exchanging insults and occasional volleys of small missiles with a sizable band of Communist workers, brandishing a red flag, immediately beneath. A small column of *Gardes Mobiles,* debouching from the river embankment, headed toward the Communists, swinging their rifles. A whistle blew on the terrace near where I was standing, I heard the field captain of the young royalists shouting some kind of orders to his troops, and immediately afterward they broke into a cheer as the workers stood off the charge with volleys of stones. Then the *Camelots du Roi began* breaking up the stone benches in the gardens and handing down fragments of them to the Communists to use as munitions against the guardians of the Republic, the common enemy; I have had many occasions since to recall that scene.

I did not see how the shooting started; in the vast roar of the mob I did not even hear the first scattered shots, which may have come from the crowd. There was a confused melee near the bridgehead—for a few moments it looked as though the mob had broken through the police lines and was sweeping onto the bridge. Then I heard an irregular rattling sound—like thousands of other overexcited witnesses on the spot I mistook it for machine-gun fire—and noticed a series of bluish flashes from the bridge as the front ranks of the mob turned back in a stampede for safety. They were pushed forward again by the pressure from behind. Again the rattling sound was heard and there were two or three curiously light taps on the trunk of a tree near which I was standing. I heard a yelp from one of the nearby *Camelots* and saw one of them walk away from the parapet holding his sleeve. "It's a massacre," someone screamed.

Shortly after that, a series of police charges cleared the Place de la Concorde, then the *Gardes Mobiles,* opening the gate to the Tuileries Gardens, were upon us. I foolishly tried to get behind them by waving my press badge, then dodging in time, turned and ran until I could get my breath no more.

The battle on the Concorde was the most spectacular phase of the riots but the decisive incident occurred about the same time on the Left Bank, when a disciplined column of war veterans belonging to the *Croix de Feu*, the strongest of the right-wing leagues, forced its way to the gates of the Chamber where the deputies were still in hysterical session. The intent of the assailants, or what they thought was their intent, was merely to "spank" the deputies and drive them out of the Chamber, but far graver violence could hardly have failed to take place if the *Croix de Feu* had actually broken into the building. One brave man, a colonel of the *Garde Républicaine*, stopped them, and thereby averted civil war in France. When refused entrance, the leader of the veterans' column, a retired colonel himself, either lost his nerve or recovered his senses; in any case he turned back with his troops.

Out of an estimated 40,000 rioters, 16 were killed outright and 665 given as wounded, though the true number of wounded was probably a good deal higher. Casualties among the various law enforcement agencies amounted to 1,660 wounded, one fatally. In the face of a threat from the leaders of the insurrection to arm their troops and renew the attack the next day, Daladier handed in his resignation, and President Lebrun placated conservative opinion by calling one of his predecessors, Gaston Doumergue, out of retirement to head a national union cabinet. The riots continued for several days, but this time it was the left that was calling its forces into the streets and the disorders were contained for the most part in the working-class quarters.

The more militant or fascist-minded organizers of the conspiracy felt that they had been betrayed by the moneymen and the politicians, who had no hankering for a revolution, not even an authoritarian one, but public opinion was not behind them. The *Croix de Feu* leaders probably held the balance of power between classic right and radical right; once they had turned back from the brink of civil war, the fate of the insurrection had been settled. In a sense, therefore, February 6 was a mere episode of passing sound and fury that changed nothing in France. It turned out, however, to be a catalyzer of grave changes. The *revolution manquée* of the extreme right not only planted the seeds of the Popular Front in France but also transformed a puerile and almost benign form of political conspiracy into something much deadlier. It is only a small exaggeration to say that the fascist fifth column which was to play an important role in the collapse of 1940 came into being on February 6, 1934, or in its disillusioned aftermath.

As for myself, this direct contact with the forces of social chaos made a deep and lasting impression. In the early 1930's, like many young men in Europe, and like a few in the United States, I had come to have serious doubts about the validity of the democratic ideal. Exposure to the swamp life of French politics had inevitably sharpened them. I had, however, acquired a clearer realization of what the most currently fashionable alternative to democracy implied. It was not only democracy that was terrifyingly fragile, I now saw, but civilization itself. The lesson was soon reenforced by what I saw and experienced during a new assignment to Germany.

7

The Innocence of Evil

Even to the most charitable eye, the National Socialist state that began to take shape when Adolf Hitler was named Chancellor of Germany on January 30, 1933, represented an unmistakable regression. During its first year of existence, however, the regime, understandably preoccupied with consolidating its still tenuous hold on the German people, displayed neither the monster traits nor the frightening power of attraction it later developed. Its barbarities, though numerous and unpleasant enough, seemed little more than political rowdyism compared with the Pharaonic contempt for human suffering that had marked Stalin's recent "liquidation" of the Russian kulaks. It was difficult, at least for an American, to feel any active sympathy with the uncouth Nazi experiment, but as far as I was concerned, the need for looking on it with loathing and dread had not yet been demonstrated. My personal attitude toward the story I had been assigned to cover, up to the moment I stepped off the train in Frankfurt am Main early in March, and perhaps for a few days thereafter, was very close to the open-mindedness toward the new or unfamiliar that is one of the traditional ideals of American journalism. I was determined to find and report with equal care all the good and all the bad aspects of the Nazi revolution. The bad ones were only too apparent, but I felt an important part of my assignment was to ascertain whether they were really as bad as they looked; as to

National Socialism's good features, if any, I realized they would be much harder to discover, but this made the effort seem all the more essential.

My visit to Germany in 1931 had been too short to give me anything but a vague sense of menace, which was identified in my mind with German nationalism as a whole, rather than with National Socialism in particular. Some of my French friends, especially in the circle of young intellectuals around Daladier, believed that the Nazis were more socialist than nationalist, but that at the same time they represented the "real," that is, the essential and eternal, Germany. Hence, if through reasonable concessions France could win them over to some realistic latter-day version of Briandism, they would prove more dependable partners than the leaders of the Weimar Republic. Laval, who had been sadly disappointed both in Bruening and in his successor, von Papen, held similar views.

The feeling, or belief, that honest nationalism offered a sounder foundation for peace than rhetorical internationalism was a new intellectual growth in postwar Europe, reflecting both disillusionment with the League of Nations and the continuing strength of the peace movement. An interesting ideological transposition—which ultimately became an inversion—was beginning to take place between left and right in Europe. Pacifism, originally identified with the liberal or socialist left, had imperceptibly taken root in the alien soil of nationalism and was putting out slightly mutant blossoms in the form of fraternization between ex-enemy veterans of the Great War, based on the memory of their common ordeal. Similarly, the thesis of left-wing intellectuals in the victor nations that the more or less legitimate grievances of the vanquished should be appeased through some liberalization of the peace treaties had begun to win acceptance in conservative business and political circles where formerly it had been considered near-treason.

Agents of German nationalism in Britain and France had been encouraging the general trend toward what later became "appeasement" even before Hitler came to power; in France they had not yet won many converts on the extreme right, where foreign affinities were chiefly Mussolinian, but they had achieved some impact on the little group around Daladier—a curious nexus of ideological unrest, Jacobin and pacifist, *dirigiste* and vaguely welfare state—that I have already mentioned. Like a number of my French friends, I was intrigued by the possibility of a virile *rapprochement* between France and the New Germany—though I was more skeptical about it than some of them were—and I shared their interest in the dynamic Nationalist Socialist version of a planned economy; in the winter of 1933 almost any alternative to the depression nightmare of laissez-faire capitalism seemed worthy of sympathetic consideration. The Nazi emphasis on social welfare and solidarity, from what I had read, likewise sounded attractive, despite its narrowly racist framework.

Similarly, the Nazi critique of democratic vacillation or paralysis in trying to cope with the challenge of the depression struck a responsive chord in my mind, after what I had witnessed in France and read about developments in my own country. (Roosevelt had not yet had the opportunity to demonstrate that democratic leadership can on occasion be as bold and trenchant as any autocratic variety.) I could even sympathize to some extent with what many foreign observers considered Hitlerism's most regressive feature: its blatant, sometimes grotesque, appeal to subliminal tribal instincts and mass emotion. Western democracy, indeed Western civilization generally, had long been suffering, it seemed to me, from the dessication of collective enthusiasm and from a hypertrophy of the rationalizing faculty.

I had not, of course, read Hitler's book, *Mein Kampf;* its turgid prose would have hopelessly overtaxed the smattering of German I had acquired (it had not yet been translated into French or English), and even if I had been able to read it, I lacked the background in contemporary German political history to evaluate it. It is rare, indeed, that the real destiny of a political movement is wholly implicit in the ideological manifestos upon which it is ostensibly based. Reading accurately between the lines of public text and utterance— discerning the hints, the overtones, the emotional associations, the displacements of stress, the complements of context—is never an easy task. In the case of Hitler's utterances—those in *Mein Kampf* and those in his more philosophical speeches up to March 1933—I am by no means convinced, even today, that we are warranted in reading into them a clear forecast of all the horrors that Hitlerism eventually brought forth. Nevertheless, they are marked at times by a perverse moral earnestness, and a deadly sobriety in their delusiveness, that renders them much graver and more ominous than the usual rantings of extremist demagoguery.

Such was the impression, more chilling than outraged or derisive, that *Mein Kampf* made on me when somewhat later I finally got around to reading it. Several of my American colleagues in Berlin—among them Edgar Mowrer of the Chicago *Daily News*, the late H. R. Knickerbocker of the Hearst papers, and Sigrid Schulz—had correctly interpreted the gravity of the National Socialist phenomenon even before Hitler came to power. The judgment of such observers, together with their factual reports on the Nazi barbarisms and oppressions, could not be brushed aside. I thought it possible, however, that precisely because they were observing the National Socialist revolution at close range, many correspondents might be unable to see it in proper perspective. Anne Morrow Lindbergh had not then coined her subsequently famous metaphor, in which the less agreeable features of National Socialism became merely scum on the wave of the future, but if she had I suspect I might have felt more sympathy with the idea than I did in 1941.

There was, too, a necessary trace of journalistic opportunism in my attitude. My German assignment was peripheral—covering developments in the Rhineland. I was a latecomer to the Nazi story and there was no reputation to be made by plodding in the footsteps of my betters in Berlin. A more balanced and less systematically unsympathetic look at the Nazi revolution, as seen from its fringes, would be something fresh. I may have had some reason to think that Col. McCormick would be interested in this open-minded approach, but there was no pressure from the home office; the idea was my own. It goes without saying that such sordid motives operate at times in the minds of American correspondents. For that very reason, the American reporter is touchy about any implication that he may be prostituting himself. As with his British counterpart, you cannot bribe or twist, thank God, the U.S. journalist . . .

Irritation at the mixture of heavy-handed flattery and intimidation that marked the attitude of minor Nazi officialdom played a role in the evolution of my attitude toward the regime. When I paid a courtesy call on the press spokesman of the Frankfurt police department, for example, I was treated to a half-friendly, half-menacing lecture on the duties of a foreign journalist in the Third Reich. Correspondents who ventured to criticize the government, I was warned, could get into serious trouble. "But I don't imagine you will have any trouble," the spokesman said, "since you are not a Jew." I promptly filed a dispatch citing this conversation as one example of official interference.

A grotesque, and for a few moments somewhat frightening, misadventure that befell me toward the end of March pointed up the difficulty. (History is always more convincing when you hear it whizzing about your personal ears or find it pointed at your private belly.)

With another American correspondent, an old friend from Paris, I had lunched at a restaurant on the old cobbled square facing the Römer. The Römer, a block of fifteenth-century buildings that, with its dependencies, once served Frankfurt as a city hall, was one of Europe's minor but authentic cultural treasures destroyed in World War II. When I revisited Frankfurt in 1951, the Römer, and with it the whole medieval heart of the former imperial city, were little more than a vast heap of rust-colored rubble; restoration of the Römer itself and of several other outstanding monuments around it gives today's tourist an idea of what was lost, but of course cannot resuscitate the vanished charm. In 1933 the little square, haunted by the luminous shade of Goethe, where we lunched was perhaps more quaint than beautiful, but it was a harmonious blend of ages and styles. The chief attraction was the red sandstone facade of the old

Rathaus, a solid, earthy, bourgeois version of Flamboyant Gothic, a fine piece of workmanship of its kind. The ensemble was so steeped in tradition, in mellowed authority, in *Gemütlichkeit,* that gaping at it one felt delighted with one's own involuntary impersonation of a nineteenth-century tourist. The Römer and the square were at their best in the golden haze of this splendid March. My friend and I sat outdoors for a long time in the warm sun, talking a little in the way of old friends, drinking the flat, hard cider of the region, and looking at the little fountain in the center of the square which used to run with red and white wine when the coronation of a German emperor took place; then we moved indoors for serious eating and drinking. It was one of the numerous occasions when my rootless, quasi-nomadic existence in Europe seemed a good way of life.

Walking away from the restaurant after lunch, we heard a hue and cry behind us and were roughly halted by two auxiliary policemen, accompanied by several Nazi Storm Troopers in their brown shirts. A twisted little man, almost a dwarf, whom I had noticed while we were lunching, and vaguely suspected of eavesdropping, was dancing around in a frenzy, pointing his finger at us and gibbering something about hate propaganda and Czechoslovakia. We had not the faintest idea what the trouble was but it seemed to be serious: The Storm Troopers looked grim and an excited crowd had begun to gather.

The leader of the Storm Troopers wanted to take us to his headquarters for questioning; the auxiliary policemen thought we should be taken to the central police station. The timely arrival of a regular police sergeant tipped the scales in favor of orthodoxy. Probably it was a lucky thing for us; Frankfurt, as far as I had been able to discover, had no SA centers comparable to the infamous Brown Shirt torture chambers that flourished in Berlin, but questioning by these neurotic bullies in the privacy of their own barracks might have proved unpleasant. It was none too pleasant, in fact, being hustled through the center of Frankfurt followed by a growing mob of beefy, hysterical Germans. Everyone appeared to be in a wild state of excitement, and none of it made any sense to us.

At police headquarters, where we were finally confronted with our accuser, the background of all the insanity came to light. I was told that the twisted man had seen me in the restaurant writing out a telegram which, from overheard scraps of our conversation, he believed to contain atrocity stories about conditions in the New Germany intended for an international slander-mill in Czechoslovakia. The telegram part was easily explainable: During the meal I had remembered that my funds were running low and had drafted on a piece of copypaper the text of a message I meant to send the *Tribune*'s business office in Paris. The reference to Czechoslovakia baffled me, until I recalled that I had voiced aloud the hope that the *Tribune*'s check could be cashed at a German bank without too much *red* tape. Perhaps the "red" in "red tape" had likewise suggested to the eavesdropper some shadowy, Communist-inspired internationale of defamation that might, logically enough, have its headquarters in Czechoslovakia. The atrocity stories, however, had no source but the twisted man's overheated imagination, tormented, possibly, by the memory of some act of long ago that might now imply disloyalty to the New Germany. A wave of such irresponsible denunciation was sweeping Germany about this time; in Berlin, I have been told, it amounted to a mass psychosis.

I exhibited my passport and press credentials and explained about the telegram. The police official who was questioning me seemed to find the explanation satisfactory but the twisted man continued to screech his conviction that I was guilty—anything so normal as a foreign journalist wiring his office for money seemed beyond his imagining—and the SA men were still dubious. If the telegram was as innocent as I claimed, their leader said, why didn't I produce it?

The message was still in my pocket, of course, but because I had been frightened by this madness and violence, I now was angry. Letting these brown-shirted louts read my private correspondence with my office seemed an affront to journalistic dignity. I refused to show anything, or to answer any further questions. Put me under arrest and let me call the American consul, I said, or dismiss the charge and let me go. Legalism, especially tinged with arrogance, still had some magic force in the New Germany, but not quite enough to prevail without external assistance. We were at an impasse; the Nazis would not let us leave, the police would not book us for detention, and my friend and I refused to talk. Finally a compromise was worked out: I agreed to furnish local references for my journalistic *bona fides,* and cited the editor of the Nazi party organ in Frankfurt, who had received me with unexpected cordiality the day before. The Nazi editor was called, he certified that I was an authentic, and seemingly objective, American newspaperman, and the incident was closed. After handsome apologies from both the police and the leader of the Storm Troopers, my friend and I walked out of the building without a stain on our names; the twisted man was retained for further conversation with the police, and they were the ones whose faces now looked grim.

That night I wrote up the whole ludicrous episode and cabled it to Chicago. "In Russia it's 'sabotage,' " my dispatch began. "In Germany it's 'propaganda' and 'lies.' " It was my first unequivocally hostile report on the Nazi revolution. No doubt a sense of outrage at the *lèse majesté* committed against an American correspondent—particularly one for whom I had such high esteem—in the lawful exercise of his functions was largely responsible for my attitude, but there was also something else. The hulking brute who seemed to be the leader of the Storm Troopers, in apologizing for the incident, had said something to me that I had already heard a number of times since my arrival in Germany. "We've nothing against you," he had explained, "but in times like these with all these Jews spreading propaganda and lies abroad, every foreigner is under suspicion."

I was getting tired of being told that of course I was all right because I wasn't a Jew. Without quite realizing it, I had come to resent the Nazi insinuation that I shared their racist delusion. My resentment was fed by a personal factor which, if somewhat primitive, seemed to me in no way disgraceful. While still quite young, I had married an American newspaperwoman who was a Jewess, and though the marriage was now breaking up, as correspondents' marriages often tend to do, one tie remained that could not be broken: I was the father of what from the Nazi viewpoint were two half-Jewish children.

I had known before I came to Frankfurt that anti-Semitism was an essential feature of the Nazi doctrine, but I had not realized how obsessive it was, nor what an ignoble stamp it was putting on the mind and face of the New Germany. From a distance it had seemed possible to hope that anti-Semitism along with other ugly elements of the National Socialist ideology would gradually lose their virulence as the Nazis were brought face to face with the realities of power; either that, or the German people would soon spew out Hitlerism in disgust. No honest observer on the spot, however, could find evidence to encourage either of these hopes. Nazi anti-Semitism was plainly growing more, rather than less, rabid; and it was contaminating the German masses more, rather than less, widely. The anti-Semitic campaigns that had been launched almost as soon as the Third Reich was born were not the work of irresponsible fanatics or of a revolutionary scum; they were unmistakably organized, with Germanic thoroughness, from the top down. The orderly, and for the most part nonviolent, character of these campaigns was the most sinister thing about them.

Though few of Frankfurt's 30,000-odd Jewish citizens appeared to have been physically molested before my arrival in the city, or during my stay there in 1933, their plight was particularly tragic. Frankfurt, the birthplace of the international Rothschild dynasty, was one of the oldest centers of Jewish culture in Western Europe; since the late Middle Ages its Jews had enjoyed more liberty and wielded greater influence than in most other German cities. By the early twentieth century the business and intellectual elite of Frankfurt Jewry had achieved a commanding position. Now, as I bluntly put in one of my dispatches, these Frankfurt Jews, accustomed to lives of freedom and power, were facing return to the ghetto. "This," I wrote, "is what the triumph of fourteen years of anti-Semitic propaganda by the Nazis and their predecessors means to the Jews of Frankfurt—and for that matter of all Germany."

I interviewed not only official leaders of the Jewish community in Frankfurt but prominent Jews in every walk of life. All were grim, bitter, indignant or furious; a number looked to the future with dark foreboding. Almost without exception, the Jews of Frankfurt feared new and heavier financial exactions, worse humiliations, and the curtailment of their freedom; but I cannot recall encountering a single German Jew at that time who expressed fear of systematic, government-directed, physical violence—as distinguished from occasional acts of hoodlumism. I do not think that the possibility of mass extermination occurred to anyone. In 1933 that was an almost unthinkable thought.

The Nazis' treatment of their purely political enemies in the early days of Hitler's Reich was a good deal more brutal than their treatment of the Jews, but even in this respect they often demonstrated a concern with what Jefferson called the decent opinion of mankind that seems surprising in retrospect. Some murders and beatings of anti-Nazis undoubtedly had high-level sanction; more, perhaps, were the work of undisciplined elements in the party, particularly in the SA; and quite a few were the invention of adverse propaganda or the inadvertent exaggerations of hasty reporting. The picture of the New Germany thus presented in the world press was a black one, and many Nazi officials were understandably disturbed by it. When unofficial censorship and attempts at thought-control failed to improve the situation, they sometimes fell back on the truth, reasoning —correctly enough—that what the press actually saw could never be as bad as what it imagined. For this reason I was allowed, without restrictions, to interview the political prisoners in the Frankfurt municipal jail, and eventually, after pulling a number of wires, to visit one of the new concentration camps that were springing up all over Germany.

The camp that I was finally authorized to visit was near a village called Heuberg in the rolling Württemberg hills about sixty-five miles south of Stuttgart. There were others nearer Frankfurt, and I no longer remember how Heuberg was selected for me. I suppose it was considered something of a model camp—model from the humane viewpoint rather than from the normal Nazi one—but I believe the accidents of personal contact had even more to do with the matter; away from the capital, a good deal of local initiative, not to mention cross-purpose and confusion, was tolerated in the Nazi organization at that time.

I took the precaution of bringing along my own interpreter, an elderly Frankfurt pedagogue and part-time journalist whom I had already used as a helper on several stories. He seemed to me almost the typical civilized, "decent," non-Nazi German of the older generation caught in the toils of a revolution that was too barbarous to be espoused but too authentically German to be disavowed, and I thought his reactions to the camp might be interesting. They were. My assistant—let us call him Dr. Mueller, and peace to his ashes, for I suspect that one way or another he finished as ash—started exclaiming as we neared Heuberg over the beauties of the Swabian countryside: the green, gently rolling meadows, the blooming pear and apple orchards, the dark woods flecking the higher slopes, the quilted clouds of April floating on the south wind against a sky of tender blue, and above all the air, the wonderful air, bracing as in the high mountains, noted for its health-giving virtues. The 1,800 actual or potential enemies of the Nazi revolution held at Heuberg were lucky, Dr. Mueller implied, to be interned in such charming and healthy surroundings. I was willing to accept his hint. "It is a spot," I wrote in my story for the *Tribune*, "where no one could complain about spending an enforced vacation—if he did not have to spend it behind barbed wire."

Most of the barbed wire was newly strung, tinny in the sun, but there were also rusted strands left over from the war, when Heuberg had been a camp for Allied prisoners. Wire fences, higher than a man's head, not only surrounded the camp but divided it internally into separate blocks, one for every two buildings, with an exercise yard of bare earth between. Both the prisoners' barracks and the administrative buildings were three-story white cement structures, cracked and weather-stained for the most part, with more recent additions in unpainted board. Dr. Mueller had not been a very astute propagandist: The prettiness of the site made the camp seem all the more beastly.

The prisoners were still wearing the clothes they had on when they were arrested. Their shirts were frayed and dirty, their faces unshaven. I had come prepared to see some grim sights, but I was shocked by all this squalor. From one viewpoint, perhaps, it was encouraging. The concentration camp had not yet become a permanent institution of the National Socialist state and its theory was still vague in the minds of the Nazis themselves. Many of the early camps opened by the SA were merely emergency detention quarters where enemies of the regime could be bullied and terrorized for a few weeks—and as William Shirer* has reported, sometimes held for ransom—before being released. The sordid conditions at Heuberg, therefore, did not seem to reflect a deliberate aim to degrade the human condition, that of prisoners and of guards alike, beyond the degradation always implicit in their relationship; nonetheless, the impression I inevitably carried away from the camp was of a place where men of their own choice had forsaken the smaller as well as the greater decencies of life.

The camp commandant, an SA officer named Major Kaufman, kept apologizing for the lack of paint, laundry facilities, proper washrooms, regular uniforms for the prisoners, flower beds in front of the administrative buildings and other prison camp amenities, like a hostess who has not had time to tidy up. He, too, seemed a fairly decent German, the type who would never condone brutality except when ordered to.

I was allowed to interview the prisoners, individually or collectively, at random or any way I liked, and though Major Kaufman rarely left my side a number of the interviews were in English or French, which he did not understand. The appearance of the prisoners was painful. Their pallor, the caged look in their eyes, and above

---

* *The Rise and Fall of the Third Reich*, Simon and Schuster, New York.

all their listless bearing gave them the aspect of long-term convicts, yet their imprisonment dated from a few days to at most a fortnight or so. I noticed that they snapped nervously to attention, not only in the presence of the commandant but whenever an officer of the camp guard appeared. The officers were mostly SA Storm Troopers but there were a few regular police and some members of the nationalist Stahlhelm as well. Discipline in the camp was evidently strict, not to say harsh, but it was apparently enforced by solitary confinement and deprivation of food rather than by beatings or other physical torture. Prisoners throughout the camp were treated "humanely and in a manner corresponding to the situation," as a Jewish former district judge from Stuttgart put it to me. He was a militant Socialist and an inmate of the special block reserved for "intellectuals."

The Heuberg standard of humane treatment was not, of course, excessively high. I saw a guard kick a prisoner struggling along with two heavy soup pails, for not moving fast enough. A prisoner who was doubtless a Communist—the Communist internees were generally the least cowed or demoralized in the camp—created a commotion by revealing in the presence of Maj. Kaufman that a guard had beaten one man with a club because he caught him smoking a cigarette in violation of the camp rules. Such flagrant brutality seemed the exception, however, rather than the rule. All the prisoners except the "intellectuals" were theoretically obliged to work, but few seemed to mind doing so, and a number complained of sitting around all day because no tasks had yet been found for them. The food was universally denounced as bad and scanty but was probably little worse than normal German prison fare.

The real origin of the terror that unmistakably reigned in Heuberg gradually emerged in my interviews with the prisoners. Though treated like common criminals, none of these men were charged with any crime. To the Communists and other militant anti-Nazis who had fought a civil war against National Socialism and lost it, being treated as prisoners of war in their own country might not seem entirely illogical, but the arbitrariness of the procedure underscored the archaic nature of their status; in the most primitive and literal sense, they were captives at the mercy of the victor's whim. Many inmates of Heuberg lacked even the meager satisfaction of being able to identify a rational cause for their predicament. "I don't know why I am here or what I have done," a one-legged weaver from Stuttgart said to me. "The police just came for me one morning and took me to jail. Then I was brought here. I am treated all right, but it's hard just the same." To such prisoners, and there were many of them both at Heuberg and throughout the rest of Germany, it must have seemed that they were the victims of some indefinable, unpredictable, Kafka-esque malevolence, that the clock of civilization had been turned back in Germany not only to a time before law, but to an age before reason. I wish that my dispatch to the *Tribune* on my visit to Heuberg—something of a scoop in its day—had evidenced a more authentic compassion with the victims of National Socialism I saw there, but I think it was useful in conveying some of the sense of random menace, or menacing randomness, loosed upon the world that I brought back from the visit, and indeed from my whole stay in Germany. For, if anything in the first months of the Hitler regime should have forewarned us of its later course, it was precisely this element of unpredictability.

I returned to Germany in the late spring of 1934. This time my attitude toward the Nazi phenomenon was a good deal less open-minded. The main reason for the change was naturally my own impressions from the 1933 assignment; what I had witnessed at the Place de la Concorde on February 6, 1934, had also helped. I had, moreover, felt the pull of a growing current of opinion that was beginning to run in Europe, especially in France. Appeasement was continuing to make progress beneath the surface, but the cumulative impact on the public mind of the daily news from Germany, of the tragic or shocking reports on conditions in the country brought out by émigrés, and of the purposeful exploitation of all these data by left-wing and Jewish propaganda organizations was more noticeable.

Hitler's decision, brusquely announced on October 14, 1933, to withdraw from both the League of Nations and the Disarmament

Conference had further antagonized international opinion, even though French intransigence on the issue of German rearmament was held to be at least partly to blame. The Kremlin was at last beginning to take the German menace seriously, its attitude was altering the propaganda posture of the Communist parties in Western Europe, and somewhat paradoxically, the upheavals of February 1934 had for the time being led to a certain parallelism of outlook between the classic right and the far left in France. It was the influence of traditional French nationalism in the Doumergue cabinet—thanks mainly to the presence of Tardieu—that on April 17, 1934, caused Foreign Minister Louis Barthou to reject the principle—favored by Britain and the United States—of an international convention conditionally legalizing German rearmament. The tension between France and Germany was now higher than it had been since the French occupation of the Ruhr in 1923.

There is still a debate going on between the surviving—or reviving—apologists of appeasement and the more fanatical anti-Nazis as to whether the Western powers lost their chance to achieve "peace with honor" during the first year of the Nazi regime by rejecting Hitler's overtures for an agreement on limited German rearmament, or whether they threw away their best opportunity for painlessly crushing aggressive German expansionism by not applying collective sanctions against Germany after Hilter pulled out of the League. It seems a futile controversy. The weight of the evidence is undoubtedly against the appeasement position, even in its respectable 1933 or 1934 version; this evidence, however, was not available at the time.

That Hitler had taken Germany out of the League and the Disarmament Conference (without refusing to continue direct negotiations for the limitation of armaments), that he had his action plebiscited by the German people (who gave the Nazis a ninety-two percent majority in the Reichstag elections of November 1933), that he had concluded a nonagression pact with the hated Poles (clearly aimed at disrupting the French diplomatic glacis in Eastern Europe) provided neither legal nor moral justification for effective sanctions against the sovereign German nation. As far as public opinion was concerned, even Germany's secret rearmament, which Hitler was speeding up, would probably not have sufficed; though disturbing, it was not yet proven, and was therefore controversial. Even if a violation of the Versailles Treaty had been finally established and submitted to the League, it is doubtful that Baldwin's England would have agreed to coercive action, and virtually certain that Roosevelt's America would have refused to cooperate in making it effective. (Britain's reluctance to join in international sanctions against Japan in 1931, and France's repudiation of its war debt in 1932, had exacerbated American isolationism, already intensified by the world economic crisis.)

Though I had ceased myself to be an isolationist, I do not believe that as a correspondent I would have supported League sanctions against Germany in 1933, had they been possible. By June 1934, when I returned to the Rhineland, I might have done so. It was the savage and sanguinary revolutionary crisis of the regime, Hitler's so-called Blood Purge of June 30, 1934, and its aftermath that changed me from a critical observer to an outspoken adversary of National Socialism. Once more the personal factor was important.

I had arrived in Munich from Frankfurt in the latter part of June and was actually in the Bavarian capital on the early morning of June 30 when Hitler swooped down in person on the nearby resort town of Bad Wiessee where the Brown Shirt leaders were gathered, arrested their supreme chief, the notorious homosexual soldier of fortune, Captain Ernst Roehm, and ordered his companions to be shot on the spot, thus launching the nationwide "purge." Like every other newspaperman in Germany at the time, I knew a showdown was impending within the regime between the turbulent left-wing elements headed by Roehm, the commander of the SA militia, and the more conservative forces that had been backing Hitler, notably the army. I assumed, however, that the eventual violent clash between them—if it came to a clash—could not occur without ample warning. It never entered my mind that Hitler might be planning to settle the dispute in his own fashion. The thirtieth of June was a Saturday, and I too had plans for the weekend. I had been working hard writing feature stories and "think-pieces" as I traveled about Germany, and felt that I deserved a rest in the country. A woman with whom I was very much in love had come to Munich specially to share it with me. We took the train, as scheduled, early Saturday morning while most of the city still slept.

On the way to the station I had noticed a number of military trucks and staff cars dashing through the streets, but the sight was not an unusual one at the time. Perhaps if my attention had not been so heavily engaged elsewhere I might have been struck by the fact that the troops sitting in these vehicles all wore the black, silver-trimmed uniforms of the SS, the elite para-military corps commanded by one of Roehm's rivals, Heinrich Himmler; the ugly, familiar, brown uniform of the SA had vanished overnight from the streets of Munich. I could not have cared less in the clear sunrise of that June morning.

It was late in the day, and quite by accident, when I learned that the brutal cleanup of the SA had begun, that Roehm himself, though he was one of the Führer's earliest comrades, had been murdered in jail, that the SS firing squads were busy throughout the land, slaughtering anti-Nazis along with undisciplined or suspect elements in the party. Sigrid Schulz, I knew, would be covering the main story from Berlin, but the *Tribune* would expect at least a short "color" piece from me, giving the local street scene and reactions in Munich, the sacred city of National Socialism. My weekend was finished, almost before it had started. Newspapermen are accustomed to such private disasters in times of public upheaval; they are also trained to quick recoveries when they are caught short in an emergency, but this time it was a close call. No hard news beyond what the Nazis were officially releasing in Berlin was available in Munich, and there was not much visible "color" in the terrified city; its citizens were staying home and reacting as little as possible to anything, including telephone calls. There were no other American correspondents in town from whose copy I could borrow essential details in the easygoing way of the profession. (Fortunately, there was the usual part-time but fully informed "stringer" of the London *Times*, the salvation of every Anglo-Saxon journalist storm-tossed on an alien shore.)

I finally got together a story of sorts, and to avoid delay, phoned my copy to my assistant in Paris for cabling to Chicago. It was around midnight before I finished. I was in pajamas and my companion was reading in bed when there was a peremptory pounding on the door of our room at the hotel. I opened it a crack, and two men with nondescript faces, dressed in nondescript dark suits, their right hands in the side pockets of their coats, shoved it back, brushing past me into the room.

"*Geheime Staats polizei* [Gestapo]," one of them said, vaguely flashing a card that I did not bother to look at. There could be no doubt about their identity.

Their manner was coolly professional but their faces were grim and wary at first. After looking at our passports they relaxed slightly, but only slightly. Though I was furious at the invasion of my privacy, something told me this was not a night for standing on one's dignity.

"Why have you been doing so much phoning?" the senior of the two said. "Why did you phone Paris just now, and what were you talking about all that time?"

I explained. The Gestapo man demanded to see the carbon copy of my message. When I handed it to him he asked for a translation; apparently neither of the two knew English. I had not thought before then I knew that much German, but I managed somehow to convey the gist of my dispatch. The atmosphere improved. I was allowed to get back in bed, in fact, ordered to, while the Gestapo men made a rapid search of our baggage. My briefcase was emptied and I had to summarize and explain every article I had written in Germany.

In the end, the Gestapo men cozily installed themselves on the foot of the bed and the interrogation, which lasted for close to three hours, began more and more to resemble an ordinary conversation, interspersed with an occasional crude attempt to trap my companion —for they cross-examined her, too—or myself in some contradiction. As the night wore on the Gestapo men became increasingly familiar, though never to the point of outright rudeness; in fact, before they finally left with a cheery *"Heil Hitler,"* they became almost friendly, in a slightly cat-and-mouse way. They realized, of course, that we were anxious to avoid the scandal that might arise if we were arrested, for whatever reason, and they exploited their psychological advantage to the hilt; we had to cooperate, whether we liked it or not, with these good fellows and broad-minded men of the world by gratifying their desire for small talk in the small hours, as well as by satisfying their professional curiosity.

Policemen—especially when they belong to any kind of political or security police—seldom have a finicky concern for human dignity; in a totalitarian state, the destruction of that dignity becomes a professional instinct and a gratifying sport. I had long been aware that this was the case in Nazi Germany, but until that night visit from the Gestapo in Munich I do not believe I had fully realized that the humiliations the regime inflicted on its victims were, in fact, offenses against human dignity and therefore, since I was human, against my own. The reminder, though disagreeable, was valuable.

Even without such personal involvements, the lessons of the Blood Purge were inescapable, and not easily forgotten. In the first place, Hitler himself emerged as a much more formidable figure than most political observers outside Germany had been willing to admit. As the complex background of the drama gradually came to light it was plain to anyone who had the slightest familiarity with Nazi Germany that in the crisis *Der Führer* had displayed not only a demoniacal energy, but also a diabolical mastery of murder as a political art. In crushing the revolutionary threat from the left, he had avoided becoming the prisoner of the right. He had used the execution of the SA leaders as an excuse for killing off potentially dangerous figures among the conservative opposition like General von Schleicher and the high-minded young Catholics around von Papen; and he had consolidated the wavering loyalty of the surviving Nazi barons—Goering, Himmler, Goebbels—by making them personal accomplices in the butchery of their old party comrades. All this bore the stamp of real political genius. A Borgia could not have managed things more astutely.

It was only in his strategy that Hitler owed anything to Renaissance Italy, however. The moral climate of the Blood Purge was a lurid and unique blend of Al Capone's Chicago and Ivan the Terrible's Moscow. The rubbing-out of individuals who knew too much about early Nazi scandals and the numerous spite killings of politically innocuous Germans that took place on the margins of the main purge seemed to me particularly revealing. I managed to get to the bottom of one of these obscure crimes: the murder of Dr. Charles Beck, director of the German Student House at Munich.

Beck, a middle-aged invalid, was kidnapped from his home on the night of June 30 by three young men in SS uniforms who, without any explanation, ordered him into their car and drove off with him. His body, with several wounds in it made by revolver bullets, was later found along the road to Dachau, a place already infamous for its concentration camp. Bruises on one arm and one leg indicated that he had been brutally kicked or beaten before being finished off. His gold watch, wallet, and rings were missing.

No official information about the crime was released and no action was ever taken against Beck's killers. The murdered man had not taken part in any organized anti-Nazi activity and was not known to have uttered any public criticism of the regime. His only offense was that he had refused, as a matter of private conscience, to exclude Jewish students from the institution he directed, despite unofficial Nazi warnings.

"The full story of the murder of Dr. Beck," I said in the lead of my dispatch to the *Tribune*, "throws a pitiless light on conditions prevailing today in what used to be one of the most civilized capitals in Europe."

A few days later, just before leaving Munich, I tried to draw some more general conclusions about the Nazi regime, and about fascism in general. The crisis in Germany, I argued, was due to inherent contradictions in the fascist system, and not to any accidental difficulties that had developed. I attributed to "politically-minded Germans" the conviction that National Socialism had only started to fulfill its tragic destiny. (The convictions of a politically-minded

American correspondent were of course unmentionable as such, though the *Tribune* appeared to share them.)

The reign of terror inaugurated on June 30 reflected, in the opinion of my anonymous sources, "the inevitable evolution of all regimes based on enthusiasm and confidence instead of on constitutional form." Back of the intrigues and rivalries of the Nazi leaders the same observers thought they detected another iron law of politics: the ineluctable tendency of political systems that overstress mystic and dynamic leadership, unaccompanied by legal checks, to produce conspiracies like Roehm's. The long-term outlook in Nazi Germany was, therefore, for new conspiracies, and more and bloodier purges. The article concluded with another significant discovery which it said many Germans were beginning to make: that fascism does not run very well in reverse.

There was perhaps a certain pedagogic intent behind my article; several paragraphs dealing with the failure of the Nazi economic experiments, in which Col. McCormick detected some parallel with Roosevelt's New Deal, would be welcome news to him, and therefore, I thought, render him more disposed to accept the thinly disguised editorializing of my broader conclusions. The affirmation of democratic orthodoxy in these conclusions was inspired, however, by more personal considerations: It reflected the now violent revulsion in my mind, not only against fascism, but against my own relatively tolerant attitude toward it of a year earlier.

Today I would be less inclined than ever to offer any justification of the political principles of fascism as embodied by the Nazi regime. I believe that I was naïve, however, in thinking that its evils stemmed primarily from its disregard of constitutional checks on dictatorial power. What I have witnessed in the intervening years makes me feel that it was with the Nazi regime—and with all political systems —as it is with men themselves. We are not merely the sum of our past actions, but they are always a great part of our present selves; we have to a large degree chosen to be what we are, though we usually do not realize it at the moment of choice. Sometimes the options that shape the pattern of our lives are decisive only in their cumulative weight, but in the face of some exceptional emergency we may rise far above, or sink far below, our normal level, thus creating a kind of mutation in our personalities and fate. I think that a mutation of major importance took place in German National Socialism and in the personality of its leader on the eve of June 30, 1934. The man that Hitler was, the political order he had created, could hardly have found any but a violent and tragic resolution to the crisis that was developing within the regime. It did not have to be that dark, that bloody, that ruthless, however. It was by a giant act of will, in the stress of dramatic circumstance, that Hitler rose above the previous mediocrity of his own bad instincts to become, perhaps for the first time, a hero of criminality, a saint of evil.

Book Three

The
Fifty-Year
Enlistment

8

Reflections on a Lost Crusade

alked up lakefront promenade to new Palais des Nations this afternoon, and en route tried to analyze secret of Geneva's elusive charm. Decor undeniably an affront to any but most naïve eye. Mellowed austerity of old Calvinist citadel and gentle Savoyard countryside with its contours of feminine abundance only accentuate marshmallow-sundae banality of Mont Blanc in background, grotesque whale spout of the Jet d'Eau, pretentious triviality of casino-style facades along the lakesides, multi-colored flags—internationale of hoteliers' salute to humanity—inevitable geranium beds, side-wheeler excursion boats toying on glassy water, white, starchy puffs of sail, prissy swans. Yet, looking at this perpetual Sunday afternoon panorama, at all this anachronistic paraphernalia of insipid holiday, one feels curiously moved. Scene moving precisely because anachronistic: atmosphere reminiscent of some pre-1914 watering place and one knows simultaneously as in a dream that enlightened lacustrian diplomacy will yet manage to save the threatened Sunday-peace of Europe, and that it did not. We believe because it is absurd to believe; we hope because we realize our doom. What happens here important because it is so futile.

Tragedy of League is that people have been misled into thinking it is real and capable of producing real results. Even now, after all we've seen happen. Running into L⸺ at the press bar, for example, and his assuring me I was wise to come: great decisions impending, Anthony Eden arriving with fire in his eye, bold schemes to refloat the League, etc. Repeated to Dell, whose white moustaches bristled with scorn: "Don't say that, my dear fellow; if Eden is going to save us again then we are quite lost." Matchless old Dell.

Partly our fault—the press—that people's hopes betrayed, but it's governments and diplomats who most to blame, especially democratic ones. Modern democracies reckless devourers of dreams. Favorite device of democratic statesmanship is to set up purely ceremonial institutions or make symbolic gestures—League of Nations, Kellogg Pact, sanctions, disarmament, resolutions, etc.—then pretend to believe they are effective ones. Public taken in, supposes millennium at hand. Perhaps pious hoaxes like Kellogg Pact do no great harm except to divert attention from real dangers, but suspect fiasco of sanctions against Italy, and with it puncturing of whole myth of collective security, have dealt League ideal its deathblow. Well played, Eton.

Like disarmament, etc., collective security has come to grief here because governments that were officially pledged to uphold it never really believed it either possible or desirable. Age-old scoundrel tradition of European diplomacy remains as deeply rooted as ever in secret fastnesses of permanent, semi-autonomous bureaucracies on which governments depend. International idealists pound pulpit, launch crusades for open diplomacy or disarmament but unable or unwilling to suppress machinery of secret diplomacy and aggression in own state services. Maybe some of frontmen who represent their countries in public sessions believe what they are saying—perhaps they are picked for that, like British finding one idealist in whole Foreign Office and making him their press spokesman—but when you talk to real professionals, diplomats or soldiers who run the delegations here, you discover vast majority of them total cynics who instinctively sympathize with every aggressor, jeer at everything that smacks of idealism. To these cynics Geneva means nothing but endless processions of shrivel-papped vestals brandishing petitions.

Actually, as I've come to know it, League more like some smirking street slut dressed in gaudy evening gown, with dirty underwear and a chronic dose of clap. Yet poor drab that she is, she still represents a threat to the doom cult of these professional world-losers, and they cannot leave her alone. Hence the permanent bombardment of sarcasms, insults, and imbecile "exposés," the excremental sneering and smearing, the fart-like explosions of "common sense" and "realism," and all the rancid exudations of old-man's grease from the Poloniuses of the press. Armaments manufacturers undoubtedly spend considerable energy and money launching such campaigns; so do leaders of some regressive political parties and permanent officials in scoundrel services of various governments. Great anarchs of press in every democratic country naturally give fullest cooperation; naming no names, of course.

PEACE THOUGHTS OF A FUTURE

WAR CORRESPONDENT

(NOTES FROM GENEVA *c.* 1937)

I no longer remember what particular disaster or betrayal had inspired these somber reflections—I had not yet started to keep a regular diary—and there is no date on the sheaf of handwritten jottings or hastily typed sheets of lined paper, torn from what looks like a schoolboy's copybook. They could have been written at any time between 1935 and 1938, but most likely stem from my usual fall visit to Geneva in September 1937. As on a number of previous occasions, I covered the sessions of the League Assembly and Council, which that year were confronted with two unusually spiny problems: the steadily widening Japanese invasion of China, and foreign intervention in the Spanish Civil War. The attitudes already manifested by the big European powers, especially Great Britain, toward these issues justified skepticism as to how firmly they would be dealt with at Geneva. Democratic morale was then at a rather low ebb in Europe, and the disillusionment expressed in my notes undoubtedly reflected a widespread mood.

There were a number of such black moments during the middle and late thirties, sometimes the uncomplicated fruit of crisis and disaster, more often the hangover from ideological debauch. The century's grand dream of human unity found its most authentic expression in the nightmare atmosphere of civil strife that overhung the power struggles of the decade. Save, perhaps, for some obscure fighting in the Paraguayan jungle that I recall only dimly, all our wars were ultimately revolutionary ones. Invariably, they were accompanied by the propagandistic excesses and the fevered group idealisms that characterize such conflicts; as their bitterness increased, they tended to become turgid crusades. The havoc on the private battlefield of the mind was not always the least gruesome. "I remember those inhuman diplomatic crises, more unnerving than war," I wrote in 1939. "I remember all those stupid, bitter political quarrels, felt like a personal grievance—quarrels about Spain, quarrels about Munich. I remember all the false hopes, all the bitter disillusionments . . . the paralyzing . . . despair which grew and grew."*

What surviving member of my generation does not carry with him such scarred recollections of a murky age? Yet most of us, I suspect, likewise feel a certain nostalgia for the thirties, beyond the normal middle-aged yearning for lost excitements. Looking back upon the sometimes naïve hopes or questionable enthusiasms we shared at different moments—both with comrades and with adversaries—is a little like recalling the bittersweet tumults of puppy love, its never entirely synthetic raptures no less than its all-too-authentic disenchantments, the instinctive awareness of ordeal accepted, as well as the magic of grace bestowed, the smarting shame of puerilities exposed, but also the half-conscious pride of growth achieved.

---

* *The Strategy of Terror*, Houghton Mifflin, 1940.

For many of us, our personal involvement in the overpoliticized public life of the day was in fact a kind of *éducation sentimentale* transposed to the civic plane. Despite—or because of—the cynicisms upon which we had been suckled, we proved in many ways to be amazingly innocent. Awakened at a relatively late age out of almost total ideological apathy, we plunged headlong into salvationary politics. We gave our hearts to more than dubious causes, thinking they served a generous ideal; we developed fetishist obsessions with tactical positions; we doted upon foolish or unworthy means for attaining enlightened ends. Above all, our imaginations endowed the institutions or factions that were the objects of our hearts' allegiance with superhuman virtues, then caused us to revile them for betrayal when their human imperfections stood revealed at last in the light of common day. Learning to recognize and treat in the political quadrant of the soul these classic symptoms of the romantic syndrome, to look at reality unveiled, without seeing it through the distorting lens of disillusion, to resist infatuation without losing the capacity for lucid dedication, count among the most difficult tasks that we have had to accomplish in order to become adult citizens of our century. The excerpts I have given from my undated Geneva notes show me at the age of twenty-nine or thereabout, confronting for the first time, and none too promisingly, this basic twentieth-century maturation ordeal.

The accents of the disenchanted lover are unmistakable. At some point in my long trek out of the coonskin world of Colonel McCormick to the frontiers of contemporary reality, a dream had taken possession of me: The wholly rational belief in the need for closer cooperation among civilized governments to meet the growing threat of neo-barbarian expansionism had acquired an element of mystique. During the European crisis provoked by the Italian invasion of Abyssinia in 1935 this internationalist mystique had crystallized into a passion as infatuate as any other.

Perhaps the simile of religious conversion is even more apt than the erotic one. Pressed to give the object of my worship a name, at one moment I might have said it was the cause of peace, at another the rule of law among nations. Sometimes I called it the League—confusing, as people do with the United Nations today, the goal sought with the institutional machinery intended to achieve it—or simply, collective security, which in my mind stood less for the good to be preserved than for the process of preserving it. In reality I was merely a sanctionist, the devotee of a newly arisen cult which held that the necessary but sufficient condition of man's salvation was to apply international sanctions against Mussolini for having invaded Abyssinia in 1935. It was one of those characteristic modern idolatries, compounded of ill-defined and sometimes conflicting idealisms, that periodically claim our devotion until experience teaches us to be more critical.

The Italo-Abyssinian conflict—or dispute as it was first termed—began with a bloody clash between an Italian military patrol and armed Abyssinian tribesmen on the borders of Italian Somaliland, in December 1934. Whichever side was mainly to blame for the immediate incident, it soon became clear that Mussolini intended to use it as an excuse for attacking Abyssinia. During the early part of 1935, the Italian military buildup in East Africa became increasingly ominous, and the Emperor of Abyssinia, Haile Selassie, finally appealed to the League of Nations—of which his country had been a full member since 1923—for protection. Ritual palavers in Geneva alternated with British and French attempts through the classic techniques of big-power diplomacy to coax or frighten Mussolini into a compromise solution of some sort. In October 1935 the Duce, defying both the Geneva institution and his two former allies, launched his armies on a full-scale invasion of Abyssinia. A few days later the League Council meeting in Geneva proclaimed the attack an act of aggression on the part of Italy, and recommended that member nations apply against her the graduated collective sanctions stipulated in Article 16 of the League Covenant.

A special committee set up to implement the recommendation agreed initially on various innocuous or slow-acting measures of financial and economic coercion. The international crisis touched off by their application reached its peak in February and March 1936 when a committee of international experts recommended an embargo on oil exports to Italy, a collective sanction that might have brought Mussolini to his knees if it had been rigorously enforced. In fact, it was never enforced at all. Early in May the Italians occupied Addis Ababa, the Abyssinian capital, and the Emperor had to flee his country. In the meantime, a second diplomatic crisis had developed in Europe, paralyzing further efforts to uphold the Covenant in Africa: On March 7, 1936, Hitler, throwing off the last shackles of the Treaty of Versailles, ordered his new Reichswehr into the demilitarized zone of the German Rhineland.

In retrospect, it is easy from one viewpoint, hard from another, to understand why the sanctions issue—especially the oil embargo—became such a dramatic one. If the League powers had really cut off Italy's oil supplies in obedience to a collective decision of the Council, it would have been the first serious attempt in history to enforce the rule of law, based on an international covenant, upon a sovereign and powerful nation. Some of the more fervent internationalists looked upon sanctions as a kind of shortcut to the millennium, an almost magic formula for ending war without war, for catching up in one futuristic leap with all the wildest hopes of the League's morning years. The fallacy in this view was that sanctions would only have been magical if effective, and effective only if the League's member governments, not to mention the Geneva idealists themselves, had been willing to risk war. (And perhaps only if these governments had likewise maintained their potential military strength at a high level of readiness, particularly in regard to those arms capable of providing what we would call today counter-deterrence.)

Like other sanctionists, I did not see the danger to the League's moral authority involved in talking about force without being prepared to use it. At first I was scarcely aware that any such danger existed. For a considerable time thereafter I was curiously insensitive both to the promise and to the hazard of the situation.

It was an accumulation of various moralistic or sentimental attitudes that had originally determined my support of the sanctionist campaign. The process started before the campaign itself, even before the Italo-Abyssinian conflict had become an acute issue in Geneva. For some time, I had been alarmed at the mounting power and virulence of the totalitarian revolution in all its forms and especially in the form of German National Socialism. I had been dismayed at the apparent fragility of democratic civilization. These feelings respectively pushed and pulled me toward the anti-fascist camp. In the middle 1930's anti-fascism and internationalism seemed to be complementary, almost interchangeable, ideologies; consequently, though I still jeered occasionally at the naïvetés of my world-saver friends, I had come belatedly to share their conviction that to uphold the authority of the League was to defend the cause of peace. Twinges of bad conscience for all the times I had proved Col. McCormick right, in print, speeded the evolution of my opinions. Various sediments of earlier experience—my adolescent cult of Shelley, my adventures in Italy with Bob, Mr. Judson's homilies on Cicero, my native American hatred of bullies—contributed to their militancy. Probably the most potent influence of all was what I might call the totemistic factor. I turned into a sanctionist chiefly because during my years of covering the League of Nations I had become emotionally naturalized into one of the Geneva clans and sanctionism had become our creed.

The group in question had, of course, no definite structure; in fact it had no formal membership and no explicit criteria for accepting or rejecting members. Its basis was neither national, though it was largely Anglo-Saxon and French, nor professional, though it was recruited mainly from correspondents who specialized in League affairs, and officials from the press or political divisions of the League itself; nor purely social, though it had the casual gregariousness of a neighborhood coterie, nor ideological, though a generally liberal outlook helped to distinguish it from other cliques in the pressroom or at the journalists' bar in the glass-walled annex of the League building (before the present Palais des Nations was built above the lake), which we called the Monkey House. A fascist sympathizer, a rock-ribbed American isolationist, or a die-hard British Tory would instinctively gravitate to some other grouping; so would most orthodox Communists or fellow travelers. There were, it is true, militant champions of the Popular Front among us—indeed, after the outbreak of the Civil War in Spain most of us became supporters of the Popular Front—and for a time we had at least one Communist brother, Vladimir Romm, the Tass correspondent in Geneva.

Romm, swarthy, hawk-faced, with a curious, shy gentleness of manner, was a special case. He was unquestionably a dedicated Communist: We covered together the bloody clash between police and left-wing demonstrators in Paris a few days after the great riot of February 6, 1934, and following one particularly close escape from the rifle butts of the *Gardes Mobiles* in a fog-choked street near the Place de la République, Romm said in his usual serious way, "That was quite unpleasant, but you know, the only thing that really frightens me in this kind of street fighting is the thought that I might get hit by a worker's bullet." Not long afterward Romm was suddenly recalled to Moscow, and later, though he was apparently spared a proletarian bullet in the back of the neck, we saw his name among the list of defendants in one of the famous trials of Stalin's adversaries. Few things did more to help us understand what was happening in the Soviet Union than reading that Romm had been sentenced to a Siberian prison camp as a traitor to the Revolution.

More than any common political faith, what bound our group together was a common attitude about politics: Under the mask of cynicism or flippancy that journalists wear as a kind of professional uniform we shared the same earnestness and the same propensity to look at political phenomena from a moral—at times moralistic—point of view.

The moral issues raised by the Italian attack on Abyssinia were self-evident, if not quite so simple as they seemed. By themselves they might not have sufficed to launch us on a major crusade; there were too many others to claim our zeal, some nearer home. The consensus among us that eventually made the Italo-Abyssinian conflict seem the master issue of the day—our challenge to make the world safe for democracy—emerged gradually and laboriously. It came out of innumerable huddles become indignation meetings at the journalists' bar, out of long, passionate discussions over the beer mugs at the Bavaria—and sometimes even the champagne buckets at the Moulin Rouge—out of interminable open-air orgies of fried fillets of perch by the lakeside, and out of starlit walks along the ramparts of the old city. We were covenanters in our fashion, but no Round-heads. Despite all the subsequent heavy-headed awakenings, the memory of those days still lies sweet in my mind, as fragrant as those thin, slight, evanescent Vaudois wines that yet warmed one like strong drafts of fraternity, as those thick, red steaks that nourished dedication, and as the heady Burgundy of group approval. There is no festival like a good cause, nothing that nourishes the enthusiasm of youth so much as expending it on something other than self, nothing that so quickens the pulse of life as the sharing of a generous indignation.

Every society has its opinion-makers, its arbiters of fashion and its guardians of public morals, with the subordinate coteries that form around them. In the loose and diverse Geneva kinship to which I belonged, these leaders usually typified in a sharply defined way some well-known pattern or tradition of political idealism. Edgar Mowrer, later a Washington columnist and writer, but then the Paris correspondent of the Chicago *Daily News* after having been ex-pelled from Germany, reembodied the fire, the incorruptibility, and a bit of the fanaticism of a New England Abolitionist. Clarence Streit, the present-day apostle of Atlantic federation, then the resident Geneva correspondent of the *New York Times*, stood for a gentler, more optimistic, and slightly hazier dream of brotherhood that has also played its role in American history. He was the self-appointed voice of the League's Wilsonian conscience, the independent but authoritative spokesman for the true-believers in the League's secre-tariat and in the national delegations surrounding it. To the non-believer he was no less a warmhearted friend, and able journalist. Wallace Carroll, then the United Press correspondent in Geneva, represented the soundest and most lucid type of twentieth-century idealist. He was the most conscientious reporter among us, the most sober analyst, in general a much-needed balance wheel. The most colorful and perhaps the best-loved figure was Robert Dell of the *Manchester Guardian,* a frail-looking but indefatigable septuagenarian with a rakish white moustache and a squeaky, drawling voice, who combined a Gladstonian outlook on world affairs with a private affectation of Edwardian naughtiness. Dell was the most passionate crusader of us all and he felt that every sound crusade should start at home. His basic credo in politics and journalism was that what the Foreign Office said was nearly always false, what it did invariably inept, what it intended generally mischievous. It is surprising, in retrospect, how often in those years Dell's rather simplistic formula proved a useful key to the interpretation of events in Europe.

I usually thought I was taking my old friend's verbal intemperances with a grain of salt, as I took Mowrer's avenging extremism or Streit's prairie idealism, but in terms of political conscience, if not of opinion, all three influenced me. All became fierce sanctionists, of course, and so, one by one, as the Abyssinian crisis neared its climax, did most of the other more respected members of our group. Sometimes it seemed to me that their attitude was determined less by the worsening of the situation than by the need to be different from those whom they disliked. Indeed, hearing some old whore like S———— sounding off at the journalists' bar about the Duce's self-restraint was enough to turn anyone into a sanctionist, particularly if he had despised the man, his paper, and his politics for a decade.

In the course of my own gradual development into a sanctionist crusader I recall no special difficulty in conforming my sentiments to the consensus of my clan brothers. For the conversion to be total I needed only the shock of some direct, personal recognition of evil. It came to me on a watery October afternoon in 1935 during a brief visit to Rome, as I stood on the Piazza Venezia in the midst of a vast crowd bemused by demagoguery, and heard Mussolini from his balcony give the signal for the invasion to his African legions, and heard, too, the crowd responding *Duce! Duce! Duce!* in gasping, interminable orgasms of ferocious submission. Somehow, the sight of the paunchy, black-shirted figure jutting its chin and strutting on the high balcony, the cunningly dosed vulgarity of the Duce's mum-

mery, the inspired fraudulence of his rhetoric precipitated my transformation. Here was no malevolent demiurge like Hitler to be con-
strained to harmlessness as one impounds the destructive forces of
nature, but the sovereign Deceiver whose ritual chastisement must
take place before we could ever hope to piece together the shattered
tablets of the law.

As a convert to sanctionism, I found myself for all practical purposes enrolled in a vast international pressure group which at times
amounted to a kind of open conspiracy. My personal contributions
to the cause were necessarily limited, but every time I could expose
the intrigues of the anti-sanctionists, or work into my dispatches
some sly attack on the premises of isolationism, I felt the glow of
belonging to an occult elite.

The real error of those who are always poking under the bed for
the secret of history is not that they are necessarily looking in the
wrong place but that they usually mistake what they find there: It
is the structureless, spontaneous freemasonries of ideal or interest,
rather than the organized networks of professional conspirators, that
most often set the wheels of change in motion, or surreptitiously
impede their revolutions.

The sanctionist lobby had no recognized central leadership but its
inner core consisted of a small, tightly-knit fellowship of Wilsonian
activists. These men were authentic revolutionaries dedicated to
promoting what they thought of as the Wilsonian revolution. They
had been working together since the days of Locarno and in some
cases since the Paris Peace Conference. They were to be found in
the government services of most European nations—Britain excepted,
where there were only a few—and in the State Department, as well
as in journalistic, academic, religious, and some business circles; but
the secretariat of the League itself was naturally their most congenial
habitat. I knew many of these zealots of the future and counted
several as personal friends; I admired, and sometimes envied, their
unquenchable idealism. I marveled at their talent for high-minded
intrigue, and occasionally wished them a little more fastidious in
fitting means to end.

The propaganda machine of the Wilsonian internationale was by no means the only one supporting the sanctionist campaign. During the relatively short time in which the Foreign Office, under the influence of Anthony Eden (Lord Avon), adopted the League as its chosen instrument for parrying the Italian threat to Britain's imperial line of communications, British propaganda was perhaps the most effective in Geneva. The urbane and seemingly objective "briefings" for correspondents given by Eden's press officer, Michael (later Sir Michael) Wright, were models of the official propagandist's art. Thanks to his bland persuasions, Eden emerged in our copy as a youthful and dapper St. George hacking at the fascist dragon in a dauntless but sportsmanlike spirit. It was no fault of Wright's that when the British cabinet pulled back from a final showdown with Mussolini, Eden became in our eyes the Lost Leader of the sanctionist campaign.

Soviet propagandists, official and unofficial, were no less active, and in the long run more successful. The greatest of them was the Soviet Foreign Minister, Maxim Litvinov, a rotund, slightly comical-looking, deceptively benign-seeming, old professional conspirator, who since the USSR joined the League in 1934 had been one of the chief stars on the Geneva stage. Soviet policy at the time subordinated revolutionary objectives—though it never entirely lost sight of them—to the need for recruiting the democratic nations as eventual allies against German aggression, and the Kremlin evidently considered that the machinery of the League could be usefully exploited to this end; hence the impassioned pleas for collective security at virtually every session of the Permanent Council, the Assembly or the Disarmament Commission that were beginning to make Litvinov seem a new Briand in the eyes of the Geneva liberals.

I came to recognize the most important transmission belts of Soviet propaganda in Geneva and I tried conscientiously to keep my dispatches free of their product. As the sanctionist crusade grew increasingly fervent, however, it became more and more difficult to prevent one's judgment from being subtly influenced by the various propaganda campaigns designed to whip up public support for sanctions; our very fervor owed far more than we realized at the time to the planned ministrations of cool minds and deft, invisible hands.

No doubt, the disagreeable necessity of producing reports on the Geneva drama sufficiently hardminded or detached to pass muster with Col. McCormick helped occasionally to keep my sanctionist enthusiasms within the bounds of reason, but not so much as one might suppose. More often, I fear, it lent to my dispatches a tone that ironically reflected the most unworldly strains of internationalist idealism. Unable to indulge—as much as I would have liked—in straightforward editorializing in favor of American cooperation with the League, I at times aligned myself (and by implication Col. Mc-Cormick) with the still-dominant pacifist wing of the British Labor Party which schizophrenically fulminated against Italian aggression, yet wrung its hands in dismay at the thought of the League's taking any action vigorous—and therefore dangerous—enough to end it. The extreme sanctionists were no less inconsistent: They proclaimed themselves in favor of peace, on the one hand, and in favor of closing the Suez Canal behind Mussolini's armies or shutting off his oil supplies, on the other. Which position finally was more unrealistic, or more immoral, remains a nice point. Later, with a conviction better suited to a prophet of the Old Testament, I castigated, for their insincerities and their backsliding, the sanctionist politicians, and particularly Eden who, beset by weak-kneed colleagues, reluctant allies, and a befuddled public, betrayed the League. When all else failed I could inject into my dispatches a tone of moralistic internationalism by reporting on the practices of the League in terms of the Wilsonian ideal.

A year after the sanctions debacle, with public confidence in the League as an instrument of collective security fatally undermined, I began a dispatch on a new fiasco in Geneva thus: "The unwillingness of the big League powers to act within the framework of the League of Nations—and the unwillingness of victims of aggression to trust their fate to the hazards of secret diplomacy—paralyzed action on . . . the undeclared war in China and on Spain's civil war." As an analysis of the immediate situation my dispatch was sound enough, but its language has a curiously archaic ring. The Wilsonian phobia about secret diplomacy seems hardly more germane to the organizing of peace in the thermonuclear age than the cult of free silver to our present-day economic problems. The Wilsonian dogma—implicitly accepted in my article—held that members of the League should not only conform their policies to its grand objectives but should also submit their most vital interests to the arbitration of its machinery. That issue is perhaps more relevant to our contemporary controversies. I suspect, however, that a realistic supporter of the United Nations would detect in it at least a trace of the millennialism that misled the architects of the League from the Paris Peace Conference onward.

I am not sure how seriously I took all the tenets of orthodox Wilsonianism in 1937—the tendency of many political crusaders to serve the cause in which they believe with arguments in which they do not is an important factor of ideological disarray—but my present reaction to that journalistic sample of nearly three decades ago gives me encouragement. Here, if nowhere else, it seems to me, is a clear indication that the passage of years and the pummelings of history have actually matured my personal outlook with regard to one of the most basic problems of our time. Many a reader on seeing these lines will claim a similar growth. For it is not we as individuals who have grown, but rather we as a whole generation of Americans. That is precisely what is encouraging—though it remains to be seen whether we have grown enough.

Our present maturity of judgment in world affairs—such as it is— unquestionably owes something to the lessons driven home at Geneva in 1935 and 1936. It is not entirely fortuitous that several of the ablest experts who helped frame United States foreign policy in the decisive postwar years had their first substantial experience of international affairs serving in Geneva under the late Prentiss Gilbert, United States observer at the League, a great foreign service officer and an important influence in the modernization of American diplomacy that took place in the 1930's.

WORK-NOTES 1963

Am I being too cynical or too flippant about a subject so pertinent to all our present-day hopes for man's future? Hard question. To the serious student of man's progress nothing is more frivolous than to nourish the delusions of facility, nothing more cynical than to condone the impostures of idealism, that so often retard it.

We are all at times unjust to ourselves as well as to others. Whether we call him me or thee, the suspect is automatically proven guilty upon being found human; the same evidence extenuates his crime. The important thing is not to determine whether we are in error, since we cannot fail to be, but to explain how we err.

I learned several things from covering the Abyssinian affair which, if they didn't cure me of my tendency to embark on political crusades, ultimately helped me to become a more responsible crusader. No political drama, for example, could have better illustrated the vices and perils of what it has since become fashionable to call moralism in diplomacy or foreign policy. Yet, viewed from another angle, what better demonstration could one find that in framing policy it is disastrous to neglect the moral factor? (I have many times since watched supposedly hardminded diplomats or politicians display the same moral blindness, and each time pay for it dearly.)

The British and French got themselves—along with the League— into a mess by promoting international sanctions against Italy because of Mussolini's Abyssinian aggression, but they probably got themselves into a worse one by condoning the offense after having failed to stop it. The loss of prestige abroad and of public confidence at home that stemmed from this dereliction was to have far-reaching practical consequences in the next few years, and it cannot be argued that these ill effects would have been averted—though they might have been somewhat mitigated—if the two governments had refused to condemn the aggression, or had denied their obligation to oppose it, in the first place. A wavering and confused policy is nearly always disastrous, whether its inconsistencies result from a clash between morality and expediency, or simply from one between two expediencies, but the error of Franco-British policy at Geneva lay deeper than that.

One element of error was clear even at the time.

"Democratic diplomacy almost always leads to paralysis disguised as action because democracies don't like to hurt people's feelings," I wrote on the eve of Munich in some short-sleeve reflections jotted down a year after the dispatch from Geneva already cited. Reflecting the same pessimism the notes continued: "Therefore they carry out a policy which merely seems bold . . . those against it will be reassured because they realize it is illusory, those for it because they think it is the real thing . . . thus the public is insulated from reality and prevented from learning by experience whether its ideal is realizable or not."

Add "moral" to bold, and we have a rough but reasonably accurate characterization of the Franco-British policy with respect to the Italo-Abyssinian conflict, as it finally emerged from the wrangling between cliques in the two governments. Unable to agree between or within themselves on either effective action or frank inaction, the two governments fell back on ceremonial: Their delegates at Geneva were instructed to carry out a certain number of ritual gestures calculated to appease the militant sanctionists without unduly provoking the anti-sanctionists (including, it was hoped, Mussolini). The fact that the sincere sanctionists who collaborated in this imposture—Anthony Eden, for instance—did not see it in these terms merely demonstrates the magic power of ceremonial, even, or especially, upon its own high priests.

Franco-British policy at Geneva was undoubtedly more moralistic than moral, as well as being unrealistic in its purely mundane aim of impressing Mussolini. We who covered the proceedings for the world press probably rendered a useful service—especially those of us who were writing for the American public—in pointing out the contradictions and insincerities. Sometimes, however, carried away by righteous indignation, we fell into a vein of moralistic debunking which probably contributed more to perpetuating the native folk-lore of foreign relations than toward forming a body of mature American opinion.

Today I have the most qualms about the Geneva dispatches written in the spring and summer of 1936 after the unexpected progress of the Italian forces in the Abyssinian highlands drove Haile Selassie from his capital. It was clear that economic sanctions had failed; the rational choice confronting the members of the League was between attempting to restore the Emperor to his throne by effectively cutting the Italian supply line—and perhaps by giving him military support for a counterinvasion of Abyssinia—or acknowledging the Italian conquest and lifting sanctions. Though a crusader, I was still too strongly influenced by my generation's horror of war, perhaps our deepest political attitude, to feel much enthusiasm for any military crusade, especially one that served the interests of the cannon-makers, the international oil trust, and the British Empire.

On the other hand, for the League to welcome the aggressor back into the Geneva concert and to recognize the fruits of aggression, as the powers in effect proposed, seemed to me an intolerable betrayal of the Wilsonian ideal. My dispatches breathed contempt for the unfortunate Eden. Pathos alternated with outrage in my treatment of Haile Selassie when he arrived in Geneva to plead his cause. In truth, the Emperor, grave, black-bearded, wearing a native cloak of pure white wool, and draped in the moral dignity of an honest lost cause, was an impressive figure as he stood at the rostrum of the Assembly confronting the stony-faced delegates of the Western democracies.

What response the League should have made to Haile Selassie's appeal (eventually, after some face-saving temporization, it was ruled out of court, Eden assenting) is not an easy question to decide even today, but in the implicit support that my dispatches gave the case for maintaining a purely ceremonial ostracism of the aggressor, I recognize one of the classic mental escape hatches of the moralistic crusader whose crusading has brought him face to face with a harsh dilemma. If I were to cover the same kind of international drama tomorrow, I think I would make a greater effort than I did in 1936 to resist the temptation of despising politicians or diplomats who choose to swallow their principles rather than to preserve them stuffed under a glass case, and I would try harder to help my readers understand its authentically tragic character, despite the seeming shabbiness of the leading actors.

There are moments in history when men who are not necessarily fools or cowards behave as if they felt themselves conscientious executors named to administer some general heritage of cowardice and folly; there are leaders whose betrayals seem to stem as much from what is sound as from what is false within. The thirties produced a number of such moments and several leaders of this sort: Besides the Eden who played a sorry role at Geneva in 1936, one thinks immediately of Bruening, von Schuschnigg, Daladier. (The Hoares, Lavals, von Schleichers, Chautemps, Dollfusses, belong in a different category: supernumerary villains.)

Underlying all these personal or collective tragedies of frustration can be discerned, it seems to me, a phenomenon characteristic of transitional ages: a lack of synchronization between ideals and institutions. Geneva in particular was a kind of historic limbo in the thirties, haunted by the wordless lamentation of aspirations awaiting some valid organizational embodiment and of loyalties hovering over the gravestones of moldering traditions. Looking back now, one can see how unreasonable it was to expect either strategic perspicacity or moral authenticity in such an atmosphere. We were doomed either to lag behind our need or to outstrip our capability, and sometimes we managed to do both at once.

Real and important changes in Western political attitudes, perhaps even in the personality of Western man—not to mention that of his Asian or African brother—had unquestionably taken place between 1914 and 1936. The rate or extent of change was not, however, evenly distributed among peoples and classes. The pseudo-heroic bombast that the Abyssinian war elicited from the rhetoric of fascist futurism sounded as artificial as the anthems of world patriotism that were composed in Geneva. Yet the intoxication of imperialism that was just beginning to take hold of the Italian people was no less real than the doubts about the legitimacy of colonial rule that were starting to sprout among the elite of the long-established empires.

The Abyssinian war played a bigger role than is often realized in the genesis of the anti-colonialist movement that has since swept the world. Internationalism was unmistakably growing as a significant political force in countries that had formerly given birth to nationalism, but nationalism, quite as unmistakably, was springing up where before the Peace Settlements it had scarcely existed. The same evolutionary dichotomy between developed and underdeveloped nations can be observed today.

At the time of the Italo-Abyssinian conflict, needless to say, it had not yet occurred to me that there was any great problem in the uniform development of those foundations of habit and custom, thought and emotion, folklore and folkway which are the support of the political and social institutions of modern nations. I assumed that save for a few temporarily misguided peoples like the Italians and the Germans, and for a scattering of retarded cases like Col. McCormick, this underpinning already existed in contemporary minds.

As for world government, my own conscious attitude toward it at that time was somewhat like St. Augustine's youthful feelings about chastity: I wanted it, but not yet. (I took it for granted that once I, and others like me, had decided we were ready, all that remained was to draft a sensible constitution; the League Covenant clearly left too many loopholes for national waywardness.) Though aware of a certain ambivalence in my internationalism, I would have been incredulous or aghast if anyone had told me that in my most basic political attitudes I was hardly less of a nationalist than Col. McCormick himself, though I may have been sometimes a less obfuscated one. It was not until several years later, when my own nation stood facing a clear and present threat to its very existence, that the truth about my inmost feelings became sufficiently respectable to bear admitting, even to myself.

At the same critical moment a curious paradox came to light. Nationalism proved to be the sole twentieth-century force capable of mobilizing effective resistance to the totalitarian imperialisms, but in the West it had become so enfeebled that it was barely capable. The breakdown or decay of nationalism, to the degree that it had occurred, had contributed more to unleashing the lust for aggression than to removing the obstacles in the path of international cooperation. The failure of the League had coincided with the decline of its principal members as world powers and as healthy national societies. The collapse of collective security had reflected not so much the triumph of national egoisms over international idealism as the victory of an internationale of wolves over an internationale of sheep.

My Wilsonian friends and I had all along been putting the cart before the horse. It was not internationalism, as we supposed, that was making national states obsolete, but the gradual obsolescence of the national state that was making internationalism necessary. International institutions were needed less to curb the appetites of the national state than to bolster its failing powers, or at least to cushion its eventual fall. Without an increasing measure of international cooperation, nations could not even assure their own survival; but without tapping the still powerful emotional dynamic of nationalism, no machinery for international cooperation could be made to function effectively. The real task facing my generation, I finally came to realize, was not to combat nationalism as an evil vestige of the past but to help make it more rational: to develop and practice it in less self-defeating, that is, more cooperative, forms.

The deflation of the futuristic internationalism that survived from the earliest days of the League occurred between 1935 and 1937. No doubt it marked a necessary, though perhaps an unnecessarily painful, stage in our education as enlightened nationalists. Men gradually learn to walk, it seems, by trying to fly and then having to pick themselves up after they have fallen. In my particular case, the sanctions fiasco was only the first of several similar, and similarly hard, lessons. Like a number of my contemporaries, especially those with a certain idealistic bent, I suspect I was a rather backward learner. Fortunately, in the history of the late 1930's and early 1940's we had an incomparable, if occasionally impatient, teacher.

A Banquet of Ghosts (2)

I do not get back to Geneva very often since the war; this visit is a kind of sentimental pilgrimage. I have been thinking recently about various friends of former times, writing about them a bit, as a matter of fact, and the need to see them again, what there remains for the physical eye to see, became overpowering. So here I am, and I have brought Vreni with me; it was her town, after all, and they were her friends, too, and it was also her war—the fifty-year undeclared war that Hemingway wrote about in *The Fifth Column.*

We are sitting in the narrow wing of the Bavaria nearest the lakeside entrance. Its walls are still hung with the cartoons of Derso and Kelen, those witty caricaturists and good drinking companions. On the right-hand wall is Prentiss Gilbert as Napoleon, reviewing his guard of future ambassadors; Romm as an altar boy kneeling before the ikon of Lenin was already there in our day, I believe, and of course, Clarence Streit with his cornflower. The large sketch across the room seems more recent: Pentman with his Yiddish fawn's face twisted in some tetanic spasm of dolorous hilarity; alas, poor Harry, we knew him well. Finally, Dell himself: venerable, silvered head, devil-may-care moustaches, leather boots and scarlet musketeer's uniform, flashing rapier, plumed hat held low, doffed, perhaps, in gallant homage to the latest-arrived Kiki or Suzy at the Moulin Rouge, perhaps in chivalrous salute to the adversary who next moment will be spitted on his blade.

It is a queer masquerade from one viewpoint—the stern covenanter as the lighthearted cavalier—but the caricature is all the same deeply perceptive. For Dell was lighthearted, as well as unbending and intolerant, saved from the "totalitarian liberalism" that claimed a number of our friends by the candid *belle époque* humanism of the bidet and the wine card that had captured his young imagination, by the irreverential Parisian ascesis of the proper sentiments that had purified his mind of cant, even the political varieties.

He was indeed our d'Artagnan, and the campaigns on which he led us into zestful battle were charges for the sake of honor even more than they were crusades of conscience. Not all of us subscribed to his twentieth-century nonconformist code of political morality, or shared his enthusiasm for the rather lumpy emulsion of Marx and Mill that seemed to be his political creed, but when he raised the standard of journalistic honor we recognized it as our true flag, and him as its peerless bearer. I am thinking of something deeper and more personal than the corporate and public honor of the press he defended with more than a hint of Gascon susceptibility, as on the memorable occasion when he stood up in the press gallery of the League Council and thumbed his nose at the Chairman—Eden himself—to illustrate, and demand moral reparation for, the insult that had just been directed at us by Hitler's representative.

Honor, of course, was not a word that we often used among ourselves. Up to a certain point this was no doubt a decent reticence, but it also reflected a kind of disdain, typical of the age, for any merely private virtue. (Honor? Well, if you like . . . But man, where is your social conscience, where is your sense of history?) Dell was one of those older colleagues who helped journalists of my generation rediscover the collective and contemporary relevances of the intimate, old-fashioned thing called honor, if not the word itself.

Some of us had begun to wonder if we had not adopted a profession that was as second-rate as snobbish Europeans supposed it to be; it often seemed, indeed, that the only truths our editors, and presumably our readers, wanted to hear from us were second-rate ones. Dell's example, among others, showed us how to give our function a new dignity by steadfastly bearing witness to the evilness of evil. The more monstrous the evil grew, the wider it spread, the more essential the function appeared; the more difficult or dangerous to bear witness, the greater the privilege of being able to do so. The very professional servitudes and restrictions, the outworn conventions and clichés that frequently hampered us in telling any really significant story made it all the more important to tell as much of this one as we could. Every fact, every thought counted; no effort was completely wasted.

We tried our best to become in reality those brave watchdogs of the truth on the frontiers of the news that our promotion departments advertised us as being. Then the phase came when people began to complain that our barking disturbed their sleep, harmed business, made dangerous enemies, gave aid and comfort to political adversaries, endangered peace in our time. In the press of the Anglo-Saxon countries attempts to muzzle us outright were rare, but it was more and more frequently suggested to our employers—and as time went on the suggestions were not infrequently accepted—that we should be instructed to bark more selectively, less antagonistically. Fortunately, Dell had taught us what was to be done in such cases: to bark our heads off.

How much difference it made to history that in the 1930's a certain number of journalists, particularly the foreign correspondents of the British and American press, came to feel it as a personal point of honor to expose the threat and evil of fascism, even when their publishers were not enthusiastic about printing what they wrote, or their readers seemingly much interested in reading it, I cannot say. I don't suppose we were the major factor in creating the anti-fascist climate of opinion that gradually became dominant throughout the West, but perhaps we were partly responsible for the speed with which it spread, and for stiffening public resistance to some of the countercurrents that developed during the appeasement period. How many weeks or months were thereby saved in mobilizing Britain or in arming America? And how many weeks or months—or days— did we have to lose?

9

The Powers of Light and the
Powers of Darkness

*T*he spirit of Franco's army is the spirit of a mob of lynchers in our own South hunting for a Negro murderer . . . Every day in Burgos, and in all the other cities held by the "Whites," men are being arrested . . . because they once belonged to some party of the left, and every night there are executions in the prisons. Franco could not win without this terror, any more than he could win without his Italian and German aviators and planes and without his Moors and his Legionnaires. Not because the "Reds" have a better army . . . but simply because the masses of the country are against Franco . . . [the Nationalist insurrection] is destroying Marxism in Spain—and liberalism—by exterminating the Marxists and the liberals. It needs foreign aid and mercenaries to accomplish this result because it has not the manpower, nor anywhere near the manpower, of the enemy . . . Franco is not conquering Spain in the same way Mussolini conquered Italy, or Hitler Germany. As a matter of fact he is not conquering Spain at all. Hitler and Mussolini are conquering Spain. Franco is merely their general in the field.

(SPEECH DELIVERED AT A LUNCHEON OF
THE AMERICAN CLUB OF PARIS ON
OCTOBER 29, 1936.)

179

I will try as best I can to resist the siren voices of middle-aged orthodoxy in looking back upon what a number of Americans today recall as an era of rampant heresy: the time of the Civil War in Spain, and of the Popular Front generally. No doubt certain opinions that we—my liberal friends and I—held about the conflict in Spain and promulgated *urbis et orbis* as articles of democratic faith were at odds with what we now know to have been the true facts. It was grave, for example, not to have seen that Spanish history and Spanish character, including the character of Spanish generals, made it implausible to view Franco as the puppet of his brother dictators, however much he needed their help. To say that we frequently oversimplified the issues is an understatement.

It is oversimplifying history no less grievously to depict the supporters of the Popular Front throughout the world merely as the dupes of Communist propaganda (perhaps, as Stalin seems to have feared, the Communists were more often subverted by their exposure to liberal idealism than we by our contact with Bolshevik cynicism) or to dismiss the eruption of generous indignations set off by the Spanish tragedy as an infantile disorder of what is now sometimes termed the liberaloid sensibility. If some of the viewpoints we expressed in those days seem puerile in retrospect, it may be because they reflected one of the delayed crises of political and moral adolescence through which my generation finally came of age.

In my case, I must confess that Spain itself was an acquired, and perhaps slightly forced, taste even before the Civil War broke out. I had been back to the country several times—usually on duty, once on a vacation—since my first assignment in 1930, and on the whole I had enjoyed, at least in retrospect, the picturesque and violent adventures one always seemed to be having there. I still recall with amusement an agitated but sumptuous luncheon in St. Sebastian with an American colleague and two erudite French gourmets whose appreciative comments on the food and wine were accompanied by intermittent musketry from the street—aimed at a sniper on the roof of our restaurant—and more emphatically punctuated from the cheese course onward by the sticks of dynamite that the sniper's friends kept dropping from the upper windows of nearby buildings.

Despite many agreeable memories, despite my respect for the brittle integrity and somber gusto of the Spanish personality, despite the haunting, lonely magic of the Spanish countryside, I always felt a kind of estrangement in Spain. I enjoyed the fine moments but was never quite able to put out of my mind the gutted horses and the blood puddles and the often messy jabbing; driving across the Spanish countryside in the brightest sun I could still sense the presence of Goya's witch-hags in the shadows, and sometimes seeing one of those forlorn Spanish villages on the horizon, I would picture myself approaching its outskirts, alone, on foot, in the gathering dusk. One was supposed to love the Spanish earth in those days, no less than the Spanish people, and I was sure I did, but the truth is, there were more than a few times when I felt in my heart that both rejected me.

I never managed to have quite the right feelings about the war— or any war—either. There was undoubtedly much to be said for it. It probably sharpened the sensibilities as much as it blunted them. Its moral values could no more be denied than its horrors. It had its moments of intense excitement, even if they were a little too likely to occur without warning when one was depressed from dysentery or lack of sleep, or was otherwise not at one's best. All in all, war was an educational experience: It helped to correct one's Ptolemaic Fallacy of Central Position (in Robert Ardrey's neat phrase), even if one never wholly lost the sense of personal injustice at being shot at by utter strangers. But there was too much thingness, too many subjects turned into objects. One accepted the dead as present objects; the pitchy magma inside a burned-out armored car, even if one was foolish enough to stop and look at it, did not necessarily denigrate the prides, the hopes, the loyalties which once as flesh had thrust it into danger. One should have felt the same about the figure in the blood-soaked khaki shirt, jerk'ng and whimpering in the dust like a dog that has been run over, but that somehow was harder, and it was harder still in the case of the adolescent with the tears streaming down his cheeks and the wet stain in the seat of his blue jeans spreading down one leg, and his fingers locked behind his head, trying to keep his legs from throwing out at the knees as he stumbled across the open field, but not succeeding, and knowing all the time it was useless in any case. Shock, pain, fear can disintegrate the soul no less than blast or fire, so why should one be more dismayed by corpses that still breathe than by those that have ceased to? No doubt the reaction was absurd.

It was equally absurd, I suppose, to be fastidious about the aesthetic appearance of the battlefield upon which one might be called to risk one's own skin, but I must admit it was a shock to me to discover in Spain what a real battlefield, at least a Spanish one, looked like. It was not a picturesque inferno landscape as one imagined from the films, but an incredible kind of tinny litter and defilement, like a hoboes' encampment beside a municipal dump, except that hoboes, as I remembered them, rarely spread their excrement around so much, including on the walls, where there were walls. A man's death can have as much dignity on a refuse heap as anywhere else, but in Spain it often took a real effort to remember that.

I had even more trouble at times keeping clear in my mind an ideological distinguo to which certain shades of liberal opinion during the 1930's attached considerable importance. My old friend Dell, with his usual, slightly mischievous contempt for cant, once put it very neatly, half in jest, half in earnest: "It isn't war that is beastly, my dear boy, merely war between nations; civil war can be quite a good thing." Though I had never before heard it expressed quite so bluntly, the attitude was familiar to me.

Like most members of my generation, I had absorbed hatred of war with the very air I breathed; almost as naturally and inevitably, I had come in the last few years to consider that a certain tolerance for revolutionary violence was the mark of a truly liberal spirit. In Spain I discovered that civil war is war, and that one cannot tell from a dead body lying by the side of the road with the flies buzzing out of a blackened crater in its skull whether it has been the victim of revolutionary or of counterrevolutionary violence. The violence practiced by Loyalist guerrillas behind the Nationalist lines was legitimate violence, of course, since it was in defense of a legal government. There was often some doubt about the combatant status of its victims, however, and in any case, was a legal government necessarily a legitimate one? I had never had occasion to ask myself the question before, and it was harder to answer than it might seem. The more I reflected upon the problem, the more I realized that a legitimate political authority is among the most mysterious and greatest blessings a people can enjoy.

The Republican regime had come to power in Spain by the most pacific of revolutions, but in 1936 it was still a revolutionary and usurping authority in the eyes of a sizable minority of Spaniards. A democratic consensus did not exist. Some of the Popular Front leaders, I knew, had no more respect for legality—at least when it was bourgeois legality—than their adversaries had, and just as few inhibitions about using violence. The only kind of republic much of the left cared about was a socialist or syndicalist one that opposed, if it did not actually persecute, the Church; the only kind of republic most of the right was willing to accept at all was a conservative, authoritarian, and clerical one. A clash between these antithetical conceptions of republican legitimacy was not only inevitable, but had already occurred: during the leftist uprisings of 1934 against the Lerroux government, when full-fledged civil war had broken out in the Asturias.

The truth was that civil war was endemic in Spain. No regime in the last century had been accepted as legitimate by the whole Spanish people; every single one—the two monarchies, the two republics, the several military dictatorships—had been conspired against or contested, arms in hand, by important elements of the population. Both factions in the present conflict were the victims of Spanish history; neither was an entirely innocent victim.

My feelings about the Popular Front were complex, like my feelings about Spain itself, and about the war there. To render them comprehensible to the reader—especially to one who did not take part in the ideological struggles of the epoch—it may be useful to recall briefly what the Popular Front was, and what it stood for in the minds of its followers. Basically, the Front, which began to take definite shape in the second half of 1935, well before the outbreak of the war in Spain, was a tactical and defensive alliance, sponsored by Moscow on a worldwide basis, between Communists and other left-wing or anti-fascist elements, including a number previously anathematized as "bourgeois." (The exact political formula varied somewhat from country to country; in France it took in the Radical Socialists, and in Spain, some Basque Catholics.) The coalition thus mirrored—and helped to implement—the new Soviet foreign policy: the "Litvinov line" of cooperation with democratic capitalist regimes that the fear of Hitler and German rearmament had inspired.

As the chief fascist powers in Europe, Germany and Italy, steadily drew together and the threat of fascist aggression became more palpable all over the continent, the sense of personal commitment to oppose fascism, everywhere and always, that the Popular Front implied to its adherents grew more militant. Naturally, the insurrection in Spain, viewed by leftists and by most liberals throughout the world as an indirect fascist aggression, strengthened the tendency to look on fascism as absolute evil, and to think of any armed resistance to it as a holy war.

The ethos of the Popular Front was not solely anti-fascist, however. Particularly in France and Spain, it was nourished by dreams of social justice, of human fraternity, of ultimate peace on earth, and of at least certain rudimentary forms of freedom that nearly all its members or supporters shared to some degree, however much they differed in terms of formal ideology. The developing twentieth-century sense of enlarged individual participation in the community of man that inspired Hemingway's *For Whom the Bell Tolls,* and the heightened awareness of human dignity expressed in Malraux's writings on Spain, were two essential components of the Popular Front idealism, at least to the intellectuals in its ranks. The eventual breakup of the Front by no means erased from the minds of my generation the moral values associated with it.

The Powers of Light and the Powers of Darkness

As an anti-fascist and internationalist liberal—even if a recently converted one—I naturally felt a good deal of sympathy with the goals of the Popular Front, especially in its early days. My reservations about it as a political movement developed gradually as the Kremlin manipulated it more and more cynically in the exclusive national interest of the Soviet Union, and as it became increasingly infected with the paranoid mentality evidenced by the Stalinist purges, including the ones in Spain. Unquestionably, the Popular Front helped to poison as well as nourish the moral atmosphere of the late 1930's. Though it was not alone in doing so, it helped to aggravate civic discord in the Western democracies, to corrupt the values of some Western liberals, and even to subvert the loyalties of a few.

Viewed as a bulwark against fascism, the Front likewise revealed a number of purely practical deficiencies. I eventually became disgusted with what seemed to me the pusillanimity of Léon Blum and other French Popular Front leaders, with the blindness of the French workers who were strong for stopping fascism, but only on company time, and only forty hours each week, and with the apparently incorrigible irrationality of the Spanish anarchists.

There was still another aspect to the Popular Front in certain countries. In France, notably, it was before anything else a movement of social and economic reform and of ideological renovation. The Popular Front parliamentary majority returned in the elections of May 1936, and the coalition socialist-liberal or liberal-socialist governments to which it gave birth, brought to France a kind of systematized and bolder New Deal. Like Roosevelt's in America, Blum's New Deal probably averted a violent revolution. During the Depression years the French industrial worker—and to some extent the French industrialist himself—had been crucified by the bankers, in Bryan's famous phrase, on a cross of gold. The patience of the worker, at least, was at an end, as demonstrated by the wave of sit-in strikes that spread from Paris throughout France after the elections, paralyzing for a while the country's economic life.

I was not greatly alarmed by the phenomenon, though for several weeks it threw large sections of the French bourgeoisie into a panic.

I visited a number of the idle plants in and around the capital, with their red flags on improvised flagpoles and their smiling workers dancing the *java* amid their workbenches to the strains of an accordion, and interviewed the members of the strike committees, or factory soviets, as the right-wing press liked to call them. It was all pretty harmless, I thought, though politically awkward for Blum, and rather fun from the viewpoint of an outside observer. Judging from the memoirs written since the war by some of the more militant participants in the 1936 strikes, it must have been a graver crisis than I realized. There was a day or two, it appears, when the old anarcho-syndicalist dream of the triumphant revolutionary general strike may have been quite near to spontaneous realization. And it was the Communists who applied the brakes in time, thereby saving Blum, the Popular Front, French capitalism, and incidentally, of course, the Franco-Soviet defense pact negotiated a year earlier by Pierre Laval.

The French Popular Front failed in many of its aims—including those of saving the Spanish Republic and of averting war—but it succeeded in revitalizing the liberal and reformist tradition of part of the French bourgeoisie; at the same time it rehabilitated the humanist ideal that had been Jaurès's in the eyes of part of the working class. These achievements seemed platonic in 1940; they probably played a considerable role in saving France from communism between 1944 and 1948.

The story of the Popular Front in France, like that of the war in Spain, thus demonstrates the need, not merely for trying to look beneath the surface of events, but for viewing them with the ecological eye of the naturalist. History is a community of antagonisms, a thicket of human purpose and cross-purpose, dense with biological ironies, in which one organism is sustained by the enemy that seeks to strangle it, another propagated by its own parasites; in which the slow worm of time transmutes the mold of fallen hopes into the food of future promise; in which today's disaster may prove the stimulus of tomorrow's triumph, while the victory still ripening in the sun already foretells the following cycle of decline.

The Powers of Light and the Powers of Darkness

[Covering the Spanish Civil War] was an adventure, an experience, once or twice an exploit. It was also something much more important: An education, short but radical and very painful; an education which changed my ideas about life and politics and journalism itself, making the responsibilities seem very heavy ones, so heavy that I can no longer write bright copy like I used to, least of all about Spain.

("SPANISH EDUCATION," IN *Nothing But Danger*,

EDITED BY FRANK HANIGHEN.)

Never try to be too honest, my dear boy; one always exaggerates so. It was overstating the case, for example, to declare that after my assignment in Spain I could no longer write "bright copy" on occasion, at least upon non-Spanish subjects. In the spring of 1937, while covering the *fiançailles* of the Duke of Windsor, lately Edward VIII, and Mrs. Wallis Simpson in the Touraine, I scored a scoop for the *Tribune* by reporting that the famous couple had paused during an evening stroll through the park of the chateau where they were staying to listen to a nightingale. My cabled story of the incident was a triumph of daring inference from available facts, rather than a stylistic masterpiece, but it was brisk enough, and my editors were properly appreciative; one of them, discussing my case with a visitor some years later, observed that my decline as a correspondent had set in irremediably only after that last flowering in the Touraine.

All the same, I did learn something in Spain. Would I have learned and grown more if I had covered the Spanish war from the side where my sympathies lay? I never had the opportunity to find out. The frontier between France and the Loyalist-held Basque provinces of Spain was hermetically closed when I arrived there from Paris, twenty-four hours after the Nationalist insurrection broke out. The frontier into rebel Navarre was likewise shut, but I had the good luck to find an unguarded cart track leading over the hills that a car driven by a nervy chauffeur might be able to take on a dry day. It was a dry day and I had a nervy chauffeur, and though I already thought of myself as a confirmed anti-fascist I was an even more confirmed reporter; in covering anything so glamorous as a war, civil or otherwise, copy came before ideology. And copy from insurgent territory was even rarer, and therefore more precious, than copy from the government side. Pamplona seemed worth a mass, or at least a few fascist salutes.

My new Spanish adventure started well. It was one of the occasions when the life of a foreign correspondent seemed to fulfill my childhood fantasy of becoming an explorer. Events can sometimes modify the moral and emotional landscape of a people so suddenly and radically that it is almost as if they had brought with them a new kind of tribal culture; this is what had happened in Spain. During the three-day news blackout before my arrival, a war civilization of hitherto unobserved type had superseded the normal Spanish one; some of its traits were familiar, even if exaggerated, but a greater number seemed completely new, or at any event rearranged in surprising new patterns. I was one of the first visitors from the outside world privileged to discover this phenomenon, and I gazed with as much wonder as if I were looking at plumed savages upon the proliferation of improvised military uniforms and insignia it had produced: the rakishly-worn khaki mechanics' coveralls and red berets of the Requetés, the Monarchist militia, the equally Carlist shotguns that the peasants waved like welcoming pennons—providing one had remembered to give the fascist salute in time—as one drove through their villages, the blue shirts with the yoke-and-arrow, red-and-black armbands of the Falangists, the scraps of red and gold cloth sewn on the tunics of sheepish-looking conscripts, the big gold crosses and Sacred Heart scapulars attached with safety pins, the young girls in black lace mantillas and Red Cross armlets upholding morale in the square of Pamplona. The very exoticism of the scene was reassuring: What was happening in Spain appeared to be at once so parochial and so unique that it was absurd to pass judgment on it in terms of twentieth-century values.

The political objectives of the various forces supporting the insurrection were all reactionary by my standards, but they were so wildly contradictory that it was hard to take them seriously. A general named Mola, whom I had never heard of, headed the insurrectionary junta in Burgos, and there was mention of another rebel force in the south led by the former army chief of staff, General Francisco Franco.

At least in the northern areas where the insurrection had some popular roots, it seemed a kind of fiesta that had turned hysterical, rather than an explosion of mass hatreds. The central plaza in Pamplona was hung with gold-red flags and banners as for a fiesta and loudspeakers continuously blared out what from the Navarrese viewpoint were no doubt patriotic marches. The people on the streets walked faster than they did in normal life, and spoke in unnaturally loud tones, with sudden gestures. As one drove south toward the supposed war front, the tempo became even jerkier; the successive images of the trip that flash back before my mind are as vividly disconnected as the sequences of some antediluvian screen melodrama.

An air raid was in progress when I caught up with the Navarrese army at Soria, after driving for several hours across a wide, red, almost empty plain. The experience was less apocalyptic than I had imagined it would be—a single Loyalist plane appeared overhead from time to time and the pilot would drop by hand a three-inch artillery shell to which metal wings had been soldered—but like the other novices, I found it unnerving at first. Along with three Nationalist soldiers, I took refuge in the vestibule of the local hospital each time the enemy reappeared. When the hum of his motor began to fade we would step out of our shelter and the soldiers would fire their rifles at the tail of the departing plane. There was a barred window on the second floor of the hospital, apparently for disturbed cases, and behind it a patient was plucking at the bars and gibbering and screaming curses at the soldiers. They started muttering back, and finally raised their rifles. Before they could shoot, a doctor wearing a white smock jumped out of the doorway and slapped the nearest soldier in the face. Then with only a slight pause each time, he slapped the second and third soldiers. They all lowered their guns and walked away, and so did I.

The main worry of the Navarrese officers I interviewed in Soria appeared to be over whether their allies from Castile or Andalusia might reach Madrid first, and on the basis of the sketchy information available, they admitted that the column from Burgos had a slight head start; the best Pamplona could hope for was to catch up with it before it reached the capital, and thus share the glory. I had acquired some allies myself; on my return to Pamplona, after rushing back to France to file my story, I had joined forces with a veteran British colleague, Harold Cardozo of the London *Daily Mail,* and Bertrand de Jouvenel, the French political philosopher, then an amiably adventurous young journalist. We decided to send one of our two cars back to France with some copy hastily typed during intervals of the air attack on Soria and to continue on in the other one to a town called Aranda de Duero, which General Mola was expected to occupy during the day in his march on Madrid.

The Navarrese were also heading for Aranda, but it seemed pleasanter and more interesting to push on ahead of them. Our road map did not indicate the route very clearly and the politico-military situation in the hundred or more miles of desolate countryside that we had to cross was known only to God. The peasants in most of the villages we traversed were armed, as in Navarre, but not enthusiastic. It was a relief to see the red and gold colors of the insurgency floating over Aranda when we arrived there.

When we learned that General Mola's mobile column had passed on and reached the foot of the Somosierra pass leading over the Guadarrama Mountains to Madrid, we sped south, worried like the Navarrese lest we miss the final assault. We knew we had reached the front at last when, just before dusk, we came upon a long file of empty trucks blocking the highway and saw field guns with their muzzles elevated toward the purple crest of the Guadarramas set up in batteries close by. The Nationalist army from Burgos, about a thousand strong, was lounging on the ground in little groups, reliving the day's heroics. There had been an unsuccessful but gallant attempt to storm the pass just before our arrival. The talk was about plans for the renewed attack that would be made next morning with the help of the Navarrese.

Officers and men greeted us enthusiastically, both because we brought them firsthand confirmation that reinforcements were on the way from Soria, and because we would be witnesses of their future exploits, which they seemed childishly eager to have the world know about. Everyone took it for granted that we were sympathetic to the cause of Christian civilization as exemplified by the Spanish National Movement, and nobody seemed to care what other credentials, if any, we carried with us. (They consisted of our passports, our Paris press badges, and slips of paper signed by the military commandant in Pamplona authorizing us to travel by car between there and the French border.)

Soon we were installed at a table in a nearby rural *fonda*, typing our stories by candlelight, while exalted young men in dusty overalls kept handing us the wineskin of comradeship and dictating accounts of their prowess in flawless French, or Oxford English. By the time we had finished our dispatches we were so full of drink and the fellowship of war that the only natural, sensible course seemed to send our one remaining car back to France with the unquestionably immortal, if slightly wine-stained copy we had just written, and to trust to luck from then on, like everyone else.

There were no beds in the village, if it could be called that, so we finally reeled out of the *fonda* and up the road to the head of the column and lay down on the bare earth, still warm from the afternoon sun. A young Spaniard wearing a big steel helmet came up and began talking in halting English, while we lay on our backs on that warm earth looking up at the starry Castilian sky. Most of the Spanish Nationalists we had talked to had seemed filled with a wild and often incomprehensible exuberance, but this young man was slow and fumbling and earnest; I suspect he had been studying for the priesthood before he joined the Requetés. He was desperately anxious to make us understand, and though we might be sympathizers, he evidently feared that as foreigners we would have difficulty in understanding. The important thing to remember about the Nationalists, he insisted, was that they were fighting for an ideal; the Marxists had none. The workers had been misled by the Marxists, but we must not suppose the Nationalists were trying to punish them; on the contrary they were fighting for the happiness of the workers since they were trying to give them back their ideal, and someday the workers would be grateful for this, because materialism never makes Spaniards happy.

Later on I had numerous opportunities to reflect on some of the less reassuring implications of this dialectic, but at the moment it merely seemed sincere and rather moving and marvelously Spanish. After a while the earnest young man went away; the firing from our outposts gradually died down as the tired soldiers negotiated their private armistices with the shadows of the night; the answering flashes from the dark mountainside grew more and more rare; soon we were asleep ourselves.

We never saw the next day's battle for the pass, except from a distance, which was probably just as well since it turned out to be confused and bloody. Sometime after midnight we were wakened by the cold and the mosquitoes. Our stirring around attracted attention, and we were arrested as suspicious presences on the battlefield. Nobody seemed to remember having ever seen us before; our credentials were patently inadequate. We were marched at gunpoint to the Falangist command post back in the village, where we spent the rest of the night undergoing intermittent interrogation—none of us were capable of any elaborate conversational effort in Spanish—but mostly just waiting. It was a long wait. When we voiced some curiosity as to our fate, the Falangists who were guarding us gave the matter careful thought, or appeared to do so, and finally said it was a decision for higher authority, but in their opinion we would be shot. Perhaps they were merely being playful, or perhaps it was an honest error of judgment.

When the attack started at first light, the guards forgot all about us and rushed out into the courtyard to watch it. They did not seem to mind when we joined them, though another Falangist who was passing by stopped to curse us at length. There was a great deal of firing and shouting, but it was hard to make out what was happening. At one point the enemy seemed to be counterattacking, for we noticed blue-clad figures with rifles running back through the village, away from the front. About nine o'clock an officer came and said he had orders to take us to Burgos. We were hospitably received at Mola's headquarters, and after nominal reproach for our unauthorized trip to the zone of battle were allowed to interview the general himself.

I bore the Spanish Nationalists no ill will for the uncomfortable end of what had started out as a good adventure—it had clearly been the consequence of our own folly—and for some time I continued wandering unescorted with two or three colleagues throughout the regions held by the insurgents, or supposedly held by them. We had a few narrow escapes in the course of these travels, but usually from enemy—i.e. Republican—bullets. The Loyalists seemingly commanded the Spanish skies in those days, and learning to huddle like rabbits in the shadow of boulders or shrubs while one of their pursuit pilots used our car for target practice, or to lie dead-still in some scarcely perceptible swale of a bare hillside, knowing the circling hawkeye above would direct the slightest movement, became familiar though never agreeable experiences. The Nationalist machine guns, the rare Nationalist plane represented protection for us, as did their occasional patrols on the roads or their sentries at night; the Nationalist soldiers among whom we lived were not only of the same flesh as ours, but that flesh was exposed to the same perils and the same indignities. It was impossible not to have some feeling of brotherhood with them, whatever one thought about their political ideas.

However, our misadventure at the foot of the Somosierra Pass— the meeting with the young soldier, the long hours in the Falangist command post wondering whether or not we were going to be shot —never completely faded from my mind. It illustrated the tenuousness of the frontier between dream and nightmare that I had noticed in Spain and reinforced my feeling that the Spanish landscape was not completely fixed; appearances could not be completely trusted; under certain circumstances, anything might turn into anything else. Moreover, it sensitized me to an aspect of the war that, in time, came to seem the most atrocious of all. In Navarre most of the population appeared to be spontaneously supporting the Nationalist cause; nearly everywhere else, even in Nationalist strongholds like Burgos, there was evidence of savage repression and sometimes of mass butcheries. On our trip to the Guadalajara front I had passed through villages where there were almost no adult males to be seen and where the surviving population seemed stupefied by fear. At the front we soon learned not to ask what was done with prisoners, not because the question was resented, but because it was answered with too much relish. As far as we could gather, the Republicans, at least in those early days of the war, were just as pitiless. "This civil war or insurrection or whatever you want to call it," I wrote in a dispatch to the Chicago *Tribune* summarizing my early impressions of the Spanish battlefield, "is something like a crusade, something like a Chinese bandit war, something like a family feud in the Kentucky mountains, or an ax murder in a basement."

At Torrijos, between Talavera and Toledo, we had lunch with the Falangists at their barracks, and after lunch as an attraction they showed us the prisoner they had picked up in the village when they entered—the only inhabitant who had remained. He was an old peasant with a silly, fixed grin on his face. The peculiar thing about him, they said, was that he thought he was among friends and would grin at them and give them the clenched-fist salute. We thought this was very queer, so to prove it the Falangists patted the old man on the back very kindly and said to him, "These señores are Russians, aren't you going to salute your Russian friends?" The old man was quite happy to salute us: he jumped up and grinned and raised his fist, very proud of himself. We said of course he must be loco, *but*

The Powers of Light and the Powers of Darkness

the Falangists got indignant and said not at all, he really believed it, and of course he would have to be shot for that eventually. They were having so much fun, though, they weren't in any hurry to shoot him.

(AMERICAN CLUB TALK)

As time went on, the conduct of the war, without becoming any less savage, grew more professional, especially on the Nationalist side. I immediately noticed the changed atmosphere of the battlefield when, like the other correspondents, I deserted the relatively static northern fronts in September and attached myself to the Army of Africa under Gen. Franco's command that was driving up the valley of the Tagus to relieve the beleaguered Nationalist garrison in the Alcázar of Toledo. The spearhead of this force was composed of the *Tercio*, the Spanish Foreign Legion, and of Moorish regulars or auxiliaries under Spanish professional officers. Both the Legionnaires and the Moors could be quite charming when you met them socially. The Moors, many of them primitive tribesmen recruited in the mountains of Morocco for the occasion, were simply mercenaries fighting for infidels against infidels, despite the Sacred Heart scapulars they often pinned to their tunics or burnouses.

The Legionnaires, though their corps had originally been modeled on the French Foreign Legion, were almost wholly Spanish. They were disciplined troops, when their officers wanted to hold them in hand, but steeped in the colonial tradition of licensed rape and pillage after the battle. In theory the Legion had been created for service in Africa (perhaps the most decisive foreign intervention in the Spanish Civil War was the help given Franco at its very outset by the Italian Air Force in ferrying Legionnaires and Moors from Morocco to Spain), but it had also been trained as an arm of last resort for suppressing domestic rebellion. The brutal liquidation of the Asturian miners' revolt in 1934 had been mainly the Legion's handiwork.

195

As an elite body of professional soldiers, the Legion had naturally been on the side of the generals against the civilians from the start of the war. Like comparable formations in other armies it had a fanatical *esprit de corps* and a kind of quasi-Pretorian ideology of service, but few Western military organizations have ever developed such a morbidly romantic cult of death. *Viva la Muerte!*, that "senseless and necrophilous cry," as the Basque philosopher Unamuno termed it on one famous occasion, was their traditional rallying call, and their corps hymn was called "Los Aficionados de la Muerte." It was a tinny but haunting tune, quite lovely to hear sometimes in the tepid evening with the Legionnaires climbing into their trucks to leave for the front and the village girls—those who cared to show themselves—waving good-by as if indeed to a bridal party. Compared with the great ideological marching songs of the modern world—the "Marseillaise," the "Internationale," the "Battle Hymn of the Republic," even the "Deutschland über alles" and the Fascist "Giovinezza"—the Legion's hymn seemed both a sickly and a tawdry statement. It is wrong, however, to sneer at such pop art of the soul. The great captains and conquistadors of the past raised and held together their armies not by loot or fear alone, but by their skill in manipulating the garish symbols and the tinsel myths that in the minds of simple men lend some measure of human dignity to a brutish life, a brutal death. The kind of military music that moistens nursemaids' eyes and makes their charges clap their hands has probably conquered more empires than the kind that makes the slave lift up his head or the scholar clench his fist. So it was to be once more in Spain. It would doubtless be oversimplifying the Spanish war in a new direction to say that the Nationalists' ultimate victory was the triumph of condottierism, rather than that of fascism, or clericalism, or feudalism, but it was unquestionably in great part the triumph of professionalism over amateurism.

The naïve Platonism that often underlies, however paradoxically, our most mechanistic interpretations of history exposed foreign liberals in Spain to the traumatic discovery, as Camus put it, "that one can be right and yet be beaten, that force can vanquish spirit."

196

(World War I, among many others, might have taught us to be less surprised, if we had not fallen into the self-glorifying habit of declaring that the victory won by our superior force was essentially a victory of the spirit.) My own experience in Spain, particularly watching the Foreign Legion in action, led me to a still more unsettling corollary: that men fighting for a bad cause can be braver than those fighting for a good one. The inexperienced Republican militiamen who faced the Legionaires and the Moors were anything but cowards; many of them, indeed, died like heroes, but the survivors, after bravely defending a position, would often turn panicky when forced by superior maneuver to retreat, and in an attack they rarely managed to equal the reckless dash of the Legionnaires. Eventually, the Legion's contemptuous disregard of enemy fire became something of a military liability, leading at times to unnecessarily heavy losses, but during the early months of the war, when the Legion was pitted against inadequately armed, sketchily organized civilians, this attitude was a major psychological and tactical asset. In heroism, as in most other things, the professional usually beats the amateur; courage, like skill, has to be systematically cultivated. That is an old lesson of history my generation has had to relearn, and Spain was one of the places where it was driven home.

Franco's Legionnaires were not merely professional heroes, however; like the Moors, they were also professional butchers. Covering the Nationalist advance on the Tagus front gave me numerous opportunities for confirming this observation and thereby—as we shall see a bit later—implanted in my mind a first seed of awareness in regard to another elementary lesson of history that contemporary thinkers often misinterpreted. The seed did not sprout, however, until some while after I left Spain; at the time my own powers of understanding were still partially numbed or distorted by the sheer horror—though a fairly mild horror by later standards—of the data they were called on to assimilate and comprehend.

Inevitably, I fell at times into cliché. There was, for example, the unfortunate, misleading simile of the mad dog, which I used in my talk to the American Club of Paris. The actual phrase referred back to an incident at the press headquarters in Talavera de la Reina during the last phase of the offensive to take Toledo and relieve the Alcázar. One evening an Italian photographer we all knew came back from a visit to the front. He was a Fascist, and like press photographers the world over, a fairly hard-boiled fellow, accustomed to violence and gruesome sights. What he had seen on this trip had shaken him, however. The Legion and the Moors were always in too much of a hurry to bother about removing the enemy dead—they took care of the wounded, of course, in their own peculiar fashion—and the Falangists, who were responsible for policing the rear and guarding the lines of communication, usually seemed to be too busy disposing of prisoners and suspects in their fashion to get around to the dead. Occasionally, the Falangists, or somebody, would sprinkle a little gasoline on the most visible corpses and set them afire, but this summary cremation did little more than give them a high glaze, making them look like painted wooden Indians in front of old-fashioned American cigar stores. They lay in this state sometimes for weeks, not only out in the fields and in the trenches, but along the roadside and sometimes in the middle of the road itself, so that one had to swerve to avoid them. The Spaniards never seemed to mind—I sometimes wondered if they hadn't a kind of African feeling about enemy bodies smelling sweet—but the effect on foreigners was occasionally drastic. There was one particularly unpleasant stretch of the road between Maqueda and Santa Olalla, two recently captured towns, that we had all been over several times, but the experience became no less disagreeable with repetition.

It was the repetition of familiar horror that had finally got under our Fascist colleague's skin. "I can't take any more of this," he said, after he had drunk down several generous portions of straight Scotch. "I am damned if I will make another trip along that road. Do you know how long those bodies have been there already? Why can't they bury them; why can't they do something with them?"

"Well, you know how the Spaniards are," someone said to quiet the Italian down; the room was full of officers of the Legion, many of whom understood English.

"I know how the Spaniards are," the Italian said, beginning to shout. "They are mad dogs, they are not men, they are just mad dogs."

I felt the same way myself, then and even later, but I should have known better. If any Spaniards were behaving at the time like mad dogs, they were members of the security squads, especially the self-appointed ones, on the Republican side, whose minds had become unhinged by the fifth-column phobia the Nationalists had done everything possible to plant in them. The same hysterical orgies of killing had broken out in some of the smaller towns and villages seized by the Nationalists in the first days of the insurrection, but now things were being done in a more orderly way, especially where the Legion operated, and there was no lack of method underlying what at first glance seemed mere homicidal madness.

Once several of us who were drinking with an officer on the staff of General Varela, the tactical commander for the offensive against Toledo and Madrid, asked him how many Reds he thought it would be necessary to shoot when the Nationalists got to Barcelona. It was a deliberately provocative question, but the officer, a captain of the Legion who had been crippled storming a Republican machine-gun nest on the walls of Badajoz at the head of his troops, took it in good part and tried to give us a sober answer. Pulling a sheet of paper out of his notebook, he made some rapid calculations. "About four hundred and fifty thousand," he finally announced. Of course, the Nationalists never got around to shooting more than a fraction of the enemies they planned to shoot, or talked about shooting, and the captain may merely have been illustrating for our unconscious benefit the Legion's slightly macabre sense of humor.

It was part of the Legion's method in enveloping an enemy position to leave a single escape route open when possible, thus encouraging his withdrawal, but to give no quarter to those who stayed behind, whether because they scorned retreat or because they were wounded and unable to run. They sometimes shot prisoners, for we occasionally came upon enemy bodies with their hands tied or wired behind their backs, but they preferred not to take any. The Moors

fought in much the same way—they and the Legionnaires instinctively employed traditional African, or simply colonial, tactics—but
occasionally with more fantasy. We heard many stories about the
picturesque mutilations they practiced on the enemy dead or
wounded. It was difficult to find incontrovertible evidence of such
outrages, though I did once see on the outskirts of Toledo the body
of a Republican militiaman whose head had been cut off—it was one
of twenty-four corpses attached to a single strand of rope. Of course
there was no proof a Moor had done that; I merely hoped it was a
Moor.

Of all those early battlefields in Spain, Toledo was the worst.
There was a savage fight before the militia broke and fled, with the
usual shootings and bayonetings in the heat of combat, more or less,
not to mention incidents. Then, after the hot shootings, there were
the cold shootings, more of them, even, than usual. When the correspondents were allowed to come in with Gen. Varela and Gen.
Franco after the Army of Africa had cleaned up the city, with some
help from the garrison of the Alcázar, we found the cleaning-up had
been thorough in some ways but not in others. Most of the bodies had
been dragged off the streets by the heels, and piled like logs in the
doorways of houses or tossed face down into the big mine craters
the Republicans had made when they tried to blow up the Alcázar.
It had not been possible to wipe up everywhere, however, and
though one could not have properly said in the old cliché that the
gutters of Toledo had run with blood, a surprising quantity of it
seemed to have trickled down certain of the steeper streets in rivulets
—who would have thought those young men had so much blood in
them?—and to have collected here and there in sticky puddles.
Homeless dogs were licking at some of these puddles in the ruined
Plaza Zocodover when we came into Toledo with the generals. (I
put the dogs into the lead of my story that night, but the censors
made me take them out.)

While some of us were being taken through the Alcázar, or what
was left of it, we saw four prisoners being brought in to an officer

of the garrison for questioning, and we stood awhile and listened. There was not much to listen to, actually. The officer cursed one prisoner and hit him in the face with his fist, and then he cursed and hit the next one, and so on. When he reached the fourth man he started all over. After about five minutes he ordered them to be taken out and shot.

There were two ways of looking at the incident. One way was to say that the men in the Alcázar had been under siege for some two months, were very near to starvation, had been shelled and mined, had had burning gasoline sprayed on them from fire hoses and, at the last moment, within a few hours of being relieved, had very nearly succumbed to a desperate Republican assault, so it was natural they should have difficulty in controlling their nerves on the day of victory. The other, more romantic way of looking at things was to recall that the officer who was punching helpless prisoners in the face was an authentic hero, one of a band of heroes, and that this, from his viewpoint, was one of the glorious dates of Spanish history. Therefore, he was befouling his own courage. I could conceive both viewpoints, but it was the romantic and therefore unforgiving one that prevailed in my mind. Perhaps that was the fault of my grandfather who had been a rebel, too, in his day, and something of a fanatic, but not, I imagine, the kind that hit prisoners.

The visit to Toledo with the generals crystallized certain convictions about the war that had been forming in my mind for several weeks. The distressing or nightmarish sights I had witnessed there might not in themselves justify any sweeping generalizations, but it seemed to me that they accurately expressed the esoteric doctrine of the Nationalist insurrection. The esoteric doctrine—or rather doctrines—of the Nationalists, as reflected in the public statements of their chief military and civilian notables, scarcely attempted, at least in those early days, to conceal their basic attitudes about the conduct of the war and the kind of society they meant to establish in Spain, but naturally refrained from spelling out all the implications of these ideas. When one talked informally with Spaniards, especially profes-

sional officers who knew the minds of their leaders but did not have
to weigh their words as official spokesmen do, one was frequently left
aghast both by their frankness and by what they were being frank
about.

The core of the matter was the definition of the enemy that
seemingly prevailed at all levels of the Nationalist movement. It
varied a little, naturally, in different sectors of the movement. Upper-
class Spaniards often appeared to view the enemy as constituting a
racial or even zoological entity. One officer-aristocrat who liked to
drink and argue with the foreign correspondents had even worked
out an elaborate private theory of the war, at once racist, historical,
and ecological, which interpreted it as a struggle between the indigenous Nordic *Weltanschauung* of the Iberian peninsula and the
Oriental one introduced by the Moors. The Nordics in the first
Reconquista had defeated and enslaved the Moors, who became the
urban proletariat of modern Spain and eventually embraced Marxism, an Oriental ideology that was, so to speak, in their blood. All
might still have been well, our aristocratic philosopher explained, had
it not been for the installation of public sewage in Spain. This unfortunate measure, by reducing the infant and general mortality
rates among the descendants of the Moors, had enabled them to
multiply dangerously, so that they were now on the point of over-
whelming their masters and imposing their alien faith on the land.
The new *Reconquista* upon which the Nationalists were embarked,
in addition to its military and political objectives, would have to
restore the biological balance in Spain. (How was left to our imaginations.)

Spaniards of more clerical outlook denied or de-emphasized the
biological factor in the struggle and portrayed it in more theological
terms as a crusade against heretics or infidels. It was not enough to
liberate Spain from the enemy; whenever possible he should be saved
from himself. Except in the case of the incorrigible enemy leaders,
shootings were to be carried out in a therapeutic rather than in a
punitive spirit. (Many condemned Reds, one was often told, asked to

make their confessions, and were generously allowed to do so before being put against the wall.)

Whether the enemy was viewed in biological, theological, or class-war terms, there appeared to be a consensus among the several varieties of Spanish Nationalist on one all-important point: The enemy was not an idea, a system, or a mere organization, but a practically homogeneous mass of people termed Reds, and in theory every Red had to be shot. That was the unofficial but fundamental code of the Nationalist rebellion.

Various influences, I knew, were at work beneath the surface to temper the inhumanity of this code, but up to the time I left Spain shortly after the fall of Toledo they had made little progress that I could detect. (I think I underrated the historically important role that the Falange was already beginning to play within the Nationalist movement in gradually substituting political for metaphysical criteria of the enemy, thus making possible the eventual reintegration into Spanish society of a good many rank-and-file "Reds.") The horrors I had witnessed were not the inevitable by-products of social hate that civil war always engenders, I concluded. They were rather the logical end products of hatreds nourished and structured by a world outlook that it was a grotesque understatement to call merely reactionary. Civilized German, Italian, Portuguese, and other foreign advocates of the authoritarian state whom I encountered in Nationalist Spain often seemed no less appalled by what they heard and saw there than I was myself. It was not merely the political and social superstructures of post-medieval civilization that were being challenged in Spain, but the foundations. My duty as a witness was clear: to reveal and explain the nature of the challenge.

Neither I nor any other correspondent with the Nationalist forces could give a full picture of the war as seen from our side and expect to stay in Spain. Supervision of the foreign press corps was getting closer all the time, and the censorship tighter. More and more pressure was being put on us to make our dispatches conform to the themes of Nationalist propaganda. There must be no mention of homeless dogs licking blood puddles, of enemy bodies with their hands roped, of wounded being dispatched and of prisoners stood against the wall. Such subjects might be discussed over drinks in a bar or restaurant without arousing suspicion—indeed they often appeared, sometimes graphically illustrated, in the Nationalist-controlled Spanish press—but they were not suitable for foreign readers. It was no longer permissible in our copy to call the Nationalists rebels or insurgents, or even Nationalists—though Spanish National Forces was all right—or the other side Loyalists or Republicans; Reds was good enough. Many of us evaded the censorship by handing in only routine messages or brief "flashes" for cabling from Nationalist territory and sending our important dispatches by car to France. Even in these uncensored reports it would have been suicidal to write with compelte frankness, and sending them out at all was getting to be a risky business.

Every correspondent who has to operate under censorship in a totalitarian regime faces a moral and professional dilemma. To remain indefinitely is to serve inevitably in some degree as an involuntary instrument of that regime's foreign propaganda. To leave or invite expulsion may let down not only one's paper but one's readers, who are thus deprived of the often vital information that an ingenious correspondent can usually manage to pass through even a hostile censorship. The greater the moral implications of the facts one has to suppress, the more painful the dilemma becomes. At times to keep silent is to lie, as Unamuno said in that heroic speech of his at the University of Salamanca, replying to a characteristically demented outburst from General Millan Astray, the crippled founder of the *Tercio* and the inventor of the famous *Viva la Muerte*. (The incident happened while I was still in Spain, but I only heard of it long after.) What I had seen at Toledo, it seemed to me, was something that it would have been a lie to keep silent about. I tried to compromise with my conscience for a while by sending out a long and uncensored dispatch on Toledo that was not a lie, yet not the whole truth. For another fortnight or so I wrestled with the decision that confronted me, until one night, in the course of a long drive from Talavera up to the French border with some more copy, there suddenly seemed to be no more problem and the decision took itself.

You can forgive men for acting like mad dogs in time of war, especially such a terrible, savage civil war as this one is, when there is so much savagery on the other side, too, and such terrible atrocities. What I can't forgive is acting like mad dogs and making speeches to the world about saving Western civilization. What I hate most, what any newspaperman hates most, is hypocrisy and cant and all kinds of lying propaganda. No matter how good a cause is, when I hear men telling lies about it, I want to expose those lies. I don't want to attack the Spanish Church or Spanish fascism, I just want to tell you how the Spaniards on that side are defending the Church and defending fascism, and then you can judge for yourself whether the propaganda that has presented the Spanish Civil War to the world as a great conflict of principles interesting the whole world is justified, or whether these principles are just being used on both sides as a convenient pretext for turning into mad dogs.

(AMERICAN CLUB SPEECH)

My decision to tell the uncensored story of what seemed to me a willful retreat from civilization in Nationalist Spain was not dictated solely by the voice of conscience. There was a grain of worldly and professional calculation in it. The fall of Madrid, if the capital fell, was still some time away, I knew, and for a while at least there would be a relative lull in the fighting. It was a good moment for a vivid exposé of conditions behind the Nationalist lines. No really complete and authoritative one had appeared in America since the war had taken on its new professional aspect. The evidence of large-scale and steadily mounting German and Italian intervention that I had gathered made it all the more likely that my series—it would have to be a series, of course—would prove a major scoop.

Col. McCormick dashed these hopes. He granted my request to be relieved of the Spanish assignment, but was strangely unresponsive to my suggestion of a dramatic series on conditions in Nationalist Spain. What interested the *Tribune's* readers, he indicated, was an exposé of conditions behind the Republican front. I should have no difficulty in collecting material for it from Spanish refugees in France. I knew what that meant.

In itself the Colonel's new assignment was legitimate enough. I had no illusions about how enemies, or suspected enemies, of the Republic fared in many areas held by the Loyalists. The crimes against the human person committed there might be less calculated than those on the Nationalist side; they were no less atrocious. The *Tribune*, moreover, had kept its readers better informed than the American public at large about the way in which the Nationalist forces were restoring Christian civilization in Spain: In addition to my own reports, it had earlier published a spectacular scoop by its Madrid correspondent, Jay Allen, on the mass shootings in the bull-ring of Badajoz after the Army of Africa took the town. It was fair enough to give the Loyalist conduct of the war some critical attention. As far as I was concerned, however, it was out of the question to substitute the series on Republican atrocities the Colonel evidently wanted for the one on Nationalist atrocities I had proposed. It was more than a matter of conscience in the usual sense; my daemon had spoken and its voice had been unmistakable. Somebody else would have to interview the refugees, and since the *Tribune* would not let me use its columns for the purpose I would have to find some other way of bearing witness to the abominations on which I had some personal evidence.

My Spanish ordeal had brought me a little closer to facing the heavy responsibilities which in an age like ours lie on anyone who claims the privileges of a free mind. I wanted to keep my job if possible, but I was now ready to sacrifice it, if necessary, to my good conscience. My real problem as an independent witness, I soon discovered, was a problem of communication. By October 1936 the war in Spain had begun to polarize opinion throughout the world. Col. McCormick's reaction to my suggested series was symptomatic. Just as liberals and socialists of every variety in all countries tended to equate the cause of the Spanish Republic with that of human freedom, so the adversaries of Roosevelt's New Deal or Blum's *Front Populaire* were increasingly coming to look on Franco as a palladin of traditional Western values (including, of course, property values.) Even staunch anti-Nazis like Winston Churchill or that fiery and authentic French patriot, Henri de Kerillis, the editor of the right-wing *Echo de Paris*, made no secret of their Franquist sympathies. Neither did Pope Pius XI, another outspoken enemy of German National Socialism. Col. McCormick was in good company on Spain.

My own private sympathies were with the Loyalists, but my public duty, as I saw it, was not to help the Republican cause; it was to expose a new betrayal of the West's traditions, at once more flagrant and more insidious than the Nazis', a kind of blasphemy against the very cause of man. Punishing the blasphemers or even preventing their triumph in Spain seemed less important than keeping the habit of blasphemy from spreading to other lands, and thus corroding all of Western civilization. It was a rather new; and therefore puzzling, point of view to many at the time. The readers or listeners I had to reach with my testimony were not those whose opinions had already been molded by Popular Front propaganda and their own dreams; they were those whose consciences were beginning to be befuddled by Nationalist propaganda and their own nightmares.

The invitation—quite fortuitous—to talk to the American Club on my experiences in Spain seemed to offer at least a partial solution to my problem. The club's members were for the most part respectable, prosperous, and politically conservative American businessmen in France. Regardless of the impression I made on my listeners, their luncheon table offered a modest but useful sounding board for getting my message to a broader audience. General Franco and Col.

McCormick would both hear of it, but I trusted I was out of reach of the former, and I was prepared to brave the wrath of the latter.

The reactions of both my distant listeners were somewhat unexpected. A day or two after lengthy extracts of my American Club speech, featuring the mad dogs, appeared in the Communist *l'Humanité*, the liberal *l'Oeuvre* and other French papers sympathetic to the Republican cause (a result of the friendly, if not wholly welcome, machinations of an old League of Nations acquaintance, an active member of the Wilsonian mafia, now converted into a pro-Loyalist mafia), my colleague Alec Small, who had replaced me in Spain, was arrested crossing the international bridge from Hendaye to Irún. Taken to the office of the redoubtable Major Troncoso, the Nationalist chief of security along the French border, Small was treated to a maniacal harangue and the information that as soon as it was finished he would be stood against the nearest convenient wall and shot as a self-confessed collaborator of that notorious Red propaganda sheet, the Chicago *Tribune*. Fortunately, it was lunchtime when Troncoso finished his harangue and the firing squad was getting hungry; Small's sentence was commuted to instant, ignominious, and perpetual expulsion from Spanish National soil. (The incident taught me one of the basic moral imperatives of our age, and perhaps of every age: When tempted by righteousness, think of your family and friends.)

Col. McCormick expressed his displeasure more temperately and selectively—TAYLOR WHATS THIS ABOUT YOU MAKING SPEECH AT AMERICAN CLUB PARIS QUERY—though he, too, in later years occasionally referred to Small's misadventure as if the unfortunate Alec had somehow been a witting accomplice in my transgression. To his characteristically worded cable I sent a respectful reply, enclosing a copy of my speech. The Colonel answered with an uncharacteristically lengthy letter beginning with a somewhat headmasterish reprimand and ending on a philosophic note. "In the case in question," Col. McCormick wrote, "aside from the facts of the matter, people in deadly combat are highly excited and afraid, and they are not judicial. You cannot act as though they were rational beings."

It was more of an explanation of his position than the Colonel usually deigned to give his underlings, and between the lines I thought I could detect a trace of bad conscience for his refusal to print my proposed series.

The fact is, neither of us was wholly right or wholly wrong. It was true, as the Colonel pointed out, that given the conditions prevailing in Spain, particularly the shootings of hostages, suspects, and passive Nationalist sympathizers by the Republicans, the Nationalists should not be censured too severely for their often irrational reactions. I made some allowances for the factor of war-madness in my American Club speech, but probably not enough. I likewise underrated the independence of the Spanish national temperament, the long-term role of the Church in moderating the excesses of Spanish totalitarianism, the no less important role of the Falange in substituting a political for a biological concept of victory, and above all the strange mixture of prudence and fanaticism in Franco's own character.

On the other hand, the cruelties and the horrors I had witnessed in Nationalist Spain could not be attributed, as Colonel McCormick and other apologists of the rebellion supposed, solely to the stress of the war. It was a disciplined hate that had launched the war in the first place, and one directed against many political, moral, or simply human values to which the Colonel was no less attached than I. The fourteenth century in which the Franquist crusade had its roots was not the same one in which the Colonel was said to have his heart; the Christian civilization that the Spanish Nationalists claimed to be defending was not the one to which both he and I belonged. It was not only Col. McCormick's political judgment that failed him in this instance, but his usually keen sense of news. The same delusion of normalcy that had often paralyzed the critical judgment of observers in Stalin's Russia or dulled the perceptions of those in Hitler's Germany blinded him, as it did many others, to what was happening in Franco's Spain. He mistook the moral malignancy that had developed there for a simple inflammation.

There were of course aspects of the problem to which I in my turn was insensitive, but this did not make Colonel McCormick necessarily right. In the first place, while I was sympathetic in principle to the sufferings of those Spaniards in Loyalist territory who were the victims of Anarchist mythology, Communist ruthlessness, or sheer mob hysteria, I am afraid I did not think very often about their fate. As Ernst Juenger justly remarks, the essence of being a victim of history is being an unfashionable one, and in the circles I mainly frequented at the time only the victims of Franco, Hitler, or Mussolini were in fashion. Later, when the Communists in Spain started liquidating non-Stalinist elements of the *Frente Popular* on a large scale, our sympathies broadened slightly. The countercurrent of democratic humanism set in motion throughout the West by the Spanish Civil War was an important event in the moral history of our age. Those members of my generation who in some way contributed to it have no reason to be ashamed of their role. It would have been still more glorious, however, if our idealisms had been a little less pretentious and intolerant, if we had tried harder both to understand the motivations of our adversaries, and to be more honest with ourselves about our own.

Moreover, in denouncing the Franquist secession from Western civilization I and many of my liberal contemporaries fail to foresee, or rather refused to admit, that it was not necessarily definitive. No doubt, a barbarized Spain within a Europe dominated by German neo-barbarism would have remained barbarian, or worse. Spain's apparent return to the concert of civilized, if not exactly enlightened, nations owes something to the sheer exhaustion of war, and more, probably, to the beneficent effects of twenty years' ideological containment by the overwhelming strength of the free world. No matter how one explains and qualifies the change today, the fact is that in 1936 many of us would not have believed it possible. Underlying our error was not only a curious pessimism about the Spanish people, whom we claimed to admire so extravagantly, but a lack of faith in the evolutionary possibilities of that versatile creature, man, whose cause we thought was our religion. It is true our error seemingly had no grave consequence; indeed between 1936 and 1939 it may have inadvertently saved Europe. But it is worth recalling, for the same basic fallacy, in a different context, today might destroy a world.

The Art of Recall

It must have been quite late in the afternoon when I left Talavera. A few miles out, there was a puncture near an olive grove, and I remember sitting in the dust under the filigree shade in the late heat and thinking about a number of things. I thought, it is only a puncture, but sometimes a small thing is enough. Then I thought a bit about the dogs in Toledo (I thought about them again several times later during the ride), and wondered about them. I tried imagining myself in a dog's mind, feeling puzzled and afraid of being punished, but with an old, stealthy feeling starting to come back. I tried to put these thoughts away then and thought of the chauffeur who was fixing the tire and wondered a bit about him. He was a queer-looking Spaniard, tufted and jerky, and sometimes he sounded as if he were talking in several foreign tongues. Usually I managed to catch a few words in almost any kind of Spanish, but not with him when he started talking that way. I was a fool in any case to let him take the fork through the mountains, especially after we had lost time with the puncture, so near to sundown.

Except for one being a little safer than another, if that mattered, it would have been the same on any other road, I suppose. Any road in Spain when the sun went down, or anywhere on earth. Any earth, in fact, or any sun. I recalled former occasions: certain evenings at the farm in Missouri, and perhaps some even earlier time in childhood I could not place exactly, and the night I camped on top of the cliff in New Mexico, and driving back in that strange red dusk after covering the tornado in Illinois, and other times that had not come yet, but would come, and come again, time without end, so it was no use dying. The same feeling could come on anywhere, of course, or any time, but it was most likely to come at a certain moment after sundown, expecially if the air was dry and moted, and the sky that dusky, inflamed red. It always subsided when night fell at last; this time, too, but then things turned queer in other ways.

That chauffeur was worse than a fool, I'm sure now he was a little mad, perhaps from fear. Somewhere in the middle of the mountains he tried to turn up a little canyon on what was obviously a cart track, leading nowhere. It was true there had been a big guerrilla attack, or series of them, just after dark I think, all along the road we had picked. A staff car had been shot up quite near a village and had run off the road down an embankment and was tilted over on its side in a little snowdrift of broken glass, splattered with blood. Several bodies had been thrown out, or taken out, and a crowd of peasants were standing around with guns and lanterns; presumably not the guerrillas. We stopped and I started to get out of the car thinking there might be some wounded, though it hardly seemed likely, but the peasants screched at us like banshees and almost seemed to threaten with their guns, so we drove on. I don't know what was the matter with them. After some of the other things I had seen in Spain the overturned car with the bodies alongside didn't seem horrible or frightening, but extraordinarily topsy-turvy somehow, and the whole landscape from then on appeared a bit unhinged.

Once, that lunatic chauffeur drove past a roadblock at the entrance of a village with the guards yelling and waving, and it was a miracle I managed to make him stop halfway down the main street, before we were riddled. Another time we stopped quite correctly at a roadblock and then it was the local militia who appeared to have gone crazy. Trying to read our passes with a small flashlight, they got everything mixed up in their minds and decided for no imaginable reason that the chauffeur and I were Red guerrillas escaping after the raids down the road. That is what they seemed to be saying, in any case, but I suspected they had really forgotten their own identities. Things were unsettled like that all along the way.

Not knowing what the chauffeur, or anybody, would do next kept me awake, though I was worn out from several nights without much sleep, and on account of what I had seen in Toledo, and from wondering what to do about it, though one part of my mind was constantly wandering off as if it were dreaming. Sometimes I seemed to be covering the continuing debate with myself about whether I should remain in Spain and go on watching the Army of Africa winning battles and taking towns, or whether I should stay out for good after this trip and really write about it. The way it went on it sounded quite like some of the debates I had covered in Geneva, with my honorable colleague saying this, and my good friend saying that.

More often there were simply pictures in my mind, and snatches of talk vaguely overheard as if from another room, and occasionally a kind of rudimentary puzzling about things that was not quite thinking. The subjects of these sequences were usually the dogs in Toledo, and some of the bodies along the roads that I now remembered were even more like the glaze on an overdone frankfurter than like that of a wooden Indian, and the girl prisoner who was said to have been locked up in a room with the Moors, and the nuns that the papers claimed had been stripped and then covered with tar and burned alive by the Reds somewhere or other, and similar Walpurgis-thoughts, suitable to the occasion. After a while I stopped being bedeviled by them, or anything, and simply sat in the car looking out at the moonlit landscape.

When we finally stopped at an unmarked crossroads we were somewhere north of the mountains but not recognizably near anything else, and our gas was getting low. The chauffeur was not sure we were lost, but neither was he sure that we were not. He no longer seemed sure of anything, not even of his fear of himself, and was merely dejected and resigned. I felt quite certain of where we were, though I don't think I had ever seen the crossroads before, and to prove it I climbed up a low ridge, some fifty, or at the most a hundred yards above us, and looked across the moonlit plain marbled with heavy boulders. In the distance there was another height, or so it appeared, and I thought I could make out a high wall with battlements and some dark towers or spires beyond it. It even seemed to me there were faint lights, though the hour was late—one or two in the morning perhaps. At any event it was what I had expected to see, though I was not quite sure whether it was Ávila or another ancient town, if it really was a town.

What mattered was that it was a splendid and solemn vision in the night, and that an unmistakable feeling was linked with it, as the other feeling was linked with the special moment after sundown, remembered, too, as the other was, from former and future times, but averring that all was well. I sat for a long moment with my back resting against a boulder enjoying the flood of peace, feeling the chill air and knowing it could not chill me, realizing the night was full of dangers and that none could harm me. I scarcely heard the chauffeur blowing his horn, but finally, knowing he would drive away and leave me if I stayed much longer, and not caring very much, but feeling it as a reluctant duty, I walked slowly back to the car.

The chauffeur had recovered the identity of his fear, and now I understood, more or less, what he was saying, despite his atrocious patois. I told him the right road to take, as if I actually knew it, and climbed into the back seat and slept most of the way to Burgos. There didn't seem to be any more problems, or anything left to worry about. One problem in particular that I had been turning over and over in my mind for many days or even years, had been settled for good. I had been wondering, without quite putting it in those terms, whether there was really anything in men, including myself, that checked us on certain occasions, or might check us, from turning back into lemurs. Now I knew, though I was as far as ever from knowing what it was.

10

The Delusion of Normalcy

*P*rague surely most beautiful and baffling of all Central European cities. A treasury of stone, like Florence or Venice, and
not so far behind them, either. At same time, living twentieth-
century capital and people's national shrine. Superb blendings of late
Gothic and enhanced baroque; of German order and Slavic sensitivity, with leavening of Italianate. Iron and leaden tragedies of history
transmuted into golden art. Longer I stay here more I am moved and
captivated, but less I feel capable of explaining what moves and
captivates me. Too many resonances.

Story of Nazi threat in Czechoslovakia, latest variation on Slav-
German theme—but are they the same Slavs, the same Germans?—
equally hard to come to grips with. Suppose my off-the-record interview with Beneš high spot of my visit so far, from professional
viewpoint, but can't help feeling vaguely disappointed by it.*

---

* Eduard Beneš (1884–1948) had been the chief assistant of Tomáš Masaryk,
the founder of Czechoslovakia, and had succeeded Masaryk as president of the
republic on Masaryk's retirement in 1935. He was in office at the time (November–December 1937) of my assignment to Czechoslovakia, which had been inspired by reports of a growing pan-German and National Socialist opposition
movement, headed by Konrad Henlein, among Czechoslovakia's large German
minority. (The so-called Sudeten Germans.) Beneš, who was regarded, especially in League of Nations circles, as a major European statesman, was driven
into exile by the Munich accords less than a year after I interviewed him. He

Personal impressions: as Gunther says, Beneš essentially a wrestler, a gymnast. Dominant traits: balance, control, alertness. Mind neither specially hard nor brilliant, it seems to me, but fast, springy, precise. Bullet-headed, piercing deep eyes deep-set under bushy brows, artisan's hands. Wiry movements; never fidgets. Alternately leans back to study you, forward to convince. Jumps straight into interview, inviting questions, awaiting your attack.

Beneš's view on international situation: Europe now at critical turning point. With breakdown of League over Ethiopian affairs and Spanish crisis, 1936 was fascists' year; 1937 started badly but tending toward equilibrium as it approaches its close. Will 1938 be year of democracies? B. seems to imply, though didn't quite say so. In any event, believes present equilibrium between fascist powers and democracies will last some time, two or three years most likely, thus giving democracies breathing spell. Important they put this period to use to seek general European détente. Depending on their success, situation in Europe will either take a definite turn for better or swiftly get much worse. Not very successful in drawing him out on this general statement, but did get one interesting hint: crux in relations between Nazi Germany and democracies is colonial question, says B. Adds that Germans have exhausted dynamism of Nazi revolution and must consolidate gains and reinforce their situation before any major new moves. Expects similar pause in Far East: Japs will halt expansion in North China, seeking armistice while they too consolidate. Mussolini busy digesting Ethiopian conquest. Little Entente ties stronger again, and has no doubt Little Entente powers would back France up in military showdown if necessary. Altogether favorable moment for democracies to explore constructive solutions.

Asked what solutions he envisaged for Sudeten problem, B. replied that of course this was a purely internal question which Czechoslo-

---

returned to Prague after the Liberation in 1945 and was reelected president, but became the victim of a second national and personal tragedy in February 1948, when a local Communist ultimatum, backed by Moscow, forced him to install a Communist government in power.

vakia not prepared to negotiate or even discuss with any other government. At same time fully aware Czechs themselves must grapple with it seriously. Basic principles governing Czech approach to problem stated by B. as follows:

(1) Duty to defend democracy in interests of German minority itself as well as that of Czechs; no ideological concessions possible. Hence no backing down to demands of [the Nazi-instigated] Henlein party, which B. feels is already losing momentum and will continue doing so until it has slipped back to its pre-Hitler strength.

(2) Practical concessions to minority on such points as giving them more jobs in state service until fair representation attained, getting German children out of Czech schools and into their own ones as fast as possible, no more building of Czech schools in German areas, gradual education of Czech majority to better attitudes toward their German fellow citizens, economic help for depressed industries in German-speaking areas, etc.

Regarding danger of European war in next years, B. soberly optimistic. Another war very unlikely in our generation, he thinks, because it would be too destructive for everyone; even Hitler must realize that.

Walked back to hotel from Hradčany Castle through old town after interview. Day cold but sunny, sheathing city in a golden haze. For once Prague really Zlata Praha, Prague the Golden, as the Czechs call it; they never need any special light to see it that way, of course; always glowing in their minds. Thinking over what Beneš had said, decided he was reasonable as always, but still am not wholly convinced. Like other liberals, B. tends to credit his adversaries with being as rational and civilized as he is himself. Maybe he's right about Hitler being too sensible to start a new world war, but even in short time I've been here I've learned enough about how the German minority feels to be pretty sure that the kind of palliatives Beneš was talking about won't be adequate to counteract Nazi influence on them. Like other Central Europeans all these people prisoners of their own past. Believe my friend K——— was sounder à propos of Nazi agitation in Sudetenland when he said to me, "The

World War is still being fought in this country, only military opera-
tions have been suspended for the moment." Yes, and the Hussite
wars, too, and the struggle against the Habsburgs and the age-old
clash of Slav and Teuton tribes. Only the Turks out of the picture
for good. The one Central European problem that has ever been
permanently settled.

(WORK-NOTES CZECHOSLOVAK TRIP

AND ANSCHLUSS: 1937–1938)

My stay in Czechoslovakia seemed merely interesting while I was
there; memory gives it the quality of a tragic dream. As a student of history I am not sure that Beneš, for all the drama of his life
—and death—was the ideal prototype of the doomed *homme de
bonne volonté* of the 1930's, yet in my mind's eye his stocky figure
and his shrewd peasant's face loom out of the two-dimensional
grayness of the past with an extraordinary density of presence. The
interview itself turns into an archetypal experience, a scene from
some modern Everyman's life story: the impressive, almost awe-
inspiring room that suddenly felt a little empty, the voice of wisdom
heard articulating the wisdom of Polonius, the chilling revelation of
a heritage of doubt, the distant view of spires and gables, golden in
the haze—Everyman's Jerusalem that each generation has to lose,
and regain for itself.

Few men, of course, realize the gravity of their predicaments,
starting with the predicament of mortality. No matter how black
things look, we tell ourselves that our salvation is somehow still at
hand. When hope is manifestly impossible, we anesthetize ourselves
with a comforting despair: Like the Viennese of the times I have
been writing about, we declare that the situation is hopeless, but not
serious. This failing of the human mind is so nearly universal that
dwelling on it adds little to our understanding of historic process; the
vanquished are generally unable to see their doom until it is upon

them, but the victors in their turn are no different. Hitler had no more realization of imminent disaster in June 1944 than Beneš had in December 1937 (or, no doubt, in December 1947).

What I have called the delusion of normalcy is a more specific infirmity. Essentially, it is the inability to see or the refusal to recognize a crisis situation of some kind when it has already developed. In December 1937, Dr. Beneš could not be expected to know that Hitler would invade Austria in March and formally demand annexation of the Sudetenland in September; Hitler did not yet know himself. Considering, however, that Beneš was widely regarded at the time as one of Europe's most astute statesmen, it seems remarkable that he felt so little sense of urgency about the general European situation, and especially that he understood Hitler's character so little as to imagine that some vague colonial concessions on the part of the French and the British would appease the Führer's appetite. (This particular bit of wishful thinking was perhaps based on reports the Czechoslovak government had received of a conversation, shortly before my visit to Prague, between Hitler and Lord Halifax, which had somewhat bemused that readily-bemusable British diplomat.) The truth is that by the end of 1937 the democratic nations were already confronted with a grave threat to their existence and independence; the very fact that a man like Adolf Hitler was the ruler of a nation like Germany under the conditions then prevailing was in itself an extreme crisis, calling for the most energetic remedies. Perhaps this had been true since 1933; by 1937 there was no excuse for not seeing it.

All the essential elements of the situation were fully known, and a few men had already fitted them together into a coherent picture of the Nazi menace. Among these men were prophetic figures like Winston Churchill and Charles de Gaulle, but there was also a scattering of clear-sighted observers, diplomatic and otherwise, such as André Francois-Poncet, the French Ambassador in Berlin, or William C. Bullitt, the United States Ambassador in Paris, or among my own colleagues, William L. Shirer, Edgar Mowrer, and Hamilton Fish Armstrong. Dr. Beneš, despite his great reputation, seemingly did not belong to the select company, any more than did Lord Halifax, or Léon Blum, or even Anthony Eden.

My Spanish assignment the year before, and the German ones before that, had opened my eyes to some aspects of the developing European crisis. I realized that it was a delusion to expect the Nazi and Fascist leaders to confine their actions or policies within the accepted norms of civilized behavior, unless compelled to do so by superior force. I was less confident than Dr. Beneš that they could always be counted on to act in accordance with the dictates of rational self-interest, or of what seemed to us their rational self-interest. He seemed not to be aware of the ruthless dynamic of National Socialism.

The delusion of normalcy, in my case at least, was primarily strategic. Since 1918 the world had come to regard the military preponderance of the victorious democratic powers as the normal state of affairs in Europe. For several years, however, the real power balance had been steadily shifting; by the end of 1937 only a slight further weakening on one side, a relatively small increment of strength on the other were needed to upset it. Yet scarcely a handful of experts realized fully what had happened and what was impending. The rest of us simply assumed, as men usually do, that whatever had been, still was, and must continue to be.

The core of our delusion was more magical than logical—that is precisely why it was delusive—but it was reinforced in our minds by various lucid fallacies or half-truths, the misread or ill-digested lessons of recent history. The World War, we frequently reminded ourselves, had conclusively demonstrated the superiority of defense over attack; in any new conflict the cards would therefore be stacked against the aggressor from the start. War itself, that is, war between civilized peoples, was in any case unthinkable. All Europeans still remembered too vividly the horrors of the trenches. The dictators might bluster and rant, but confronted with a new Armageddon, their troops would not march.

Underlying such misconceptions, I now think I can perceive the broader decline of historical culture—as distinguished from mere historical science—among the twentieth-century western elites that Ortega y Gasset denounced. It was probably no accident that many of those who were the most percipient about the nature of the totalitarian threat had a sense of history closer in some ways to that of the seventeenth century than to that of the twentieth. The limitations of such an outlook are apparent at times in both the policies and the writings of men like Churchill and De Gaulle, but they were nonetheless able to comprehend the outstanding historic phenomenon of the period better than many whose historical science was more sophisticated and whose minds were more contemporary.

The deficiencies in historical perspective from which I suffered were due to sheer ignorance rather than to any excess of scientism. Even so I was not wholly free from its superstitions. In every age there is a certain intellectual fallout from scholarly error against which even illiteracy is scarcely a protection, and while the brevity of my exposure to higher learning in America had perhaps preserved me from some of the befuddlements that often seemed to afflict Americans of my generation, I had not escaped all of them. In particular I tended—as many American specialists in international affairs still tend—to disregard or underestimate the human factor in power equations. Power itself I unconsciously equated with economic mass, which is only one of its ingredients and by no means always the decisive one.

The mechanistic naïvete of my outlook was complicated rather than offset by the equally naïve and equally dehumanized idealism that is another specific vice of American strategic and political thought. That idealism had been shaken, but not destroyed, by my experiences in Spain. Like many of my fellow countrymen at the time—and since—I had a superstitious confidence in the self-implementing power of ideas only a shade less strong than my belief in the magic of production graphs. Ideas cannot be stopped by bullets, I had been told since infancy, but only by better ideas, and undoubtedly our side had the best ideas; somehow they seemed to march together with the big battalions.

My 1937 assignment in Czechoslovakia did not immediately or

completely dissipate my own delusion of normalcy, but it proved something of a milestone in my education as a political reporter by helping to clear my mind of the misapprehensions that fed it. My confidence in ideas as soldiers of democracy, for instance, got a rude shock when I discovered during the assignment that certain ideas which hitherto had been most highly trusted within the democratic camp had in a sense defected to the enemy. Thus, national self-determination, which had been the chief explosive principle in Wilson's Fourteen Points, was now being damagingly exploited by the German Nazis to break apart the model Central European democracy that the Fourteen Points had helped to establish in 1919. Hitler's propagandists aimed their disruptive attack not only at Czechoslovakia's German minority but also at the large Hungarian one, and at part of the Slovak population as well. The republic's vulnerability to these tactics suggested to me that it was not quite such a model republic as the West supposed. By prevailing Central European standards, it was nonetheless a bastion of political enlightenment.

I interviewed Konrad Henlein, the chunky, spectacled, former bank clerk and gymnastic instructor who was the *führer* of the Sudeten Nazis, and then spent several days touring the main German-speaking areas of Czechoslovakia, conscientiously exposing myself to the propaganda with which his lieutenants bombarded me. The trip left me with no doubts as to the gravity of the Sudeten problem. Whether because of the original sin in drawing Czechoslovakia's frontiers as they had been drawn at the Paris Peace Conference, or because the Czechs in numerous petty ways had discriminated against the German minority, or because Nazi propaganda had poisoned their minds, considerably more than half of the 3,500,000 German-speaking citizens of the Czechoslovak republic were unquestionably disaffected. Offered self-determination, they would opt for Germany—even a Nazi Germany. From what I had seen of them, I doubted whether any Czech economic or other concessions at this late hour could win them over.

My observations in the Sudetenland had equally convinced me, however, that the Henlein party was, as the Czechs alleged, financed and manipulated from across the German border. To a reporter who had had the opportunity of studying the Nazi techniques of semi-overt conspiracy in the Saar and in Austria, the Sudeten pattern was unmistakable. Whatever Henlein's followers—and even Henlein himself—considered themselves, their party apparatus was Nazi. The orders it had been created to execute came, I was certain, from Germany; the interest it served was that of the Berlin government, not that of its membership. The Sudeten grievances had probably once been real enough, but the sense of grievance which the Henlein party cultivated among its supporters was largely synthetic. Within limits, it could be—and was—allowed to simmer or brought to a boil as Hitler's plans required. "So obvious Berlin using Henlein party to blackmail Prague government that no need to illustrate," I wrote in my notes on the Sudeten visit.

Clearly, such a situation reflected a perverse exploitation of the self-determination principle by the Nazis; yet their cynical abuse of the Wilsonian ideal did not appear to detract from the effectiveness of their propaganda. Good ideas, I concluded, could undoubtedly be made to serve bad causes. In political struggles, few if any ideas were good or bad per se; both their moral implications and their effectiveness in moving men depended largely on the immediate context. We must fight for our ideas because we think they are good, not count on them to fight for us. When they seem to, all too often we discover later that they were not the ones we thought we believed in. This viewpoint, as I have just formulated it, has gradually taken shape over the years, but it was my 1937 visit to the Sudetenland, I think, that planted its germ in my mind.

Book Four

A
Time to Seek
and
a Time to Lose

11

The Sweet and Bitter Years

N ow, in the spring of 1940 as I am writing, we are living an
unfinished nightmare that began roughly in the summer of
1938 . . .

*The war in Europe . . . was preceded by a long period of tension
and by three separate crises that the papers called war scares. I
covered all three of them, including the last fatal one, and they were
bad, but I can think of something worse. I mean the whole nightmare mentality of our epoch, the passionate ideological conflicts, the
political and social convulsions, the sunspot atmosphere of unease,
violence, terror, frustration and inner emptiness . . .*

(WORK-NOTES, 1940–1941,

FOR A BOOK TO BE CALLED

Awakening From History)

I close the folder, lean back in my chair, and shut my eyes, repeating an already familiar experiment. The images that follow
one another upon my inner screen relate to the last years before the
war, yet none of them evoke a sunspot atmosphere. There is sun, it
is true, in the sharpest of these imaginary snapshots from the past,

but it is a clear and youthful sun, falling upon the most untroubled meadow in the whole of France. A placid river winds beyond it; there is an ancient willow that Corot might have painted, a herd of tranquil, grazing cows, and standing somewhere nearby a young woman smiling; at least her smile is there, implicit in the quietness and verdure. I have no trouble in recognizing that landscape; it still exists: My wife and I revisit it from time to time, and on a bright day the same quiet smile still lingers over it. The meadow in question lies along the Seine below Paris, between Mantes and Les Andelys, where the river, out of sheer reasonableness as Jean Giraudoux says, describes a series of symmetrical loops beneath the high, gray-white chalk cliffs that line its right bank. Giraudoux had been one of the tutelary spirits presiding—along with Colette and Jules Romains— over the early days of our acquaintance, and walking or picnicking in this poetically reasonable countryside, or in the nearby valley of the Epte, was a minor act of piety for us, as well as a pleasant way to spend a Sunday. We also had a more practical reason for adopting the region; it was comparatively near Paris and easy to reach in a small car. During the crisis summers of 1938 and 1939, when one's vacation time was measured in hours, those were all-important considerations for a newspaperman in Europe. Even in May 1940 we still felt we could afford to expend some of our jealously hoarded gasoline ration on a last visit to our favorite cliffs, our favorite meadow, our favorite willow. Occasionally when I close my eyes and try to recall them, there is a small puffy cloud, the kind made by a bursting antiaircraft shell, hanging in the sky above one corner of the landscape. There is no pathos or irony in the image; the cloud seems as natural and appropriate as any other.

How is one to reconcile such mental pictures with all that "unease, violence, terror, frustration and inner emptiness"? There were, unquestionably, occasions when the political air in Europe became almost unbreathable, when the skies crackled with civil spite and the earth rumbled with herd passions. At such moments to take any part in public life, if only as an observer, might indeed seem a torment to the soul. There were other moments—more numerous, I think—

when participating in the great quarrel of the age seemed not only a solemn duty but a privilege of history. Some personal relationships were corroded by ideological or factional passion, others were deepened or enriched. The conflicts and disasters on the battlefield of the mind that were the essential theme of nearly all my non-journalistic writing in those days were real enough—real, that is, both as a private and as a collective ordeal; what I failed to record was the inner growth—my own and that of my contemporaries—which necessarily ensued, plus the emotional rewards that went with it. Learning to face reality is always a liberation and an enhancement, however bitter or tragic the reality may be.

In my case, there were other, more personal factors that helped to give my memories of those last years on the brink of world war their somewhat paradoxical coloration. One was that I shared them with Vreni; our marriage, even more than most, involved a kind of mutual adjustment to history, as well as to one another, from the very beginning.

It was the sanctions crisis that had first brought us together. From one viewpoint this was a banal enough occurrence. Young women who dream of journalistic careers often contrive—with or without international crises— to introduce themselves into pressrooms, which they think of as romantic spots; there they are likely to encounter reporters, who impress them as romantic beings. On occasion, the reporters in question may be tempted to respond no less romantically to such a flattering delusion, especially when they are in their declining years—their late twenties for example—and rightly or wrongly feel that a premature graying of the sensibilities is setting in.

The trouble in our case was that though the stars appeared to wish us reasonably well, every human obstacle that the mind can create for itself seemed to stand between us. I cannot imagine what we could have opened our hearts to each other about if it had not been Laval's iniquity or Eden's lapses. The fact that we were in agreement on such matters was not in itself significant; everybody in Geneva was in agreement—everybody one spoke to. What counted was the kind and weight of the feelings that went with one's opinions. One had to be earnest, but not rigid; one had to be able to laugh at it all, but only at the right moments. It would have been shameful not to protest such fascist affronts to human dignity as jeering at the Negus from the press gallery, but one might well hesitate to link one's destiny with that of a compulsive signer of anti-fascist manifestos.

By the end of the League's fall session in 1935, Vreni and I had already reached the metaphysical core of our problem, and with it the end of our agreement. She believed there might be hope for Eden —and inferentially for humanity—despite his, and its, repeated self-betrayals. I doubted it, and likewise thought it unlikely she and I would ever meet again, though we had agreed to continue our argument in Paris, where Vreni had decided to pursue her journalistic ambitions.

Again and again, it seemed that my pessimism was only too well founded. Vreni came to Paris after all, but fell ill and had to leave almost at once. During the long winter Eden proved himself to be the same old Eden, sanctions collapsed, and the League went from bad to worse, but incredibly Vreni returned in the spring, and together we witnessed the burgeoning of the French Popular Front, man's new hope. The outbreak of the war in Spain appeared to cut it short; Eden was up to his usual tricks, and Blum followed his sorry example. Vreni and I decided to marry anyway; then after my speech at the American Club, Col. McCormick exiled me to Rome for the winter, and we were separated once more. I never really believed our marriage would take place, but just when my hopes were at their nadir—I happened to be covering Mussolini's visit to Libya at the time—the Loyalist forces in Spain routed the Duce's Black Shirt "volunteers" near Guadalajara, and the future smiled on us once again. We rushed things through then, before some new disaster should befall humanity, or the leaders of the West discover new pretexts for betraying the common cause.

Shortly after our marriage we decided to find an apartment and furnish it. I had been living for years in furnished flats or hotels and I was a bit skeptical about a foreign correspondent having possessions, but Vreni said a place of our own was essential, and I concurred; I supposed there was some kind of female gland that determined such things. Eventually she found a suitable place for us, a small apartment in an ultramodern building, gleaming white and quite beautiful in its way, on a hilltop overlooking the Seine above St. Cloud. It was less than half an hour's drive from my office but the surroundings were agreeably rural and it had immense windows giving out upon the Bois de Boulogne in the distance. It was pleasant, too, to look down from the little glassed-in balcony where I had my worktable and see the barges gliding past on the river below us. We moved in just before I left on the Czechoslovak assignment.

Being married, of course, did not really solve any problems—it seldom does—but it modified our outlook upon the political scene in certain respects. I suppose that like most lovers and young home-builders we became for a while shamefully self-centered. My log-books for the period—up to the summer of 1939 in any case—are mostly laconic and intermittent notations of professional activities, interspersed with monosyllabically lyrical travel comments; my wife's are largely filled with listings of the restaurants where we had lunch or dinner, along with the names of the friends who shared our meals; sometimes a menu or the recipe for a favorite dish is included. A casual reader might conclude that it was gastronomic rather than political passion which ruled our lives. After restaurants, the most numerous entries were walks in the country, or trips we took together. Thus, on May 23, the date of the first alarm in what was eventually to become the Sudeten crisis, my wife's diary reveals that were hiking in the forest of Fontainebleau with Captain Flint. The captain was not one of my military sources but a newly acquired, city-born, six-month-old Scotch terrier whom we were initiating into the ancestral world of gorse and bracken, of hare and pheasant, of moss-covered boulders and heraldic beeches. Thus too, in that same month of May 1938, when we drove to Geneva to cover a particularly dramatic, if characteristically futile, session of the League Council, the things about the trip that seemed to me most worth recording were an evening stroll together along the ramparts of Vézelay; the look of the light fading on the queen mother of French cathedrals; the discovery on the way down of a restaurant for cattle dealers unknown to the Guide Michelin in a small market town lost in the region of lush marshes and birch-ringed ponds called Les Dombes; the slabs of thick, juicy, grilled Charollais beef we ate there that merited a star; and the delightful return visit on the way back. The restaurant, moreover, was decorated with bright, poetically naïve murals panted, apparently, by some local disciple of the Douanier Rousseau, which would have made ideal illustrations for Alain-Fournier's romantic classic *Le Grand Meaulnes*. (Unfortunately, in our enthusiasm over the food and the decor of our restaurant, neither Vreni nor I bothered to note down the name of the town in which it was situated. When we made a special pilgrimage to Les Dombes after the war to revisit our youthful find, some enchantment had confused the roads leading toward it and erased all the remembered landmarks; town, restaurant, *filet de Charollais* and naïve masterpiece had vanished into the same mists that swallowed up the chateau where the adolescent Meaulnes first encountered Yvonne de Galais.)

How frivolously nostalgic such small personal reminiscences appear in the light of all that has happened since, indeed in the light of what had already happened then! Vreni, of course, was mainly to blame for the far-too-frequent escapist interludes in our existence as a serious-minded anti-fascist couple. I had permitted myself enough distractions of all kinds, including romantic ones, before I knew her, but at least they had the strained or somber or violent character appropriate to the times. Except for certain of my purely intellectual interests, I had, in short, been living like a barbarian, like a Visigoth, as Vreni put it. Though not completely obsessed, as many American females are, by the passion for making over the male along more refined lines, Vreni evidently felt it her mission to subject me to the gentling Mediterranean influences with which she identified herself. I submitted to the civilizing process much of the time with reasonably good grace. Under her guidance I discovered—or rediscovered —those minor delights of the mind's palate and of the lucid senses that the French call *les menus plaisirs*. Even my taste in natural scenery changed. Previously I had felt strongly attracted only to the rugged, the unreal and the austere: the shifting dune, the Druid coast, the windswept mesa, the shimmering marsh, the naked, rolling down. Now, for the first time, I came truly to appreciate the more intimate harmonies of the Île-de-France, of Normandy, and of the Loire.

My reading habits likewise underwent a certain modification about the same time, History, sociology, and psychology had for some years largely supplanted my earlier, more literary bent. I continued to read or reread Dostoevski, Tolstoy, Stendhal, a little Balzac, and some English poetry or drama, mostly Elizabethan, but until I met Vreni, hardly any current fiction except Lawrence, Hemingway, and Faulkner. Though I had lived in France since 1928, and had some familiarity with the French classics, I was grossly ignorant of twentieth-century French literature, apart from Gide and Proust, of whom the former bored me and the latter gave me mental hives. Vreni, whose schooling had been mainly French, took a keen delight in the modern French writers, including some of the most recent ones. Naturally, I soon came to feel that I must be on terms of courtesy with these privileged visitants of her imagination. (In return I brought her the Sartoris family, the green hills of Hemingway, the awkward magic of Dostoevski's early *feuilletons* and, once we were safely married, the revelation of the Sonnets, along with some of Donne.) In time I suppose I might have got around by myself to Jules Romains, Saint-Exupéry, and Bernanos; Malraux was already required anti-fascist reading, like Silone and Orwell, and so in a sense was the fallen angel, Céline. Without Vreni, however, I might never have discovered *Le Grand Meaulnes*, and I would probably have gone on indefinitely snorting at Giraudoux and ignoring Colette. Reading these and other contemporary French authors with Vreni, and especially reading them at that particular moment in history, was a more important educational experience than one might have expected.

I doubt whether any of the French novelists I have mentioned will be counted in the future among the giants; it was not an age of giants, after all, only of monsters. All of them, however, undoubtedly deepened and broadened the range of my sympathies, caused me to love more lucidly what I had always loved and to understand better what it was I hated. Probably, they sharpened my sense of history, that is, my sense of history as tragedy.

I have been tempted on occasion—indeed I have sometimes yielded to the temptation—to maintain with Nietzsche that happiness was fit only for cows and democrats. The famous clause in the Constitution of the United States guaranteeing the rights of its citizens not merely to life and liberty, but also to the pursuit of happiness—the only truly revolutionary statement in an otherwise admirably prudent text—seems to me, even today, among the ambivalent legacies of the Age of Reason. Certainly, the European bourgeois ideal of happiness that Nietzsche had in mind rotted away on the battlefields of World War I. Undoubtedly, the commercially stimulated mystique of self-pampering that threatens to replace it in present-day America has perils both for the private soul and for the national security. Yet, whenever I look back on the brief span in my own life between my marriage in 1937 and my return to the United States after the fall of France in 1940, I find myself, despite certain reservations, standing once more on the same side of the fence with the cows and the democrats.

Even the seemingly frivolous enjoyments that loom so large in my recollection of the period—the *bistro* meals with friends, the outings in the nearby countryside that Vreni and I took together, the books and plays and films we shared—were an essential element in our preparation for the trials of all kinds that lay ahead.

The trials were not long in coming.

12

The Geopolitics of Appeasement

*B*efore I got back to my hotel dead tired at five o'clock that
morning, I said good-bye to at least two Austrians I am afraid
I shall never see again. There was nothing I or anyone else
could do to help them, and I knew it, and they knew it. They might
have tried to escape. It was easy enough that night and for several
nights later. The Czechoslovak border is only an hour by car from
Vienna—easy enough to take a taxi or even a train to within a few
miles of the frontier and then walk across the fields at night. I suggested that to one of my friends, but he just shrugged. It was something I just couldn't understand. Scores of Austrians who knew
themselves marked to die when the Nazis came in made no serious effort to get away—just went home and waited like rats in a cage. As
near as I could come to figuring the thing out, they just didn't feel it
was worth the trouble with Vienna gone . . . I don't think Americans
would have reacted in quite the same way. I think they would probably have found some use for all those extra cartridges in the clip
before firing the last one . . .

(EYEWITNESS ACCOUNT FOR THE

MUTUAL BROADCASTING COMPANY)

The forced *Anschluss* of March 1938—that is, Hitler's military occupation and annexation of Austria—was a less barbarous, or at least a less bloody, crime against humanity than those to which the wars in Abyssinia and Spain had already accustomed us, but for many members of my generation, and no doubt of the older one too, it marked a particularly sinister milestone on the road to a new Armageddon. There is a revealing difference between the tone of my reports on the Austrian tragedy, which I covered in Vienna, and that of my series on Czechoslovakia, written only three to four months earlier. In an eyewitness account I gave the Mutual Broadcasting Company of the chaotic night (March 11) when Chancellor Kurt von Schuschnigg resigned in compliance with Hitler's demand and the local Nazis took over the Austrian capital, I fear I even crossed the thin line between indignant reporting and incendiary editorializing.

It would probably be exaggerating to say that I felt the loss of Austrian independence as a private tragedy, but it touched me closely, more closely than any story I had as yet covered in Europe, except the war in Spain. I had been back to Vienna several times since my first visit in 1931, and my heart for some reason had put down roots there. After Paris and Rome, it was where I felt the most at home. I had both friends and memories of friendship in Vienna; a number of my friends were Jewish, and nearly all were bitter adversaries of Hitler. To stand by helplessly while they were driven from the city they loved, or to see them resigned to a miserable death, was not an agreeable experience. It was hateful to think of Vienna itself falling into hands so brutal and so corrupt. In the rape of this once glorious capital, I truly felt myself diminished.

More than anything else, I believe my reporting from Vienna expressed a reaction against the tide of appeasement, then running very strongly in Paris and London. Even before I had left for Prague the previous fall, part of the French press had launched a campaign in favor of reconsidering France's post-Versailles commitments. Hitler's reoccupation of the Rhineland in March 1936, it was belatedly discovered, had foreclosed all possibility of French military intervention in Central or Eastern Europe to uphold the territorial status quo: French losses in trying to storm the newly built Siegfried Line would be prohibitive. The argument was not completely fallacious, but the strength of the fortifications that Hitler had so far established on his western border was exaggerated in the appeasement press. I had found the Czechs particularly disturbed over an article by Pierre Dominique, a well-known Radical Socialist journalist reputed to have good contacts with Daladier's entourage. France, Dominique had argued, was safe enough behind the Maginot Line because it would cost Hitler 2,000,000 men to pierce it, but it would cost France just as many to break the newly built Siegfried Line; therefore, no effective military help could be given to Czechoslovakia or Austria in case of a German attack upon one or both of them. The only hope was for the Big Four—France, Britain, Germany, and Italy —to agree on peaceful settlements of Europe's territorial and other problems.

By February, French and British defeatism about maintaining the Versailles order in Europe had increased astonishingly. A former French premier, Pierre Étienne Flandin, had returned from a private visit to Berlin convinced, as he put it in talks with French officials and politicians, that France must reach an understanding with Hitler which would allow the Germans "freely to develop their energies in Central Europe and the Danube Basin." The idea was not new, but Flandin gave it both new weight and new respectability. A moderate center-right leader with important business connections, Flandin was too substantial a figure to be dismissed either as a Nazi gull or as a Nazi stooge; insofar as he was thought to seek inspiration abroad, it was from the Foreign Office and the City. He often professed admiration, no doubt sincere, for the statesmanlike doctrines and methods of Neville Chamberlain, whose star was then rising toward its zenith. (Eden, the chief adversary of appeasement in Chamberlain's cabinet, was maneuvered into resigning on February 21.) Though Flandin had been out of office since the Popular Front victory of 1936, I knew that it would be a mistake to consider him simply as a voice crying in the French political wilderness. Appeasement, plainly, was no longer merely a political slogan or a diplomatic theory; it had become an insider's speculation on the patterns of the future.

I was myself more influenced than I realized by the curious mixture of cynicism and self-delusion rife in the main democratic capitals during the early weeks of 1938. One of my first dispatches to the *Tribune* from Vienna, a few days after Hitler's brutal interview with Schuschnigg at Berchtesgaden on February 12, reflects the prevailing mood not only in Austria but in the West. (By threatening to invade Austria if his demands were not met, Hitler had bullied the Austrian chancellor into accepting a number of stipulations, including the appointment of a local Nazi as Minister of the Interior, that seemingly doomed the country's independence.)

"As matters stand now," I wrote, "there is only one policy for Austria—and eventually for Czechoslovakia—to follow. This is to tip the cap and say yes, sir, when the Führer gives orders. If he wants to, Hitler can put every Austrian and every Czech into uniform— some kind of uniform. He is apparently going to tell them that if they carry the ball for Germany in foreign affairs he won't insist on the uniforms. That is a good bargain for them. They will accept it and so will other denizens of these parts until some new development has altered the European picture."

Like many other people in Europe at the time I was already resigned to the inevitable. The inevitable, however, as we pictured it to ourselves, did not mean an outright German occupation of Austria, much less of Czechoslovakia. As my dispatch implied, it was supposed that Hitler would content himself with making vassals of the Austrians and the Czechs, leaving them nominal independence and a measure of internal autonomy. This extraordinary delusion was not only current in Vienna—encouraged by Schuschnigg's equally extraordinary reluctance to reveal what Hitler had actually said to him at Berchtesgaden, and thus to mobilize world opinion in support of Austrian independence—but apparently in London and Paris. Chamberlain, Halifax, Flandin (and no doubt the current French premier, Camille Chautemps) shared it; there is some evidence that even Mussolini did.

If Hitler had contented himself with forcing Schuschnigg from office and imposing a cabinet of local Nazis, the appeasers in London and Paris would doubtless have discovered numerous excuses for his action, however brutal. At Berchtesgaden, Schuschnigg had agreed —under duress—to a certain course of action. In calling a plebiscite on Austria's independence he had unquestionably violated the spirit if not the letter of this agreement. It was natural the Führer should be angry, and when angry it was well known that he was sometimes impulsive, even excessive, in his reactions. The wretched Schuschnigg had thus tempted fate, and the appeasement mentality had little sympathy for those who tempted fate.

Sending the German Army into Austria after Hitler's essential demands had already been accepted in Vienna and then formally abolishing Austrian independence were more serious misdeeds. Hitler, it appeared, had once again gone out of his way to shock opinion in the democracies; the fellow seemed to positively relish the indignation his behavior aroused, with never a thought for the embarrassment it caused his friends and apologists abroad.

There was controversy, of course, over whether or not the whole operation had been coldly plotted from the first. We know today that while Hitler probably intended all along to absorb Austria into the German Reich at the first good opportunity, the 1938 *Anschluss* was improvised from one step to the next to a degree that few political observers at the time would have believed possible. If we had known the whole truth we might have been even more alarmed than many of us were. All too often we suspected a devilish calculation where in reality there was a still more hellish chaos.

The lesson that my generation learned when Hitler finally sent his tanks rumbling across the Austrian border is one that we can never wholly forget. It was one thing to argue in the abstract about the implications of German hegemony in the valley of the Danube. It was another to stand on a balcony of the Bristol Hotel in the precocious March sun watching the victory parade of primitive steel monsters (with those other monsters that looked like healthy, blond young men half-emergent from their open turrents), gazing down on the crowds of cheering Viennese massed along the Ring, faithful in their very fickleness, and witnessing once again the materialization of the familiar, sinister, comic figure in the brown shirt, with the stiff automaton's arm, out of some recurrent nightmare that seemed to follow wherever one went.

"The Platonic protests by Paris and London against the use of armed force in making Hitler's dream of *Anschluss* come true do not mean much," I cabled (or telephoned) the *Tribune*, "but what is grave is that the European equilibrium has been upset. History teaches that such upsets inevitably lead to war, and the wind which blows over Central Europe tonight is a war wind. The changes in the map of Europe which yesterday's ultimatum ushered in are far from finished."

I was back to Bismarck, or more accurately, to Grotius and Vattel, supported in all probability by the more immediate influence of John Wiley, the United States Minister in Vienna at the time of the *Anschluss*, a brave and clearheaded, if traditionalist, diplomat. We all turned out to have been right, of course, but were we right for the right reasons?

I have asked myself the same question a number of times since that troubled spring of 1938. Today, as I reread these words in another troubled spring, I feel a good deal less certain of the answer than I used to. If there are laws of history as there are of physics, there seem to be discontinuities in both. Wilsonians, at least those of my youth, believed that the balance of power was one of those self-fulfilling axioms of Old World diplomacy that were largely responsible for the tragedy of 1914. Perhaps they were right. But the fiasco of appeasement in 1938 taught my generation that disregard for the strategic and psychological realities underlying the doctrine can be no less fatal to peace.

A few days after Hitler's triumph in Vienna I was en route to Prague once more. Vreni—who had joined me in Vienna on the eve of the annexation—and I had driven to Bratislava, just within the Czechoslovak border, and then on to Brno, where we had taken the train. The warm sun of March fell on newly plowed fields, and the fruit trees were beginning to bud across the rolling Moravian countryside, promising the fullness of summer, but at first I scarcely noticed them. The drive to the frontier had been tense because we were accompanying my friend, Marcel Fodor, and his wife, Martha, to see that they got across safely, and the parting with them had been a sad occasion. I thought about what life in exile from Vienna must mean to them, and from time to time I thought about what continuing to live in Vienna would mean for other friends, if they stayed alive. There had been no real violence in Austria because once Schuschnigg had fallen there had been no resistance, and the prompt arrival of the German Army and SS units had put an end to the rowdyism of the local Nazis. Himmler had arrived even before the formal proclamation of the *Anschluss* to take personal charge of the police cleanup, and Julius Streicher had flown in to organize the anti-Semitic campaign in a methodical Prussian way. There was to be no more haphazard hating or persecution in Austria, no settling of purely private scores, no looting of Jewish shops or casual beatings in the street; everything would be legal and orderly, according to plan. The day of the Eichmanns was at hand.

Too preoccupied by such ruminations and forebodings to enjoy the spring landscape with a poet's eye, I nonetheless studied it with a reporter's, particularly in the border area between Bratislava and Brno, noting the marching columns of Czech infantry, the trains of artillery, the occasional khaki-colored figure sprawled on a hillside behind a light machine gun. As I expected, the Czech Army was taking the *Anschluss* seriously. I would have some good copy for Colonel McCormick when I reached Prague. In the meantime I had a new thought for myself. Henceforth, the possibility of maintaining a minimal level of decency in social, and even personal, relationships in Czechoslovakia, and perhaps throughout the whole lower Danubian valley, depended on whose army controlled the Moravian Gap. Six and a half million Austrians had been condemned to live in permanent betrayal of themselves and of each other, not so much because of their own weakness or the shilly-shallying of the Western democracies in the recent crisis—by then Austrian independence was already doomed—but because Germany had been allowed to re-militarize the Rhineland in March 1936.

I had been in Paris on the day Hitler marched his troops into the zone still demilitarized by the Treaty of Versailles, and had covered for the *Tribune* the debate within the French government over whether or not to oppose the German move by force. The risk of French firmness leading to all-out war would have been slight, and if war had occurred a speedy victory for France and her allies seemed nearly certain, with the elimination of the National Socialist regime as its reward. Merely forcing Hitler to withdraw by a show of strength might well have proved fatal to his prestige. These argu-ments, which in hindsight look so unanswerable, had been put for-ward by the "hawks" of the day within the French cabinet, but the bureaucratic conformism of the French General Staff and the tragic mediocrity of the Sarrauts, Flandins, Chautemps, and other more or less begrimed doves who at the moment were in power had prevailed.

I had been almost completely blind myself to the broader implica-tions of the hectic, semi-public, all-day discussions in the French government. Though I was already a convinced anti-fascist, I was still at heart a pacifist. All I could see in the story—surely the most momentous one I had covered up to then—was that attacks of "war fever" had flared up intermittently during the day in Paris, but had happily subsided by nightfall.

With Austria's freedom lost and Czechoslovakia's threatened—I would not yet admit doomed—the real historic dimensions of the Rhineland crisis two years earlier had become apparent.

13

The War in the Mind

*P*ropaganda is many things, but . . . it stands today chiefly for
a kind of magical warfare, aiming at dominion over the souls
of men. By propaganda, the will of one man or of one group
of men is substituted for the wills of other men, without their realizing it. A spell is cast over them, the sword drops from their hand, or
is snatched up to transform defeat into victory.

(EXCERPT FROM DRAFT INTRODUCTION TO
The Witchcraft of Nations, UNPUB-
LISHED, WORK-NOTES, 1938)

Life in Paris in the last two years before World War II was neither
all crisis nor all home-building and *bistros* and Giraudoux. My job
as correspondent for the Chicago *Tribune* was both more demanding and more frustrating than ever before; I was beginning, too, to
try my hand occasionally at magazine writing and at radio journalism. In the autumn of 1937, shortly before I left on my Czechoslovak assignment, the idea came to me to attempt a study of
propaganda. Exactly how and when the project germinated in my
mind, I can no longer remember; it must have been quite hazy at the
beginning. My original intent, as far as I can recall, was to apply to

the contemporary international scene some of the viewpoints of the American pioneers in propaganda analysis, like Harold Lasswell and Leonard Doob, whose work I had recently discovered. My own mood of disillusionment after the collapse of the sanctions crusade had made me particularly receptive to the influence of the debunking school of historians and social thinkers then ascendant in the United States.

What I saw of Nazi techniques of propaganda and subversion during my Central European assignments both sharpened my interest in the subject and altered my approach to it. Exposing the petty trickeries of press officers and pressure groups no longer seemed an adequate objective. It might be true, as I put it in one early note, "nothing ever what it seems" and, concerning distortion of the truth, "democratic governments just as bad as totalitarian," but after witnessing the skill with which Goebbels and Hitler had befuddled world opinion and paralyzed the Austrian will to resist, such statements no longer sounded adequate. It was hard to avoid the feeling that there was something akin to witchcraft in Nazi propaganda, and in one way the analogy was not wholly fanciful. The primitive witch doctor had been, in fact, the first propagandist. In my book I proposed to trace the history of his evolution up to the present.

The project was foredoomed in the ambitious form I conceived it, but the work I put into it turned out to be rewarding from several points of view. One immediately useful by-product of my study was that it caused me to read Hitler's book, *Mein Kampf*, which I had only skimmed, more closely than I might otherwise have done. I never had any doubts about the gravity of the Nazi threat after finishing it. The argument then going on in the United States and in Europe as to whether or not *Mein Kampf* should be taken as a blueprint for conquest seemed irrelevant. The author might or might not be expressing his literal intent (though as A. J. P. Taylor rightly observes, the literalness of Hitler's thought was one of the most dangerous things about him); he could not help revealing his compelling goals. To Hitler these goals unquestionably were not negotiable; destiny never is.

I had underestimated Hitler, I decided after studying him, and so had most of my anti-Nazi friends. He evidently had a murky mind, not a shallow one. Hitler's dreams—or delusions—of anachronistic conquest had to be taken seriously because he appeared to have both the regressive kind of character and the freshness of strategic intuition that matched them. In certain ways he was more in tune with his age than the rest of us.

My propaganda research had led me at one point to delve into the history of colonial wars, and this reading had not only sensitized me to the psychological element in all warfare and conquest, but had called my attention in particular to the role of what might be termed cultural surprise, which was often decisive in clashes between European and "native" forces. Usually it was the discipline, the advanced weaponry, and the sophisticated tactics of the White Man that threw his adversaries into disarray, but from time to time, especially in guerrilla campaigns, the elusive, unpredictable hill or jungle fighter, with his crude arms and his blood-chilling cruelties—so different from one's own—succeeded, at least temporarily, in demoralizing the colonialists. The examples were even more striking if one broadened the field of inquiry to include the occasions when Europe itself had been the victim of Afro-Asian colonialist expansionism. Technologically, the heavy armored cavalry of the Middle Ages in the West represented a more developed stage of civilization than the mounted archers of Genghis Khan, yet the latter almost invariably routed the former whenever they clashed. Everything about the demonic raiders from the East was disconcerting to a Christian warrior: their tactics, their treachery, their toughness, the cowardly way they turned from battle, the animal ferocity with which they fought when cornered, the indiscriminate ruthlessness with which they slaughtered knight and villain, their equal contempt for the laws of God and the rules of strategy. The analogies between the military doctrines of Genghis Khan and Hitler were striking; those in the behavior patterns of their respective victims perhaps even more so.

In the end, it is true, Hitler not only overreached himself, as most conquerors do, but contributed to his own downfall by a series of crude blunders and by fits of indecision at critical moments. In the art of conquest, however, he displayed real flashes of innovating genius. Both the concept and the tactics of modern political warfare* owe a great deal to him. Hitler was one of the first to see and to demonstrate that in our century, under certain conditions, the strategic will of a powerful nation can be broken without the direct use of force by means of political, psychological, economic, and other similar pressures.

Munich, of course, was his masterpiece, though its success was probably due more to the unwitting cooperation of his adversaries than to conscious planning. It is the only example, so far in our time, of a major political warfare victory achieved entirely without military intervention or internal coup d'état. The precise combination of circumstances that made such a triumph possible may never occur again. Nonetheless, Munich contributed more than a new term of abuse to the vocabularly of my generation; it marked another vital stage in our political education. Thanks to my study of propaganda, as well as to my recent assignments in Central Europe, I had a head-start, but I still had some drastic unlearnings to master.

I realized in a dim way that Hitler's final aim was not merely to recover the 3,000,000 Germans of the Sudetenland for his new Reich, but to destroy Czechoslovakia as an independent nation, and to break the spirit of the Western Allies in the process. Naturally, I looked on the French and British appeasers as his witting or unwitting accomplices. In trying, however, to explain to my editors. or readers how this crisis was different from other diplomatic conflicts the world had seen, and why the new Nazi techniques of psychological assault

* Political warfare, psychological warfare, and propaganda warfare are sometimes used interchangeably. In what seems to me the soundest contemporary usage, political warfare is the most comprehensive term, exploiting all non-physical means for breaking an adversary's nerve or will. It includes propaganda, of course, but also other psychological manipulations, along with various techniques of subversion—e.g., personal bribery or blackmail of key individuals —deception, that is, misleading the adversary as to one's real intentions, and various forms of military or diplomatic intimidation whether practiced against whole populations or merely their leaders.

were a real menace to the democracies—including ultimately the United States—I was not, I am afraid, very convincing. Probably I still fell short of total conviction myself.

The friends or informants whose opinions carried the most weight with me insisted that Hitler was not merely bluffing (and even today one cannot be quite sure they were wrong). The real issue in Paris and London was, therefore, whether to accept diplomatic defeat or to risk a war which at the moment the Western Allies were technically ill-prepared to fight. There were men of good heart as well as of normally good judgment who believed it might be wiser to yield, in order to arm for more effective resistance later. In retrospect, it now seems to me that even such lucid defeatists were wrong, but determining the lesser evil was not at the time as easy as one might suppose. Hitler was demonstrating the effectiveness of what we would call today a strong counter-deterrent force in paralyzing the reactions of an eventual victim to a peripheral or indirect agression.

I myself felt the impact of the counter-deterrent principle—without recognizing what it was—every time I thought of the bombs falling on our apartment in St. Cloud. Decorating and furnishing the apartment had been a challenge to the imagination, especially as we had little money to spend on it. The enterprise had developed well on the whole; Vreni and I were pleased both with the result and with each other. Progress, however, was naturally slow; there was still much left to do. When the September crisis came we were in the process of installing a rather ingenious system of indirect lighting, and we were made aware of how white and conspicuous our building was, even at night, and of what an admirable landmark it must be for locating the great Renault automobile works, only a mile or so up the Seine, where most of the French Army's tanks were produced. The heart of Paris appeared, if anything, less exposed.

At the peak of the crisis I packed up my notes and a few books and moved them to the emergency office I had taken with several other correspondents near Saint-Germain-en-Laye. If the bombing got too bad, Vreni and I could sleep there, and I could file the story of Paris being destroyed. Thus, I did not really have much to worry about. I worried a bit all the same, and in the last day or two before Munich I often thought about our pleasant apartment being turned into rubble along with Paris itself.

(In 1938 Hitler scarcely had the capability to destroy Paris from the air—certainly not at the same time his ground forces were storming the Bohemian bastion—but Nazi propaganda had worked skillfully and effectively on the Western public mind to transform the real menace of the Luftwaffe into a magic dread. This irrational fear of the enemy on the part of the British and French peoples, especially the latter, was one of the reasons why the Munich settlement proved a psychological disaster for the West.)

In its immediate military and diplomatic consequences Munich was probably as significant a victory for Hitler's Reich as Sadowa had been for Bismarck's Prussia. France's gradual, twenty-year decline as paramount power on the Continent had reached an end; she was no longer paramount, and scarcely even a power. The issue for France was no longer rank in the European pecking order, but survival.

Some of the ill consequences of Munich became apparent only much later, but many were visible almost at once, especially in France. My own first spontaneous reaction to the news that agreement had been reached in Munich was the same feeling of "cowardly relief" to which Léon Blum confessed. Agreement meant no war, no bombs. I could take my papers and books back to St. Cloud and resume work on them, sitting in the morning sun on that pleasant balcony above the Seine.

The discovery soon came that relief had been unwarranted, as well as cowardly. Few foreigners who witnessed the political, moral, and social disarray of France in the weeks after Munich are likely to forget the spectacle. "After Munich, France as a nation seemed to be stricken with something like collective locomotor ataxia," I wrote a few months later, and, looking back on it, I do not believe I exaggerated much. The psychic wounds of Munich were probably deeper than I realized.

My own morale was weakened for a considerable time. The post-Munich period subjected my faith in democratic leadership, in the kind of political elite that democratic society produced, in the viability of democratic institutions, and even in the democratic ideal to a sterner test than any it had yet undergone.

One of the things that helped prevent disillusion from crystallizing into ideological apostasy or complete cynicism was another assignment in Central Europe that I undertook a few weeks after Munich —this time in Hungary and Yugoslavia, with stopovers on the way back in Rome and Zurich. The timing could hardly have been better. It proved to be one of those between-the-acts moments in history when the curious spectator can, as it were, stroll around backstage and talk casually with members of the cast whom one normally sees wearing their official masks and striking postures to impress the audience. Few of the persons I interviewed played any important role—the real show after all was in Berlin—but their viewpoints were often extraordinarily enlightening.

The young Nazis or Nazi sympathizers I encountered, for example, were all bubbling with a self-confidence that was itself highly significant. "The democracies are finished," one of them told me in Budapest. "The democratic conception of war is old-fashioned. The fascist conception is modern . . . Our wars are won before they start." Having just watched Hitler win a war before it started, and without firing a shot, I could not help but be impressed when I heard *Der Führer's* Central European—or Latin—admirers brag about taking over the world with his invincible new technique of bloodless warfare. "Blowhards," I wrote in a letter to my wife, "but some of them give me cold chills down the spine." I think it was in the course of this assignment that for the first time the thought of Hitler as a potential world conqueror entered my mind. There were, I realized, more important tasks for an American correspondent in Europe than sneering at Neville Chamberlain's umbrella or being ironic about the rottenness of the French bourgeoisie.

One such task, inspired by my study of propaganda, was to discover and expose the mechanisms by means of which the Nazis were exploiting in Central Europe the political and psychological fruits of their victory at Munich. I was exceptionally lucky in my investigations, and what I learned from them made a lasting impression.

"The real German menace in the Danubian countries," I wrote in a series of articles summarizing my findings, "is the revolutionary influence of Germany on the political and social life of its vassals. Slowly, but remorselessly, they are being Nazified . . . The organizing work of German agents does not cease when Nazi economists by the skillful juggling of frozen credits and by exploiting the greed of individual capitalists have got a stranglehold on the foreign trade of a country, and when Nazi diplomats have concluded a political alliance with the government of that country.

"On the contrary, the real work only begins then. Friendly business and diplomatic relations have opened the door to German propaganda. German advertisers contribute to the support of local newspapers, and these in return are asked to publish Nazi propaganda articles. Cultural organizations set to work helping the natives to adapt Nazi ideology to local taste. Anti-Semitism is one of the most effective mental disciplines for achieving this purpose, since it is almost impossible to imagine anyone being strongly anti-Semitic without being pro-Nazi."

In Belgrade I had actually had a glimpse of the wheels turning. I was sitting in the cluttered little office of a senior editor of *Vreme*, the semi-official organ of the Yugoslav government, when another man walked in and with a few curt words in Serb handed him some sheets of copy. When the editor started to protest, the other man simply shrugged and walked out. "That was our business manager," the editor told me. "And this is what I am going to have to print." He handed me a clipping from a German newspaper, a pseudo-sociological explanation of the Jewish menace to Western civilization, explaining that the "must" copy he had just been given was a translation of it.

In all the countries I visited I found a strong undercurrent of resistance to the Nazification of national, social, and cultural life. It was fortified by the widespread indignation among civilized Europeans over the pogrom in Germany that the Nazis had instigated in retaliation for the assassination of a German diplomat in Paris by a young Jewish refugee. Only a limited number of German Jews had actually been slaughtered during the pogrom; but some of the killings had been particularly bestial, the evidence that the outbreak had been systematically organized at the highest party level was overwhelming, and the whole affair had marked a spectacular aggravation in the barbarization of the German people. The revolt of the European conscience as I had heard it expressed during my trip sometimes came from the most unexpected quarters. Listening to the sense of outrage voiced by certain Hungarian aristocrats, Serb politicians, Swiss businessmen, even sometimes by fascist diplomats or journalists in Italy, I realized more clearly than ever before that what Hitlerism was threatening was not merely the democratic pattern of society to which I remained deeply attached, despite the weaknesses in it that Munich had so cruelly brought to light, but the permanent values of Western civilization itself.

Underlying the protests against totalitarianism, I reported in my *Tribune* series, was a kind of "naïve rediscovery of the importance of all things that lend security and dignity to individual life: respect of political and property rights, codes of behavior, culture and religion." Perhaps the naïveté was my own.

It was, after all, the moral and human implications of Hitler's entry into Prague on March 15, 1939, that made the date a fateful one. From the strategic viewpoint, the dismemberment of Czechoslovakia and the proclamation of a German protectorate over Bohemia-Moravia changed nothing in Europe. The violation of the pledge given at Munich to respect Czechoslovakia's independence was flagrant—if less cynically premeditated than we supposed at the time—but a mere breach of diplomatic faith on Hitler's part would not have sufficed to reverse the tide of appeasement. It was the realization that owing to the cowardice and blindness of Western leadership some 9,000,000 Czechs had been delivered into an anachronistic form of collective bondage under a brutal, neo-barbarian despot that produced an explosion of public indignation in the capitals of the West. And it was

251

largely the pressure of this indignation that pushed the French and British governments, especially the latter, into the series of diplomatic countermoves, culminating in the British guaranty to Poland, which were to make war virtually inevitable.

In terms of political and intellectual maturation the six months from Munich to the final dismemberment of Czechoslovakia were hardly less important than the previous six months had been. Naturally, they made me feel even more urgently that my first duty as an American correspondent in Europe was to help my readers realize the seriousness of the Nazi threat. The period likewise added substantially to my own understanding of the threat. Up to then, when I heard European anti-Nazis speak of the ethos and institutions of National Socialism as a form of neo-barbarism, I had taken the expression as an illuminating metaphor; now I realized it was a literal description of an extraordinary sociological phenomenon. Not all Nazi attitudes, even in the political and cultural areas, were barbarian in the strict sense, but a number were; the National Socialist mystique of race was, of course, the most flagrant example. Hitler's ideas about war and conquest as social institutions, in fact his whole concept of what could only be termed intertribal relations, along with his theories of propaganda as a magic arm, seemed to me almost equally striking examples.

In technology, in bureaucratic organization, in social controls, even to a considerable degree in science and art, the German people under Hitler remained members of a high civilization; in many other areas their patterns of thought and feeling appeared to have regressed —or to be regressing—to a primitive level—a level I had recently studied as background for the book on propaganda in the works of the French anthropologist Lévy-Bruhl. The new barbarians who were menacing the citadels of Western civilization were self-made and in a sense part-time ones, but that made them all the more dangerous.

Many things about the rise of the Nazi movement in Europe continued to baffle me. Events since Munich, however, had revealed certain essential factors of its dynamism. Success had not merely strengthened Hitler's hold over the German people; it had accelerated the regressive, barbarian trend of Hitlerism, and in so doing, had seemingly made it more contagious than ever to Germans and non-Germans alike.

The papers here haven't forgotten the anniversary of the World War. As in Germany, they are making calculations to show that the position is more favorable than in 1914. Indeed it seems to be as far as material forces are concerned. Still there is a strong undertone of gloom in the press. "1914 all over again," even if the chances of victory seem more immediate and certain, can only evoke a feeling of hopeless fatality. France and England did not get much out of their victory last time except the soon-faded dream of a better world. Now we are back where we started facing the whole thing over again.

All our bright dreams have faded, all our utopias of collective security have collapsed. Two disillusionments have merged in one bitterness. We are still suffering the hangover from the idealistic 1914–1918 wartime and prewar slogans, and on top of this, there is a new hangover, the depression following the collapse of the anti-fascist "fronts," to save Abyssinia, Czechoslovakia, Spain; the shambles of the New Deal in America, and the rout of the Popular Front in France. The purge in Russia has disgusted many idealists of the left; the internal dissensions of the Spanish Republic, which was the symbol of our united resistance to the new barbarism, have disheartened us. Our one hope was America. Roosevelt's defeat over the Neutrality Bill has destroyed this hope, for the time being at least. These are times of intellectual and moral disarray like the last days of the Weimar Republic in Germany . . . Doubt and suspicion spring up overnight like monstrous moral toadstools.

(War Diaries, August 2, 1939)

In August 1939 the military leaders of the West were preparing, as usual, to fight the last war; the politicians, the diplomats, the journalists, the intellectuals were resigning themselves no less anachronistically to losing the last peace. I had started at the beginning of the month keeping a diary of the new European crisis—over Danzig and the Polish Corridor this time—that was primarily intended to capture from day to day the effects on me of the events I was covering as a reporter. A few months later, after the crisis had turned into the second world conflict, I found that my diary (together with a parallel one I had persuaded my wife to keep) provided much of the raw material I needed for the book I was starting to write on the war in the mind—the clash of ideas, of wills, and of nerves—accompanying the military one, and I exploited it accordingly. Today, rereading the same entries that I drew upon in *The Strategy of Terror*, I am mainly struck by them as examples of cultural lag, including a form of it that I had earlier termed the lag in the heart. Like many of my contemporaries, I kept reacting to August 1939 as if it were July 1914.

The sense of doom that nearly everyone in Europe felt was natural enough; up to the last minute—and even a little beyond—we might suspect that the crisis would end in a new Munich, but from the first a new Armageddon had seemed a good deal more likely. There was some justification, too, for the feeling that, as in 1914, human blunders and misunderstandings had contributed to make an eventual collision inevitable; what was misleading was the nature of the blunders.

The European order that perished in 1914 had collapsed into international anarchy essentially because its peace-keeping institutions—including those in the minds of its political elites—had been too rudimentary, or too obsolescent, to deal successfully with the complicated clash of national interests, fears, passions, and mythologies provoked by the Sarajevo assassination. The Versailles order of Europe fell apart during the thirties because the victors of World War I who had imposed it failed to agree between—or even within—themselves either on the concessions to the vanquished that might have halted Hitler's rise to power, or on the mobilization of over-whelming force to contain his regressive lust for conquest and domination. Once Nazi Germany had been allowed to rearm and to occupy the key positions in Central Europe, the only choice facing the democracies was between surrender and fighting for their lives.

My diary of the 1939 crisis reflects, among other things, my generation's dismay, verging on despair, when events began to force on us the realization that the causes of war were both deeper and more complex, and therefore less controllable, than we supposed. Even more traumatic was the discovery that humanity had not taken the lessons of World War I as deeply to heart as we had imagined.

Nearly two years after my interview with Beneš, I still could not bring my reason utterly to reject his optimistic theory that even a psychopath like Hitler would not be mad enough to launch his people into a European war. If it turned out that Hitler really was such a lunatic, then surely the German people would refuse to march at his order. (In July 1914 many European Socialists had similarly believed that the German workers would proclaim a general strike if the Kaiser ordered them to march.) The shock of war itself was not sufficient to shatter immediately the false optimisms—along with the false despairs—about history and human nature that since the twenties had distorted our judgment in world affairs. Witness the entry in my diary for September 1:

"The war we have been fearing so long, without ever really believing in it, started at dawn this morning on the Polish frontier, but it is only by a kind of algebra that we can accept the reality of it at all. Some people frankly do not accept it despite the general mobilization proclaimed at noon, despite the ineluctable evidence of the dispatches and the communiqués. Many ordinary Frenchmen still believe that it will all blow over somehow after a day or two of fighting in Poland.

"The general mobilization decree got home, however, and people went around in the afternoon with sick, gray faces like a boxer who has been fouled. They know it is true now but they can't feel it. The idea of going to war in cold blood out of intellectual conviction against an enemy they don't really hate seems so monstrous that it really staggers the imagination. Hitler would make everything easy for us if he started to bomb, but without that there seems to be no way of whipping up a war spirit. Not that anybody grumbles against the official thesis. On the contrary there is complete unanimity, unanimity in conscious acceptance of a useful and necessary war, unanimity in unconscious rejection of an absurd and monstrous war.

"Though I have long felt that the horror of war was the central political attitude of our time I realize now that I have underestimated the depth of this feeling . . .

"If the feeling in Germany is the same, and according to all reports it is even stronger, I don't see at the moment how either side can last more than a few weeks, and it is just a question of which cracks first . . ."

The stunning German victories in Poland, the early Nazi atrocities there, the apparent acquiescence—not to say enthusiasm—of the German people in Hitler's conquest, gradually revealed the real nature of the war that had begun on September 1, 1939, and consequently of the Nazi threat to the Western democracies. The same developments likewise brought home to us some hard truths concerning the nature of contemporary political and social reality, the state of twentieth-century civilization, and the degree of evolution attained by the human animal in our age. The mind-clearing effect of all these lessons was intensified in some respects, confused in others, by a series of secondary shocks resulting from the unforeseen collusion between Nazi Germany and Communist Russia that opened with the announcement of the Ribbentrop-Molotov accord of August 22, 1939.

Though often in sympathy with the Popular Front, I had thought that I had no illusions about the totalitarian nature of the Soviet regime under Stalin. Like other Western liberals, I had been horrified by the Stalinist purges of 1937 and 1938, and what I had learned from Anarchist, Trotskyite, or other extreme left-wing friends about the Communist role in Republican Spain made me deeply suspicious of the Communists as allies. Nonetheless, again like many other liberals, I was reluctant to draw any practical conclusions from evidence that my critical faculties accepted in theory. "I admit Stalin is a murderous swine, maybe worse than Hitler," I wrote in one of my work-notes sometime in 1938, "but refuse to countenance anti-Communist activities."

The announcement of the Moscow accord had a shattering moral impact that I find almost impossible to communicate in terms comprehensible to anyone who did not himself participate in the fevered polemics and idealisms of the Popular Front period.

"Ribbentrop's psychological bombshell burst upon us in the weakness of the night, at the end of a long day of clutching fear and of unnerving hopes," I wrote in my diary for August 22. "My reaction and Vreni's the same: the bottom has fallen out. Now we are up against it, we have to fight for our lives. In anticipation we already saw a monstrous alliance between the two barbarisms sweeping over the whole world, destroying what is left of our civilization. Reaction from fear: upward surges of hate, now against treacherous Bolos [Bolsheviks], now against stupid and crooked old men who had made this tragedy inevitable . . ."

The entry of the Red Army into Poland, patently concerted with Hitler, appeared to confirm the darkest suspicions inspired by the signing of the Moscow Pact and the publication two days later of its terms. On that day my wife wrote in her diary:

"The Russians have entered Poland. 'Fourteenth day of the war against Hitlerism' says the *Daily Express*. It looks more like the fourteenth day of the Thirty Years' War. Now at least we don't have to worry about the meaning of this war . . . we are fighting for our skins. New vistas open up: the war spreading from one country to another, the U.S.A. sure to come in very soon now, and what that is going to mean to Ed and me, Switzerland reduced to the state Poland is in today, with ruins and shell holes spreading even to the remotest valleys, to the Engadine . . . We must try to shed now all our loves, all our memories, like old garments. We have already given up our worldly possessions. I went to the flat today and had a bath, and then, while cooling off went through a mess of papers and letters, filling the wastebasket. I stored away the books that were lying around, and the personal trinkets. Now all looks tidy and impersonal like a waiting room. A week ago I thought with melancholy of my curtains, and two weeks ago I sent away my silver. What importance have they now? My only regret is for the books. But on the whole, all that is sacrificed easily. Thoughts of a future life in a house of my own, in the country, with children coming in at four o'clock asking for bread and butter, and us being young parents still, are more difficult to blow out. Yet the only thing to do is to face this new kind of thunderstorm naked, like when it is raining and we are out camping. Naked, and with one single thought: win this war and stay alive. Or maybe the staying alive part is also superfluous."

The assumption implicit in my wife's diary, more directly voiced in mine, that the two totalitarian powers had formed a kind of neo-barbarians' league proved to be delusive, like my earlier belief in the pacifist sentiments of the German masses. Such swings from optimism to pessimism, from dreams of innocence to nightmares of satanism, are symptomatic of my generation in the 1930's. Counter-error, however, often supplies the antithesis to previously accepted error, from which comes the synthesis of closer approximation. Thus, while my 1939 nightmare proved to be nothing but that, it nonetheless helped me in my political education. My progress as an observer of world affairs had for a long time been blocked by my refusal to admit that if Hitler was a barbarian, or a paranoiac, Stalin was another, and consequently that there were essential similarities between the neo-barbarism of Nazi Germany and the debased Marxism known as Stalinism.

The liberation that I owed to the direct impact of events was helped along by an upheaval in my journalistic careeer, ironically provoked by my new anti-Communist convictions. Though the Chicago *Tribune* had continued to print most of my dispatches without editing them to the point of emasculation, I had been bombarded from Munich onward with letters and cables from the paper charging that I had let myself be deceived by Allied propaganda and in consequence had lost my objectivity in reporting the power conflicts of the Old World.

In the spring of 1939 a grotesque little incident had occurred in connection with an assignment from Colonel McCormick, who considered the relationship between United States Ambassador William C. Bullitt and the French government suspiciously close. I knew that Bullitt's contacts with the French were even closer than the Colonel suspected, but saw nothing disturbing in that, and had myself developed a quite confidential relationship with Bullitt, whose intellectual vigor and brilliant, if erratic, political insights I respected. In my embarrassment, I called on the ambassador and explained my dilemma. He was amused and volunteered a wealth of background about his contacts with Daladier, now premier again, Finance Minister Paul Reynaud, and the French General Staff. Some of the material seemed to me so incendiary, in terms of American domestic controversy, that I began to doubt whether Bullitt had really intended it for publication, so I took the precaution of letting him read my dispatch before sending it. He ostentatiously picked up a pencil and corrected several errors of punctuation; otherwise he changed nothing. I then sent the article to Colonel McCormick and received a reply a brief, savage note terming it "nothing but gossip and hearsay."

I had resigned myself to what seemed my rapidly approaching break with the *Tribune* when the Moscow Pact, followed by the German invasion of Poland, put a new light on the international situation. Surely, I reasoned, the scales must now fall from Colonel McCormick's eyes. When Stalin pounced upon the stricken Poles to claim his hyena's share of living flesh, and then launched his aggression against Finland, which was widely though erroneously assumed to have Hitler's blessings, my hopes for the Colonel's conversion soared.

A few days after the start of the Finnish war I fell upon what in my mood of exalted indignation seemed plausible as well as sensational evidence of the sinister ties between Berlin and Moscow. A young White Russian émigré, stopping off in Paris en route from Switzerland to Finland to volunteer as a freedom fighter, had given me an exhaustive summary of a confidential report received from the Berlin agents of an international anti-Communist organization to which he belonged. I knew the young man well and had solid reasons for trusting his personal integrity; I had mixed feelings about his organization, which was subsidized by Swiss and other private European business interests. I had long been somewhat suspicious of the group because of the links certain of its members appeared to have with Nazi Germany, but this gave all the more weight to the information my young friend had brought me.

The gist of it was that there were secret protocols to the Moscow Pact amounting to a de facto military alliance between the two signatories. These subsidiary accords, it was said, provided for a substantial degree of cooperation or coordination between the German and Soviet governments in their foreign propaganda operations, in the exchange of military intelligence, and in economic affairs. There were also delimitations of spheres of influence, and understandings regarding future territorial expansion of one or the other partner in the Balkans, in northeast Europe, and ultimately in the Middle East.

Later, after my own wartime experience had familiarized me with the techniques of so-called black—i.e. covert—propaganda, I would have recognized the pattern. Many of the factual elements that the Russian émigrés in Berlin had collected from their German sources were accurate, and some of them previously unknown, at least to the general public in the United States or Europe. As the Wilhelmstrasse archives were to reveal after the war, there really had been several more or less formalized understandings (though not in the form of actual protocols to the Moscow Pact) between Nazi and Soviet authorities along the general lines indicated in the émigré's report, and it is possible that there were other, still more secret ones that have left no trace in the surviving German files. Exaggerated or distorted details of this collusion had been artfully interwoven with accurate ones in the version I was given, and skilled hands had erected a towering structure of innuendo on a modest substratum of fact.

Soberly presented and critically analyzed, the report might have provided me with the basis for an interesting diplomatic think-piece. The two lengthy dispatches that I sent the paper—at full cable rates—failed, however, to evaluate the material as critically as they might have, and were spiced with thinly veiled editorial suggestions that the United States should join the European democracies in a moral and diplomatic front against the totalitarian aggressors.

When a furious cable arrived from Chicago rejecting my dispatch as a "bedtime story," I realized that my hopes of an ideological reconciliation with the Colonel had been naïve, and that the time had come for the inevitable divorce. I thereupon filed an intransigent, not altogether polite, cable in response to the *Tribune*'s, defending my think-piece as a valid scoop and suggesting that its publication would further the political education not only of the paper's readers but "more particularly that of its editors." Colonel McCormick's reaction was not long in coming. The wording of my cable, his message said, my recent dispatches, and "other vagaries" had led him to conclude that like several other American correspondents in Paris, I had fallen victim "to a mass psychosis hysterically trying to drag the United States into war." On the basis of this diagnosis the Colonel offered his valedictory recommendation that I join the Foreign Legion or take a rest cure.

Looking back on the incident, I find a good deal to be said on the Colonel's side. As an editor he was justified in spiking what was undoubtedly an overemotional, tendentious dispatch presenting largely uncorroborated information of a sensational nature from a dubious source (even though some of it turned out to have been true). The fact that it conflicted with the *Tribune*'s editorial policy could be considered as incidental; after all, there is no reason why any editor should go out of his way to provide his readers with ammunition against the ideological positions he is trying to uphold.

On the broader issue of policy itself, I naturally feel more strongly today than ever that I was right and Col. McCormick wrong, but the ironies surrounding our disagreement prove how complex it was. On the one hand, the Colonel's isolationism-first had for the moment led him into bed not only with the American apologists for Hitler, but with the native liberals or leftists who deplored any American intervention in an imperialist war even on behalf of such a patent victim of imperialist aggression as Finland; I, on the other hand, had a motley collection of Polish hyper-nationalists, White Russian counterrevolutionaries, French *cagoulards,* and even Spanish Carlists between my own ideological sheets. The truism that politics makes strange bedfellows is never more true than in a period of upheaval like the one through which we are living, though I wonder whether in our political, as well as our sexual, lives there is not often some unsuspected and paradoxical affinity beneath such conjunctural misalliances.

Giving up my job as the *Tribune*'s Paris correspondent was a painful wrench in several ways. Though I had little doubt that thanks to the war I would eventually find another, more rewarding job in Europe, I had no immediate prospect. Furnishing our apartment in St. Cloud had used up all the financial reserves that my wife and I possessed; in fact, we were in debt. I was sorry, too, to put aside my newly purchased war correspondent's uniform in which I had already made two visits to the curiously nonlethal front in what was then known as the Phony War.

It was a relief, on the other hand, to be freed from the nightly gymnastic of searching for some perspective on the day's events that would be compatible enough with Col. McCormick's to run the gauntlet of the *Tribune*'s copyeditors, and at the same time valid in terms of my own professional or political conscience. Moreover, as was to be expected, in abandoning the hopeless struggle to open the Colonel's mind to the truth as I saw it, I eliminated a factor of excess and distortion in my own.

Above all, the enforced hiatus in my career as a reporter gave me the leisure to start writing the book, a topical offshoot of my broader propaganda study, that had gradually been taking shape in my thoughts. I was by no means certain that I would find a publisher for such an odd kind of reportage, stressing the human element in the war of nerves that accompanied the shooting war and implicitly refuting the premises of American neutrality, but I decided to write it anyway and then see if I could sell it. Vreni encouraged me; perhaps she did not feel as strongly as I that such a book needed to be written, but she saw that I needed to write a book about something near and present. She helped in other ways, too. Shortly after the outbreak of the war, she got a temporary job covering Paris for a Basel daily whose regular correspondent had been called up for active duty in the Swiss Army. Her salary, though modest by American standards, was enough to pay our food and rent bills for a while, and that is always helpful to a writer. So Vreni became a foreign correspondent, which had been her early ambition, and I sat on the balcony in St. Cloud and became a "writer," which had once been mine, and we were both content. "Now that all those damned international crises are over and the war has finally started," Vreni wrote in her diary on the last Sunday in January 1940, "we enjoy a quieter, more peaceful, and on the whole happier existence than in any of the last few years." I felt the same way.

14

The Eye of the Hurricane

Individual participation in mass ordeal may either retard or foster personal growth; often at different levels or in different ways it does both. One of the reasons why my exposure to the terminal crises of the Versailles order, the outbreak of war, and finally the military debacle of 1940 was a valuable experience in terms of both personal and professional growth is that I was at the same time studying my own inner reactions to the public drama on which I was trying to report. Such tumultuous occasions are not normally conducive to fruitful introspection. In this case, introspection from mid-1930 onward was to a large extent a by-product of the book I was trying to write, but the book itself was in a sense the by-product of another undertaking and another experience.

Like most members of my generation, I had already been strongly influenced by the ideas of Freud by the time I came of age. The concepts and doctrines of psychoanalysis had seeped in a diffuse form into nearly every layer of educated Western society; they probably influenced the thought of the twenties and thirties to about the same degree that those of Marx or Einstein did. I was content for the most part to take the latter two at second hand, but I read—and not infrequently reread—with close attention the major works of Freud himself, along with those of his leading disciples or ex-disciples, especially Adler and Jung.

Partly from intellectual curiosity, partly in the hope it might release creative energies that I felt lay dormant in me, I was tempted to undergo analysis myself. A brief experiment in Vienna with Wilhelm Stekel, the most flamboyant of the Freudian epigones, further whetted my interest in the psychology of the unconscious. So, for less subjective reasons, did my study of propaganda.

If I sought a complete analysis, of course, I had to find an analyst in Paris, where the choice was limited. From what I could find out, the most suitable one for my purpose was Dr. René Allendy, a prolific writer on professional and philosophical topics. I read two or three of his books, which I found stimulating but not wholly convincing, and for some time hesitated to approach him. The 1938 crisis decided me. It was not that I felt I needed help in adjusting myself to what seemed an increasingly pathological world, but I instinctively sought to steady myself by affirmation in the face of an increasingly uncertain one. My propaganda study and the unfurnished apartment in St. Cloud were affirmative gestures; so from one viewpoint was my marriage itself. Starting analysis would be another. Thus it was that one hot afternoon shortly before the tensest phase of the Sudeten crisis I found myself stretched out on a worn leather couch in an oddly deserted-looking villa in Auteuil, the haunt of ceremonious cats. (Allendy, I discovered later, kept a parrot, in addition to being a cat-lover.) Momentarily forgetting the woes that Hitler and Col. McCormick were inflicting on me, I was trying to dredge up those of a long-buried past, under the discreet prompting of an enigmatic, bearded stranger whose profile, viewed from a certain angle and in my current mood, bore a disquieting resemblance to that of the late Monsieur Landru, a twentieth-century Bluebeard whose lurid crimes and air of bourgeois respectability had captured the French imagination, a few years earlier.

It was the beginning of a curious and in a sense romantic adventure of the mind. The circumstances alone, the gathering storm over Europe, the naïve faith in the future that the whole enterprise implied would doubtless have sufficed to make it that, but there were other specific elements of drama, tragic or lyric, that concurred; above all, there was the personality of Allendy himself.

At the time I started my analysis Allendy was forty-nine. He was a man of medium height, deceptively thickset in appearance, with a large intelligent head, a deeply lined, sensitive face framed by a neat beard—the Landru aspect really called for gross prejudice in the mind of the viewer—and pale, grayish eyes that were introspective rather than chill: the eyes of Merlin. He had a strong, analytical mind, accompanied by a no less powerful Celtic predilection for the hermetic and the otherworldly. Even within a profession whose cultural standards in Europe were then notably high, he seemed an exceptionally cultivated man. He had taken an advanced degree in Nordic languages before studying medicine and was widely read in literature, philosophy, and several branches of science. Temperamentally distrustful of all authority and hostile to every orthodoxy, Allendy, after getting his M.D., had practiced as an homeopath, though he appeared to be as allergic to homeopathic dogma as to every other. Fairly late in life he had graduated from homeopathy to psychoanalysis and what is now termed psychosomatic medicine. Though a Jungian by natural bent, he followed, if somewhat loosely, the Freudian routine of analysis.

During the First World War Allendy had served in the trenches and been badly gassed. His lungs failed to heal; he developed tuberculosis and finally was sent off to a sanitarium to die. He obstinately refused to comply with his superiors' prognosis, however, and eventually cured himself by a sheer effort of will, aided by various heretical treatments of his own prescription. The experience had left him with a passionate hatred of war and a quasi-mystic faith in the power of mind over microbe.

Allendy appeared to consider Paracelsus his true master, rather than such contemporaries as Freud or Jung and had made a particular study of the medieval alchemists. His scholarly apologia, *Paracelsus, le Médecin Maudit,* was greatly admired in certain European intellectual circles. I found some of his esoteric interests a bit disconcerting, but as a child of the age, I was reassured by reading his *Capitalisme et Sexualité*, a thoroughly contemporary work that attempted implicitly, if not quite successfully, to reconcile Marx and Freud; on the plane of analytical theory, nobody could accuse the author of underrating the libido. Beneath the book's clinical jargon, however, the perceptive reader could detect an idealization of romantic love, a loathing of the sordidnesses or hypocrisies that debase it, and an impatience with all social trammels constraining it that recalled my adolescent idol, Shelley. A later work entitled simply *l'Amour*, which Allendy completed during the Battle of France at the military hospital where he was mobilized, is an even bolder as well as more mature hymn to every form of love, rising in its closing pages to an etherialized, almost Franciscan fervor that the orothodox Dante himself could scarcely have disavowed. Such was the highly atypical twentieth-century Virgil I had found to guide me in my oddly timed wanderings through the underworld of the mind.

The analysis had to be interrupted several times by the analyst being called to the colors, or the analysand running off on distant assignments; even when both were in Paris, the hurly-burly of events often disturbed it. On the other hand, the sense of urgency inspired by the onrush of history and the resurgence of archaic emotions under the stress of war probably facilitated it, at least from a pedagogic viewpoint. So, perhaps, did certain conflicts or bereavements of my personal life at the period. There are times when it is useful to confront the whole haunting pack of one's private ghosts and demons—to have to meet all one's tests at once.

Though I had yet to learn how limited is the direct light thrown by the sweeping incertitudes of individual psychology, whether Freudian or Pavlovian, on complex social and political phenomena, I found that analysis rarely contributed to my immediate comprehension of the collective tragedy I was living through, and trying to study. There was one notable exception, however, one area of significant overlap between self-knowledge and the understanding of history.

From reading Jung and Freud, I had already learned that there were numerous similarities between the thought patterns of children and savages and those of the unconscious mind in civilized man. Until my analysis, however, I had never fully realized—one never does—the accumulation of myth, magic, and illogic that cluttered the garrets of my own mind.

The unsettling discovery was that much of this primitivism was not in the least unconscious, and did not need the interpretation of dream symbols or the shadow play of analytical transference to bring it to light. My waking, daylight mind was quite aware of many of the Stone Age heirlooms that it walked about with in the twentieth-century world; only their inventory produced a shock. Or rather, what produced the shock was the inventory itself, along with the fact that in drawing it up one often came upon evidence suggesting that an unseen hand was still somewhere at work producing or refashioning these heirlooms from a supposedly prehistoric past, as traditional artifacts in certain regions continue to be manufactured by tribal artisans for sale to tourists.

During one of my last sessions with Allendy, in the spring of 1940, the air-raid sirens went off, but we had got used to false alerts by then. Besides, as I remarked jokingly to him after glancing at my watch, it was one of the invulnerable hours of the day for me, and presumably my magic umbrella would protect him, too, if any bombs actually fell. Perhaps that was a slight exaggeration, I continued, relaxed on the couch but listening with one ear for the warning drone in the sky and the lumbering thud of mammoth hoofs approaching. There was no positive guarantee of safety at any hour, but by contrast with the zone of death marked on the watch's dial, one felt relatively secure the rest of the time. Ah, said Allendy, with a wheeze of pleasure, and what was the zone of death? The 3,600 seconds between four and five, I answered, morning or afternoon. It was a purely private superstition as far as I could make out, and comparatively recent; I had never noticed it until the war in Spain. It derived from a dream I had while I was there, from a voice heard in the dream. Not a known voice, not the voice of any figure in the dream, simply a voice saying, between four and five, but nearer to five, not particularly ominously, but very slowly and distinctly, not in English either, or any known tongue, yet clearly heard and understood. There had been more to the dream, since forgotten, but remembered on waking, and I had tried to analyze it as I lay in bed. Nothing could be simpler, after all. It was a precognitional dream—there seemed to be such things, did there not?—foretelling that my death when it came would come between four and five, but nearer to five, morning or evening. So, ever since, whenever any danger was near, I always looked at my watch, or at least recalled the hour, and felt safe or menaced accordingly.

There was no need for Allendy to comment. The enormity of what I had said struck me, and struck me for the first time, with full force. The Stone Age man who still lived in the deep caves of my mind was not only untouched by the light of modern reason but was capable—at least in the stress of war—of twisting the latest tools of twentieth-century thought into ritual implements for a shaman's panoply.

Suddenly, it seemed to me that I understood mankind's contemporary predicament, as well as my own, better than I ever had before. What Nazi propaganda was doing to the mind of Germany (probably after Hitler had done it to his own), was closely analogous to what I had done to mine in forging my private hour-magic. The terrifying ease with which I had subverted reason and science—even if rather dubious science in this case—to the service of ancient darkness—perhaps still more, the insouciance with which I had consciously accepted the regression—illustrated how vulnerable twentieth-century civilization was to the literal neo-barbarism that Hitler was spreading in Europe, with the word and with the sword, the sword, as he put it, of spiritual violence.

Allendy accepted my interpretation of the anecdote, but he did not draw quite the same conclusions that I did in terms of opposing the new barbarians—by the word and by the sword. He was too much a man of his generation for that, too marked by his own experience in the first war, above all too aware of how war replenishes barbarism, even when it is fought to defend civilization against barbarians.

Deeply as he hated war, however, Allendy played his personal part with antique fortitude in the second, as in the first one. My last image of him is wearing an ill-fitting French officer's uniform, holding a basket of cats under his arm (it even seems to me, though I scarcely dare credit the surrealist vision, that there was also a caged parrot on top of his baggage), as he left to take command of the base hospital in Normandy to which his military orders, for the second time since the summer of 1939, had assigned him—no longer Virgil, but a modern Socrates, walking with firm and manful tread despite his unmartial impedimenta, unhurriedly trailing his spear point in the dust of defeat.

15

The Shock of Growth

The fall of France was not the end of the world for Vreni and me, as it was for some of the friends whose existence we had shared, but it was the end of a world, one that had seemed good while we had it. The way the end came, moreover, amplified its cataclysmic repercussions in the mind. To a contemporary eyewitness the French collapse appeared a tragedy of the absurd, a kind of fetal monster of history. The breakdown of military and social order laid bare an underlying, hitherto unsuspected anarchy of events themselves. The most dispassionate observer could not escape a bruising sense of shock, and Vreni and I were neither dispassionate nor simple observers. We took part in the final debacle as refugees among millions of others, like all of them physically and emotionally uprooted from the familiar humus of sustaining attachments we had learned to call home.

Situation critical but maybe not yet hopeless. Mass interview for U.S. correspondents with Reynaud's new Minister of Information [Louis] Prouvost at Continental. Said Weygand highly pleased with stubborn resistance of troops, insists every village and town in France will be defended like fortresses even if they razed to ground one by one. Admits some members government leaving Paris for Tours but

271

government as such not fleeing. "As for myself, gentlemen, I hope to have pleasure of seeing you several times more in this office."

Basically same note from Mme. L. who telephoned Vreni today advising us to leave at once for Tours because shelling of Paris about to start. She claims city won't fall, however, so no need pack up everything: "We'll all be coming back in a few weeks."

(WAR DIARY, JUNE 9, 1940)

Returning to the Ministry of Information less than twenty-four hours after Prouvost's statement (I had finished the book and was back on the job as a correspondent, this time for the Columbia Broadcasting System), I found that most of the staff, including the minister, had slipped out of the capital during the night. The discovery jolted my relative optimism of the day before, but failed to shatter it. Later in the day, Vreni and I decided to drive separately out of Paris, naïvely planning to rendezvous the next morning in Tours; we still shared the conviction of her telephone informant, who had a close family connection with one of the resistance-minded ministers in the Reynaud cabinet, that the city would withstand the impending siege and eventually be relieved by fresh armies building up behind the Loire. Accordingly, we followed Madame L.'s advice and took no belongings with us on the exodus, except our two Scotties (Capt. Flint had by now acquired a consort), clothes, and a few light, easily lootable items from the St. Cloud apartment, such as Vreni's jewelry and some silver. I even neglected to pick up the spare cash in my checking account in a French bank.

Vreni left around midafternoon, in our baby Simca, taking the dogs and accompanied by Maité, the wife of a French officer serving with his regiment at the front, whose children they were to pick up at Laigle, some one hundred miles west of Paris. Laigle, as far as I could make out from the scanty information available, was still a safe distance from the zone of battle, and the road from there south to the Loire was thought to be less encumbered and therefore less subject to air attack than the main highway from Paris to Tours. I was relieved to see Vreni go: The semi-deserted capital, already overhung by a pall of thick, greasy smoke from the burning storage tanks of fuel oil down the Seine, was looking more sinister by the minute. I had to stay behind to help my CBS colleague, Eric Sevareid, collect what concrete news we could find for the broadcast to the United States he was scheduled to make that night—the last one, we had been warned, before the technical staff of the French state radio packed up and left for Tours. Thus, it was past midnight, in the early hours of June 11, when Eric and I took to the road ourselves.

Grim as the silent, blacked-out city had seemed to us, the kind of frozen stampede of a whole panic-stricken nation that engulfed us beyond its gates was even more unnerving. By the time we reached the suburbs, we found we had joined the tail of a motorized procession two hundred miles long. Every driver in it wanted to press the accelerator down to the footboard and never release it until he was south of the Loire. Instead we crawled along without lights at ten or fifteen miles an hour.

Slowly as we crawled, we managed to pass hundreds of cyclists and even pedestrians, some pushing perambulators or wheelbarrows loaded with their belongings. Thousands of others had given up the struggle for the night and dropped in exhaustion by the side of the road.

We got tangled up with military trucks traveling in convoy, with ambulances rushing south to evacuate the wounded or rushing north to collect them, with tanks and artillery and peasant carts. Once we had to lie in a ditch while unseen bombers droned overhead, then released their load of thunderous death on some more distant objective. Peasants rendered hysterical by bombings or simply by the roar of passing bombers ran about in the village streets brandishing pitchforks and shotguns, threatening to slaughter anyone who even lit a cigarette.

The peasants hated the refugees because they passed over the land like a swarm of locusts, buying up all the food in the shops, draining the precious gasoline out of the pumps. And because they were thought to attract enemy bombers. And most of all, in fact, because just seeing them go by frightened the countryfolk. It frightened them so much that many of them joined the procession with their clumsy carts, thus further slowing down its pace and reducing the chances of those behind.

Military police on the main roads struggled to maintain some kind of order and to prevent traffic snarls, but the government, in the excitement of packing its bags and leaving, had neglected to take any effective, large-scale measures for regulating the exodus. In the end, the roads became so blocked with civilian refugees that vital military movements were paralyzed.

Sevareid and I had an almost miraculously uneventful trip. We passed through the chief danger zone just behind one vicious bombardment and just ahead of another. By quitting the main highway as soon as possible and threading our way across the countryside on secondary roads, we made the three-and-a-half-hour run to Tours in a trifle over nine hours, possibly a record for the period.

What I had seen on the way down from Paris, together with the confusion and demoralization I found on arriving in Tours, the somnolent, provincial center that had become the new, all-too-provisional capital of France, dissipated my last illusions about the military situation. General Weygand's army was not defending the sacred soil of France city by city, village by village, house by house, as the Minister of Information had rashly assured the press it would. With the exception of the fortress troops locked up in the Maginot Line, what remained of it after Dunkirk and the Wehrmacht's new breakthrough between the Aisne and the Seine was splintered into uncoordinated, often leaderless masses fleeing from the enemy along roads hopelessly clogged with civilian refugees. There would be no miracle on the Marne in this war, nor along the Loire either. The Battle of France was lost.

During the August crisis the year before, there had seemed some danger that a German blitzkrieg might succeed in smashing the French Army while it was mobilizing. Later, one worried over the possibility that a combination of political warfare and massive air attack might break civilian morale in France and thus force a disastrous peace. Once, however, the French Army was fully mobilized, and the British Expeditionary Force solidly established on the Continent—particularly after the Allies had enjoyed eight months of respite from attack to complete the training and equipment of their forces—the chances for a decisive German victory through a classic ground battle in the West appeared remote. That the Germans in four weeks of fighting and with relatively light casualties to themselves might succeed in annihilating all hope of effective military resistance in metropolitan France had appeared inconceivable to experts and laymen alike.

I had lived so long in France, and had unconsciously adopted so many French viewpoints, that with most Frenchmen I had come to think of the country as virtually invulnerable to invasion. My conducted visits as a war correspondent to the elaborate underground fortresses of the Maginot Line had given me a confidence in their impregnability greater, if anything, than that possessed by the average French newspaper reader. I realized, of course, as the average newspaper reader probably did not, that the Maginot Line protected the nation's eastern frontiers only along the Rhine and in Lorraine; the official information and explanations I had been given about the staunchness of the military shield from the Ardennes to the Channel had sounded convincing, however. The piercing of this shield in the original German breakthrough near Sedan, and the total French collapse in the north that soon followed it, had therefore been a stunning shock to me, as they had been to the entire French people, starting with its military chiefs. It was not merely an illusory security that had been shattered by the German panzer divisions, but the whole nineteenth-century bourgeois civilization of security based on a concept of linear defense against destiny that France had supremely exemplified. That civilization had deep roots, some going back to childhood, in my own mind; the Battle of France wrenched them loose. A private drama within the general one made the experience momentarily more harrowing but ultimately perhaps more fruitful.

*

I was only mildly worried at first when I reached Tours and found no news of Vreni. Though she and Maité had left Paris nearly eight hours earlier than Eric and I, they had had farther to go and their car was slower than ours. Or they might have had a puncture, or simply have spent the night in a hotel somewhere. As the day wore on, however, I began to grow uneasy. The news that the Germans had crossed the Seine west of Paris and were wheeling south along that same roads that Vreni had planned to take turned uneasiness to dread. I cursed myself for having let her go. Until late that night I shuttled distractedly between the pressroom in the Ministry of Information, set up in a requisitioned post office, and the Hotel de l'Univers where Vreni and I had agreed to meet, hoping vainly for a message from her.

I waited all the next day again, though scarcely hoping any longer. There was a heavy air attack on Tours that night, I think, but I did not get up for it. There was no shelter in the private house where Eric and I had found beds and none nearby; in any case I felt so worn out that nothing seemed to matter.

The wire from Vreni arrived early in the morning on my third day in Tours. It helped only a little. It had been sent forty-eight hours earlier from Alençon, a large town about one hundred miles north of Tours, where Vreni was stranded, her car having been wrecked in an accident. It seemed unlikely that she would still be there, with the Germans coming straight on; she would doubtless have found some kind of southbound transportation by now. She might be anywhere, and anything might have happened to her, since she had sent her wire. The only thing that seemed important after those last two days of waiting for her in Tours was being together again, whatever was happening around us, and there was a risk that if I missed her in Alençon and she turned out to be stranded in some new place I would not find out in time to rescue her before the German Army drove between us. Still the risk had to be taken. For one thing, I could not have faced the prospect of sitting in Tours another day waiting for word from her. Accordingly, I borrowed the CBS car from Eric, managed to find a service station in town that still had some gasoline, and set out for Alençon.

There were fewer refugees on the road than I had encountered coming down from Paris, but the exodus seemed even more of a folk migration than before. Many of the refugees had trucks or tractor-drawn carts filled with household belongings; even the passenger cars often had a mattress lashed to the top, perhaps a kind of magic shield against strafing aircraft. Especially outside the towns, I noticed groups of men and women walking south, carrying bundles. There seemed to be no cars, not even military traffic, heading north; the southbound troops I passed were gray-faced under the dustcake and stubble. A number of them were wearing dirty bandages of some sort, and sometimes there were requisitioned civilian trucks with wounded lying on the floors. The roadside was an interminable cemetery for every kind of vehicle, some twisted in the agony of a final collision or riddled with holes, others, apparently, simply abandoned where they ran out of fuel. As I neared Alençon I felt like a motorized Orpheus approaching the portals of some twentieth-century Hades.

As I had feared, Vreni had checked out of her hotel, that same morning, it seemed. There was no message saying how she hoped to reach Tours; doubtless she had had no idea herself. My heart fell when I came to the main square and found a crowd of several thousand refugees struggling to get on three or four buses that were about to leave for somewhere. Suddenly I heard my name called, and turned and saw at last my Eurydice, grimy but unhurt, accompanied by a black miniature Cerberus that on closer inspection turned out to be two Scotch terriers entangled in each other's leashes. Vreni had just been about to board a bus departing for Angers, on the Loire below Tours. Obviously nothing could happen to us from now on, not if one had the slightest faith in magic.

Forgetful of what had happened to the original Eurydice, we even tempted fate by driving back northward along the road to Verneuil, looking for the Simca. Vreni had had to abandon it, leaving most of the luggage inside, after she and Maité, on their way to Laigle, had collided with a peasant cart in the blackout. Some soldiers from a motorized antiaircraft unit falling back on Alençon had dropped Maité in Laigle, then brought Vreni on.

We knew we were entering the zone of battle, or at least of the enemy, when there were no more refugees on the road, no peasants, no soldiers, nothing to mar the deep country peace. Larks soared above rich meadowland in a cloudless, pentacostal sky; cuckoos in the shaded thickets ceaselessly humored the gentle obsession of their kind; we even thought we heard a belated nightingale when we halted briefly in a little wood to eat a sandwich. The wild roses were flowering in a natural hedge, and across the road from us stretched a field of bluish, rippling wheat, reddened with poppies. This was the French countryside that Vreni and I loved, taken from us by war, and now given back.

The villages we passed through looked deserted. I stopped in one to fill the radiator of the car, and entered the local *bistro*. Several old peasants were sitting around wooden tables, some of them drinking wine. No one said anything. I went into the kitchen and filled my bucket and then stood at the *zinc* and ordered a glass of wine. *"Monsieur est Allemand?"* the proprietor asked. *"Non, Americain,"* I answered firmly. The proprietor said nothing. "You are not American," one of the peasants said. "You are a *Boche*." There was no menace in his voice; he was just telling me that he knew. "I'm not a *Boche*," I answered. "I tell you I am an American—an American journalist." *"Bon,"* the proprietor said, shrugging. *"Monsieur est Americain."* The old peasants looked at one another. *"Americain et journaliste,"* one added. I paid for my wine and picked up my bucket and walked out. "They must have thought you were a parachutist," Vreni commented when I related the incident to her. I guess that was part of it.

I expected to see a German tank come trundling down the road long before we reached the abandoned Simca. The prospect did not seem very alarming now that Vreni and I were together again, especially after I had come so close to missing her in Alençon. That had been a portent of some kind, not of invulnerability, exactly but of assured recovery, whatever might be lost. I wondered whether there might not be something besides magic in that feeling, and what Allendy would make of it if I related the whole incident to him, and whether I would ever have the chance to relate it. I wondered, too, whether he was still at his hospital in Mortain, not far away from where we were, but much nearer to the enemy, and if not, what had happened to him in the retreat.

Then as we were driving along I thought about Maité and her children, with the Germans doubtless in Laigle now, and about her husband Albert, most probably in the mountains with his *Chasseurs Alpins,* fighting against the Italians. I also thought of many other friends, French and British and American and Spanish and Swiss and Greek, with whom Vreni and I had eaten meals in *bistros* and covered conferences and crises together, and sometimes taken trips or walks in the country. A few of our friends were still in Paris, others with the army or on the road somewhere as refugees. There had not always been time for good-bys, so I was taking leave of them now in my mind as we drove along. Thanks to the countryside of France that the war had taken away from us and then given back, I took leave in the same way of the places that we had loved the best; the quiet meadows along the Seine near La Roche-Guyon and the chalk cliffs above them; the great beeches in the forest of Fontainebleau and the thick carpet of moss beneath, where you lay and looked up at the sky through the filigree of the leaves; the morning light on the Loire; the grave splendor of Vézelay, and the swallows in the evening sky when we walked along the ramparts; the white, dusty roads and the olive groves of Provence, and the thyme-scented hills around Les Baux; the mellow Savoyard landscape sloping down to the Lake of Geneva.

The little Simca looked hopelessly crumpled when we found it at last, but on closer inspection I discovered the engine and steering rod were undamaged. By wrenching off the fender jammed against one of the front wheels I was able to get the car running again.

The two heavy suitcases that Vreni had been obliged to leave behind were still there. They had been opened, of course, but not everything had been looted out of them. Vreni's jewelry and the silver were gone, except for a few unmatched spoons, and my best winter suit was missing. The looters had spared, however, the morning coat I had bought for my wedding and never worn since (the striped trousers had been borrowed from a friend); probably they were not anticipating a demanding social season for the immediate future. Vreni and I laughed at the coat, which had been thoughtfully refolded and still smelled faintly of mothballs. Then I tossed it in a ditch, and we transferred one of the suitcases with what seemed salvageable into the CBS Renault. Vreni took the wheel, with the Scotties in the back seat, and I got into the Simca, and we started back for Tours, traveling this time in close convoy.

On the way I took mental leave, finally, of the flat in St. Cloud and of the books and other belongings we had left there. I felt lightened and gay, and from time to time hooted the Simca's horn in greeting; Vreni hooted back. The war had become a kind of tumultuous, sometimes uncomfortable country outing for both of us, a vacation from the past and the future, from responsibility and anxiety, from habit and recurrence, from the vexations of society and the spider web of relationship, from the toils of civilization; from the burden of humanity if one let oneself go; from the despotism of self, if one took advantage of the opportunity: the oldest, most total, and most intoxicating of all man's holidays.

In one sense, I remember clearly following the last, lamentable exodus of the French political and bureaucratic elite from Tours to Bordeaux, and covering the final collapse of France's military resistance there. The scenes of those days remain hard-edged in my memory, but they are discontinuous: a mosaic of fragmented happenings and fragmentary beings, like Picasso's *Guernica*. .

It was a vivacious, chattering kind of defeat, not because of French frivolity but because everyone was together in one place for the end and everyone knew everyone. Because *Tout-Paris* had fled to Bordeaux it naturally met *Tout-Paris* there; the cafés, the lobbies of the hotels, the shady public squares, and even the air-raid shelters, when the bombs were not crumping too near, were filled day and night with Parisian chatter. At moments one had the impression of attending a garden party in a lunatic asylum during an earthquake.

From the reporter's point of view Bordeaux semed at first a kind of news paradise. In the republic of misfortune that the city had become, one could buttonhole the nation's great on any street corner. The most cautious politician, the most inaccessible civil servant, the most aloof poet, the wealthiest banker, or the reigning beauty would often unburden himself or herself without inhibition to a foreign journalist remembered, if at all, only as a vague background face at press conferences or in the lobby of the Chamber. All too often, however, he or she had nothing to say worth listening to; one began to suspect that it had always been so, and that one should have known it all along.

It was much the same with the censorship. As the French state fell apart, the minor bureaucrats responsible for preserving its secrets from a domestic press that had virtually ceased to exist and from a body of foreign opinion that no longer mattered grew every day both more irrational and easier to evade. In the end, Sevareid and I ceased bothering about getting our copy censored; in fact, we practically stopped writing copy. Whenever there was something new to report, one of us would rush to the overseas broadcasting section of the state-controlled radio network, install himself in the first unoccupied studio, and start talking into the microphone, heedless of whether our words were being beamed to Latin America or to Japan, hoping only that someone somewhere would pick them up and repeat them to New York. One needed faith for this kind of hit-or-miss journalism, and on occasion one had to be ruthless as well as lucky. Several times when I had a major news flash I found a dark, plump little woman crooning in Spanish in the only functioning studio. The first time I tried for a while signaling her through the glass door to break off. Thereafter, I simply walked in and pushed her away from the microphone when there was need. It was harsh as well as ungentlemanly, I suppose. In her fashion, the crooner was being no less true to her trust under difficult circumstances than I was to mine, and I suppose from her viewpoint these intermittent assaults by a maniacal stranger must have seemed among the weirdest episodes of a lunatic period.

All this has little significance today. Even at the time, the finale in Bordeaux seemed rather the epilogue than the climax of the French tragedy. For a day or two, I hoped that the Jacobin democrats, the anti-Nazi liberals, and the old-fashioned patriots among the nation's political elite, including those in the Reynaud cabinet, would save honor if nothing else by evacuating as much of the French Army as could be saved to North Africa and moving the seat of government there. When Reynaud, yielding with misplaced correctitude to what was doubtless the authentic will of the majority, resigned in favor of Pétain and the defeatist clique around him, I knew that as far as France was concerned the war was finished, and French democracy along with it, until it should be restored by foreign arms.

Sevareid and I reported Pétain's appeal for an armistice. Then the studios were closed down, and our assignment in Bordeaux was at an end. We both decided to leave France while it was still possible to find transportation. The tragedy of France would continue, and eventually no doubt it would be possible to resume reporting it, but our cruel reporters' instinct told us that what the French people suffered would no longer be really important news in America. What mattered now was how the British people would resist, and how soon the American people would awaken from the isolationist thrall.

There were strong and sensible reasons for returning to America. *The Strategy of Terror* was about to be published, and I naturally wanted to be on hand to exploit whatever success it achieved. I thought, too, that after what I had witnessed during the fall of France I had useful things to tell my fellow countrymen. There was also a deeper, not wholly rational motive that I think weighed more heavily. Neither then nor later did I feel the sense of almost personal betrayal with which many American Francophiles reacted to the French collapse. After sharing some of their trials during the exodus from Paris, I felt more pity than contempt for the French leaders whose nerve or will had failed them in Bordeaux. The France that I had known was dead, however, and I had no wish to linger beside a corpse, even a beloved one. France was dead—until the distant, unpredictable day of resurrection—and the life that Vreni and I had lived together in Paris was shattered beyond repair. We would have to begin a new one; it was better, therefore, that it be in a new land. The very fact I thought of my country as a new land proved that I had been away from it too long.

Each generation revises the hopes and fears for humanity it has inherited from all former generations in the light of its own experience; every social group continually reshapes its doctrines of survival on the basis of the ordeals it has survived. The more tragic the experience, the more catastrophic the ordeal, the more indelible the mark it leaves upon the organizational or racial memory. So the wisdom and the madness of nations accumulate; so the collective personality of man grows and grows twisted; so, no doubt, it has always been, since that initial genetic shock—if it was the initial one—that forced our remotest ancestors to remold their own ancestral habits around the awkward, upright posture.

On the professional plane, one important lesson, which the military and political catastrophe of June 1940 brought home to me, has again and again demonstrated its lasting validity. The fact that the French collapse came as such a stunning surprise to me suggested that as an observer of French affairs, I had not been sufficiently hard-minded or skeptical in evaluating available information, and sometimes not aggressive enough in reporting it. I had noted the main political and psychological weaknesses of France, but had failed to give them all the weight they deserved. Sometimes, especially while I had been working for the Chicago *Tribune*, I had been reluctant to write everything that I knew or suspected, for fear that it would damage the French or anti-Nazi cause. Earlier in the year, Lord Beaverbrook, the publisher of the London *Daily Express* and the *Evening Standard*, in some respects a more enlightened British analogue of Col. McCormick, had commissioned me to travel around wartime France and do a series of articles for his papers; he had appeared to feel that an American reporter would be more free to say what he thought than a British one. I had been intrigued by the assignment at first but had soon given it up, precisely because what I observed about French morale and attitudes toward the war during my travels seemed too disturbing to print, especially in an Allied newspaper. (And what one hesitates to write, one finally hesitates to believe.) Abandoning the assignment, however, had helped neither the French nor the British cause, nor that of freedom itself. In trying to be cognizant of his social responsibility, a reporter should never forget that his overriding responsibility is to the truth as he sees it.

Among the more general lessons impressed on my mind by the fall of France was the supreme importance of leadership and morale, the human factors par excellence in even the most mechanized forms of power struggle between competing social groups. In my first dazed reaction to the catastrophe I had just witnessed I tended, perhaps, to oversimplify the role that these two factors—always closely related and in some situations almost interchangeable—had played in it. Yet it cannot be denied that French leadership as a whole failed the nation in 1940. Morale cracked—under tremendous pressure it is true—and it started cracking from the top down, both in the military and in the civilian establishments.

Since warfare first became total in modern times, no great power has acquiesced so totally in its own defeat as France in 1940. The fall of France was essentially the breakdown under stress of the nation's power elite. And though some members of this elite had never given more than lip loyalty, if that, to the cause of French democracy, many others, I knew, had belonged to what was virtually the priestly caste of the republic; their collective abdication in the face of temporal defeat was an ideological betrayal.

As an American democrat, I could not help but be deeply shaken by the apparent evidence of basic weaknesses in the democratic system itself which the French defeat brought to light. My own faith in democracy had often wavered in the past, had in fact only recently put down conscious roots of strong conviction, and what I saw in France might easily have destroyed them. Somehow, it did not, even if my more liberal sensibilities were to a certain degree blunted or coarsened. At the deepest, most metaphysical level—that of a concept of society founded on the recognition of universal human worth—

my emotional attachment to the ideals of democracy hardened in direct proportion to my growing awareness of how difficult in our age, perhaps in any age, it is to defend them. Among all existing political and social ideologies, democracy was the peerless daylight cause precisely because it was the most vulnerable to the forces of the night.

One reason why democracy is nowhere safe on earth, I concluded after the fall of France, is that the democracies in modern times had become suspicious of the very idea of leadership and had to a considerable degree abandoned it to the enemy. Another reason why we often lacked vigorous leadership when we needed it most was that we failed to realize that crisis in our age was endemic. Finally, we failed, or simply refused, to recognize that democracy still possessed—perhaps would always possess—real enemies on earth, and that these enemies, by definition as it were, would always attack us in non-democratic ways. Merely seeking to perfect democracy, therefore, would not suffice to protect it against these attacks, and might in some cases even contribute to weakening it. Ideological enemies who did not depend on their ideas alone to destroy us could not be defeated merely by better ideas; better arms, better leadership, higher morale, and sounder strategy had to be marshaled against them.

". . . We have come to look upon history as an irreversible process of automatic progress or evolution culminating in the democratic system," I wrote shortly after Pearl Harbor for a new edition of *The Strategy of Terror.* "We have blindly assumed that just as nature labored for countless eons to produce the pithecanthropus, so have tens of thousands of patriarchies, matriarchies, oligarchies, despotisms, and monarchies since the first syllable of recorded time labored to establish through our world the system of government and society called democracy—to some a goal, to others a half-way house to a yet more perfect system called socialism. Awed by this vast teleological edifice, we have held it unthinkable that any man or group of men could undo the work of millenniums . . . We forgot that democracy was not established upon earth by the millenniums but by the blood, sweat and tears of our ancestors—plus a good deal of sheer luck. What all these things won can be lost by their absence

. . . That is what the French had forgotten, what we have all forgotten. We have even refused to believe the evidence of our eyes that there were authentic anti-democrats left on earth . . ."

To save America—and whatever else remained of the free world —from suffering the fate of France, the Allied war effort must be based, I concluded, on the obsession of victory. The greatest weakness of the French democratic leaders had been their flickering, uncertain dedication to the victory of democracy. Because they had lost a battle, or at worst a nation, they had been willing to surrender a civilization.

Today I am more conscious than I used to be of the dangerous, unresolved, perhaps unresolvable contradictions implicit in such a militant ideology of democratic victory, and the exaltation of my 1942 prose rings a little unnatural to my ear. That is so, at least, when today happens to fall in one of our quieter years. Everything seemed a great deal simpler in 1940. Indeed, I cannot recall any period of my life when the future, including my personal future, seemed so free of problems as it did in the weeks immediately after the French collapse, when the only collective problem of humanity seemed to be the survival of freedom, and my only private one, untroubled as I was with a home, a job, or a career, was how I could contribute to it.

On this score I felt a good deal of confidence. I had learned quite a bit in the last few years, and particularly during the last few weeks in France, about the forces that make or unmake a nation's will to win over the enemies that imperil its existence, and that of the values to which it is attached. My job, my career, was to communicate this learning, to help my country master some of the more recondite twentieth-century arts of survival with which my experience in France had, at least to a limited extent, familiarized me. I first became aware that I had taken this decision on the ship from Bordeaux to Liverpool which I boarded with Vreni and Eric Sevareid. The sense of purpose and participation that this gave me—a birthright of which my generation had largely been deprived—no doubt explains why that hazardous and scarcely luxurious voyage remains one of my brightest memories.

We had been lucky—luckier, even, than we realized at the time—to get passage on the *Ville de Liège*, a fast modern freighter under American ownership but flying the Belgian flag to comply with the requirements of the Neutrality Act. She was, I believe, the last vessel bound for England to sail from the Gironde, save for the British destroyers and corvettes that escorted us for a few miles out into the Atlantic. Eric had heard from someone in a bar that the *Ville de Liège* was anchored in the river a few miles from Bordeaux and was about to leave. We drove to where she lay and asked her skipper, Captain Jorgenson, a tough, friendly, competent-looking Norwegian, to take us with him, wherever he was going.

Jorgenson immediately agreed, but wanted to make sure we realized the risks. He had arrived in France with horses and munitions for the French Army; the horses had been debarked, but when Jorgenson discovered what had become of the French Army he had decided, apparently on his own initiative, that the munitions would be more useful in England. (Jorgenson's wife had been caught in Oslo by the German occupation, and the Nazis were not his type of Nordic.) The *Ville de Liège* was thus effectively as well as technically belligerent shipping; moreover, Jorgenson had agreed under charter to evacuate the survivors of the Czechoslovak Legion in France. Except for the first few hours off the coast of France the ship would be traveling without naval escort, steaming straight out into the mid-Atlantic off the main trade and escape routes, relying on her speed to dodge any submarines that might be lurking in her path. For a day or two German bombers might be a problem. Liverpool was Jorgenson's immediate destination; he thought his chances were good, but could not say just how good.

Jorgenson's steady look and his clear, sensible way of talking would have made the chances of arriving anywhere seem good to us after the panic and mass hysteria we had been living in for the last ten days. We abandoned the two cars on the riverbank then and there, and came aboard, the three of us, with our scanty luggage and the two dogs. We spent the night at anchor off the Pointe de Graves, near the mouth of the Gironde, in the midst of a British convoy.

There was a spectacular dive-bombing attack by Stukas, eventually fought off by the antiaircraft guns of a British light cruiser supported by those of the merchantmen and smaller escort craft. It was a magnificent sight, the first and last air raid of the war that I unreservedly enjoyed watching.

The next morning the Czech Legionnaires, many of them wounded, came alongside in a small lighter that ferried them from the beach, threading its way carefully among the bits of floating debris that were the result of the previous night's air raid. The Czechs brought along a few of their women and children. They were accompanied also by several Polish women and by a badly wounded Polish general whose aide asked Jorgenson to let them all come aboard.

He accepted the whole party, but the beach was still lined with refugees from all the countries of occupied Europe, and soon another lighter arrived alongside, loaded almost to the waterline with haggard, hysterical civilians who said they were Belgians and pleaded desperately to be taken along. Jorgenson hesitated a moment, then gave in. The empty horse stalls could be converted into dormitories for an even larger number of passengers, but food was limited and space in the lifeboat and rafts even more so. It was Jorgenson's duty to his ship, his crew, and the passengers already aboard not to overcrowd; he stretched a point in accepting the Belgians, but that had to be the end.

"That's all," Jorgenson ordered the crewmen manning the rails. "Don't let any more aboard." A number of small boats or rafts packed with refugees were now bobbing around the *Ville de Liège*, however, and the occupants of one large raft had made fast to the rope ladder hanging over her side and were trying to scramble up. One refugee, a large blubbery man, had succeeded in shoving himself on deck and was on his knees with the tears streaming down his face, screeching in German like a child in a temper tantrum. The sailors tried halfheartedly to push him back onto the ladder, then looked at Jorgenson, who hardened his face and said *"Nein."* The sailors tried to push some more, then suddenly they stopped and stepped aside. Jorgenson said nothing, but his face looked relieved.

The rail was lined with members of the crew representing a dozen different nationalities, some of them not belligerent, and they all looked relieved as they watched the refugees clawing their way up the ladder. Several score made the deck before Jorgnson finally insisted that it be pulled up. By that time there were over three hundred human beings on board the *Ville de Liège*, with lifeboat accommodations for about one hundred. The crew all looked cheerful and had started on their own initiative to bring cups of hot bouillon to the women and children.

The weakness Captain Jorgenson had shown in dealing with the refugees made him seem stronger than ever, and I felt there was an important lesson in the incident. The obsession of victory was merely an obsession like any other, I now saw, unless at all times it included the victory of humanity, that of the only humanity a human being ever fully knows, his own. Perhaps that was dangerously overloading with qualifications the simple, ruthless notion of victory, one side winning, the other losing, one living, one dying. But the *Ville de Liège* was also dangerously overloaded because of Jorgenson's humanity, and yet one did not thereby feel endangered. On the contrary, I actually felt safer with all those extra refugees aboard, all those women and children who would be in the lifeboats if we were torpedoed, because I had inwardly acquiesced when the sailors stood aside and let them come aboard, as Captain Jorgenson himself had acquiesced, as Vreni and Eric had, and everyone, I imagine, who had witnessed the scene. We all felt safer.

At the same time, danger was very close and we knew it. By late afternoon the French coast was out of sight, and so was the smoke of the huge, slow-moving convoy with which we had steamed out of the estuary. We were alone on the great empty Atlantic, but not quite alone, for our radio antenna still linked us with the world of war and death beyond the horizon. A whole wolf pack of U-boats, the radio warned us, was prowling along the coast from Brittany to the mouth of the Gironde, for some distance out. Six ships had already been sunk in the area within the last twenty-four hours. From time to time the radio operator of the *Ville de Liège* brought Captain Jorgenson little slips of paper reporting new torpedoing. One was that of our sister ship, the *Ville de Namur*, about 200 miles to the northwest of our position at the time, too far away, Jorgenson decided, for us to try to pick up the survivors.

Somehow these grim reminders of our own hazard merely fortified the feeling of security—or at least of a kind of secure precariousness —that had been growing in my mind since I came aboard the *Ville de Liège*. The feeling was not one of magic invulnerability like that conferred at times by the watch ritual I had related to Allendy; it was not a metaphysical cloak like the one that had enveloped me once for a few intense, timeless moments the night in Spain when I had climbed the hill near Ávila; it was not the lyric exaltation that had welled up in me after I found Vreni in Alençon. My present euphoric mood was both more sober and more lucid than any of these earlier adventures of the soul in the uncertain borderlands of awareness; above all it was more durable, and during the five days it took the *Ville de Liège* to complete its lonely zigzag course out into the mid-Atlantic and around the west coast of Ireland I often tried to analyze the factors that might account for it.

Several were easy enough to identify, and virtually self-explanatory when one had done so. Any sea voyage is a holiday from the servitudes of terrestial life, as war itself is, and this wartime voyage between a life frame that had vanished and one that had yet to be created was thus a holiday within a holiday. At the same time it was the joyful rediscovery of an ordered human society after the social *Walpurgisnacht* in which the French breakdown had culminated. A torpedo might hit the *Ville de Liège* at any moment, but with Captain Jorgenson in command one felt confident that reason and humanity would continue to prevail, panic and delirium to be held in check, as long as she stayed afloat. Death, if it came, would not come as alienation. One felt oneself the member of a community of hazard.

Life aboard the *Ville de Liège* was more than a purely symbolic reintegration into society for me, however. In retrospect I can perceive more clearly than I was able to at the time that the halcyon imprint it left on my memory, the tourist-folder vignettes of endlessly smiling skies and of sparkling, wine-dark seas that flash before my eyes when I recall it, reflect above all else the sense of enhancement that we always feel whenever we break through some of our own inner barriers.

I was not immediately aware of all that I found beyond those barriers, but I did perceive that I had found myself in several important respects during those sessions of serene introspection on the *Ville de Liège*. I both repatriated myself as an American and enlarged the image of America that I carried in my mind; the vicarious experience of defeat had made me both a franker nationalist and a more authentic internationalist than I had been before. I was a more dedicated, as well as a more disillusioned, democrat. Because I had seen how fast and how far man can slip back down the ladder of progress, because I had been able to measure more realistically than previously the immensity of the effort required to achieve each step up he takes, my faith in his capacity to climb, in his aptitude for progress, grew strong and clear, where in the past it had often wavered or turned dim.

At a more intimate level I felt a new sense of security, of being at home in an insecure world, precisely because I had learned at last how profoundly unsettled the world was, and would doubtless remain for the rest of my lifetime, and perhaps that of my children. I had shed my delusion of normalcy: The world I was living in, I had discovered, was not what I had been brought up to think of as a normal world, and in my life it never would be. Yet living in such flux of history did not mean one could never put down roots anywhere: it simply required learning to put them down wherever one might be. It was not necessary to renounce all one's attachments; it was essential to multiply them. It was not the goal of happiness that one had to abandon, merely the claim to happiness, the childlike expectation of happiness.

I was still a considerable way, perhaps, from being able to look at the twentieth-century world with truly adult eyes, from participating in twentieth-century history with a truly adult sense of responsibility, but I had come a considerable way, too, the last bit of it rather fast.

Book Five

The
School
of
War

16

A Certain Loss of Innocence

The Second World War seems to have been on the whole a less tragic experience for my generation than the first one was for our fathers—it was too inescapable, and we were already inured to upheaval—but it was nonetheless a formidable ordeal to live through, if one did live through it. At least 30,000,000 human beings did not, and no merely human mind, least of all a contemporary one numbed by repeated surfeit of catastrophe, could possibly compute exactly how or how much such an immense sum of death has diminished each of us survivors of the holocaust, or to what degree it has impoverished the generations of man to come. Viewed as a crisis in the evolution of twentieth-century civilization, the conflict is even more difficult to gauge. While there are staggering losses, there are also some gains to balance them, if only because a certain amount of cultural wreckage from the earlier war which was stifling reconstruction was finally razed, and because some moral wounds that had been festering since 1914, or even longer, were at last cauterized. In terms of dead and maimed, of cultural and economic treasure destroyed, of lives uprooted, World War II was undoubtedly the most costly that man has so far waged against himself. From the Western point of view it brought about, or helped bring about, a substantial and unwelcome shift in the global balance of power. From the viewpoint of humanity as a whole it fostered—though at times it also exorcised —habits of violence, ruthlessness, and herd suspicion that still bedevil us. The very fact that before it was over all the belligerents had come to look upon the obliteration of whole cities by air attack as a normal combat practice represented in itself an appalling, if inevitable, regression form the already debased standards observed during the 1914–1918 war. The Nazi death camps so far exceeded any remembered norms of barbarity that they stigmatized not only their authors but even the civilization from which the German leaders had seceded. In opening the Pandora's box of nuclear weapons, the United States loosed on our planet a menace without precedent in man's whole history, and revived an apocalyptic terror the Western mind had scarcely known since the Middle Ages. All these horrors and disasters—along with many others—were part of the price that my generation paid, and that our children and our children's children will go on paying, for saving ourselves and them from the two most extreme manifestations of contemporary neo-barbarism, German National Socialism and Japanese militarism.

Yet our struggle, and the victory that crowned it, won some positive rewards (apart from the reward of survival), not only for the victors, but for all men. One of the most significant, it seems to me, is the expanded world-consciousness that the Second World War brought to millions, if not to hundreds of millions, whose mental horizons had hitherto been bounded by their native villages, or at best by the frontiers of a single nation. It was not quite the One World of human brotherhood some of us had dreamed about, but it did reflect a substantial "planetization"—in Teilhard de Chardin's sense—of man's self-awareness, and that, perhaps, is a necessary prologue to more effective progress toward human unity.

Nowhere was the enlargement of territorial horizons and interests or the ripening of political attitudes more dramatic than in the mind of America. World War I had made us for the first time a great power in the classic sense, but in failing to join the League of Nations it seemed to an internationalist that we had recoiled from the traditional responsibilities of our status, perhaps from the sheer anguish of power, like some overgrown adolescent terrified of his own hulking body. In World War II, with our power suddenly expanded beyond that of any traditional model, save Rome itself, we finally learned to accept the responsibility and to live with the anguish.

Whether America's emergence as a superpower was an unalloyed blessing for the world at large or even for America itself; whether on overall balance the war barbarized the minds of men in some respects more than it raised them to a higher level of civilization in others; whether from the evolutionary viewpoint the recognition of genocide as a crime against humanity outweighed the ghastly scale of its perpetration in our time; whether the growing condemnation of war as a criminal activity compensated for the ever-increasing frightfulness with which we still persist in waging it; whether it was a real progress to discover new human rights while the oldest ones were being more widely flouted than ever; these are questions we ourselves cannot hope to answer.

What should be possible for those of us who are survivors of the century's second Armageddon is to look back on it—before it is too late—and to identify some of the particular experiences within the general ordeal that in the light of our present maturity, such as it is, seem either to have stunted us or to have helped us grow. Such experiences—and the kinds of growth or stunting that they fostered —naturally are conditioned both by individual destiny and by historic circumstance. The losers in a war do not have the same remembrance of it that the winners have; both may feel proud or bitter or anguished to recall what they have felt or seen, but it is never the same pride, the same bitterness, the same anguish. The growth ordeals of a civilian are different from those of a soldier, even when the former is more exposed to the dangers and savageries of combat than the latter, as was not infrequently the case in that war. The impression of a given military action gained from a front-line foxhole not only bears little resemblance to what is portrayed in a headquarters war room but also diverges in many respects from the view of it that the general gets flying over the actual battlefields; in fact, the perspective from the foxhole itself changes according to whether its occupant is a combat infantryman, a staff observer, or a war correspondent.

One of the most important psychological frontiers in war—or indeed, in any collective enterprise of historic proportion—is that which separates the spectator from the participant. Up to 1941, I had been a professional spectator of power struggles and of organized violence in various forms, but no matter how deeply my sympathies were involved, I had never had to accept my share of moral responsibility for the things I saw or hoped to see happen. My heart was pure, my hands were clean. Thus, I could upbraid the League of Nations for betraying its ideals in Abyssinia with little danger of someday having to ask myself whether I had not betrayed my own ideals in helping to draft or execute plans for bombing, or at least starving, Italian women and children into respect for the Covenant. When the United States entered the war—to be exact, a little before that—I crossed myself the invisible border between observation and action, between the critic and the players. For the first time in my existence, I found myself confronted with the moral problems that arise when one takes a direct, active part, however modest, in helping to shape or to carry out group decisions involving the use of power. The resultant loss of innocence and gain of adult awareness stands out in my mind as the most significant lesson in self-understanding of my war years. It was a traumatic one at certain moments, brightly colored at others.

My exposure to the apocalyptic aspects of the war—the great cities swept by man-made fire storms, the German horror camps, the frozen hell of the Russian front, the jungle hells of the Pacific—was no greater than that of any contemporary newspaper reader. Physically, I lived a comfortable staff officer's life most of the three or so years I spent overseas, but without the monotony of such an existence. The main dangers and fatigues were those of frequent and prolonged travel, often in wild regions and in every kind of weather, in the still rather primitive military transport craft of the period. The little military action I saw myself was small-scale and reassuringly old-fashioned. The real terrors and atrocities I encountered were of a different sort. Like several other episodes in my life, my wartime experience was, from the twentieth-century American viewpoint, at once typical and atypical. The disillusionments—including the self-disillusionments—that I had to surmount, the choices I had to learn to make, the temptations I had to overcome were in the main more political than military, and sometimes only remotely related to the outcome of the war. But for these very reasons they were often in miniature—and sometimes in caricature—those that history itself was forcing on the mind and conscience of America, or at any rate on those of American liberals.

17

Indiscretions of a Democratic Well-Poisoner

The Japanese attack on Pearl Harbor, December 6, 1941, undoubtedly effected a revolutionary change in American psychology; it was then, for the first time in our existence as a nation, that many Americans acquired a consciousness of national mortality. As far as I can recall my own feelings on the occasion, however, the realization that a kind of magic invulnerability had been shattered forever did not dawn with the first reports of the Japanese raid; it developed gradually, over the following days and weeks, as the momentarily critical nature of our strategic predicament became apparent. Probably the news was somewhat less of a shock to me than it was to most of my fellow countrymen. In my mind we had already been at war with the Axis powers—and fighting for our national survival—for some time; it was natural enough that one of them should eventually seek to formalize the situation. I had lived for too long too far from the United States, and too close to the European dictatorships, to feel any very strong sense of outrage at the thought of an inevitable adversary choosing to strike the first blow and to strike by surprise. Any other behavior on his part would have seemed surprising. All in all, my thoughts and sentiments were quite different from what they had been twenty-six months earlier when Hitler launched his blitzkrieg against Poland. I felt no sense of doom such as I had experienced in 1939—and scarcely any awareness of heightened danger, either to America or to myself. I think I was more relieved than anything else.

Since my return from France some eighteen months earlier, I had been one of those Americans who believed that if we were to save what was left of European civilization and safeguard our own, it was imperative to enter the war as full belligerents at Britain's side. Our greatest fear had been that because of constitutional and political difficulties President Roosevelt, who we assumed shared our view, would not be able to act in time. Now the Japanese had swept away all such obstacles; my relief was therefore natural and, in retrospect, not wholly unjustifiable.

I happened to be in England then, and owing to the time lag in the United Sates, I did not learn of the Japanese attack until late in the afternoon, well past the blackout hour. Pearl Harbor Day for me is therefore one without a morning, a day when history began at dusk; it has a faint reek of boiled cabbage and warm gin before breakfast, along with more appetizing associations. No doubt my mind has telescoped the impressions of an all-too-lighthearted wassail with the somewhat queasy awakening that followed. The English friends with whom I celebrated the occasion were no more conscious that we were drinking to the knell of Britain's imperial rule than I that we were hailing the birth pangs of a new world superpower which Americans of my generation would sometimes find difficult to recognize as the land of their fathers. I only recall a sense of comradeship that seemed the promise of the general human brotherhood our joint victory would one day help to found. Perhaps the oddest of memory's vagaries is my feeling that I had been let in on a portentous secret known only to a handful of initiates. It is true that the first report reached me—or reached the British colleague who rushed to tell me—on an official telephone from some high-level source in London, but by the time we had finished the first round of gin and bitters inspired by it, the BBC had already broadcast the news and millions of Americans had heard it hours before. The secret was not the fact of the Japanese attack; it was the nature of the place where I happened to hear about it: a small bar, adjacent to a large, smelly canteen, set up in what I believe was originally one of the servants' eating halls at Woburn Abbey, the Duke of Bedford's ancestral country estate. Known familiarly as the Ostrich Farm—because of the Duke's extensive private zoo, many of whose inmates roamed the stately park in virtual freedom—the premises had been requisitioned for the Political Warfare Executive, a secret wartime agency embodying some features of the venerable scoundrel tradition in British diplomacy that had scandalized me as a correspondent in Geneva during the Abyssinian war. I was myself on mission from a fledgling American analogue (then called the Coordinator of Information) as a kind of apprentice-scoundrel. I had started my war service some months before my country was officially at war. The transatlantic fellowship mellowed that raw December night in warm gin and warmer beer symbolized the coming fraternity of man from one viewpoint, but from another it was merely the professional bonhomie of an inernationale of witch doctors and well-poisoners.

Perhaps the characterization is too harsh. The Political Warfare Executive was technically a secret service, but it was largely staffed with journalistic amateurs or high-minded Oxford and Cambridge dons. Richard Crossman, the future Labor minister, was supervising the German section at Woburn Abbey in my day; Ritchie Calder, a left-wing Socialist who after the war became a prominent figure in British UNESCO activities and in the international movement for nuclear disarmament, was one of the chief PWE planners, and my former Paris colleague of the *Daily Express*, Sefton Delmer (whose memoir *Black Boomerang* is the fullest account of the agency's operations I have seen in print), was in charge of the so-called "black" German programs. Black propaganda is essentially calumny and provocation, the age-old crafts of tyrant and conspirator, spread with the help of twentieth-century technology. A case in point is one of Delmer's most notable operations, the covert radio station *Gustav Siegfried Eins*, which pretended to be the true voice of the traditional German officer class, broadcasting from somewhere in occupied Europe. *Gustav Siegfried Eins* was a kind of electronic forgery dependent for its effectiveness less on plausibility than on an inspired scandal-mongering which Cesare Borgia, Richelieu, or Fouché, Napoleon's police chief, would have admired. One shudders to imagine what nineteenth-century Russia would have been like if the czarist Okhrana had been able to give its crude fabrication, the mythical Protocols of Zion—a blueprint for an imaginary Jewish plot to achieve world dominion—a comparable living voice. My earlier propaganda studies in Paris naturally brought such historical analogies to my mind at Woburn Abbey. Sometimes I even felt myself plunged back into the witch-haunted world of Lévy-Bruhl's "primitives."

I can recall in particular a meeting of the PWE Sib Committee I attended during my stay in Britain. "Sibs" (from the Latin *sibillare:* to whisper) were rumors dreamed up by the planners at the Abbey and intended for unattributable launching by "black" radio, by secret agents, or by the resistance networks in occupied countries, and in other ways. Rumors, I learned at PWE, were a very tricky business: If they were carelessly handled, strategic intentions might be inadvertently betrayed and resistance activities compromised. Moreover, what was an effective "sib" in one area might backfire in another: To launch, for example, the rumor that Hitler and Mussolini were united by bonds of homosexual lust might merely serve to enhance the prestige or glamor of the two enemy dictators in certain parts of the world. Experience—no doubt bitter—had led to the establishment of a rather high-level interministerial and interservice committee that met every fortnight to winnow the latest crop of "sibs" grown in the closes of Woburn Abbey. It was impressive to watch the eminent, and eminently respectable, bowler or brass-hatted servants of His Majesty who sat on this committee arriving for the occasion in their black official limousines—I recognized several of them from various international conferences I had covered before the war—and I was duly conscious of my rare privilege in being admitted to their highly secret deliberations. The Sib Committee was one of the most taboo political warfare mechanisms or activities in Britain, and I am surprised that Delmer was, evidently, authorized to reveal its existence in his book a mere seventeen years after the war. I found the "black" propaganda that they were engaged in producing, and even many of the British "white" programs, more imaginative and frequently more ruthless than any Nazi psychological warfare I had studied. The mixture of bureaucratic solemnity and schoolboy best with which the business of the meeting was conducted helped to make it memorable for me.

The atmosphere of creative nightmare in which my PWE friends lived; the romantic isolation of their country retreat behind its invisible walls of secrecy; the incongruous splendor of the Abbey with its echoing, deserted corridors; the dreamlike, autumnal park that surrounded it; the raucous cries of the peacocks; the lordly, hieratic stags—all these influences and impressions, I found, tended to lure one's rational mind along a labyrinthine way back to a world where magic, white or black, became the true causality. Usually the unshakable British common sense and the fundamental British decency that underlay even the delirium of twentieth-century political warfare sufficed to set at rest my faint qualms about the whole business. From time to time, however, I could not help asking myself certain questions. One, which I wondered about quite a bit but tactfully refrained from putting to my hots, concerned the basis of operational doctrine upon which PWE had been so quickly, yet apparently so solidly, built. The agency was strictly a wartime administrative creation but almost everything about it—except, perhaps, the personalities of its staff—bespoke an ancient experience in the techniques of dissension and demoralization. From what secret peacetime drawers had the British taken out all these recipes for exploiting human weakness, all these mental philters, all these scoundrel skills accumulated through centuries of power struggle in every quarter of the globe which they were now so generously making available to an upstart ally and potential successor?

I never discovered the full answer—the problem of how power attitudes and certain power skills are transmitted within large organizations such as states falls in one of the least-explored borderlands between history and sociology—but I had already gathered from my earlier readings that political warfare, at least in a rudimentary form, had been part of the British secret service tradition from the start. Somewhere in the world, Britain for centuries past had always been waging political warfare, though perhaps only on a local scale, and practicing the various arts of subversion connected with it. Whenever a major threat to British power had developed, as during the Napoleonic wars or in the First World War, there had thus always existed the indispensable foundations for rapid expansion: a pool of trained personnel, a current technology of clandestine operations, and the necessary structures of administrative control.

The situation was quite different in the United States, as I had good reason to know. Some months earlier, in researching an article for *Fortune*—a plea for the creation of a permanent American political warfare service—I had unearthed a number of picturesque examples from the early history of the republic demonstrating that Yankee ingenuity—and lack of scruple—in the clandestine aspects of war or diplomacy were capable of meeting the most exacting Old World standards. Neither John Paul Jones nor President Polk had founded a permanent secret intelligence service, however; there had never been a peacetime American equivalent of Britain's MI–6 (secret intelligence service). The Army's G–2 and the Office of Naval Intelligence constituted a nucleus of sorts for the development of wartime espionage activities, but there were no administrative cells in the United Sates government before 1941 capable of serving as an oganizational memory for storing whatever experience in political warfare we acquired in our successive wars or foreign adventures. In consequence, both the theory and the machinery of political warfare had to be built up anew each time the need for them was felt.

That was only half of our difficulty, however. Whereas the British ruling classes, in the course of time, had largely come to terms with their own consciences over the moral issues raised by diverse ungentlemanly but useful adjuncts of British power, had learned when to close their eyes and when to cry a halt, in the United States, as late as 1942, the very principle of a secret service was abhorrent to many, including professionals in the armed forces and the State Department. Secretary of War Henry L. Stimson himself had earlier manifested an insurmountable repugnance against suggestions for reestablishing the U.S. "black rooms" of World War I in an attempt to break the Japanese diplomatic and naval ciphers. Gentlemen, Mr.

Stimson felt, do not read other people's private correspondence. Several of the senior American military or civilian personalities with whom I had official dealings before and after Pearl Harbor impressed me as being no less anachronistically high-minded in their opposition to any government-sponsored U.S. programs that could be considered political or psychological warfare.

My own attitude with regard to the moral implications of such programs had evolved—or at least changed—since I had begun to study the subject in Europe. After the fall of France, I was more convinced than ever that Nazi political warfare was a threat to American democracy calling for urgent measures to strengthen our defenses against subversion and demoralization. "Under certain conditions," I warned in a lecture early in 1941, "it might be essential for national morale to put some of the IRA [Irish Republican Army] chiefs in this country in front of a firing squad.* The same measure might have to be taken with respect to the Communist fifth column . . . Conversely, there are the oft-denounced indulgences of American conservatives for treason in its reactionary, anti-New Deal manifestations." (I sometimes wonder today how I would have felt if I had been called on to command one of those firing squads I recommended against fellow Americans guilty, at least in my eyes, of a type of treason unmentioned by the basic laws of the land, on behalf of an enemy with whom we were not then officially at war.)

I was also active in several of the Administration-encouraged volunteer committees—a characteristic and often picturesque phenomenon of the epoch—that were simultaneously agitating for U.S. intervention in the war and trying to fortify domestic morale. One of these groups attracted me particularly because of its special concern with the problem of political warfare. Called the Committee for a National Morale, it had been founded by an elderly specialist in

* The Irish Republican Army, a clandestine nationalist organization fighting principally for the unification of Ireland, had members and sympathizers in the United States who in their fanatical hatred of Britain were willing to work— or were suspected of being willing to work—with Nazi agents against the Allied cause.

Iranian studies, Dr. Arthur Upham Pope, a man of irrepressible energies and evidently of diverse enthusiasms. Pope's missionary fervor had somehow prevailed on a number of distinguished American intellectuals, including such honorably atypical representatives of the social science community as the anthropologists Margaret Mead and Gregory Bateson, to join with him in what finally became a sort of lobby for the establishment of a national morale service. (Not all members of the committee, needless to say, shared our chairman's ambitious concept of the proposed addition to the New Deal bureaucracy.) My recruitment was due, of course, to my recent book. Having written about political warfare, I naturally qualified as an expert in the field, and in those years of national innocence there were probably not many Americans whose visible qualifications were much higher. The Pope committee had a tenuous link with Washington through Secretary of the Interior Harold Ickes, who encouraged us—as his comments were transmitted by our chairman—to believe that we were drafting the blueprint for a revolutionary and beneficient administrative innovation, calculated to assure the national salvation. Somewhat more parsimoniously, Mr. Ickes, or someone, supplied us from time to time with funds, presumably from White House sources, for our expenses. The most unworldly member of our group could scarcely fail to be visited at moments by daydreams of a spacious office in the nation's capital, complete with scrambler telephone.

My niche in our imaginary tables of organization was in the division responsible for undermining enemy morale. (The committee was on the whole more interested in constructive, nonauthoritarian techniques for strengthening the home front.) As far as I can recall, the assignment had fallen to me by common consent, without any particular seeking on my part, largely, I suppose, because having described and analyzed the Nazi psychological offensives, I was assumed to be capable of plotting the American counteroffensive. Once I started thinking about how it might be organized, I began to believe in it; function produced the concept, practice—or at least experiment—the theory. No doubt, if my mind and conscience had actively recoiled from the idea of fighting Hitlerism with Hitler's favorite weapons, I would have refused my role as the Committee on National Morale's specialist in counter-political warfare. Since I accepted the role, I soon became the advocate for my speciality that others supposed I had been from the start. And since my advocacy had to overcome the ideological or moral scruples of the government officials and opinion leaders the Committee was trying to influence, I naturally had to begin by stifling my own, such as they were. In the process I found myself carried along by my psychological momentum toward positions more extreme than some of my colleagues approved or than any with which I would earlier have chosen to identify myself. The article in *Fortune*, along with various lectures and unpublished memoranda from the same period, reflect my transformation from an exposer of mental terrorism into one of its apologists.

The broad and unrestrained kind of political warfare I argued for was close to what Colonel (later Major General) William J. Donovan, a prominent Wall Street lawyer, Republican political leader, and dashing combat officer of World War I, had been championing in Washington, though I was not aware of the fact until I was summoned to meet him in July 1941. Donovan offered me a job in the new office of the Coordinator of Information he had just been appointed to set up. The organization was to have far-reaching, if somewhat vague, responsibilities in a field ranging from foreign propaganda programs and information to subversion and secret intelligence. That, at least, was how Donovan read his charter. The propaganda wing, called the Foreign Information Service, was to be headed by Robert E. Sherwood, the noted playwright and one of President Roosevelt's most talented speechwriters. I knew Sherwood slightly, from some of the overlapping interventionist committees with which we were both connected, and admired him greatly. With Donovan's concurrence, he invited me to become one of the three special assistants that had been allotted to him in the organization chart of his division; I would have particular responsibility for advising him in the area of true psychological or political warfare, as distinguished from straightforward information programs.

I reported for duty at the COI's temporary Washington office late in August. Some two months later I was sent on the study mission to Britain. On my return, shortly before the end of the year, I wrote a report for Sherwood summarizing what I had learned in Britain and concluding with recommendations that our own operations be based as far as possible on the PWE doctrine of all-out political warfare.

My proposals stirred up a certain amount of dissension within the COI camp. Sherwood himself, despite his evangelistic New Deal convictions, reacted favorably, as I had expected, but many of my colleagues seemed baffled, and some were horrified. The upper echelons of COI's Foreign Information Service, by then installed in a seedy Madison Avenue office building in New York, were staffed in large part with earnest and somewhat doctrinaire American liberals, for whom psychological warfare apparently meant radio sermons on President Roosevelt's recently proclaimed Four Freedoms, and folksy chats about the neighborhood drugstore as a national cultural institution. (Later, when the Foreign Information Service of COI grew into the Office of War Information, headed by Elmer Davis, a more contemporary and hard-minded type of liberalism swept away most of the intellectual fuzz, but the nostalgia for native corn continued to crop up from time to time; indeed, faint traces of it can still be found, it seems to me, in the output of the present-day United States Information Agency.) Naturally, this Chautauqua outlook—as I thought of it—seemed naïve and anachronistic to me. My attitude doubtless appeared cynical and reactionary to my office adversaries.

From one viewpoint, they were right. It was not a lack of ideological conviction, however, that led me to advocate fighting the enemy with his own weapons. It was rather an excess of political activism, reinforced by the feeling I had brought back from France that democracy was in imminent danger of perishing from this earth. To save it, all means were democratic. It was thus neither the organization man's assumption that the organization is always right, nor the authoritarian *raison d'état* that sometimes paralyzed or distorted my conscience, but something closer to the Jacobin doctrine of *salut publique* in the French Revolution, the "obsession of victory" I mentioned in my last chapter. I was ready to apply Bolshevik standards and methods, complete with Cheka if necessary, to defend the democratic revolution.

In the COI context, the controversy was in many respects futile. If the purely ideological approach to political warfare made little sense, the ruthless Machiavellianism I often championed had its drawbacks, too. Some stratagems or devices of political warfare which looked diabolically ingenious on paper turned out to be as unrealistic as the fuzziest daydreaming of the ultraliberal faction. After COI split up and I joined Col. Donovan's Office of Strategic Services, I was haunted for weeks—no doubt a fitting chastisement for my earlier sins of witchcraft—by a single-minded fanatic, the inventor of a scheme for putting the Japanese Army to flight with elaborately contrived nocturnal apparitions simulating a luminous fox, a symbol of ill omen in Japanese culture. More than once I was put to flight myself by the author of the project who, during his all-too-frequent visits to Washington, liked to sit in a corner of my office practicing sound effects on the foxcall he had had specially built at Abercrombie and Fitch.

Certain "black" programs that PWE might have been able to carry off were simply too complicated and tricky for an American government agency to attempt, even behind the screen of wartime censorship. Still others, I came eventually to realize, were self-defeating for a democratic society defending itself against totalitarian neobarbarism. Today I can scarcely recall without a shudder one "black" project that was seriously discussed, though fortunately never put into execution, during my COI days. This tortuous scheme was based on a kind of double deception that might be characterized as induced character assassination. With the help of the British clandestine services, a low-powered, amateurish-sounding broadcasting station, pretending to be an underground Nazi one, was to have been set up on British soil in the Western Hemisphere, as close as possible to the United States. Its programs, partly in German, partly in English, would be beamed to the U.S. and would purport to emanate from within the country; ostensibly, they would be addressed to American Nazis, fascist sympathizers, and militant isolationists. The basic propaganda line and most of the editorial material were simply to be lifted from recent and authentic Nazi propaganda broadcasts, but from time to time the pseudo-fifth columnists were to interpolate unattributed extracts from anti-war editorials in the American press or from the speeches of isolationist leaders, especially those who had been most actively connected with the militant America First committee and who continued after Pearl Harbor to subvert the national morale with appeasement propaganda.

Whenever possible the extracts in question were to be taken from editorials written but not yet printed, and from speeches not yet delivered; they would be obtained with the help of undercover agents previously planted or recruited in the target organizations, and their use in the "black" broadcasts would be so timed that they slightly antedated the normal release. The speakers and publications thus plagiarized without their knowledge would be compromised by appearing to have got their inspiration from a clandestine and flagrantly subversive Nazi propaganda station operating in gross violation of federal law. Effective smear campaigns could then be organized against the target individuals and groups; public pressures could be generated for stern repression of the whole Nazi fifth column in America, along with its accomplices and sympathizers.

I doubt whether any record of the sinister project survives in the national archives; officially, indeed, it never existed. COI had no charter to operate on the domestic front, and if such an operation had been submitted to Col. Donovan he would have been horrified at its political implications. As far as I am aware, only one employee of COI besides myself had any guilty knowledge of the embryonic conspiracy: Robert E. Sherwood. One U.S. government official outside the agency—Harry Hopkins—was involved to the extent that Sherwood consulted him; he promptly advised Bob to forget the whole business. A British clandestine liaison officer in the United States was unofficially sounded about the possibility of obtaining the outside help upon which the realization of the scheme depended, but played no part in its elaboration. The reason I happen to know all these details myself is that I was the sole author of the plot, the person who discussed it with the British agent, and the one who proposed it to Sherwood.

The only excuse that can be offered for the execrable design is that it reflected the alarm bordering on panic felt by many American anti-Nazis after the early German victories in Russia and the series of Allied military catastrophes in the Pacific. I hatched the scheme in late December 1941 or in early January 1942, shortly after my return from England. I believed at the time—and I suppose Sherwood did too—that what might be termed the democratic will to survive in the United States was gravely threatened by a conspiracy of foreign and domestic enemies. The conspirators, I thought, were seeking to exploit the momentary American and Allied reverses in order to build up public pressures for a negotiated peace that would eventually open the way to a kind of American Vichy regime. The danger was not, I think, wholly imaginary, but it was surely more remote than I considered it. Even if it had not been, there was no demonstrable need for organizing what in effect would have been a para-governmental counter-conspiracy to discredit the purveyors of defeatism and perhaps of a certain ideological disaffection whom I looked on as virtual Nazi fifth columnists. The implicit definitions of treason, subversion, and conspiracy that underlay my appreciation of their political activity were as perilously metaphysical as those which were later responsible for some of our more irrational anti-Communist witch-hunts, with all their private injustices and national humiliations. Perhaps demagogues like the late Joseph R. McCarthy owed more than was generally realized to the anti-Nazi witch-hunters of an earlier day, among whom I was neither the most nor the least respectful of due process.

From the moral viewpoint, my abortive enterprise recalls the demimonde of *agents provocateurs* and bureaucratized conspiracy responsible for such synthetic nightmares of history as the Dreyfus affair. As I write, there flashes again before my mind's eye the sallow features and tarnished look of the French police official who had tried to sell me those curious anti-Communist forgeries I mentioned in an earlier chapter; he and his disquieting Russian accomplice Nikho would doubtless have admired my ingenuity and accepted me as a worthy disciple—if only I had not overlooked the profit angle. Who knows, though; perhaps there was a time when Nikho and the Chief, too, spun their shadowy plots not for private gain but in the service of a political ideal.

Another ghost face from the past floats before me now; I remember that doughy pallor, that fixed look of sincerity, as if glued on, and that peculiar sad ennui, like a kind of body odor that somehow went with them. I never knew the man well and though he is linked in my memory with the Chief and Nikho, unlike them he never did or said anything to capture my conscious imagination. His name, I discovered later, was Otto Katz, but I knew him as O.K., or sometimes André, Simon. He was a German-Czech Communist who at the time of our acquaintance was the Paris correspondent of a Spanish Republican news agency. I suppose he cultivated me because of my American Club speech against the Spanish Nationalists. While the war in Spain lasted he used to drift into my office from time to time, give me some minor and usually accurate bits of information—often to the discredit of the Communists—and then simply sit for long minutes without speaking a word, looking sad and bored and sincere.

Many years after the war I learned from the memoirs of a British ex-Communist newspaperman (Claud Cockburn) who had worked under Katz-Simon that he had been one of the Comintern master propagandists in Western Europe during the Popular Front period, specializing in the "gray" and "black" range of press activities. Some of the most lurid anti-Nazi and anti-Franco atrocity stories of the times—there was no dearth of them—had been spawned in Katz's fertile brain and planted by him or his assistants on unsuspecting colleagues of the bourgeois press. He had been particularly artful in contriving to get anti-fascist fabrications printed in right-wing papers. No doubt, I figured in the operational plans he submitted to his superiors as a potentially valuable dupe who should be saved for some major coup and until then supplied only with factual items, to build up confidence.

As I realize now, Simon-Katz, like Nikho and the Chief, was thus another colleague before the fact, in terms of my 1941 role. Like myself, but unlike the other two conspirators, he was plotting for a cause—perhaps even a cause he still believed in. After the war he was hanged in Prague for treason, the usual party term for mistimed fidelity. I suppose he was still wearing his sincere look when the trap fell.

There, but for the grace of God . . . The three memory phantoms —the venal anti-Communists and the dedicated professional revolutionary—have risen out of the pit to bring me the same comminatory reminder: All conspirators are fellow conspirators, even those against conspiracy.

It is always useful to be reminded that whenever we fight an amoral enemy with his own arms we risk putting our cause on the same moral plane with his. Yet in an age like ours, which combines some of the most sinister aspects of the power struggle in Renaissance Italy with those of the Thirty Years' War and the French Revolution, such moralizing reminders are only a negative contribution to the problem of survival with honor. The underlying issue is perhaps not so much ethical as sociological and psychiatric.

Judging from the experience of our times, an open society cannot defend itself effectively in many circumstances against the subversive attacks of a closed one without in some measure adopting the latter's tactics and operational code. To limit the unavoidable moral and political regression, it is necessary, among other things, to measure accurately the scale of the threat, including the adversary's real capabilities and intentions, and to analyze coolly one's own vulnerabilities, in other words, when we look under the bed to see only what is actually there—if there is anything at all.

The ability to assess objectively a covert, or partly covert, and therefore conspiratorial menace to the community one belongs to and to the values one holds sacred is among the essential political skills that an adult citizen of the twentieth century should possess. Mastering it is also a significant key to a certain kind of psychological balance and maturity. Clearly, I had not made much progress toward

such maturity of mind when I went to Sherwood with my proposal
for what amounted to an electronic frame-up of the critics of Roosevelt's war policies. Possibly my acclimatization into the overlapping
worlds of the amateur witch-hunter and the professional witch
doctor exposed me to influences that set back for a while my moral
and emotional development. If so, my subsequent wartime service in
an organization dedicated in part to still stealthier arts of conspiracy
and in part to the most brutal techniques of militarized murder may
have acted as a kind of psychological antidote, or counter-poison.

18

The World as Conspiracy

Battles Long Ago: North Africa

The molecule of twentieth-century experience with which the present chapter deals is a complex one. Particularly for the reader who belongs to a generation later than mine, it may help understanding if I preface the personal, essentially subjective mind history I am trying to relate with a brief, summary glance at the general event history that frames it. For the first part of the chapter, the key background event is the successful landing on the coast of French North Africa—Algeria and Morocco—carried out in the second week of November 1942 by a combined American-British task force under the command of General Eisenhower. (The background in the later parts of the chapter concerns Southeast Asia.)

The North American expedition was the first large-scale action of the still-raw United States forces in the European theater since our entry into the conflict. It marked a turning point in the history of the war. Coordinated with the westward drive of Field Marshal Montgomery's Eighth Army through the Egyptian and Libyan deserts, the establishment of the Allied beachhead in Algeria and Morocco led within a few months to the liquidation of the German-Italian forces in all North Africa and prepared the way for the invasion of Italy.

My concern, of course, is with the political and psychological implications or repercussions of the operation. At the time, French North Africa (Tunisia, Algeria, Morocco), along with the vast territory south of the Sahara then called French West Africa, were under the control of the Vichy regime in unoccupied France, headed by the aged Marshal Philippe Pétain. Though a German-Italian armistice commission kept a vigilant eye on all local affairs, and meddled in some, no Axis military units were stationed in the area. French forces, substantial though poorly armed, were still garrisoned there, with Axis permission, to preserve order and maintain a French colonial presence.

From the United States viewpoint, Vichy France and its overseas possessions were neutral territory, and we maintained courteous diplomatic relations with the Pétain government, despite its evident subservience to Nazi Germany. An influential bureaucratic faction in the Roosevelt administration manifested a sympathy for the Vichy regime that often seemed warmer than considerations of diplomatic and strategic expediency could account for. American public opinion, however, was generally anti-Vichy, both because of the regime's pro-Axis—or apparently pro-Axis—leanings and because of its anti-democratic, crypto-fascist political philosophy. British opinion, both public and official, was even more adverse: The British looked on Vichy as a virtual German puppet state, backed the Free French movement of General Charles de Gaulle, and waged unremitting political warfare against the Pétain government. Bitter clashes between British—or British-supported Free French—and Vichy armed forces had already occurred, notably in West Africa and in Syria. Frenchmen, particularly French professional officers, who were loyal to the old Marshal but hostile to the Axis, were scarcely less hostile to the British, though usually friendly toward the United States.

Because of these and other complexities in the situation, when it was decided between Washington and London to mount the North African operation it was agreed that the British, though their military contribution was essential to success, should remain in the background politically, and that the Free French should be kept out of the picture altogether. Originally the landings were conceived in purely military terms and it was assumed that there would be some resistance on the part of the local French commanders. Later, in the hope of winning cooperation from some or all of the French authorities in Algeria and Morocco (landings in Tunisia were finally ruled out for logistic reasons), an ambitious program of underground diplomacy and subversive political warfare was grafted onto the military plan.

As numerous memoirs and studies have related, the political side of the operation was only partly successful and led to a vast, continuing imbroglio. On the eve of the landings Admiral Jean-Louis Darlan, the key figure in the Vichy regime after Pétain himself, unexpectedly arrived in Algeria, where his son had been taken gravely ill, and his presumably fortuitous presence in North Africa upset all the carefully laid plots of the Allies and their French partisans. The French armed forces not only failed to welcome their Anglo-Saxon liberators, but put up a far more stubborn and effective resistance than anyone had foreseen. Military expediency dictated a negotiated armistice with Darlan, recognizing his political authority in North Africa in return for his rather perfunctory cooperation against the Axis. This arrangement aroused almost equal indignation in the enemy capitals and among the masses in the United States and Britain—not to mention those in France. Hitler reacted with characteristic, uncomplicated brutality to what he considered a French betrayal by invading the hitherto unoccupied zone in France and by forcibly converting the Vichy administration into an out-and-out collaborationist one. The feeling of moral outrage aroused in the West by what the liberal press denounced as the "Deal with Darlan" had less immediately dramatic consequences. Ultimately they were found to be even more far-reaching—and in several respects tragic.

An extensive literature exists on the background and aftermaths of the Darlan affair. On the basis of my own firsthand impressions of it, I can offer at best a minor and peripheral footnote. My aim in the following pages is not, therefore, to contribute significant new material evidence in regard to a still shadowy, if much-studied, episode in contemporary history, but to bring out an aspect of the complicated and turgid drama that in my opinion has not been adequately stressed: its extreme moral ambiguity as paradigmatic of an essential twentieth-century ordeal of growth.

*

The hybrid COI split apart—not without some bitterness between Sherwood and Donovan—early in 1942 when the Office of Strategic Services was created, and I elected to join the new organization. Though I had grown fond of the fumbling, slow-speaking, but sensitive and witty Sherwood, and though his passionate Lincolnism was much closer to my own political outlook than Donovan's blend of Wall Street orthodoxy and sophisticated American nationalism, the General's personal charisma had proved overpowering.

I stayed in OSS—though sometimes attached to it by nothing more tangible than the invisible presence of Donovan in my mind—until some months after the end of the war. The experience was, among other things, the most prolonged and intensive exposure to the world of backstage power intrigues and rivalries, bureaucratic and national, that I have ever had. I suppose it was my relatively long period of service, from September 1943 to February 1946, in India and Southeast Asia that was most educational in this respect, but when I look back on the period as a whole it is an earlier mission in North Africa that comes to my mind as most pointedly illustrating the moral and emotional hazards involved in all secret service work. In reality, the hazards were to a large extent those of being an agent of power in any capacity and at any level; from another viewpoint they merely illustrate how dangerous it is for a writer to lend his pen to any organizational cause, especially one he believes in. For it was in my capacity as a technician of words that my personal involvement, at first a very superficial one, in the North African tragedy began.

One typical, hot, somnolent Washington weekend in the late summer of 1942, Gen. Donovan called me to the office—I was serving at the time as one of his special assistants—to collaborate with a distinguished overseas visitor, Robert Murphy, then the U.S. Consul General in Algiers, in drafting a memorandum for the President. Murphy, whom I already knew from Paris, had been supervising the activity of several OSS agents, disguised as vice-consuls, stationed in the chief cities of French North Africa, and was himself in direct clandestine contact with certain French Resistance elements. He and Donovan both believed in the potential military value of their underground allies. The recent British-U.S. staff talks, inaugurated with joint landings on the North African coast in view, had so far taken little account of this asset, except as a source of intelligence. Hence the memorandum for President Roosevelt, with whom Murphy was scheduled to have a talk at Hyde Park.

My role was to help Murphy and Donovan make the document as persuasive as possible. The General, for some reason, thought I had a certain talent, akin to that possessed by the authors of travel folders and real estate prospectuses, for this kind of administrative prose, and he urged me to give it full rein in the present instance. The injunction was unnecessary. At the time I believed as firmly as Donovan himself in the theological virtues of conspiracy, subversion, and insurrection, and I had a special enthusiasm for the French Resistance. Murphy's basic proposal for supporting the Anglo-American landings with an armed uprising of the French underground forces in North Africa, to be headed at the decisive moment by General Henri Giraud, fired my imagination. Gen. Giraud was an apolitical military personality, supposedly a popular figure in the French armed forces, thanks to his recent spectacular escape from a German fortress-prison. I would have preferred myself that Gen. de Gaulle's Free French movement in London be more closely associated with the scheme— several of Murphy's North African friends were Gaullist sympathizers—but knowing from bitter experience the almost hysterical anti-Gaullism prevalent in the State Department and the White House since the Free French occupation of St. Pierre and Miquelon at the beginning of the year, I considered Murphy had already gone as far as possible in the direction of undermining our official Vichy policy, even if that was not exactly his aim.

What finally emerged from all these pressures and maneuvers was the compromise, later the source of bitter controversy, whereby Murphy was authorized to organize his proposed *putsch*, and Giraud was to be smuggled out of Vichy France to serve as its standard-bearer, but none of the French Resistance leaders party to the conspiracy were to be told the exact time and place of the landings until a few days before they were due to occur. The secret Franco-American partnership for the liberation of North Africa was therefore an unequal one from the start; it involved an implicit deception of the junior partner by the senior, since the French were inevitably led to suppose that the invasion was not scheduled to be launched before sometime in 1943. We also encouraged our French allies to believe that the invasion force would be much stronger than in fact it was to be, and somehow in the course of the complicated underground negotiations with Giraud, that ill-starred and uninspired patriot was given cause to suppose that he, not Gen. Eisenhower, would be the Supreme Allied Commander in North Africa. De Gaulle, of course, was not consulted.

I followed the developing imbroglio, first from London where I had been sent by Gen. Donovan to represent him on the interallied subcommittee charged with planning the political warfare aspects of TORCH (the code name for the North African invasion), next from Gen. Eisenhower's headquarters at Gibraltar (I reached there in time to see the vanguard of the invasion armada steam through the straits in the November dusk), and finally from Algiers, where I found myself assigned to the recently formed Psychological Warfare Branch attached to AFHQ (Allied Force Headquarters). Boasting the assimilated rank of colonel, but condemned to wear a hybrid uniform with a distressing YMCA look to it, I was put in charge of the unit's intelligence section. My successor in Sherwood's office, now part of OWI, an intelligent and sensitive former correspondent in Europe named Percy Winner, headed its operational—i.e. censorship and information—wing. A veteran U.S. cavalryman, Colonel C. B. Hazeltine, was put in overall command of the branch with the foredoomed mission of keeping Winner and myself inside the bounds of official orthodoxy.

It was, I believe, two days after the cease-fire so unexpectedly negotiated between General Mark Clark, advised by Murphy, and Admiral Darlan, that the three of us—Colonel Hazeltine, Winner, and I—flew into Algiers. I was too busy at the moment to record my impressions; in the disarray of the epoch—and of my own feelings—they probably were not worth much. I can remember being a little disappointed with myself for not being more deeply—or less turgidly

—moved by the occasion: After all, it was the first time I had set foot on French soil, or breathed French air, if they were that, since Bordeaux. Nothing in North Africa, however, seemed clear, or whole, or wholly authentic, least of all an American's private memories of France.

I think I had arrived expecting to find dramatic visual contrasts between the purifying impact of liberation and the lingering traces of Vichy moral squalor. Save, however, for a few fresh bullet scars on an occasional building front and the burgeoning of Allied uniforms, liberation did not appear to have greatly marked the physical aspect of the city. As for Vichy squalor, unless one counted the omnipresent photography of the Marshal under that heading, it was hard to distinguish squalor from mere colonial seediness. One widespread image of corruption had, it is true, a kind of baroque vividness that stamped itself upon my mind: the bare, tanned, otherwise appetizing legs of the girls and young women cankered with purulent sores. It would have been dishonest, though, to read any profound moral or political symbolism into the phenomenon, the result of a minor skin infection picked up on the bathing beaches and untreated owing to the scarcity of medical supplies in Algiers at the period; in any case one soon got used to it, wartime being wartime. Perhaps there was something a little corrupt in the climate, too. A curious local version of Indian summer, gradually merging into the Mediterranean rainy season, still lingered over the coast for two or three weeks after the landings. The days were Southern European or Levantine, sticky but generally harmless, despite the menacing fertility of the leaden clouds that gathered in the afternoon; the nights were chill and starry, dangerously African; sometimes the skies blazed for hours on end with antiaircraft fire, and the earth shook with the thunder of heavy bombs, punctuated at intervals by the crash of falling masonry. My most vivid auditory memory of those bombardments, however, is the crowing of the cocks throughout the city, which on occasion never ceased from shortly after sunset to sunrise. It was a natural enough phenomenon—owing to wartime shortages, everyone in Algiers who could kept chickens wherever he was able to, and the racket from the bombs and guns often woke them prematurely—but one could also read into it whatever symbolism of betrayal seemed most apt to one's personal situation.

The political and emotional atmosphere in North Africa for the first few weeks after the landings was no less ambiguous than the weather. The unfortunate Giraud, who had been brought out of France to assume supreme authority in North Africa, had yielded his place with a kind of heroic meekness to Admiral Darlan, an officer of higher rank and a Vichy personality presumably more endowed with the mana of Pétainist legitimacy. Darlan, whose unexpected presence in North Africa had scrambled all our laboriously contrived political warfare plans, had thus officially become head of the government, holding power in the name of the old Marshal, now considered a prisoner or hostage of the Germans, while Giraud served as his army chief. Most of the Vichy officials or military commanders had been confirmed in their posts. Room near the top, however, had been saved or made for several of Murphy's original co-conspirators. Darlan's Secretary—i.e. Minister—of Police, for instance, was Henri d'Astier de la Vigerie, the main organizer of the brilliantly successful though ultimately futile *putsch*, whose youthful partisans had arrested the Admiral and held him prisoner for several hours when they took over the city just before the Allied landings during the night of November 7–8.

The improbable—and to many, scandalous—denouement of the invasion drama seemed to have engendered an almost universal sense of betrayal that was all the more bitter because it was based in a number of cases on the feeling of having been tricked into self-betrayal. Among the Resistance elements who had worked with Murphy before the landings there were realists—perhaps it would be more accurate to call them addicts of power—who adjusted themselves with almost suspicious ease to the presumbaly unintended outcome of their machinations. The idealists or fanatics—liberals, leftists, Gaullists—could not resign themselves to what they looked upon as at best a *modus vivendi* between honor and shame.

By now I had learned that in most cases, whatever the errors of men, the chief villain is history itself. Seeing the difference between TORCH as planned and what actually happened during the operation had made me more aware than ever that there is a substantial margin of unamanageability, and therefore of moral nonaccountability, in nearly all large-scale collective enterprises, that there are moments in history when a kind of quantum-skip in the causality of events occurs, unrelated to the planned intent of any human participants in them. Consequently, I thought it unjust to castigate Murphy for his "deal with Darlan," as if the circumstances had permitted a cool and lucid appreciation of possible alternatives—assuming there were any—and clamoring one's indignation over the immorality of the arrangement, as liberals all over the world, including many of my PWB colleagues in Algiers, were doing seemed to me almost as futile as denouncing the immorality of a tidal wave.

Yet I recognized that the moral havoc wrought by the accord was extreme, and though I could not share the indignation of those who felt the most betrayed by it, I found their sense of betrayal all too understandable. I could not help feeling a certain tinge of shame, almost of guilt, over my own role, insignificant as it had been, in the whole sorry North African adventure. Beating one's breast, however, served no useful purpose. What the situation called for most urgently was to reassure our friends in the anti-Vichy Resistance, and as their suspicions and resentments gradually subsided to effect by stages an authentic reconciliation between them and the less corrupt pro-Vichy elements in the army.

The most crucial of the anti-Vichy Resistance groups—or at least the one that most engaged my own sympathies—was the band of Algiers *putschists* headed by D'Astier de la Vigerie. They were also the most disaffected: After having worked closely with Murphy for months before the landings, and having lived through the drama of the *putsch* with him, they now felt abandoned. Though it was no part of my official duties, I decided to appoint myself a sort of unofficial liaison officer to this group, to listen sympathetically to their grievances, and to do what little I could to obtain redress for them. It was a brash and hazardous decision—how hazardous I was still too unfamiliar with the jungle of underground French politics to realize. I kept Col. Hazeltine informed of my activities, after a fashion—he had the great, if rare, military virtue of being loyal to his subordinates as well as to his chiefs—and from time to time reported my impressions through unorthodox channels to Gen. Donovan, but in reality was my own agent.

In contrast to most of the other French factions in North Africa the D'Astier group was unquestionably pro-De Gaulle, but it would have been an oversimplification merely to call it Gaullist or to pin any collective ideological label on it. Some of its members possibly considered themselves Gaullists above all else, but I think they were a minority; most were hyphenated, and in varying degrees conditional, Gaullists. A certain number might conceivably have been termed liberals, in the sense of being politically a little left of center, but none as far as I could make out were moderates in any sense (that was part of their charm). A few were definitely leftists in their opinions and either joined the Communist Party later or were secret adherents or sympathizers at the time. Several key figures in the group had in addition to any other anti-Nazi and anti-Vichy motivations that of being French Jews with strong Algerian roots and of belonging to a cultivated, relatively cosmopolitan local elite. In this category were José Aboulker, a twenty-two-year-old student who had acted under D'Astier as the field commander of the *putsch* squads his chief lieutenant, Bernard Karsenty, and Guy Cohen, alias Calvet, a shrewd, cheerful, enigmatic little man, the proprietor of a fashionable couture shop where Murphy often used to meet with his fellow-conspirators, who served as an unofficial liaison between the ex-*putschists* and the emotionally pro-Allied but politically somewhat addled *Deuxième Bureau* of the French Army in Algeria. Finally there was an important right-wing element reaching, in fact, so far to the extreme right that it included monarchists who in many of their political attitudes seemed strangely akin to the Spanish Requetés. Among the latter was a frail young Jesuit priest with an almost girlish voice and the face of a Botticelli angel, called Father (Abbé), or Lieutenant, Cordier. He had captured the central telephone exchange at gunpoint in the Algiers *putsch,* and later had volunteered for service on the Tunisian front in a special French commando unit created after the landings. Finally there was, of course, D'Astier himself.

Henri d'Astier de la Vigerie, then in his early forties (he died shortly after the war), was a tall, slim man with an aristocratic profile and flashing dark eyes. He had, or affected to have, a Castilian nobleness of manner, mitigated by a certain natural warmth. In a sense he was the reactionary equivalent of the Communist professional revolutionary: A large part of his adult life had been spent in conspiring against the French republic, mainly, though perhaps not exclusively, in the interests of the Bourbon Pretender—until 1940 the Duc de Guise, then his son, Prince Henri d'Orléans, Comte de Paris. Before the war D'Astier had been a Cagoulard, but his patriotism must have been deeper than either his authoritarian convictions or his personal ambitions. In any case he was one of a handful of extreme right-wing French activists who had turned away from Vichy soon after the armistice and joined a Resistance largely influenced by the political and social ideals they had formerly combated. D'Astier had been one of the earliest recruits to the pro-Allied underground in North Africa, and the ideologically heterogeneous band of devoted followers he had assembled demonstrated at once the sincerity of his anti-Vichy sentiments and his personal magnetism. All in all, he was both a colorful and an attractive, if anachronistic, figure, half crusader, half condottiere. Asked how D'Astier had spent his day, one of his colleagues in Algiers in the period just before Darlan's assassination is said to have replied: "As usual. In the morning he went to mass; in the afternoon he conspired."

The plots D'Astier hatched in his afternoon hours did not worry me at first, since I supposed they were aimed merely at counteracting Vichy influence in the North African regime or at promoting the Gaullist cause. I am afraid I joined in some of this kind of plotting myself, as did most of my colleagues in the Psychological Warfare Branch. On one occasion I even helped D'Astier conspire against himself by arranging, quite arbitrarily and illegally, to have some

youthful Gaullists arrested by American military police, technically
for curfew violation, and held in comfortable confinement for a few
days for having painted or plastered *Vive Roosevelt, à bas Darlan*
and similar slogans on the walls of Algiers. By taking this action I
not only spared D'Astier the embarrassment of being obliged to
make the arrests with his own police, but, as one of his assistants explained to me, saved the young culprits from a long, harsh term of
imprisonment in a penitentiary controlled by unreconstructed
Vichyite officials.

I am less proud of my part in forcing the arrest of Charles Bedeaux,
the 1936 host of the Duke and Duchess of Windsor, and at least in
those days a familiar of Hitler's foreign minister, von Ribbentrop.
From acquaintances in the *Deuxième Bureau,* responsible at the time
for counterespionnage activities in Algeria, I had learned that
Bedeaux had been stranded in Algiers while on an economic mission
to West Africa on behalf of the German High Command in France.
Since he was a naturalized U.S. citizen—though a Frenchman in
every other respect—there appeared to be a prima facie case of
treason against him. The *Deuxième Bureau* professed to be mildly
surprised that the American authorities were uninterested in the
matter. Its own interest, however, was no more than tepid, mainly, I
gathered, because Bedeaux was a frequent dinner guest at the tables
of several influential and politically conservative French hostesses
who were currently launching the post-invasion social season in
Algiers; several of my superiors on Gen. Eisenhower's staff, it was
intimated, were on occasion his fellow guests. That, as far as I was
concerned, made Bedeaux a convenient symbol of the unwholesome
political promiscuities and of the collusion between defeatism and
resistance that the Murphy-Darlan accords had inevitably encouraged. He was also reported to have close associations with several Vichy technocrats known to be members of the so-called
Synarchiste movement which was viewed at the time—somewhat ex-
aggeratedly—as a kind of sinister and powerful ideological mafia
with fascist overtones. Without looking deeper into the affair, I
made up my mind to have him put behind bars, and eventually, by

327

grossly misrepresenting the French feelings about him to the Americans, and the American attitude to the French, thus making each side feel its good faith was being questioned by the other, I succeeded. Bedeaux committed suicide while being brought back to the United States for trial.

Perhaps I would not have been so ruthlessly vindictive, nor have resorted to such shoddy methods, if I had not still been haunted by the nightmare of a shadowy yet tightly organized international conspiracy working for a compromise peace, and with it the consolidation of German hegemony in Europe and the creation of a crypto-facist holy alliance against world communism. It was the specter of such a plot that had inspired my COI project for a bogus "black" radio in America. Whereas in 1941 I had sought to neutralize the American wing of this supposed defeatist internationale, now it seemed to me that the chief threat came from its French branch.

I have digressed a bit from the account I had started to give of my own relations with the D'Astier de la Vigerie group, but the degression lays a foundation for explaining some of the events that follow. My first warning that I was becoming involved in something that later might require a good deal of explanation came, I think, about the middle of December, possibly a day of two earlier. One morning José Aboulker and Bernard Karsenty, the two members of the group with whom I had the most contact, arrived in great agitation at the Hotel de Cornouailles, a modest establishment on a quiet side street which served as the PWB headquarters and phalanstery, to report that one of D'Astier's plots was getting out of hand. He was now, they told me, involved in a conspiracy aimed at setting up the Comte de Paris as the head of a de facto French provisional government in Algiers. The idea was to persuade Darlan to step down as chairman of the French Imperial Council, the supreme governing body in North Africa since the landings, and then have the Bourbon Pretender—though not in that capacity—elected by the other members in his place. A restoration of the monarchy as such was not contemplated—at least until after the liberation of metropolitan France. If

Darlan would not resign of his own accord then he was to be removed by some unspecified but presumably nonviolent means. The project, if it succeeded, was certain to revive long-dormant political passions in France, the two young men explained, and thus would shatter the unity of the underground resistance. Much as they admired D'Astier, they could not let him commit such a catastrophic blunder; hence their intervention.

There was thought to be a royalist majority on the Imperial Council, so there was a real danger that the scheme, wild as it looked, might go through unless it was scotched in time by an American veto. It was also possible that D'Astier, if he encountered too many political obstacles, might attempt an armed coup d'état to achieve his objective. The need for fast counteraction was all the greater because the Comte de Paris, at D'Astier's instigation, had already arrived secretly in Algiers from his home in Spanish Morocco and, installed in a bourgeois flat as Monsieur Robin, had begun his consultations. I reported the information to AFHQ where it turned out to be already known, thanks to Murphy, who assured me he was taking the necessary steps to neutralize the intrigues of D'Astier and his Monsieur Robin. I am afraid both of us underestimated the real gravity of the Comte de Paris's bid for power. I am certain that I did. It is always hard for twentieth-century minds to realize that an anachronism—or what we assume to be an anachronism—can be dangerous.

The next warning—somehow I failed at the time to connect it with the first one—came a few days later when D'Astier invited me to lunch with several of his young followers, veterans of the *putsch* and for the most part volunteers in the recently formed commando unit, the Corps Franc d'Afrique. We met on the heights above the city at a little suburban restaurant, esteemed for its black market contacts. We sat outside, under the flowering mimosas in the warm December sun that did not feel like December, sheltered from a fresh wind that flecked the Mediterranean below us with a crinkled webwork of white foam, like the cracklings in the ancient blue of some rare porcelain. We had a mountainous bowl of *couscous*—the strongly peppered native North African dish built up from a base of steamed cereal which, like the Englishman's curry or the Dutchman's *rystaffel,* had become for the French in Algeria a symbol of digestive colonialism—washed down with an abundance of the strong Algerian wine. The atmosphere during the meal was like the weather and the food: warm with good-fellowship but gusty, intellectually nourishing, spiced with an excess of passion that bit the tongue. The underlying theme of our table talk, insofar as it had one, was how long, oh Lord! how long!, our affliction, of course, being Darlan. I tried to hold out some reasonable hope for a fairly near future; there were increasingly numerous signs, I said, that Washington at last was beginning to realize the urgency of replacing the "provisional expedient" in North Africa, as Secretary of State Hull had just termed it, with something less objectionable to the democratic conscience and to the ideals of the Resistance. My optimism was too pallid, however, too merely reasonable, to prevail against the fanaticism of my hosts.

"I know it is a terrible thing for a priest to say," burst out Abbé Cordier, from across the table, "but, oh, I could kill that man with my own hands!"

I had heard similar threats against Darlan uttered on a number of occasions by various members of the D'Astier group, but never with such a passionate intensity of feeling. That was not what disquieted me the most, however. Cordier had been about to add something and suddenly cut himself off; I noticed that he was blushing like a convent girl who realizes she has said something improper. The whole boisterous table fell silent for a moment, a little too obviously, I thought, then D'Astier shifted the conversation to some innocuous topic, and Darlan's name was not mentioned again during the rest of the meal; in fact, from that instant on none of my friends in the group talked to me about him at all, whereas in the past it had sometimes seemed to me they talked of little else. A curtain of some kind had definitely fallen between us. The abrupt change in the atmosphere around the table, the expressions—or lack of expression—of the faces, a certain flatness in the voices, were enough to justify suspicion. It was not suspicion, however, that I carried away from that lunch; it was conviction. I knew, though to this day I cannot explain how I knew.

There was no bureaucratic formula, of course, for translating my subjective certainty into the kind of intelligence report that might be taken seriously at AFHQ, and thus give timely warning of the impending tragedy. I thought of Darlan's murder as a tragedy not because of any regard or compassion for the man himself, nor because I wholly accepted the official thesis of his continued usefulness to the Allied cause in North Africa, but because I could plainly foresee—no great perspicacity was needed—at least a few of the politically disastrous consequences it was bound to have. I tried talking to Murphy, and even suggested to him—rather fatuously as I look back on it—that perhaps the conspirators would defer the execution of their plan if he simply asked them in to share a bottle of whiskey, as he had sometimes done in the past, and explained Washington's real feelings about the provisional nature of the Darlan expedient. Murphy listened patiently, but did not seem much impressed either by my apprehensions or by my suggestions for averting the crisis I saw looming ahead; there was little reason why he should have been, and in the light of what is known today about the background of the assassination it seems unlikely, to say the least, that any move on Murphy's part to renew his once warm human contact with the conspirators would have changed things. The murder was not, as I naïvely supposed at the time, a kind of political *crime passionnel*, but almost certainly a deliberate act of policy conceived by a ruthless and subtle, if slightly chimerical, mind—precisely such a mind as had hatched the irresponsible though not necessarily unrealizable scheme for a camouflaged restoration of the French monarchy in North Africa.

The inexorable occurred, inexorably. (I sometimes wonder how many persons, besides myself and the actual assassins, in North Africa or elsewhere knew that Darlan was doomed—Darlan himself seems to have been one of them—and of this number how many chose at the time to say nothing, see nothing, do nothing.) Darlan was shot and fatally wounded in his office on December 24, 1942, by a young royalist-Gaullist named Bonnier de la Chapelle, soon identified as a member of the Corps Franc d'Afrique and a follower of D'Astier de la Vigerie. Condemned to death by a hastily summoned court-martial, the boy was hustled before a firing squad at 7:45 A.M. on December 26. Several high-level but curiously inept appeals for clemency or delay, including one by the Comte de Paris himself, who had not managed to wake up in time, had failed to save him. Giraud, who had the authority to grant a stay of execution, ordered instead that the court's sentence be carried out with military dispatch. Whatever hopes the Pretender and his supporters had left were shattered when Giraud, though a monarchist himself, took over Darlan's powers as High Commissioner with the unanimous consent of his colleagues on the Imperial Council.

By a predictable irony, Darlan's assassination marked a temporary triumph of the Vichy spirit. General Jean Bergeret, perhaps the most reactionary personality of the Darlan regime, almost immediately emerged as the real power behind Giraud. Put in charge of the investigation into the background of the crime and apparently abetted by the Minister of the Interior, Jean Rigault, up to that time known as a supporter of the Comte de Paris and perhaps the most quintessential conspirator of them all (D'Astier was not trusted for all too obvious reasons), he exploited the assignment to persecute every faction of the anti-Vichy Resistance in Algiers.

Early in the evening of December 29, we were tipped off at the Hotel de Cornouailles that flying squads of *Gardes Mobiles*, on orders from Bergeret, had arrested a number of the November 7 *putschists* in their homes at gunpoint, handcuffed them, and whisked them out of the city. Their immediate destination was the concentration camp at Laghouat, some 150 miles to the south, but that, I was informed, was intended to be only the first stage en route to a penal colony in the Mauretanian Sahara, notorious for its murderous climate. There seemed to be a real danger, moreover, that some of the prisoners, who included José Aboulker and other prominent members of the D'Astier group, might not reach Mauretania at all:

Bergeret, it was said, planned to have them tried by a summary court-martial at Laghouat and executed on the spot for an alleged new conspiracy to kill Giraud, himself, and Murphy.

Bergeret's sanguinary intent may have been as fictitious as the assassination plot his investigators claimed to have uncovered probably was— probably, alas, is still all that one can say—but in the prevailing climate of Algiers one could not afford to take anything for granted. After trying every bureaucratic channel, political and military, formal and informal, in a vain attempt to make AFHQ realize the catastrophic effect on world opinion if we tolerated this vindictive Vichy counteroffensive against the underground allies who had risked their lives in our common cause a few weeks earlier, the already half mutinous psychological warriors of the Hotel de Cornouailles turned to direct action. The American and British correspondents in Algiers, the recipients of numerous earlier "leaks" of classified information aimed at generating domestic political pressures on the theater command, were alerted in suitable terms to the latest outrage. For my part, I telephoned on my own nonexistent authority to the U.S. military police post at Blida, an inland town through which the prisoners' convoy had to pass, demanding that it be intercepted on its way south and that all its members, including guards and chauffeurs, be detained pending new instructions. PWB, I explained, had reason to suspect a kidnapping of pro-Allied sympathizers carried out by Vichy or German agents disguised as French *Gardes Mobiles*. All but the last carful of prisoners in the convoy had passed out of the territorial jurisdiction of the Blida MP's before I got through to them, but the incident may have helped sensitize both French and Allied authorities to certain implications of the situation. If there had ever been a scheme to have the prisoners shot in Laghouat or en route to the Sahara, high-level attention focused on them by my unauthorized intervention made it riskier to carry out.

A less controversial and possibly more useful activity in which I took part that night was driving around the city with one of my British assistants collecting weapons from the homes or offices of

Resistance friends who had not been arrested but who we thought soon would be. The arms in question had usually come from Murphy or the OSS in the first place and had been used on our behalf during the November 7 *putsch*. Under a recent High Commission decree their possession by French civilians was technically illegal; the owners risked heavy prison sentences or even the firing squad. A cold, steady rain kept falling as we made our rounds in an open jeep and I already had the grippe; two days later I was down with pneumonia.

The climax of the long night's drama, from my viewpoint, came in the early hours of the morning when I was waked by a knock on my door at the Hotel de Cornouailles. Accompanied by one of his young lieutenants, D'Astier walked into the room, and after apologizing for the intrusion with his usual aristocratic courtesy— but, I thought, with less than his usual aplomb—asked if I could keep him out of view for a while. Police and security agents sent out by Bergeret were looking for him, he said, with orders to shoot him down on sight.

It was the first time I had seen D'Astier since the lunch in the little outdoor restaurant, and I studied him curiously. There was no doubt in my mind that both he and the Abbé Cordier had been deeply involved in the murder of Darlan, but the confession (or alleged confession) written a few hours before his execution by Bonnier de la Chapelle specifically naming them had not yet come to light. Exactly what D'Astier's role in the crime had been did not seem to me at the time to matter much—it was only later that it began to weigh on my thoughts—and it would have been both cruel and futile to cross-examine him about it then. He was unquestionably frightened, though there was a certain romantic and aristocratic quality even in his fear, a hint of some menace at once less vulgar and more sinister than the guns of Bergeret's uniformed killers. He likewise had a slightly puzzled look as if in some remote, shadowy corner of his conspiratorial world something—and not merely something political—had gone unaccountably and dramatically wrong. Perhaps it was simply the common light of reality that he dreaded to face. In any event we canvassed the situation from every angle and weighed the relative merits of half a dozen more or less practical schemes either for keeping D'Astier in hiding or for allowing him to give himself up to the authorities under circumstances that would rule out the possibility of a camouflaged police murder.

The major obstacle to both courses was that officially no charge had yet been made against him—in fact he was himself still the nominal chief of the policemen who were unofficially seeking a chance to kill him. Either to surrender publicly or to go into hiding would appear a confession of guilt. As the morning light grew stronger, D'Astier seemed to lose some of his nervousness, and finally he left the hotel without having adopted any of the plans we had discussed, though he accepted my offer of a PWB jeep to take him to the Cathedral for mass, just to make sure there was no mishap on the way. It was not until more than a week later that he was finally taken into custody, along with the Abbé Cordier.

During all that time I lay in bed with a persistent fever and cough. Night and day my room at the Cornouailles continued to be filled with French and American fellow conspirators who came to report the latest inhumanity, the latest injustice, the latest absurdity committed in poor Giraud's name, or to seek a redress that I was less than ever able to obtain. Whether the plot against Murphy, Bergeret, and Giraud was real or imaginary, there was a case of sorts for temporarily neutralizing a certain number of the more dangerous anti-Vichy hotheads. There was no excuse for treating them like desperate criminals, for dragging them out of their homes in chains, for packing them off to some Devil's Island of the Sahara. The punitive intent was unmistakable, and it was just as plainly directed not only against real or presumptive insurrectionists but against even the most innocuous Gaullist sympathizers. One morning the wife of a young French journalist and historian I had known in Paris, Louis Joxe, came to the hotel to tell me her fears for her husband's life. Joxe, who had held an important administrative post in the High Commission under Darlan, had been arrested in his office by the *Gardes Mobiles* and sent off under escort for duty as a reserve officer on the

Tunisian front. The circumstances of this strange mobilization fully justified the suspicion that he might be in more danger from French than German bullets in Tunisia. Yet Joxe, though an avowed Gaullist sympathizer and a participant in the pro-Allied *putsch* of November 7, had no close relations with the D'Astier activists and was one of the soberest and most prudent of men. Years later he became a minister of Gen. de Gaulle and one of his most heeded foreign policy advisers.

In cases like Joxe's I tried to get AFHQ to intervene, but the immediate response was usually negative. The more diplomatic of my interlocutors sometimes expressed a mild, humanitarian concern, counterbalanced by a reluctance to interfere in "a purely French domestic affair," but others made no effort to conceal their spite. Those Gaullist troublemakers and conspirators, it seemed, were no better than enemy agents. They were against United States policy in North Africa, therefore they were sabotaging the Allied war effort. Whatever was being done to them, it served them right. Darlan had been our son-of-a-bitch, and Giraud was now, and who-ever was against an officially approved son-of-a-bitch must *ipso facto* be against us.

One example of the grotesque and odious predicaments into which this kind of Cro-Magnon Machiavellianism led us made a particular impression on me. D'Astier's lieutenant, Bernard Karsenty, had succeeded in evading arrest—we kept him hidden for several days at the Hotel de Cornouailles—but a police search of his home had led to the discovery of a revolver, and if caught he faced conviction on the grave wartime charge of illegally possessing firearms. The particular firearm in this case happened to be one given to Karsenty by Murphy during the November 7 *putsch*, when he had made both valiant and effective use of it. It was thus capable of serving as the kind of symbol that appeals powerfully to the French mind and sentiments; if it figured as material evidence in a court trial leading to the young man's conviction, the symbolism, I realized, would be devasting to our interests.

There was no use in trying to explain such subtleties—or such simplicities—to the legalistic-minded bureaucrats, military or civilian, at the Hotel St. Georges, where Gen. Eisenhower's staff was housed. Consequently it was essential to make sure that Karsenty did not go on trial in Algiers, even though it meant becoming an accessory to his infraction. Since he wanted to get to England to join the Free French forces there, I arranged through a British officer on my staff for him and one of his comrades, who was also being sheltered at the Cornouailles, to be smuggled onto a British freighter that was on the point of leaving.

The two young men were hardly out of the hotel before a British sergeant from the AFHQ security staff showed up in my room—I was still convalescing in bed—and with an apologetic air said he had orders to investigate information alleging that I was harboring suspects wanted by the French police. I assured him the report was unfounded and invited him to see for himself by looking in my wardrobe and under my bed. He solemnly did so, asked a few perfunctory questions to which I could scarcely have given incriminating answers had I wished to, and left in evident relief. I never discovered what well-wisher on the AFHQ security staff had arranged to send me a British rather than an American interrogator. It might have been an accident, though I doubt it. In any case, the punctilious manner in which the interrogator carried out his mission, taking proper British care to see and hear nothing that might cause complications, was a useful lesson for a somewhat shaken Yankee neophyte in the art of what might be termed para-diplomatic *savoir-faire*.

I would have written this chapter quite differently, I suppose, in 1948, and differently again in 1958; if I should still be alive in 1978 I shall doubtless be surprised at certain omissions, amused by certain labored demonstrations of the obvious, abashed by certain residual naïvetés. One of the indications that we have survived a growth-ordeal is precisely that every time we look back on it we see it from ever-higher ground. In the case of my North African experience this kind of retrospective insight has, of course, merged over the years with the plain hindsight of history as new facts have become known and new chains of consequence have become discernible. At the end of January 1943, when I left Algiers, an observer who was open-minded but also sensitive to the currents of local French opinion could have suspected that U.S. policy in North Africa was self-defeating even from the short-term viewpoint and would leave lasting scars on Franco-American relations. By allowing or, I am even afraid, encouraging the anti-Gaullist excesses at the beginning of the Giraud regime, we rendered the worst possible service to the estimable mediocrity whom we were trying to impose on the French people as a leader, and assured the early triumph of his formidable rival, whom destiny seems to have endowed from birth with both the creative qualities and the harsher attributes of historical greatness. No doubt it was to drive home this lesson of the past that some national tutelary genius equally equipped with a sense of justice and a sense of irony dispatched Robert Murphy, by then a senior diplomat unencumbered with warriors, to Europe in 1958 as a "mediator" in the Franco-Tunisian quarrel—in reality the Algerian war—thus detonating the insurrection in Algiers that returned De Gaulle to power. By the same token, our self-defeating efforts to defeat De Gaulle succeeded all too well in embittering him, and inevitably exacerbated the tendencies toward morbid suspicion, cynicism, and ruthlessness in a mind that was already too prone to them.

Looking back on the whole affair from the high ground of the present, I would hesitate to say categorically that the slightly hyperthyroid idealists at the Hotel de Cornouailles—of whom I was by no means the least active—were right, and the military or diplomatic Machiavellis at the Hotel St. Georges wrong. I think that perhaps we were a shade more realistic and Machiavellian in the true sense, because we recognized that ideals and ideas, along with moral or human values like justice, generosity, and compassion, are genuine elements of power, without at the same time denying—even if we sadly underestimated their importance—that so are violence, ruse, and sheer force. Like most Americans, especially in those days, both parties in the controversy were weak not only in the sense of history, but in the sense of nuance. We could not have picked a better training ground than North Africa at a better time for learning to be on guard against this latter weakness.

Gen. Giraud, for example, probably came nearer to representing complete moral integrity (his misfortune was that he represented nothing else) than any of the other chief figures in the North African drama. Yet he inadvertently became for a while the champion of the most corrupt, as well as the most reactionary, elements in North Africa. The anti-Vichy Resistance, both in North Africa and in metropolitan France, wrote a heroic page in modern French history, but as subsequent events have demonstrated was not in all respects a school of civic virtue. Many of the same persons I had known as conspirators against Vichy were conspiring against the Fourth Republic when I revisited Algiers in 1957, and some of the same conspirators who had been involved in the assassination of Admiral Darlan were already plotting to assassinate De Gaulle—or at least plotting with those who were—when I went back to Algiers on the eve of independence in 1962.

Even today some things in the background of the Darlan affair remain mysterious, and up to the end of my stay in Algiers the whole episode was naturally more obscure. In some areas, however, the shadowy truth could already be felt or divined. Of the persons involved in the assassination with whom I had direct contact, I doubted, and still doubt, whether any were capable of sending a comrade to his death in cold-blooded deceit. The same intuitive apprehension that in my eyes absolved the conspirators of a more nightmarish crime behind their crime, convicted them, however, not only of the truly criminal recklessness that had futilely sacrificed a clean, young, human destiny, along with a checkered, old one, but of a kind of willful self-deception akin to that of the bank teller who confidently expects to make good his defalcations from what he is going to win at the races. The revelation that came to me during the last days of my convalescence in Algiers of this delusive, sub-Dostoevskian world of conspiracy, with its petty moral embezzlements, its emotional shams, and its self-betrayals, helped exorcise some of the demons that had begun to invade my own mind.

Battles Long Ago: Southeast Asia

Politically, the Southeast Asia theater of war, in which I spent the greater part of my overseas service, had little in common with the North African one. Psychologically, from the viewpoint of an American serving there, it often raised similar problems. The moral relationship with the enemy—Japanese military imperialism, in which no sane Westerner could feel any secret and corrupt appeal— was healthier than in North Africa or Europe, where one fought against one's unacknowledged Nazi, or facist, or crypto-Vichy self, but inter-Allied relations were fully as complex, if less dramatically so.

By September 1943, when my Asian assignment began, the Japanese were already being pushed back in the island world of the Southwest Pacific by the American sea and ground forces under General Douglas MacArthur, but they were in firm control of China's richest, most populous provinces, from Manchuria to the Yunnan border in the south, and they occupied Burma—threatening India—the Andaman Islands in the Indian Ocean, Malaya, and Holland's vast Indonesian empire. In Indo-China—comprising present-day Vietnam (North and South), Laos, and Cambodia—French administration subsisted only under Japanese military control. Thailand was a nominal Japanese ally under de facto Japanese military occupation. India and Ceylon remained under British control and most of the population cooperated in the British war effort, or at least refrained from actively opposing it, though the top leaders of the nationalist Congress Party in India, including Gandhi and Nehru, were in prison. Neither Britain nor any other European power had as yet renounced its imperial claims on any part of Asia.

By agreement between Washington and London, Southeast Asia was recognized as primarily a British military responsibility, while the more active and important Southwest Pacific was an American one, and China that of the Chinese national government based on Chungking and headed by Marshal Chiang Kai-shek (supported logistically and politically by the United States). Though U.S. officers were attached to the nominally inter-Allied Southeast Asia Command headquarters staff under Admiral Lord Louis Mountbatten (Earl Mountbatten of Burma), the United States military interest in the theater was focused on the long supply line that stretched from the port of Calcutta into Nationalist China. A small American operational force based in North Assam, on the Burma border, was trying to open a land route to China across the jungles and mountains of northern Burma and Yunnan (the so-called Ledo road), and to secure it from Japanese harassment.

All U.S. military activities and personnel in India and Burma, whether logistic or operational, were under the authority of Lieutenant General Joseph W. Stilwell, who was simultaneously, and confusingly, supreme commander of the United States China-Burma-India theater while serving as deputy to Admiral Mountbatten in the southern, British half of his command and to Generalissimo Chiang Kai-shek in the northern, Chinese half. A colorful, salty, testy, old professional soldier who had abundantly earned his army nickname, Vinegar Joe, Stilwell labored with missionary zeal against foreign aggression and native corruption in the cause of his arrogant, suspicious, unteachable, Chinese overlord, while he voiced nothing but scorn and aversion for the pomps, the shams, and the greeds of British colonialism, symbolized in his eyes by his royal-blooded, south-of-the-mountains, British supreme commander.

The Office of Strategic Services units that Gen. Donovan had insisted on establishing in Southeast Asia—without noticeable enthusiasm on the part of any authority concerned—were subject both

341

to Admiral Mountbatten's operational approval and to Gen. Stilwell's nominally administrative but effectively political control. One OSS group operated under Stilwell in direct conjection with the U.S. forces in northern Burma. In theory there was also an OSS liaison and supply unit in Chungking attached to the Chinese police and intelligence services, but it was headed by a U.S. regular navy officer and was only formally responsible to Gen. Donovan.

If it had not been for the personal influence of Gen. Donovan, I think I would have quit OSS and turned my back on the whole world of secret service and political warfare after my experiences in North Africa. As it was, I very nearly did resign, and for a while I had an ambiguous assignment half in and half out of the organization.

Immediately following my return from Algiers, I had been appointed by Donovan to head a small unit in Washington called the Planning Staff. We did little planning in any strict sense of the word, but attempted, not very systematically, to formulate some basic doctrine for OSS activities, particularly in the still-uncharted field of political warfare. The effort could have been mildly useful if anyone in OSS, starting with its chief, had cared more about doctrine in any field. Unlike many American men of action, Donovan had a high regard for intellectuals and those he considered "artists"— for some curious reason he appeared to count me among the latter— but like nearly all of his fellow countrymen, what he wanted from his intellectuals and artists was not standards or systems or general concepts—much less self-questioning—but "ideas," meaning formulas for getting something done, and above all incantations for making his projects look irresistibly attractive to others.

After a few months on the Planning Staff I grew restless, and since for the time being there appeared to be no interesting OSS assignment for me overseas, I accepted an offer from Major General Albert C. Wedemeyer—subsequently U.S. theater commander in China—to serve with him in the newly created Southeast Asia Command, then based in New Delhi. Admiral Lord Louis Mountbatten, the glamorous ex-Chief of Combined Operations (Commandos) was the theater commander, and Wedemeyer, a brilliant young protégé of General George Marshall, was going out as his American deputy-chief of staff. I was to be the deputy of the British staff officer responsible for coordinating Allied clandestine and propaganda activities in the theater. Donovan approved my transfer but without notable enthusiasm; in my new post I would not be officially representing the interests of OSS, but would have to pass judgment on its operations in the interests of an inter-Allied military headquarters. Though I developed from the first a particularly happy relationship with the official OSS representative in Southeast Asia, Col. Richard P. Heppner (since deceased), a young New York lawyer on leave from Donovan's own firm, I had reason to believe that the General still resented my administratively equivocal assignment and suspected me—unjustly as it turned out—of potential impartiality. I half expected to be treated as a renegade when he showed up in New Delhi, a few weeks after my own arrival there. That, however, was not Donovan's way, as some notes I jotted down on his visit make clear:

NOVEMBER, 28, 1943

General Donovan arrived from Cairo in the Supremo's* plane about 1730 on November 28, a bright, windy afternoon. Heppner and I were waiting at the airport to meet him . . . . The General stepped out of the plane looking as fresh and matter-of-fact as if he had left the Administration Building five minutes before, and his greeting to us as we saluted him contrived to give the impression he was resuming a conference with us that had been interrupted only a few minutes before.

We followed him to Faridkot House (Lord Louis's official residence), my first glimpse of this bleakly gaudy and gracefully modernistic palace, and Lord Louis with his casual courtesy asked us into the living room for tea, enquired how I was getting on with

---

* Supremo was a favorite local nickname for SEAC's Supreme Commander, Admiral Mountbatten.

P_____, took a quick and curious inventory of Dick Heppner, whom he must have heard of as the local bad boy, and then left us with the General. The General, Heppner, H_____ and I adjourned after a few minutes to Lord Louis's office where we were joined after a while by L_____ and F_____. Local color at this conference was provided by an endless stream of exceptionally ragged Indian coolies who kept filing in and out of the Supremo's office in connection with some mysterious work going on in the next room. This exotic touch, so characteristic of India but calculated to give gooseflesh to an American officer schooled in Washington ideas of security, left the General completely unruffled.

I suspect there is one slight exaggeration in my notes. The General nearly always looked fresh in the sense of being alert and untired, but as I see once more in my imagination the stocky figure in the carelessly worn, slightly rumpled khaki uniform with the blue ribbon of the Congressional Medal sewn on the breast of the tunic, the adjective does not seem quite appropriate. Sitting relaxed but straight at a Washington conference table, wearing one of his impeccably tailored, fastidiously neat Wall Street suits, Donovan looked like what—among other things—he was: a natural fighting man, a natural leader of men, a natural athlete who kept in permanent training. Dressed in his general's uniform he appeared incorrigibly civilian; the silvered, man-of-distinction's hair, the slightly florid cheeks with the smooth, barbershop glow, the sleek, deceptively fleshy jowls suggested neither the dashing warrior nor the ruthless spymaster of his public image, but the moderately successful Republican politician and the prosperous, able corporation lawyer that he actually was, the *bon vivant* he was not. In the prejudiced view of professional soldiers or diplomats who feared his encroachments, the perhaps slightly too candid blue of the General's eyes, the bland courtesy of his smile sometimes suggested the bridge club shark or even, in cases of extreme provocation, the shady stock promoter. To me, at one time or another, he seemed all these things, and several more.

344

. . . That afternoon the General took Dick [others], and myself to Agra (sightseeing). We flew, and arrived back in time to attend a staff dinner for the small OSS group in a private dining room of the Imperial Hotel. The General made a short talk on the role of OSS in the war and on the opportunities in this theater. In a deprecatory tone he mentioned that he had pledged the fullest assistance to Gen. Pownall (Lt. Gen. Pownall, Mountbatten's chief of staff) and had told him that if at any time he wanted something done for which he could not spare two or three thousand men, just to call on OSS and we would send in twenty or thirty men to do the job . . .

From my own knowledge of Donovan I have no doubt that he actually had said something of the sort to Gen. Pownall, probably in such a manner as to leave the studious, soft-spoken Britisher uncertain whether or not this kind of hyperbole was a form of transatlantic humor. Speaking to his own officers at an informal staff dinner, the General was confident he would not be misunderstood. As everyone in the agency was aware, he was a prudent realist who knew that a minimum of fifty or sixty OSS men would normally be needed to do the work of 2000 or 3000 trained British—or for that matter, U.S.—soldiers; he would never dream of sending in only twenty or thirty—not unless the circumstances were quite exceptional.

Perhaps Donovan was to some extent the prisoner of his own heroic legend, but the mystique of audacity that he took great pains to build up in OSS was at least partly founded on a thoughtful reading of military history and on a basically democratic faith in the unexploited capabilities of the common man, including, but by no means restricted to, the common Wall Street lawyer or Newport playboy. The para-military and guerrilla aspects of the OSS mission probably interested him more than any other. By combining unlimited nerve, Yankee ingenuity, and self-reliance, the American tradition of frontier warfare, and the most advanced twentieth-century science or technology, Donovan believed that effectively unconventional solutions could be found to almost any strategic problem. Above and beyond his other, sometimes mutually incompatible goals, Donovan, I think, hoped to demonstrate through OSS that the normally untapped reserves of individual courage and resource, and the dynamism of the individual will to win constitute the basic raw materials of victory, and that in an increasingly mechanized world, human dignity is still not only a moral but a strategic quantity.

As far as I was concerned Gen. Donovan's demonstration was conclusive, and it made an abiding contribution to the development of my personal outlook on the unending struggle for survival among nations and civilizations, institutions and ideologies, that we call history.

DECEMBER 9

The General returned from China about 2320. Dick and I met him at the field again. We had assumed that he would want to go straight to bed after a flight of nearly 2000 miles but he asked us to come back to Faridkot House with him. Lord Louis was waiting in the drawing room when we arrived and Gen. Wedemeyer, etc., who had all gone to the airfield too late, came in shortly. While Mountbatten stood with his back to the fireplace and Dick, H_____ and I sipped highballs, the General recounted his trip to China. He had removed Miles as OSS representative, the General told Lord Louis, and negotiated a new agreement with the Chinese whereby clandestine activities would be directed by a triumvirate—Gen. Tai-Li (Chiang Kai-shek's secret police and intelligence chief), Capt. Miles as representative of the U.S. Navy, and the newly appointed OSS chief. The General had given the Chinese six months in which to produce some tangible evidence of cooperation, failing which the famous "wampum," in the form of tommy guns, wireless sets, etc., which some observers feared were intended for use against the Chinese Communists rather than against the Japs, would be cut off. [Gen. Donovan had long been dissatisfied with the arrangement in force up to that time whereby OSS was nominally represented in China by a U.S. Navy liaison group, headed by Capt. M. F. Miles, U.S.N., whose activity —in the General's view—amounted to little more than operating as a procurement office for the Chinese Nationalist secret service, under Gen. Tai-Li.]

Lord Louis was particularly amused by Donovan's spirited account of his dealings with the famous Tai-Li, whom legend had built into a fabously sinister figure, a blend of Himmler and the once-popular movie villain, The Insidious Doctor Fu Manchu. To Donovan, Tai-Li appeared a sentimentalist if not a softie, a mediocre policeman with medieval ideas of intelligence work, but apart from this a rather likable fellow. "I said to him" (Gen. Donovan speaking) "General, I want you to know that I am going to send my men into China whether you like it or not. I know that you can have them murdered one by one, but I want you to know that will not deter me."

The General chuckled as he related this talk but his face became serious and determined as he added, "I mean that, too. I'm going to start sending men up there right away. In fact I'm having Taylor go up in a few days to organize an intelligence network." Lord Louis cocked a whimsical eyebrow at me but refrained from comment . . .

Gen. Donovan had informed me of my new assignment in the car driving back from the airport. We had already agreed in principle before he left for China that I should not look on my current post in SEAC as a permanent one, but in my heart, ever since my return from North Africa, I had not been quite certain that I looked upon my attachment to OSS as a permanent one, either. The General's offer—phrasing it as an order was a delicate compliment—to send me to beard Tai-Li in his lair was not only irresistible in itself, but it swept away my last doubts about continuing to belong to OSS as long as he headed it.

Whether Donovan himself took my Chinese mission seriously is difficult to say. That I knew nothing about China, had never organized a secret intelligence network anywhere, and had never even attended an OSS intelligence school could scarcely have seemed major disqualifications to him. He was a great believer in learning by doing, and his inspired amateurism helped create an atmosphere in OSS that sometimes recalled the satiric writings of Compton Mackenzie or Evelyn Waugh; on the other hand the fact that so many untrained, or undertrained, young Americans survived the hair-raising missions on which they were launched by OSS, achieving creditable or even impressive results in the process, suggests that the Donovan philosophy was not completely unsound.

In casually mentioning his new plans for me to Lord Louis and to Gen. Wedemeyer, Donovan was quite aware that while my soul might be his for the duration, my body, administratively speaking, belonged to them, except for a couple of slices. One of these could be considered the property of the Bureau of Navy Personnel in Washington because I had been commissioned in the Navy shortly before going overseas. The other would be the property of Gen. Stilwell, who as chief of the U.S. China-Burma-India Command, which overlapped with SEAC, had nominal authority over all U.S. personnel stationed in India. Possibly due to the difficulty of reconciling these conflicting allegiances, I never got to China, where I would have been obliged to match wits not only with Tai-Li but with Capt. Miles, another redoubtable sentimentalist in his own way. Talking about me as if I were his vassal, and his alone, was the General's manner of bringing his interlocutors to recognize a subtle change in my status: Even if I remained on Lord Louis's staff instead of going to China, I was hereafter to be considered as Donovan's agent and unofficial representative there. At best, however, as I fully realized, I was being used as a very minor pawn in a large and ambitious maneuver.

The vital issue for Donovan in SEAC was not who represented him, or how, on Mountbatten's staff, but whether or not OSS was to conduct independent operations in the theater. An OSS unit in Assam had for some time been recruiting and training the subsequently famous Kachin Rangers and other guerrillas in northern Burma, who were to provide one of the most convincing demonstrations of Donovan's theory of unconventional warfare. This activity, however, was in close support of Stilwell's military offensive to open up the Burma Road, and under his direct authority. Donovan wanted authorization for the unit Heppner was assembling in New Delhi to launch operations of wider strategic significance elsewhere throughout the vast theater. He was, of course, prepared to clear his operational plans through Mountbatten's staff—that was where I came in —but he insisted that they be carried out solely under OSS control. This the British were understandably reluctant to grant. The more conservative elements in the British colonial establishment and in the regional branches of the British secret services opposed any American clandestine presence in Southeast Asia.

Donovan's main purpose in gossiping about his conversations in Chungking was to warn Lord Louis, just as he had warned Tai-Li, that if OSS were not allowed to come in by the front door it would, according to a favorite Donovan formula, slip in through the transom. There was no doubt that Lord Louis got the point, but he seemed amused rather than offended by his houseguest's colossal cheek. The two men had quite a bit in common.

Though there was an element of bluff in the General's implicit threat, I realized that he had analyzed the complex factors in the situation with his customary shrewdness. Stilwell was no less reluctant than the British traditionalists to see OSS operate anywhere in the theater outside of northern Burma, dreading that we would somehow be contaminated by British colonialism, and Mountbatten was having difficulties of his own with the hard-bitten old U.S. soldier. The Supremo's good-humored reaction to the Tai-Li ploy told us by indirection that he recognized that back in Washington Wild Bill Donovan might be a useful counterweight to Vinegar Joe Stilwell; a deal could therefore be made with him to let OSS operate in his theater. Donovan concluded it before he left New Delhi.

Donovan, as usual, was empire-building throughout his Asian trip, but not just for himself. In the back of his mind he always had the long-range goal of founding a permanent U.S. intelligence and political warfare service, but neither the President nor any other constitutional authority, as far as I know, had explicitly authorized him to work toward it. If OSS or something like it were to continue in existence after the war, it should jealously preserve its independence at all times, and be strongly organized in as many areas as possible. If the aim were only to help win the war as soon as possible, at the least cost to the people of the United States, it would be more efficient to think in terms of combined or integrated U.S.-Allied clandestine and para-military operations, particularly in a British-French-Dutch colonial area like Southeast Asia. If, as Stilwell and his State Department advisers believed, it were injudicious for the United States to expose itself to such a colonialist taint, then the rational and economical course would be for OSS to refrain from entering the theater at all and to concentrate its available resources elsewhere.

In any case, the decision, whatever it should have been, was a matter of high national policy. Any U.S. para-military and political warfare activity in Southeast Asia, whether independent or in association with the British, was likely to lead far—has, in fact, led far. Yet, to the best of my knowledge, no comprehensive long-range policy in regard to the issue was ever formulated in either Washington or London. Policy just grew, where basic national policies much of the time do grow, in the field. And I think perhaps I witnessed one of the irreversible stages of its pupal development that night in the drawing room of Faridkot House, in December 1943. Donovan was building—or inheriting—a bigger empire than he realized.

Gen. Donovan's contribution, through the organization he founded, to the Allied cause in World War II was far from negligible, but the wartime activities of OSS were sometimes even more significant, it seems to me, in establishing a precedent, or a pattern, for United States intervention in the revolutionary struggles of the postwar age. The Donovan influence on U.S. foreign and military policy has continued to be felt even since his death; for good and ill he left a lasting mark on the mind of the nation's power elite. However

350

indirectly, many of our latter-day cold war successes, disasters, and entrapments can ultimately be traced back to him.

The General was a complex, colorful personality. He had an authentic ideal of civilization and a ruthless ethic of victory. His character was a unique blend of restless ambition and selfless patriotism, of recklessness and lucidity. He was an intrepid innovator and a prudent conformist, a remarkable twentieth-century American phenomenon, as well as an outstanding American public servant. There were surely elements of greatness in him; at times he seemed to me a modern Cortes who had never quite found his Mexico. Take him for all in all, he was a man. Serving under him was a privilege and an adventure, though not always one that promoted peace of mind. Perhaps that is why it was a growth experience.

The alliance within an alliance concluded between Gen. Donovan and Lord Louis was too great a policy paradox to hold together for long against the contradictory pressures of national destiny. OSS continued to expand its operations in Southeast Asia with the formal approval of the British-dominated theater command, but as time went on the relatively cordial relations that the Donovan-Mountbatten agreement had instituted between OSS and its British counterparts —or at least those elements in the British clandestine services responsive to the Supreme Commander's personal influence—soon reverted to their original, and in a sense normal, state of rivalry and suspicion. More and more, the British and American cloak-and-dagger agencies resorted in their bureaucratic duels to the conspiratorial trickery that was after all their reason for being, though it was officially supposed to be reserved for outdoor use against the common enemy. On occasion, my resources of ingenuity were severely taxed to produce for my SEAC superiors an innocent explanation for the presence of some accidently discovered OSS intelligence team or guerrilla base in an area where no such operation had yet been authorized; fortunately, the same occasion was generally exploited by one of its British rivals to "surface" some equally unsanctified activity of its own, so SEAC could give its retrospective blessings to both. All this, of course, was in the classic secret service tradition which OSS had largely inherited from its British mentors in the first place, and up to a certain point it was not dangerous, each side cheated to about the same degree—though the differing national patterns of deception sometimes caused misunderstanding—and usually with a certain gentlemanly restraint.

What poisoned inter-Allied relations in the theater was not the irresponsible intrigues of British and United States clandestine organizations competing as it were behind their respective governments' backs; on the contrary it was their most disciplined machinations conducted in accordance with the strict, though sometimes unavowed, aims of national policy and under high-level, if left-handed, official supervision. There had, perhaps, been some element of bureaucratic waywardness in Donovan's initial maneuvers to establish OSS in the theater more broadly than Stilwell and his State Department advisers, the guardians of traditional U.S. Asian policy, thought wise; but once the General's objective was achieved, OSS thereafter did everything possible to atone for its original sin by becoming the faithful secular arm of their anti-colonialist fundamentalism. The reconciliation between OSS and Stilwell was finally consummated—I played a modest part in helping to bring it about—when the former proposed and the latter approved a rather bold scheme for parachuting a secret agent into Thailand in an attempt to subvert the Thai government from its nominal alliance with the Japanese. Our British rivals had already slipped an agent of their own into the country without official sanction—or so we feared—and could be expected shortly to "surface" the operation; then they would be able to shut off OSS from any high-level contacts in Bangkok by claiming that any new Allied activity there would risk compromising the security of the clandestine link already established with the Thais. That, it was pointed out to Stilwell, would isolate the leaders of the Thai resistance from any liberalizing U.S. influences and make them little more than native mercenaries of British imperialism; the proposed OSS operation aimed on the contrary at ultimately bringing Thailand into the war as a kind of secret member of the United Nations, thus assuring its national independence and dignity after our common victory. The argument—in which I firmly believed myself—proved irresistible to Uncle Joe, and from then on his fear of OSS succumbing to the contagions of Western colonialism in Asia gradually dwindled.

From the short-term viewpoint, there was, in fact, little to fear. The longer we stayed in the theater the more OSS became permeated with the suspicion and disapproval of Western imperialism that characterized the new generation of Old China Hands in the State Department. In Southeast Asia as in China, United States policy, it seemed, was to dissociate ourselves as often as possible from the imperial aims of our colonialist allies while vigorously asserting on occasion our claim to enjoy equally with them the commercial—and implicitly the strategic—rewards of colonialism, in the measure that the institution survived our disapproval. It was not always an easy policy to uphold, especially within the framework of a wartime alliance, but OSS did its best.

I had arrived in New Delhi with a quite different outlook. In principle I adhered to the Wilsonian—and Rooseveltian—doctrine of self-determination for all peoples, including those under colonial rule, but I was prepared to leave the timing of its application to the liberal conscience of our allies. Colonialism and imperialism, insofar as they figured in my thoughts at all, meant those of our Axis enemies, or, as in North Africa, the kind of unconscious colonialism that marked the attitudes of certain Americans toward the French. I looked on the British as allies against both forms of the evil, and one of the things that had attracted me in the SEAC assignment was the possibility it seemed to offer for promoting a durable partnership between Britain and America. Gradually my mind underwent a change that I observed myself, at first with some distress, then with detached irony, and finally with a kind of self-satisfaction in growth achieved. I was wryly aware that a critical observer might detect certain analogies between the magnanimous American political strategy in Thailand, which I enthusiastically supported, and the sordid indulgence toward the spirit of Vichy which I had opposed— to the brink of mutiny—in our North African policy, but I was not greatly troubled by the inconsistency, if it really was one. In August 1945, a few days before the Japanese surrender, when I was sent on a clandestine mission to Bangkok, ostensibly to make arrangements for the rapid evacuation of American prisoners held by the Japanese in Thailand but no less, I gathered, to stiffen Thai resistance to any British encroachments on the nation's sovereignty, I scarcely thought of my original motive for accepting the SEAC assignment two years earlier, except to note that I had come a long way since then.

A number of different factors helped bring about the transformation. The confrontation with the dejected grimace that I took for the true face of British colonialism in India, and my vicarious exposure to the miseries and humiliations underlying the revolt of Indian nationalism—two essential themes of a postwar book which I called *Richer by Asia*—unquestionably made a deep impression on my mind. The direct emotional reward of working with Asian leaders, as I did in Thailand, to recover or preserve the freedom and dignity of their peoples likewise contributed to this mind chemistry, especially when it was spiced with a dash of adventure and virtuous intrigue.

What strikes me the most forcibly in retrospect, however, is my almost complete failure during the whole of my wartime experience in Asia to recognize the historic nature of the influences—one can almost call them fatalities—that were so drastically remodeling my ideological cosmos, and even in a measure my personality. What I thought of as a series of essentially private discoveries, I now recognize as the characteristic ordeal of an American mind largely shaped by the traditional values of liberalism—and still slightly befuddled by the anachronistic mythology associated with them—that was laboriously groping its way toward accepting the revolutionary intellectual and emotional implications of America's newly generated, wholly unprecedented power.

I never realized during my Asian tour of duty or for several years afterward that as the conscious servant of my country's consciously anti-imperialist aims in Asia I had been unconsciously helping to enlarge the frontiers of our existing Pacific *imperium*. It did not once occur to me, for example, that the OSS wartime operations in

Thailand with which I had some connection were already starting to forge postwar sentimental, political, and ultimately strategic links with Southeast Asia that from the United States' point of view would eventually turn into bonds of something strangely akin to imperial responsibility.

I would probably have been horrified in 1946 if I could have foreseen the pattern of 1966—as horrified as many contemporary American liberals are when they first become aware of it today—yet it was easily foreseeable. I reached the very brink of awareness myself, before pulling back in dismay, just before my return to the United States at the beginning of 1946, in a valedictory report to Washington attempting to summarize both the trend of developments in the theater since the end of the war and the lessons of the OSS wartime experience there. The Allied victory over Japan had not restored the prewar order in Southern and Southeastern Asia, I pointed out. Britain had already granted Burma's independence and was obviously preparing to grant India's. French rule was gravely threatened in Indo-China, and Dutch colonialism probably doomed in Indonesia. The era of European domination in Asia was unmistakably nearing its close. It would probably be some time, however, before the indigenous successor states achieved stablity. In the interim a potentially dangerous power vacuum was developing in the area.

It should not have needed even the modest knowledge of colonial history that I had acquired by then to predict what must happen when an expanding zone of power, however reluctant its previous expansion has been, borders on a developing vacuum—especially when a rival and less reluctant expansionism is also approaching its edges. My vestigial memories of high school physics should have sufficed. .

Secret agents rarely make history, but they frequently indicate its hidden trend. The amoral *raison d'état* that is their professional code is all too often the unacknowledged ethic of the governments that employ them. Officially controlled conspiracy, like illegally organized but tolerated prostitution, reveals the unsanctified needs, the secret cynicisms, and even to a certain degree the unavowed values, not only of the states, but of the societies on behalf of which it is conducted. Sometimes it may express the unconscious purposes of peoples themselves.

Most governments are themselves governed by moral dichotomies of which their peoples and even their members or servants are largely unaware. Their official personalities are usually a mixture, in varying proportions, of Dr. Jekyll and Mr. Hyde, and their policies reflect a balance—or sometimes a cyclical alternation—between the overt and the covert components.

My wartime exposure to the seamier aspects of international life not only broadened by understanding of power realities, but sensitized my mind to what might be termed the psychiatric factor in power conflicts. Men engaged in underground work, I observed, frequently developed delusions about the intentions and capabilities of their adversaries that closely resembled the symptoms of clinical paranoia. It was not merely their secret thoughts that acquired a delusive taint but all too often their official reports and their whole professional outlook. The atmosphere of secrecy, suspicion, and violence that overhangs most conspiratorial activity, official or otherwise, seemed to foster paranoid attitudes, and therefore delusive appreciations of reality, in even the healthiest personalities.

Clandestine operatives were not, however, the only sufferers from officialized delusion, as I gradually discovered. Soldiers, diplomats, statesmen—in short, all men whose business was power—often displayed the same symptoms. A certain measure of delusion seemed chronic, almost normal, in human thinking about power problems, apart from cases where it stemmed from misinformation, or from accidental errors of logic in processing information. In official bureaucracies or political organizations subject to a kind of bureaucratic discipline, once delusion was accepted as reality at a certain hierarchic level it automatically became institutionalized, sometimes in a permanent form under the name of tradition or doctrine. And a great deal of the time these bureaucratic deformations had a self-fulfilling character that made them all the harder to recognize and eradicate. Above all, they possessed—by the very fact of their in-stitutionalization—a rigidity akin to that manifested by the delusive systems in the minds of real paranoiacs. Hence the theory of institu-tional delusion as a chronic malady, not only of secret services, but of armies, states, even sometimes of whole civilizations set forth in *Richer by Asia*.

The theory has undergone a good deal of revision over the years —at one time I was not far from believing that all power conflicts and every form of violence were in essence delusive, which itself is probably a delusion—but I have never ceased to find it valuable both in analyzing political phenomena and in policing my own attitudes toward them. Though I no longer believe—if I ever did—that war is basically a disease of the mind, calling for psychiatric treatment or prophylaxis, I am more convinced than ever that there are nearly always pathological elements or trends in war, and in the power struggles leading to war, that do in fact call for a collective effort of mental hygiene if civilization is to survive on our planet.

19

One World Revisited

*T*here is a kind of mental gravity that weights awareness, and binds our perceptions closely to the places where we live; travel releases them. This is particularly true of air travel, I have found; at least it used to be true when planes were slower and gave time to find one's thoughts. To detach oneself from groundling servitudes and safeties, to replace our normal linear view of the world by a three-dimensional one, to discover the cloud-continents of the sky and float upon the atmospheric oceanstream—these are exercises that can hardly fail to enlarge the mind. Sometimes they do more.

Under certain flying conditions, embryonic organs of imagination may stir to life in our brains; the film of ages lifts from some latent inner eye and for a few moments—anticipating the space perspective of tomorrow—we see the earth as a star among stars, the planetary habitat of man. From such perceptions no doubt will one day quicken the germ of a global patriotism; every fatherland is first of all a living space, and needs some river, some mountain range, or some galaxy, perhaps, to frame its boundaries. In any case the air traveler after skirting in his thoughts the fringes of infinity returns to our human world with a glad sense of homecoming and an enhanced awareness of his kinship with the fellow humans he encounters at his several landings.

One World Revisited

The discovery of the universal humanness of man beneath his sometimes monstrous diversity of custom and appearance, the repeated finding of Friday's footprints upon the desert shores of the imagination—and the accompanying discovery that with unessential differences they are one's own, that the spoor of the Stranger is merely one of the variant traces of the Self—is among the great rewards of air travel, to some degree of all travel in our day.

(*Richer by Asia*, EXCISED PARAGRAPHS)

The fact is I have always loved a nomad life. Since my first Spanish revolution and the long, cold, solitary day in December 1931 that I passed riding in an antiquated first-class railway compartment, looking out the window at the Navarre hills muffled in rain, I have spent a good many hours of my life traveling. A number of trips have been lonely and tiring and uncomfortable like that early one in Spain, some have been hazardous or even monotonous, but I cannot recall any that I would have preferred not to make. Purpose and destination have mattered little, as I think back. The act of wayfaring is in itself a deep satisfaction, and often at the same time a kind of ascesis. Each journey, even when it was the repetition of familiar experience, seemed to offer its unique reward: discovery of some fertile, hidden valley of the world of mind within, revelation of some hitherto arcane grace or principle of justice in the world of sense without, perception of latent relevancies.

The particular travel episodes that inspired the fragment with which this chapter began date back to my first trip to India, starting from Washington in September 1943. That was the longest air voyage I had made up to then, and the relatively low-speed, low-ceiling, military aircraft in which I flew offered me a panorama of oceans, islands, continents, and watersheds that was impressively vast, yet rich in detail. The multiple works of man and the multiform variations of

359

nature beneath us were usually quite distinguishable—I remember a great herd of wild creatures, giraffes possibly, galloping in panic flight from the plane's pursuing shadow on the ground somewhere in the heart of Africa—but occasionally we had to climb so high that the last reassuring reminder of an ancestral habitat was erased. Once or twice I caught a glimpse of the earth from the then-unfamiliar altitude of 14,000 or 15,000 feet; it seemed incredibly remote. There were long hours flying in darkness or cloud when earth's very existence became a doubtful abstraction. I felt it as an awesome triumph of human reason over cosmic indeterminacy when the rugged, volcanic cliffs of Ascension Island, a lost speck in the South Atlantic that was the sole and indispensable refueling station on our route, suddenly loomed out of the mist, uncomfortably close to the wingtips of the converted Liberator bomber in which we had taken off from Natal on the hump of Brazil some twelve hours earlier. On an earlier trip, returning from my mission to England in 1941, I had landed briefly in Bolama, in Portuguese Guinea, and there experienced a kind of abrupt animal possession of Africa in the tropic dusk. This time, flying—with frequent, often deliciously prolonged halts —across its whole width from the Gold Coast to the coast of Eritrea, looking down on forest and savanna, on the reedbeds of Lake Chad and on the old, dull, serpent Nile, skirting the high, escarped battlements of Ethiopia, I saw all its marvelous abundance and gauntnesses unveiled. And after Africa there was Asia across the shallow trench of the Red Sea: the oven-breath of Aden, the Persian Gulf set in mother-of-pearl, the deserts and plains and sacred rivers of India.

Today, nearly a quarter of a century later, the afterglow from my impressions of that trip still lingers faintly. I can recognize, however, that the fragment superimposes a number of subsequent emotional experiences upon the memory traces of my first flight to India, and reflects a variety of influences (including, of course, that of St. Exupéry, a writer whose invisible presence seems to have been particularly vivid in my mind during my war years in the East). While many of these experiences were travel adventures of some kind, my explorations in search of the undiscovered tribe of man were not always so literal. Such progress as I made—or thought I had made—reflected various experiences of my wartime life, especially during the two and a half years I spent in India and Southeast Asia.

The end product of the experience as a whole was the mood of almost metaphysical optimism and enlargement that I brought home from the East in 1946, but some of the elements that nourished it were strange, almost to the brink of paradox, and others were mutually contradictory from the viewpoint of pure logic. My exposure to the secret service world of treachery and violence, for example, inspired an easily understandable inner search for a wholly different kind of world that no doubt on some occasions led me into mere idealistic escapism or overcompensation, but which at least a few times helped me, I think, find under the surface of the real the more real.

Similarly, if my personal discovery of Asia—and particularly of India—seemed an emotional, as well as an intellectual, enrichment to me, it was in part for two nearly antithetical reasons. One was that the special circumstances of my initial contact with Asia subjected me early and not too painfully to a kind of cultural de-colonization. By cultural de-colonization, I mean chiefly learning to respect the things—other than power—cherished or revered by peoples weaker than our own, especially when their skins are a different color from ours. For Americans, this de-colonization of the mind has sometimes —as in my own case—provided indirect rewards if anything greater than the direct ones. To cure oneself of what I came to think of in India as the sickness of being a sahib, one must first recognize that one has it, and the nature of the disease is such that if one really throws it off in India there is small chance of suffering a relapse in, say, Alabama.

What may seem odd is that in at least the early phases of my cultural de-colonization I was helped by a sort of romantic fascination with the new world of the imagination I had discovered in Asia in which today I recognize a classic pre-imperialist phenomenon. Numerous Americans before me had experienced the same fascination with Japanese or Chinese or Philippine—or in the case of Melville, Polynesian—patterns of culture and destiny, as our commercial and strategic horizons in the Pacific began to broaden. India had not yet deeply stirred many American imaginations, or aroused many American sympathies, because until the war it had seemed solely and securely a European sphere of interest, with little relevance to any American concerns. Before Pearl Harbor, South and Southeast Asia as a whole was an empty quarter in the American cultural mind, or, rather, one peopled vicariously by British, French, or Dutch aesthetic and intellectual reactions. The more the course of events incited an American observer to think of the area as a likely postwar power vacuum, the easier it was for him to see its peoples, its landscapes, its cultures, and its history in a new, romantic light, at once akin to, and subtly different from, that which had bathed it for his European predecessors when their dreams of empire were young, and like his own, not yet fully realized or avowed.

India, as the richest and most enduring civilization in the whole region and as the most complex society with the most dramatic history, naturally had a special appeal for me, even if its strategic interest, from the U.S. point of view, was less direct than that of Southeast Asia. There were also, however, temperamental, almost physiological, patterns of affinity and antipathy that influenced my reaction to the country. At a certain level of being I often felt more at home in India than anywhere else on earth. At others I was as frequently repelled or irritated or horrified as I was entranced. I was consistently stimulated, and therefore almost never indifferent: What I did not love, I usually hated.

On the whole, I suppose it was the loftiest tradition of Hindu religious thought, especially the Advaita Vedanta philosophy, that came the nearest to leaving me cold. Though I did not realize it clearly at the time, it was the absence—or what I felt as the absence —of the Christian sense of tragedy in this refined Hinduism, and in most southern Buddhism, too, that mainly put me off.

If Indian philosophy in the formal sense thus had little direct impact on my mind, I was profoundly impressed by the atmosphere of religious fervor and diffuse reverence in which all Indian society is bathed. Indians have the same selfish greeds as other men, often, I thought, a bit more sordidly indulged, and the same hypocrisies, if anything more cynically manifested, but there is a level of existence at which virtually all Hindu India can be termed a nation of spiritual wayfarers, eternally in search of a self-knowledge and an ultimate truth that are not necessarily less valid goals because they bear only a coincidental resemblance to our Western concepts of self, or knowledge, or even truth. It was impossible to come into contact with such a society, however briefly, remotely, and ignorantly—providing it was also humbly—without oneself feeling to some degree the lure of the same pilgrim road, whether or not it led in the same direction.

More than anything else, however, what both moved and fascinated me in India was the modern Indian predicament. No contemporary society—except perhaps China—seemed at once so rooted and so uprooted. No great people of our age had an inheritance that was at the same time so rich and so ruinous, none had both so much to learn and so much to unlearn. No nation that I knew of appeared to have such a dramatic rendezvous with the twentieth century still awaiting it, yet at the same time India's plight and opportunity epitomized those of every other nation caught in the maelstrom of twentieth-century history. And in my eyes, Gandhi epitomized India.

It was as the pilot of India's destiny, and especially as the paradoxical leader of an Indian cultural revolution which he sought to keep authentically Indian—i.e. steeped in the religious tradition of the past, yet oriented toward the future—that Gandhi mainly captivated my imagination. Though I never spoke to him and only once saw him at close range—when I attended one of his evening prayer meetings in Calcutta shortly before my return to the United States—his thought and example made a deep impression. I did not, of course, become a convert either to Gandhi's reformed Hinduism or to his doctrine of nonviolence, but I was interested in the latter, and I think that through studying it I perhaps became more sensitive than before to what might be termed the moral fallout implicit in every act of violence. I likewise became more conscious of the role of violence in the American cultural tradition. Moreover, my mind was at least partly liberated from the Western dichotomies of attitude in regard to the whole problem of human strife, which—like those in regard to the problem of religion—had up to then confined it. Gandhi taught me that it is not through compromise or avoiding struggle with what one regards as evil that the goal of brotherhood must be sought, but through the moralization of victory, and the means of victory. That, at least, is how I interpret today his example, if not his explicit teaching, and it is a concept that stems directly from the key scripture of modern Hinduism, the *Bhagavad Gita,* which was Gandhi's favorite devotional reading.

How much my mind actually was enriched by Asia, rather than by a sort of poetic mistranslation of Asia, is relatively secondary. It was more important, I think, that my exposure to Asian cultural influences stimulated latent centers of insight or imagination. Above all, the effort I made to understand certain Asian modes of thought and feeling helped me to understand better the hitherto invisible molds in Western civilization that had shaped my own. I thus acquired a measure of cultural objectivity or perspective that enabled me on occasion to look at the traditions and the patterns of behavior that had made me a man of the West almost with a stranger's eye, as someone who has never heard a recording of his own voice before listens to it for the first time with a stranger's ear. The result was not to estrange me from the basic values I had been brought up to revere —I merely became more critical of the perversions or falsifications of them that I had hitherto accepted unthinkingly—but to end my unconscious estrangement from all those members of the tribe of man who through some accidental dispersion had been brought up to revere quite different values. Straight-haired or fuzzy, sane or deluded, free or imagining that they rejoiced in their bonds, they were all, I recognized at last, my tribal brothers. Being brothers, as I soon realized, did not necessarily mean being partners or friends, but at the worst it implied substituting a fraternal hate that admitted, even if loathed, the adversary's humanity for simple biological aggression or exploitation. The mental gravity that had previously weighted awareness within me had been chiefly that of a Western civilization unconsciously assumed to be a planetary one; the star among stars that I looked down upon with the imagined eye of an interstellar traveler during my 1943 flight to India was identified as the home of man because by the time I wrote those words I had lived long enough in India to look upon it as a home of men. The very expression "tribe of man" which I used to replace such abstractions as "humanity" or "mankind" marked by its relative concreteness a stage in the growth of the somewhat vague one-world idealism to which I had long subscribed.

There were some quite different factors of mental liberation and enlargement that I must not overlook, however. The lens of cultural objectivity I learned to use in the East was itself a product of the West. Asia would certainly not have had the impact on my mind that it did if I had not already been sensitized to the difficulties and rewards of culture contact by a measure of exposure to contemporary anthropological thought. My propaganada researches and other readings had already laid a foundation; shortly after my return from France in 1940 I had discovered—and been powerfully stimulated by—the writings of Franz Boas, Ruth Benedict, and Margaret Mead; my duties in OSS involved virtually daily association, over a considerable period of time, with anthropologists, particularly Gregory Bateson and Cora Du Bois, and other American social scientists attached to our unit. My interest in the cultures of Asia was different from theirs, but it was to some extent controlled and illuminated by the basic concepts of the scientific discipline they professed. My acquaintance with them and with their ideas certainly helped me to derive more enrichment from my Asian experiences than I would otherwise have had.

A still more paradoxical influence in widening the sense of human brotherhood which I brought back from my stay in Asia was due to the training in social cooperation that military service gave me. One of the reasons why I felt myself enriched through having learned to look upon hundreds of millions of formerly alien beings as new tribal brothers was that I had simultaneously discovered how enriching it was to intensify one's participation in the collective endeavor of a tribe—my native one. War has probably always destroyed more than it has created, and in our century the disproportion has become graver than ever, but it is not, even in our time, pure destruction; it is still destroyer and creator in one, like the Hindu deity, Shiva. The surge of internationalist idealism after each of our century's two great wars was not merely a reaction from the horrors they produced; it was also an outgrowth of the fraternities they inspired.

There are vintages in prose as in wine, and even if my discarded manuscript had not been labeled I would instantly have recognized in it a reflection of the warming summer sun of 1946 as it fell, not on Asia or Africa, but on a dilapidated old house upon the Eastern Shore of Maryland, a remote and to me exotic retreat from war and travels. It was not quite a halcyon summer—a new wall of mutual distrust was rising between the West and its late Soviet allies, there were ominous rumblings from Southeastern Europe, and the clouds were piling up again over China—but the euphoria of victory was still in the air and for an American perhaps, too, the euphoria of a recent power promotion that brought with it a certain imperial large-mindedness without as yet the bad conscience or the nagging frustrations of empire.

For all the problems or dangers that were looming up the accent was still on hope. Even those of us who had learned that there are no completely fresh starts in history felt that humanity once more had a chance to start afresh. This time, it seemed possible to hope, the bad habits of the past would be forgotten, the lessons learned from them remembered. Despite its evident imperfections, the new United Nations organization—founded the summer before in San Francisco—appeared to be sincerely trying to keep mankind's post-war resolutions, including some of those left over from the war before, which the old League had allowed to be so lamentably and repeatedly broken.

Already, of course, the San Francisco experiment, like the Geneva one earlier, had its critics and its doubting Thomases; I was one myself, in a sense, since I maintained, in referring to the veto in the Security Council, that Washington and Moscow between them had "castrated the United Nations with the shears of national sovereignty," but in my heart I suspect I felt that even such a eunuch parliament of man might someday miraculously father world government, a term which, together with One World, figured prominently in the contemporary vocabulary of public discussion. My critique of the UN was founded in part on the hard-minded realism I had acquired in OSS through studying the behavior patterns of sovereign states from behind—or beneath—the scenes, but it was also inspired by an internationalism more unworldly in some respects than that of the organization's true believers. Like my old Geneva friends, Clarence Streit and Edgar Mowrer, I favored achieving an effective planetary authority through a progressive federal union of existing nations or through direct worldwide elections, rather than through the bureaucratic gradualism of the UN. Streit's federalist formula, however, seemed to me to involve the risk of establishing Western hegemony over the rest of the world, while the schemes for a universal legislature based on weighted representation that many world government enthusiasts supported would, I knew, be inacceptable to the touchy new nationalisms of Asia.

"If we really want to realize one world in our generation," I wrote, "we must resign ourselves to including in it what we consider the political backwardness of Russia and the technological backwardness of Asia." The observation had, and still has, a great deal of truth but was not quite the reflection of a realistic world outlook that it appears to be. Its intent was inspirational rather than cautionary. Similarly, when I remarked that "the problem of One World seems one of conversion—in the religious sense—and we have to convert almost simultaneously, ourselves, our nearest neighbors, and our most stubborn foes," my diagnosis was valid; it was my implicit prognosis that was wildly optimistic, for if I had not believed at the time that such an immediate and unlikely mutation of the human personality could be achieved through a sufficiently intense effort of moral leadership, I would not have included the sentence. The fact that I did include it is revealing. Along with a good many other surviving members of my generation, I had emerged from the war with a mental image of the postwar world in which realism and chimera were curiously mingled. The One World dream that possessed us was not in itself delusive; it was one of those Pisgah-visions of a distant reality that throughout the ages have inspired men to struggle toward new and higher collective goals. Nor were we unaware of the perils and difficulties that lay in our path; in this respect our outlook was probably more sober and sophisticated than that of our fathers in the dawn years of the League. In the rarefied postwar atmosphere, however, we underestimated—just as our predecessors had—the distance that separated our mountaintop from the promised land. In consequence, our relative political sophistication was all too often tainted with a millennialism akin to that which had afflicted the Geneva elders, and which had contributed to our youthful disillusionments during the thirties. Perhaps the 1945–46 brand of millennialism was even more extreme in some respects than the earlier forms, since it fed not only on the great hopes for man's future generated by the Allied victory over the Axis, but on the great fear and the great guilt that the United States had unleashed at Hiroshima. "If in two years or even five," I wrote in the introduction to *Richer by Asia*, "the worst political and social problems of Asia have been solved by the application of the principles which many of us believe are capable of solving the gravest problems of man, then we will know that the millennium is not only possible but much closer than the most optimistic ever thought possible—that it is in fact as possible and as imminent as the Apocalypse."

Rereading these words twenty years later, I am forced to recognize that Asia has not visibly progressed toward the millennial solutions, nor the world as a whole toward the apocalyptic doom, that seemed imminent in 1946.

Book Six

The
Crisis
of
Maturity

20

Confessions of a Part-Time Contrary One

Locust Hollow Farm, the run-down property on the Eastern Shore of Maryland that I had bought after my return from India, had seemed at first a good place to try to be a writer. Its remoteness from the tensions and frustrations of postwar urban America had, in fact, proved useful as long as I was writing about the war and Asia. In a discreet, slanting light, preferably that of early morning, the somewhat featureless bayside country, which often seemed to me either too clipped and prissy or else a little sad and abandoned, had a kind of withdrawn beauty that could be quite moving. I could imagine finally putting down roots there, and from one viewpoint it would have been natural for me to do so: Several of my father's ancestors, or relatives of ancestors, were buried in the little churchyard of Rockville only a few miles away.

It was my first taste of true country life since childhood, and it tasted good. The amateur farming I practiced when not sitting at my typewriter was interesting without being too exacting. Owing to the worldwide demand for meat and dairy products at the period, and to the recent removal of most wartime price controls in the United States, it likewise proved unexpectedly profitable. My writing, however, failed to prosper, despite the relative success of my book on Asia.

The ideal reader who lives in every writer's mind seemed to change form and personality each time I tried to open a dialogue with him.

What he wanted to hear from me turned out only intermittently to be something that it really interested me to write. What I wanted most to tell him—or thought I wanted—he seldom cared very much to hear, or if he did, I found that I had unexpected difficulty in communicating it to him. Like living in the deep country and settling down in the land of my fathers, my writing career was an experiment—and, of course, foredoomed as long as it remained that. In a dim way I realized the need for deeper commitment, but the kind of fevered sterility that seemed to strike me whenever I sat down at my worktable made commitment difficult. The creative layer of my brain, like some disordered gland, alternately flooded consciousness with a superabundance of disconnected ideas or emotions and paralyzed it with a backwash of critical doubt.

Even if I had preserved no direct memory of this travail, the contents of my "Unfinished" folder would suffice to remind me that the ordeal I was undergoing involved a good deal more than the normal difficulties of postwar readjustment—though of course they were part of it—or the eternal ones that every writer faces alone with himself and the blank sheet of paper. The despairing tone of certain of my scribblings, the stridency or excessiveness of others, the all-too-frequent stretches of withered abstraction are symptoms not only of arrested progress but of a many-sided falling-back.

American civilization seemed more oppressively alien to me than at any time since my adolescence. Like every American writer or artist or creative worker of any kind—except scientists and engineers, I suppose—I kept running head on into the rigid dichotomies and obsessive compartmentations that clutter the openesses of our cultural horizon without properly framing them, like sheep corrals on the empty prairie; and because I had for so long preferred the excitements of daily journalism, of political agitation, and of war service to the hard creative ascesis, I found the experience cruel.

As often happens in the case of such deep, invisible bruises to the spirit, I tended to misplace the ache. "American civilization," I wrote in one prospectus, "has become un-American by turning defiantly insular, culturally nationalistic, like the nineteenth-century Europe which Americans of the authentic tradition have always condemned. Fear of communism is leading not only to political reaction and militarism but to the stultification of American intellectual life, to cultural timorism, and to the loss of the special American freshness upon which we have always prided ourselves. We seem to be approaching the Vichy stage of fascism, which is the most depressing if not the most dangerous."

This diatribe summarized several of the main conclusions of a projected book. My proposed title, *Confessions of a Contrary One*, and to some extent the theme, had been suggested by an anthropological study of Comanche Indian culture that had recently come my way.* "Contrary One" was the Comanche term for deviants in their society who rejected the values and ideals of the tribe. The Contrary Ones expressed their eccentricity in various ways, but the most common expression—and the one that distressed orthodox Comanches the most—combined a distaste for violence, a tendency toward contemplation and mysticism, a lack of manly ambition to collect loot, and a notable deficiency of civic spirit with respect to participation in the basic national industry of raiding weaker tribes.

There were obvious differences, I acknowledged, between Comanche foreign policy and that of the United States, but as the author of the study had emphasized, the Comanches were originally a peace-loving people who under economic and social pressures had evolved over a few generations into one of the most predatory societies in history. This cultural revolution had taken place by consensus, without any change in the democratic nature of Comanche institutions or attitudes.

Comanche society was on the whole more tolerant of deviants than American society is; even so, they were regarded as neurotic cranks or freaks by healthy-minded Comanches. Undoubtedly they were un-Comanche by latter-day Comanche standards. From another viewpoint, however, the Contrary Ones embodied a principle of

---

* *The Psychological Frontiers of Society*, by Abram Kardiner (with the collaboration of Ralph Linton, Cora Du Bois, and James West), Columbia University, 1945.

373

social health that the rest of their people had lost, and they remained faithful to ancestral ideals that the conformist majority had unconsciously betrayed. Adopting the outlook of a contemporary American contrary one, I proposed to develop in an anecdotal vein a critique of certain postwar trends, both cultural and political, that I found alarming or hateful.

Naturally, it was the current of opinion in favor of launching a preventive war against the USSR before the Soviets developed a nuclear arsenal of their own that frightened and outraged me the most. At the time it seemed a mere ripple on the surface of the nation's public consciousness, but from the personal links with official Washington that I had maintained in my country retreat I knew that there were influential levels of the Truman Administration, of the armed services, and of the business community where it flowed more strongly.

No doubt the demon that lurks in every ink bottle or typewriter ribbon egged me on to exaggerate the intensity and range of my dissent. On the other hand a number of my adverse comments on American society were probably valid—and probably, alas, remain so today. Unquestionably, they were symptomatic of a fairly deep malaise connected in some way with my attempt to reintegrate myself into American life after my years as an expatriate. Where I was most lacking in self-awareness was in assuming that my role as an American contrary one reflected exposure to Gandhian nonviolence and Eastern spirituality. In retrospect, my 1947 attitudes seem more expressive of the tendency historically endemic among American intellectuals to seek refuge from the problems and responsibilities of power in some transcendental idealism, and as Irving Kristol has noted, to bask in the moral beauty of their own protest.* In one sense, therefore, my cultural reintegration was more successful than I realized: Nothing is quite so homespun as a sound, conforming nonconformist.

* "American Intellectuals and Foreign Policy," by Irving Kristol, *Foreign Affairs*, July 1967.

Some of my proposed chapters anticipated the gentle beatitudes of civic withdrawal that have since become orthodoxy to part of the American intelligentsia, or pseudo-intelligentsia. Others—one in particular—came close to the revolutionary Tantrism of the New Left.

Perhaps if I had possessed more firmness of soul and gone ahead with my book I might today be one of the senior gurus of the Psychedelic Age. As I should have foreseen, however, the moment I started showing the prospectus around, I found myself subjected to the remorseless pressures that the American establishment instinctively brings to bear upon its deviants of literary bent: sympathetic editorial interest, in some cases bordering on mild enthusiasm, and the virtual assurance of a decent advance if I produced a sample chapter or two with enough bite in them.

Europe seemed the only escape.

In reality, it was not merely America on which I wanted to turn my back, but the whole century, and even some of the centuries that had gone before. This more radical withdrawal both inspired a decision to drop the *Confessions of a Contrary One* in favor of another project, and then ultimately prevented me from finishing that as well. It was to have been a study, part sociological, part historical, of romantic love—or more precisely, of what I termed the romantic experience—in Western civilization.

Fossils From a Private Collection

. . . this world we live in—our human earth which used to be the fatherland of poets and lovers—has become a kind of occupied province under the heel of an alien master race . . . These tyrant-rulers with the empty hearts . . . are all those who worship power and self, nakedly or in the name of some inhuman ideology, of some anonymous collective institution or of some soulless abstraction.

375

They are the haters, the despisers of man, the rejecters of the merely human. They are the monsters disguised as men who stalk across our earth with mineral tread, crushing our feelings and our lives as they go about their great affairs of power, plotting their wars against one another, hurling at their adversaries mechanical insults that are more like the gnashings of angry gears than any human rage . . .

(*Amendments to Eros,* UNFINISHED)

21

The Parable of the Mischievous Guru

The spring of 1948 was a fine one in Paris, as I remember it, but possibly because I had been away from Europe so long I found its charm gently depressive. The trees along the boulevards had already put out leaf when I arrived from Switzerland, where I had spent the winter with my family; lilacs and tulips were still flowering in the parks; the apple and pear trees trained *en espalier* against the walls of the Luxembourg Gardens seemed perpetually covered with blossoms flawless as wax, unmarred by any stigma of fulfillment; day after day a changeless, temperate sun shone down on a city delivered from poignancy.

I rose early every morning and left my drab little Left Bank hotel to walk around the streets. They came to seem familiar again and I soon recalled where everything had been. I even made some fresh discoveries. Having very little money helped; Paris, unlike many great cities, is most hospitable to those who are most dependent on its hospitality.

I was neither happy nor unhappy. I knew I had to wait, and on the whole I was content to be alone in Paris in the spring with very little money, waiting. Some of the things I was waiting for were simple enough: money from a bank in the United States, where I still had a few hundred dollars left; the final decision on a job I had applied for in Paris that sounded as if it might be interesting and would at least be comfortable; word from my publishers about a proposal I had submitted for a new book—a successor to the abandoned Comanches —that I was not very anxious to write and about another one already half written—my essay on love—that we were tentatively agreed had better be dropped; meetings with old friends who were temporarily out of Paris or whom I had not yet made up my mind to phone. What else was not altogether clear: some kind of a sign, probably. I was killing time, as the saying goes, though that was not just how I felt about it: Time seemed to be melting away too fast, if anything, like the taste of some insipid sweet.

Studying the menus posted outside the more modest restaurants of the Latin Quarter, to see where I might find the best meal for the least money, was an absorbing occupation; so was browsing through the bookstores, or among the secondhand stalls along the Seine, trying to solve the fascinating philosophical and practical problem of which books to buy when I could scarcely afford any. Such gastronomic and literary researches took up quite agreeably a good part of my day. Reading *Le Monde* and *Combat* over a cup of black coffee accounted for another part. I spent the rest of my time walking, which included a certain amount of thinking, or ruminating, or perhaps just daydreaming. Whatever way I started out, when I had any goal at all, I usually reached a point where my steps seemed to turn back in time, and the streets along which I was walking became peopled with men and women I had almost known.

One of the things that developed out of all this mind-idling was a macabre and somewhat didactic idea for a novel. I had not actually tried to write any fiction since my early Left Bank days in Paris, but from time to time I used to jot down the rough outline of some projected novel, and once or twice I had even carried the make-believe to the point of open discussion. I did not go to that extreme in the case I have just mentioned, but I did put on paper a synopsis of the proposed book—to be called *The Doctor of the Dead*—and several thousand words elaborating on various facets of the theme: the encounter between a neurotic, young American writer and a mad

378

The Parable of the Mischievous Guru

French psychiatrist, Dr. G. From the literary viewpoint, these abortive scribblings depress me more than a number of others, equally farfetched, but they convey something of the climate in postwar Europe before the success of the Marshall Plan had begun to restore morale, and they throw light on the crisis I was going through myself. After the tensions and intoxications of the Great Crusade, I found it difficult to readjust to the unenthralling, all-too-often dispiriting realities of the postwar world.

FOSSILS FROM A PRIVATE COLLECTION

In happier and more stable times life of the soul coincided in most cases with life of the flesh . . . this insured that when a soul died it was probably buried . . . now we have millions of walking dead leading their limbo-existences among the still living and refusing to admit that they are dead . . . we are not only overrun with walking dead but we have no adequate institutions for dealing with them . . . indeed there are no accepted means for detecting them . . . psychiatry? except for extreme cases psychiatrists won't admit that their patients are dead . . . they talk about treating neuroses, psychoses, etc . . . it's all right if you like but it's all poetry, it's all allegory. I tell my patients: First, learn that you are dead. Afterwards we shall see . . . same treatment for Western civilization—begin by burying.

Psychologically, modern personality is singularly ill-adapted to withstand the strains and shocks which modern society, fashioned in its image, inevitably creates. A twelfth-century or an Asian mind could live in the shambles of postwar Europe but the twentieth-century mind cannot, and since it is doomed by the laws of its own construction to produce such shambles, it is condemned to despair, madness, and death . . . Sensualist dies spiritually when he discovers that his body has lost power of enjoyment, religious mind when it

379

discovers that God is myth, and modern mind when it becomes con-
vinced that pursuit of personal happiness does not lead to happiness
... it is this last discovery that fills postwar Europe and will eventu-
ally fill America with walking dead ...

(*The Doctor of the Dead*, UNFINISHED)

I have already mentioned some of the personal problems—of course
there were others—that helped create the funereal mood of my literary fantasy; there is little need to expand on either its political or
cultural background. The misunderstandings and rivalries that had
been poisoning relations between the West and its former Communist
allies for more than two years had finally developed into the cold
war. The rejection of the Marshall Plan, imposed by the Kremlin on
its European satellites the previous summer, had concretized the
division of Europe—and of the world—into two increasingly hostile
blocs. The Moscow-directed Communist *putsch* in Czechoslovakia a
few weeks earlier (February 1948) had marked a dire new stage in
its aggravation, or as we would doubtless say today, its escalation. To
members of my generation living in Europe—especially those who
had visited Czechoslovakia in the late thirties—the *coup de Prague*
seemed a toll of doom. The implications of the threatening Soviet
blockade of Berlin—it materialized in June—were even more dramatically ominous. Not quite a decade after Munich, Europe appeared to be facing simultaneously a new Czech crisis and the
equivalent of a new Danzig test, neither of them more appealing to
the liberal mind than the old ones. Some pessimists feared that World
War III was only a few weeks distant.

My morale as an internationalist, and to some extent even as a believer in man, had, of course, been further shaken by the assassination
of Gandhi a few months earlier, and perhaps still more by the failure
of Gandhism to prevent or halt the ghastly massacres that had broken
out at the partition of India.

Logically, these horrors did not necessarily invalidate the relatively hopeful theses as to the future role of Asia in world affairs that I had developed in *Richer by Asia;* they merely demonstrated, as I had written, that grave maladies have grave symptoms, and perhaps, as I likewise suggested, that the Western doctrine of nationalism is not the right treatment. Closer, however, to the level of instinct, I feared that I had been systematically overoptimistic—and not only about Asia. "There is hope for India," I had written during the previous summer in an article for *The New Republic,* "as long as the Indians cannot control their madness sufficiently to build and launch atomic bombs with it. And there is hope for us if we can recognize in Indian madness our own dressed in Eastern garb." Such hope was hardly the kind that warms the blood.

The purely intellectual influences immediately reflected in my 1948 novel project naturally included the currently fashionable doomsday school in American and British literature and journalism —I suppose it is fair to include under this heading both Aldous Huxley, whom I had been rereading, and Toynbee, whom I had just discovered—along with even more depressant French writers, among whom Sarte and Camus were the most significant. In addition to the nightmare of a nuclear apocalypse which they shared with their Anglo-Saxon colleagues, the French pessimists were reacting to two indigenous traumas: the betrayal, as they viewed it, of the social ideals of the French Resistance, and France's decline as a world power, its Portugalization, as Simone de Beauvoir called it. The malaise of being an American was quite different, almost antithetical —the guilt of having achieved historic greatness without being quite prepared for it—but there was still enough left of the prewar roots I had put down in France for me to experience something of the contemporary French indisposition as well. Perhaps, too, as the French themselves suppose, there is always an element of universality in anything that comes out of France, including its aberrations. In any event, there are evident traces in my unwritten *Doctor of the Dead* of both Camus's plague-stricken Oran and Sartre's film *Les Jeux Sont Faits.* The Orient, still vivid in my mind from my wartime

381

travels, had supplied some of the underlying philosophical attitudes along with much of the symbolism. The title was an allusion to those metaphysical undertakers in Tibet who assist the exit of the departing soul.

At a still more archaic level I can recognize fragments of mind debris from one of my own dead lives, tinted by certain esoteric writings I once had studied, seeking a key to their comprehension that I never found. It was natural that such long-buried memories should rise to the surface of awareness at a time when I was alone in Paris, unemployed and unengaged, with all my thoughts irresistibly pulled backward toward the past, toward several pasts.

The denouement of my story (the narrator makes the inevitable discovery that it is his psychiatrist who is mad), and the ambiguous personality of its central figure, the mysterious Dr. G., reflected, of course, a persistent ambivalence in my attitudes toward my own analysis, which as I have earlier related was interrupted by Allendy's remobilization in the spring of 1940. Allendy himself, I had learned from French friends, had died in Montpellier in 1942, and I had not thought of him for some time. It was an accidental encounter with his shade during one of my wanderings around the limbo-Paris my mood had created that recalled him to my mind. I was browsing through a Left Bank bookshop, wondering whether I could afford to buy anything at all and hesitating between an account of the Darlan affair by a woman journalist I had known in Algiers and Simone Weil's wartime tract, *l'Enracinement*, when my eye fell on a slim, cheaply printed volume: *Journal d'un Médecin Malade*. The author was René Allendy.

It was a moving little book: the account of an experiment in self-analysis inconclusively terminated by the death of the analyst. Allendy was already dying when he embarked on the enterprise and as a physician must have understood the gravity of his symptoms. The analysis itself, however, seemed to me to reveal little awareness of approaching dissolution.

The shock I received from reading Allendy's book was unexpectedly violent. It served, somehow, as a concrete and total communication of his death, almost as if I had stumbled unawares upon his corpse. Though I knew he had died, I had not realized before he was *that* dead. In some inaccessible fastness of the mind I had evidently been waiting all these years for his resurrection. Perhaps, too, Allendy's apparent failure to see, or admit, that his attempt at psychosomatic self-healing was foredoomed revived my earlier transference suspicions of him as a charlatan and sorcerer. (Much later, when I reread the little book, this failure seemed to me the inevitable price of a tragic and essentially noble experiment. Allendy knew better than most men how hard it always is to find the truth; he had been a seeker after it all his life. That he had apparently been struggling with self-delusion when death surprised him merely proved that he had remained a seeker to the end.)

In an account of Tibetan religious beliefs and rituals I had been reading just before I came to Paris, there is a folktale about a famous guru who subjects his *chela* (disciple) to an interminable number of painful or humiliating ordeals. Nothing daunts the faithful neophyte until he is ordered to commit a particularly abominable crime. Then he revolts and calls his master a monster. "Imbecile," the guru retorts, whacking him over the head with a slipper, "how long has it taken you to discover it?" In that instant, the tale concludes, the *chela* attained enlightenment.

The enlightening shock I got from reading Allendy's posthumous book was less dramatic, and, of course, less instantaneous in its effects, but it was all the same an important experience. Until then part of my mind had remained linked to Allendy—and through him to other figures of a much earlier past—by ties of infantile dependence. Now the cord of analytical transference had been severed at last; Allendy had not been able to complete his own analysis, but from beyond the grave he had at last successfully terminated mine. My initial desolation was followed by a strong sense of release. And as often happens, release from one infantile, or at least immature, relationship led me to discover and free myself from other previously unsuspected ones, not only with particular individuals but with wide arcs of reality itself.

Fossils From a Private Collection

. . . Narrator becomes aware of a remarkable but at first indefinable change in his own relationship to the world. Every condition that he had learned from G. was characteristic of the limbo-world has disappeared. All material forms have lost their fossil rigidity and become clear symbols of process. Green is the color-symbol of growth, flesh the tactile symbol of cellular metabolisms . . . men and women are no longer isolated entities but multiple facets of a single personality and each fragment is a symbol of the whole . . . realization that while he must change endlessly, because the soul itself is another symbol for process, he cannot die . . .

(*The Doctor of the Dead,* UNFINISHED)

The job for which I had been waiting in Paris eventually materialized. It was at UNESCO (the United Nations Educational, Scientific and Cultural Organization), founded in London some three years before, which had recently set up its permanent headquarters in the French capital under its first director-general, Dr. Julian Huxley, the distinguished British biologist and humanist. I knew nothing about UNESCO's activities, but the friend who introduced me to the organization and briefed me on its ambitious objectives made them sound interesting, almost exciting. The fact that UNESCO was attempting to promote the One World ideal largely through nonpolitical means sounded like good sense to me—how else, in the present situation, could one go about it?—and taking part in this bloodless intellectual crusade seemed a possible solution to the problem of futility that up to then I had been wrestling with so unsuccessfully. It was hard for me to picture myself as an international bureaucrat, or as any other kind, but I could no longer see myself very clearly as a writer or reporter, either; unless the international cooperation that UNESCO and the other organs of the UN were trying to establish took shape what would there be left for anyone to write about or to report on?

UNESCO at the time was housed on the Avenue Kléber near the Etoile in what before the war had been the Hotel Majestic, one of the most sumptuously old-fashioned in the French capital. The cut-glass chandeliers in the great ballroom, the gilded woodwork, and the general impression of mildewed deluxe recalled a Sol Steinberg caricature of faded splendor. Under the Occupation, the building had served as a German military headquarters and the Gestapo was said to have utilized some of its extensive cellars as torture chambers. The darker ones were popular with thrill-seekers of various kinds during the lengthy UNESCO lunch hours. Staff discipline appeared to be somewhat lax, reflecting the easygoing disposition and casual administrative habits of the director-general, but the elasticity of working hours and priorities was at least partially compensated for by the enthusiasm of the personnel. The professional bureaucrats had not yet moved in, or were just beginning to, and UNESCO was still largely staffed with idealists, dreamers, talented eccentrics of various strains, or just plain cranks. Most of them seemed wholeheartedly dedicated, at least to their own jobs, though how their particular activities contributed to the broader objectives of the organization was not always clear to a newcomer. Even the most recondite UNESCO projects, however, generally expressed in some way the humanistic futurism that pervaded the whole headquarters. Winding one's way along the dim uncarpeted corridors of the Majestic from Fundamental Education past the Hylean Amazon, perhaps, to Human Rights or the Free Flow of Information, one sometimes had a vision of deserts flowering almost overnight; of vast and tasty new harvests from the seas; of spacious new metropolises in the jungle; of happy headhunters squatting in their longhouses reading Lorca, translated, thanks to UNESCO, into their island dialect; of reforested Mediterranean crests, freed from the ravening, millenary lust of goats by the same rational and cooperative UNESCO magic that was to rekindle the faltering sexual urge of the Andean llama on the wastelands of the *altiplano*.

I worked at UNESCO for more than two years. On the whole it was an interesting and valuable experience which, among other things, helped me to realize the gravity of the vast, long-range problems—hunger, illiteracy, overpopulation, wastage of natural resources —that threaten the survival of civilization on earth at least as seriously as do the power rivalries of the technologically advanced nations. Much of the organization's activity was probably futile in terms of immediate import, because the member nations, starting with the most directly threatened, had no real will to grapple, except verbally, with their problems.

My initial assignment in UNESCO was in the Ideas Bureau. This ambitiously named institution, a brainchild of the British writer, J. B. Priestley, conceived during the second general conference of UNESCO in Mexico City at the end of 1947, had just come into being. Intended to function as a kind of super-planning board for the Mass Communications Department—the enriched UNESCO version of an information service—and in certain respects for the organization as a whole, the Ideas Bureau reflected UNESCO's ceaseless but so far consistently unsuccessful quest for dramatic, jumbo-sized ideas capable of firing the enthusiasm of the masses all around the world for its internationalist, democratic, and humanitarian goals.

My colleagues in the Bureau consisted of three other international thinkers-at-large: our chief or chairman, W. E. Williams, a refreshingly unorthodox British adult-educator; Roger Caillois, a gifted French sociologist, critic, and prose poet; and George Voskovíc, a moody, imaginative Czech actor-producer, recently arrived in Paris from his native Prague.

From the start we formed a congenial team. At first we felt a little sheepish as we sat around the big table in Williams's office and conscientiously cerebrated. Soon, however, we got caught up in our own impersonations; the harsh noises from the real world of international conflict and conspiracy outside the Majestic's tall French windows gradually faded to a gentle background murmur for our brainstorming. It was Caillois, I think, who, despite his French intellectual's misgivings about the whole business, opened the way for our breakthrough. What was really needed to launch UNESCO, he remarked, was something to crystallize the new concept of human interdependence in the public mind as the Paris exposition of 1889 had helped crystallize the nineteenth-century myth of progress.

"Why not, precisely, a UNESCO-sponsored international exposition?" I suggested.

"A One World World's Fair," said Voskovíc.

"Lads," said Williams, "we've got it."

Before long the Ideas Bureau had worked out a detailed blueprint of the proposed One World World's Fair. Along with more orthodox features it called for such attractions as a Waxwork Museum of Culture Heroes of All Civilizations, a historical chamber of horrors with the title, Man Against Himself, and a tent for Arab storytellers with simultaneous translations in many languages.

Dr. Walter Laves, the American deputy director-general, did not seem entirely convinced when we outlined the project to him—though it was the sort of gaudy and Barnumesque device for "selling" the UNESCO ideal that the organization's supporters in the United States often clamored for—but he gamely agreed to take us into Huxley. The director-general, on the other hand, was enthusiastic. Even the warning that our scheme, if ever approved by the member governments, might cost their taxpayers half a billion dollars or more did not appear to chill him. He listened to William's presentation with undisguised enjoyment, his birdlike head cocked to one side, and repeatedly interrupted to suggest improvements that had just occurred to him. Most of them were excellent. Huxley, it has always seemed to me—at least since that occasion—has one of the most cultivated as well as least conventional minds of our century; he was not, perhaps, the ideal person to head an international bureaucracy like UNESCO, but in many important respects he was a better head than the organization deserved.

With Huxley's blessing we next arranged a dinner conference—

paid for out of the Ideas Bureau's own collective pocket—for the UNESCO Executive Board, a permanent international committee that keeps an eye on the secretariat for the member governments. It seemed impossible that we could run the gauntlet of fifteen such notorious budget butchers and program murderers and survive, but somehow we emerged unscathed. We had ordered a number of striking visual aids to illustrate our project and had also taken particular pains with the wine list. It was a brilliant performance. Williams was superb. Caillois managed to sound at once hermetic and convincing. I felt a small glow of pride over my own modest incantatory contribution. Voskovíc, who wound up our presentation, pulled out all the stops. The Board was visibly impressed, even moved. The Greek member, as I recall it, actually wept with emotion as he congratulated us. Huxley beamed like a scientific cherub; Laves looked like a man who has seen a miracle. It was a marvelous and Faustian moment.

Needless to say, the triumph of the Ideas Bureau was short-lived. As the date for the third general conference, in Beirut, approached, less and less was heard around the Majestic and in UNESCO circles generally of the One World World's Fair—except for a prominent though not particularly helpful mention in a *Saturday Evening Post* article on UNESCO entitled "Dr. Huxley's Wonderful Zoo" (Huxley had formerly been curator of the London Zoo). A trip I made to Washington to win U.S. support for the scheme proved unproductive. The end came at Beirut, where the French delegation did a scalp dance around the doomed *Bureau des Idées*, mainly, as far as I could gather, because they disapproved of the name. Huxley himself was thrown to the wolves of bureaucratic orthodoxy—though I do not suppose his sponsorship of our project contributed materially to his downfall—and was succeeded by the Mexican diplomat, poet, and educator, Dr. Jaíme Torres Bodet, another superior mind who, as his American and French backers should have guessed, was soon to make himself as unpopular with the bureaucrats as Huxley had been. (Torres Bodet resigned in 1952 after protracted arguments with the organization's leading member governments over UNESCO's budget and program.)

The fiasco of the One World World's Fair, grotesque as the whole incident appears in retrospect, marked an important psychological turning point for me, an essential, if belated, maturation ordeal. Once again my old *guru*, history, had dealt his enlightening slap at the decisive moment. There was, of course, nothing inherently foolish in the idea of trying to popularize UNESCO and its goals through the kind of international exposition that my colleagues and I proposed, but in the sulphurous summer of 1948 to assume as we implicitly did that any major government in the world, any mass of public opinion, or any influential elite group could be persuaded to take such a project seriously one had to be singularly deluded or singularly insulated from political reality. I fear I had allowed myself to become both.

A year or two earlier, before the international situation had become so desperate, when it seemed to be merely drifting toward catastrophe, I had felt some revival of interest in the protest pacifism that had intrigued me for a while in my Geneva days. The threat of nuclear doom that the postwar era faced made the pacifist movement look more relevant, if not more practical, than it had seemed in the thirties, and *Richer by Asia* had earned me a considerable correspondence from American adepts of nonviolence, of varying degrees of rationality or sophistication. None of the anti-war activities, even the most rational ones, for which my participation or support was solicited struck me as very promising, but the dedicated idealism that often inspired them impressed me. There should, I reasoned, be some way in which the Gandhian principles and techniques of nonviolence that had fascinated me in India could be adapted to crystallize the worldwide, diffuse, popular dread of a nuclear holocaust around an effective program of resistance to war. The need for such programs seemed to me all the more urgent because of the trend in favor of preventive war that I had already noted. For a few months I toyed with a fantastic scheme for promoting the establishment of a world government-in-exile, with its own clandestine radio transmitter, to wage a permanent campaign of civil disobedience against every form of officialized militarism everywhere.

I think I first broached the idea to Clifton Fadiman, then editing the short-lived, cooperatively-owned magazine, '47, as the theme for an article, and he strongly encouraged me to write it for him. The same idea was to be the basis for the final chapter of my proposed *Confessions of a Contrary One*. "In a crisis threatening peace, or if war broke out," I wrote in some private notes elaborating on the scheme, "proposed world-government-in-exile would not attempt to determine rights or wrongs of dispute but would seek to paralyze military operations of both parties by simultaneous open and underground political warfare offensives against them."

One reason I never tried to get my fantasy of universal subversion put in print, despite Fadiman's encouragement, was that I began for a while to take it too seriously myself and I was afraid that premature publicity might spoil the chances of anyone else's doing so. The greatest problem, I felt, was discovering and recruiting an acceptable underground provisional president for the world. The prestige of an Einstein or an Albert Schweitzer would be valuable, but practical experience in clandestine work seemed no less essential. (By the time, several years later, that I finally met someone in Paris who might conceivably have filled the role I had ceased to believe in the whole thing, and I am not sure it would be a compliment to mention his name.)

Bit by bit, realization of the immense practical difficulties involved in launching such a project accumulated in my mind, but the fear that whatever subversive impact it might achieve would be felt more in the democracies than in the Communist nations, and therefore might simply stimulate aggressions by the latter against the former, probably did more to put me off it. Similar objections, as far as I could see, applied to any peace movement that addressed itself to the masses over the heads or behind the backs of their governments. One-sided subversion for peace could never be anything but an hypocritical imperialism or a treason that lacked the courage to go by its true name. By this time (late 1947–early 1948) the cold war could no longer be dismissed as a mere shadow play of delusion and counterdelusion, and there seemed no use in criticizing the

United States government and people for not manifesting a more Gandhian attitude toward our troublesome former allies.

The Truman Administration as a whole could not be blamed because the United States was now unmistakably beginning to oppose political warfare with political warfare around the world; practically it had no choice. While continuing to disapprove what I termed "the lamentable Truman Doctrine" (i.e. defending Greece and Turkey), I warmly praised the Marshall Plan.

The techniques of indirect or nonmilitary aggression that Stalin was now employing against the remnants of European democracy were closely akin to those once employed by Hitler, as I had analyzed them in *The Strategy of Terror*, but whereas my exposure to Nazi political warfare had finally turned me into something close to a professional anti-fascist, I as yet felt no call to join the gathering ranks of the anti-Communists, professional or amateur. History had let me down; it would have to get along without my help for a while.

By the time I joined UNESCO I was beginning to face the developing new world crisis in a slightly more adult mood, but some emotional shock was needed to complete my recovery. Falling upon Allendy's book had been one; the bursting of the One World World's Fair bubble seems in a minor way to have acted as another. From then on my morale improved, despite intermittent regressions, both in a political sense and in more private concerns. I started coping with my own problems as well as those of the universe. Among other things I reached the decision to abandon, at least for the time being, any thought of trying to make a current living by writing, but to use the considerable leisure that my duties at UNESCO left me to get launched on a new book—which eventually turned out to be this one.

Apart from the incidental therapeutic benefits, important as these were, working in UNESCO at the particular time I did contributed to my education in two essential areas. In the first place, through the very nature of the organization's activity, it focused my attention on the problems of resistance to what I thought of as cultural

AWAKENING FROM HISTORY

subversion. With the collapse of Hitlerism it had seemed that the threat of organized regression had vanished, and I was inclined to be a little impatient of those Americans or other Westerners who continued to march about brandishing the banners of Western civilization as if celebrating some never-ending Flag Day. I felt I could serve the Occidental cause better by criticizing the deficiencies— or excesses—of Western civilization, particularly in its American subdivision, to which my contact with the Orient had sensitized me. My preoccupation for some years with the problem of cultural lag in virtually every aspect of modern life likewise tended to keep me away from the ramparts. Our civilization would have less trouble in defending itself, I thought, if its attics and cellars were cleared of some of the outdated cultural bric-a-brac that had accumulated over the centuries. There were moments when I felt myself close to those American sociologists and educators who almost automatically equate innovation with progress. It was becoming harder and harder, however, to discover anything progressive in the cultural straitjacket that the Soviet rulers had already imposed on all of Europe east of what Winston Churchill had recently baptized the Iron Curtain, and were now trying by stealth or terror to slip on the surviving democracies of Western Europe.

By 1948, Russian Stalinism was already entering its most paranoid phase, and orthodox Communists in the West, with their intellectual camp followers of high or low degree, were compulsively hailing as revelation every delusion, whim, and prejudice of the half-demented, semi-civilized Caligula in the Kremlin. It was the heyday of Socialist Realism—the most degraded form of it—in the arts and in literature; Lysenko's crank or quack genetic theories were official scientific dogma throughout the Communist world. Various branches of learning from linguistics to economics had suffered from Stalin's heavy-handed doctrinal intrusions; even physics and mathematics were not totally spared. The Nazi secession from civilization had seemed far graver, even in its relatively early stages, but it was alarming to see the same tendencies developing in the Soviet Union, and even more alarming to see how little effective resistance

392

the incipient new barbarism was encountering from Western intellectuals who before had fiercely opposed every infiltration of Nazi ideology.

UNESCO, I felt, should act as a rallying point for the world's intellectual elites in the struggle to defend the freedom of science and art. My already considerable admiration for Huxley rose still higher when he accepted an invitation—though not, of course, in his official capacity as director-general of UNESCO—to attend a Stalinist-sponsored international congress of intellectuals at Wroclaw in Poland, and took the floor there to protest against the Lysenko cult. I was on a mission to the United States at the time, and I was depressed by the negative reaction in American UNESCO circles to Huxley's courageous gesture. Half of the organization's supporters in the United States seemed indignant because the director-general of UNESCO had ventured to associate with notorious subversives, while the other half were shocked because he had taken sides in an ideological controversy. I returned to Paris gloomy about the chances for the survival of a civilization whose defenders were either so muddled-headed or so lacking in moral backbone.

Today I realize that the problem is more complex than I was prepared to admit in 1948, and I no longer believe that the conception of UNESCO's role I had then is entirely valid. I still think, however, that my reaction to the Stalinist regression was healthy. I was rediscovering the necessary limits to cultural relativism at a time when Western civilization once again faced an undeniable threat. No doubt I exaggerated its gravity somewhat: As we have since observed, civilization, even in the Soviet Union itself, had hidden powers of resistance and recovery.

The other useful lesson that working at UNESCO taught me— though in some respects it, too, was perhaps slightly overdrawn— was closely related to the first one, but more explicitly political. Until I joined the organization's secretariat, I had never had the opportunity to study Communist political warfare at the cellular level (in both the Party and the biological senses of the word). I had lived abroad all throughout the Red Decade, and though the

Popular Front had enlisted my sympathies for a while, like most newspapermen I have never been an ardent joiner of anything institutional. Consequently I lacked the firsthand experience of Communist subversion acquired during the period by members of the labor movement in the United States, and by the more sophisticated American liberals, from struggling with the Communists inside labor unions or public committees.

The Soviet Union was not a member of UNESCO during my term of service, and the organization's three Communist member states—Poland, Hungary, and Czechoslovakia—were at the time only semi-active ones. The few avowed Communists in the secretariat were mostly nationals of Western countries. Some of my new colleagues, I suspected, might be secret or at least unadvertised members of the Party—not necessarily for any very sinister reason—but even these, it seemed clear, were a small minority.

Despite their numerical inferiority and the absence of moral backing from any major power represented in the organization, the Communists in the secretariat had unmistakably succeeded in getting effective control of the UNESCO Staff Association, a nominally apolitical body representing the interests of the personnel, and were manipulating it at every opportunity for flagrantly political, if not always very consequential, ends.

The covert Communist attempts to influence UNESCO's official program were more subtle, and rarely very successful, but they could sometimes be detected in the vigor with which certain projects might be pushed in this or that staff section, or in the bureaucratic delays that seemed to accumulate in the path of others. Some outside experts were more sought after as consultants—by certain divisions —than others; some writers were more often solicited to contribute brochures or articles on subjects related to UNESCO's goals than others. Somehow, prominent anti-Communist intellectuals such as Ignazio Silone, Arthur Koestler, Manès Sperber, Malraux, Camus, Raymond Aron, and David Rousset rarely were called upon. I saw a chance to make up for such omissions when, after the dissolution of the Ideas Bureau, I was put in charge of a new staff section that functioned as a kind of international literary agency. The objections —sometimes from quite unexpected quarters—that had to be overcome whenever I proposed seeking a contribution from one of these literary untouchables—most of them former Communists and therefore doubly anathema to Moscow—proved to my satisfaction that I had correctly diagnosed the reason why their names had not previously appeared, or appeared more often, on the UNESCO rosters. As a former practitioner of underground political warfare myself, I felt sure that the blacklisting of anti-Communist intellectuals the Stalinists were trying to impose on UNESCO was not the manifestation of a spontaneous ideological reflex, but the implementation of a political directive, doubtless originating in Moscow.

The para-bureaucratic skirmishing with my Stalinist colleagues in which I engaged made me realize more keenly than ever before the need for matching Communist activism, wherever it manifested itself, with a democratic or liberal activism that was no less militant and no less adroit. The menace of communism in the West, as I was beginning to understand it, was sometimes subversive in the strict sense of the word, sometimes military or para-military, but it was always and everywhere political as well, and had to be opposed by political means, in addition to any others. It could no more be suppressed by police measures alone—or contained solely by military defenses—than it could be neutralized merely by social and economic reforms aimed at eliminating the hardships or injustices that undoubtedly favored its development. The importance of political counteraction in meeting the Communist threat was impressed all the more deeply upon me while I worked at UNESCO because the UNESCO milieu was in principle an apolitical one, meaning in practice that nobody in it thought much about politics, except the Communists, who thought of little else, day or night. The leading member governments, starting with that of the United States, were largely to blame for this state of affairs. Their foreign policy experts were too engrossed in power problems to bother with such unworldly matters as education, science, and culture, and too tradition-bound to take seriously the war in and for the minds of men. The more or less official intellectual mandarins who made up the bulk of the several UNESCO national commissions—inevitably including a number of politically uneducated educators, socially irresponsible social scientists, and historically illiterate men of letters—were thus left to their own, sometimes underdeveloped, policy devices.

I am afraid that my attempts to function as a spare-time democratic activist in UNESCO were not brilliantly successful, but perhaps they were all the more instructive for that. I recall in particular one of my brushes with the Staff Association leadership which, though trivial in itself, had some far-reaching implications. The Stalinist clique in the body had organized a series of after-hours educational lectures for the improvement of its members and had invited the late Professor Frédéric Joliot-Curie, a world-famous nuclear physicist, to deliver one of them. I had raised some objections when the project was first discussed, but had not pressed them very strongly. Joliot-Curie, it was true, was a prominent member of the French Communist Party and a leading figure in the Communist-sponsored Peace Partisans movement, but he was also a distinguished international scientist. To blackball him in this context would have seemed too much like the Communist attitude toward such writers as Camus and Silone; after all, I believed in the Darwinism of ideas, or thought I did. Besides I had been assured that the talk would be noncontroversial.

The assurances, as I should have expected, turned out to be misleading—or to put it more objectively, there was some subsequent controversy over the definition of "noncontroversial"—and I wrote an indignant letter of protest for publication in the Staff Association bulletin. One of the Association's officers, a young French Communist with whom I had amicable personal relations, tried to persuade me to withdraw it. "Don't you see what an unfortunate impression your letter would make?" he said. "Do you really want to introduce a cold war atmosphere into our association?"

I was first enraged, then fascinated. It would have been hard to find a better, more Orwellian example of Stalinist doublethink. To arrange for a notorious Communist cold-warrior to harangue an audience of UNESCO employees on the evils of United States nuclear policy, in line with Moscow's most recent directives on the subject, had nothing to do with the cold war; that was purely educational. To protest against such a misuse of the staff association of an international civil service was to introduce a cold war atmosphere into it.

What had enraged me the most, I realized as soon as I cooled off, was the fact that in one corner of my mind I agreed with my interlocutor. I had long come to feel that since the cold war was a fact of international life it was better to win it than to lose it by default, but in my heart I did not really approve of introducting its atmosphere anywhere, least of all into UNESCO, which I had once thought of as a haven from its tensions and stridencies. Hence, the reproof, however disingenuous, touched a spot in my conscience that had never ceased to be a little sore. Finding and hitting such sore spots was, I already knew, a basic element of Stalinist psychological strategy, and one that rarely failed to achieve some results, given the almost universal guilt complex that was one of the striking psychological phenomena of the period. The Lord knows, my generation had enough rational grounds for guilt; in one way or another, at one time or another, we had all been accomplices of Auschwitz and Belsen, of Hiroshima and Dresden, of Guernica and Vorkuta, of every horror and every betrayal. Survival itself sometimes seemed a kind of betrayal. An American conscience had to bear the specially heavy burden of American society's monumental, still largely unrectified injustice to its Negro members, as the European conscience still had in many cases to bear that of colonial oppression.

The Great Guilt of the postwar era, however, was too diffuse, too incompletely conscious, to be wholly rational; like the Great Fear of the year 1000 it was a kind of collective possession. In the Soviet Union, Stalin seemed to be trying to exorcize the guilt demons—on his usual Pharaonic scale—by the primitive method of transferring them to sacrificial scapegoats, but abroad, Communist propaganda was exploiting the irrational elements underlying the guilt theme in somewhat the same way that Hitler had formerly exploited those underlying his racist doctrine. The psychological havoc was fearful, particularly in Europe. During the forties and much of the fifties the intellectual beachheads of the Old World were littered with the decaying remnants of once sturdy minds and sensitive hearts that had succumbed to the guilt fog blowing in from the east.

While I sometimes wondered whether it might not be a deliberate Kremlin policy to promote a sense of guilt in the West regardless of its object or pretext, free-floating guilt as the psychiatrists say, the specific Communist aim in most cases was naturally to make non-Communists feel guilty about criticizing Soviet policies or resisting Soviet (or Communist) encroachments. At the founding of the Kominform in October 1948—an act which, as one, by no means systematically anti-Communist French historian remarks, "seemed like a declaration of war against Western civilization"*—Andrei Zhdanov, Stalin's grand inquisitor, had imposed as the ideological basis of the alliance his concept of a world irrevocably divided into only two groups: the "Imperialist and Anti-Democratic camp," whose aim was the establishment of a worldwide American hegemony, and the "Anti-Imperialist and Democratic camp." Whoever was not firmly aligned with the latter was necessarily a lackey or accomplice of the former, which meant being guilty of encouraging not only imperialism and American domination but "brigandage," "aggression," "preparation for aggressive war," etc. Any action, however violent or brutal, taken against the "imperialists" was justified because it ultimately served the cause of peace, not to mention democracy. "The Soviet Union," as the French Communist leader Maurice Thorez blandly explained a few months later, "has never been and never can be in the position of an aggressor toward any country whatsoever."

Zhdanov's extreme political Manichaeanism was not wholly acceptable to the type of European intellectual I usually encountered in UNESCO, or elsewhere in Paris ("Manichaeanism" did not acquire its present perjorative sense in Europe until some years later,

---

* *Histoire de la Guerre Froide*, by André Fontaine, Paris 1966.

when it was most commonly applied to American political attitudes), but the feeling that hampering the forces of "anti-imperialism" in the accomplishment of their self-appointed mission was almost a transgression of natural law, like incest, struck deep root. Some high-minded European non-Communists—intellectual opium-eaters chronically drugged, as Raymond Aron has remarked, by the myth of revolution—could not bring themselves, at least in public, to speak against the ruthless witch-hunt that Stalin after 1948 launched against suspected Titoists in the vassal states of Eastern Europe, nor against the horrors of the Soviet slave labor camps—then at their most monstrous phase of development—because, as one of the characters in Simone de Beauvoir's *The Mandarins* put it, "if one campaigns against them, the *bourgeois* will be too happy."

I was immune from such typically European conflicts of conscience, not only because I was at heart pretty much of a bourgeois myself, and therefore no revolution addict, but because Gandhi's teaching had if nothing else sensitized me to the kind of double-standard moralizing that underlay them. The same influence, however, made me peculiarly vulnerable to another guilt theme in the Communist psychological arsenal. I had never ceased to look back on the destruction of Hiroshima and Nagasaki as crimes against humanity; I had never stopped regretting that the United States government, in offering to surrender its temporary monopoly of the absolute weapon to international control—the Baruch plan of 1946 —had hedged an unprecedented act of national self-abnegation with legalistic qualifications that largely dimmed its exemplary virtue; above all, I had felt from the first, and continued to feel, that the very development of the nuclear arm renewed in each of its stages a monstrous ecological impiety. Like a number of my UNESCO colleagues, along with a great many intellectuals—especially scientists—in the United States, I had been vividly impressed by the threat to the biological heritage of the whole planet arising from the repeated U.S. nuclear test explosions, each one bringing the level of atmospheric pollution by radioactive fallout a little closer to the threshold of doom.

For a long time any more or less plausibly documented attack on United States nuclear policy that I read or listened to was assured some degree of acceptance in my mind, even if I suspected that it was ultimately inspired by Soviet propaganda. Though I regarded the leadership of the so-called Peace Partisans movement—one of the most notorious Communist international "front" organizations—with considerably more than mere suspicion, I recall that I was nonetheless troubled by some of the arguments in favor of an immediate, unqualified, international ban on atomic weapons expounded at its world congress in Paris in April 1949. Logically, I realized that the Peace Partisans' formula—which was of course the Kremlin's—would paralyze the application of the recently signed Atlantic Pact and leave Western Europe at the mercy of the Red Army, while offering no safeguards that the Soviets themselves would respect the prohibition. Logic, however, was hard put to resist the emotional pull of the Partisans' demand to outlaw the symbol of planetary suicide.

Unquestionably, the congress, in which artists and intellectuals from fifty nations participated—one of them was Picasso, who painted his famous dove of peace for the occasion—was a great tactical success from the Communist viewpoint. Some 14,000,000 people in France alone eventually signed the so-called Stockholm Appeal for a nuclear ban, for which the Paris congress was intended to set the stage.

As far as I was concerned, though, any mental imprint left on my thoughts and feelings by the Communist-sponsored campaigns to abolish the atomic weapon was virtually wiped out within a few weeks after the close of the Paris congress when I learned from the newspapers that the ration of radioactive iodine available to the infants of the world in their milk had just been augmented by the first Soviet atomic test explosion in Central Asia. (The test occurred in July 1949 and was officially confirmed by President Truman, from American expert observations, on September 23.) Of course, the exposure of Soviet hypocrisy did not necessarily invalidate the Peace Partisans' criticisms of United States nuclear policy, but for me, at least, it largely neutralized what had been most effective in these criticisms: their purely emotional impact on the inflamed guilt nerve of my American conscience. I had finally discovered, from personal experience, how easily conscience, which is the prerequisite of all moral growth—or simply survival—can also become the greatest temptation to self-betrayal.

I fear that the evolution—when it was evolution—of my political outlook during the years I have been writing about represents at best a limited and uneven progress. I learned to look at the world of man's strife and competition with a sharper eye than before (though the effort no doubt provoked some new distortions), and despite the more tragic image of the human condition that was thereby printed on my mind, recovered some of the belief in humanity's future that I had lost in the immediate postwar letdown. That was all, but it was something.

"Contemporary pessimists like Aldous Huxley and Orwell," I wrote toward the end of 1949, "are quite right in seeing that a bushman is at the controls of our plane . . . but they forgot that the mind which is capable of inventing an airplane is capable of teaching a bushman to fly . . . Civilization does not exist, but it can be invented . . . We are quite likely to blow ourselves to bits . . . [first] . . . but that is an inevitable evolutionary risk. Living in the twentieth century is a hazardous and even tragic experience, but it should not be a nightmare to us."

The quotation is from a letter about the new book I had been working on for some months. "UNESCO," I reported, "has re-animated an earlier attachment—the project for a book to be called *Awakening from History* . . . Now in the queer mixture of intellectual ferment and plain mold that is so characteristic of UNESCO it seems quite relevant, both to my own need and to the general state of the world . . ."

I had already made up my mind to leave UNESCO, regardless of which molds finally got the upper hand, but was not yet sure what I wanted to do. I had not even decided whether to remain in Paris or return to the United States. I was beginning to feel tempted again by journalism, but still dreaded returning to the remembered servitudes of daily radio or newspaper reporting. Though my financial situation had improved through the steady rise of real estate values in the United States—I still owned my farm in Maryland—and through several small inheritances, I needed a job of some kind. I thought I had had enough of the bureaucratic life to last me for all my days. Whether as a polemical journalist or in some other way, I felt I ought to take a more active part—more active than was possible while serving in an international organization—in the new great quarrel of the century—the constantly developing struggle between the Communist world system and our own. It was my fight, too, I now recognized, and not such a degrading one as I had once thought.

Though the Soviet nuclear breakthrough of the previous summer —along with total Communist victory in China—had dramatically increased the hazards of the conflict, as well as strengthened the overall Communist position, I no longer viewed the cold war as the ineluctable prelude to planetary suicide. The traditional dichotomies of war or peace, victory or surrender, rivalry or cooperation, that for long had imprisoned my thoughts—and those of my contemporaries—seemed to be melting, or at least softening, in the strange, rising sun of the nuclear age.

I was still debating with myself what practical conclusion to draw from all these considerations when, in the early summer of 1950, some friends of mine at the Council on Foreign Relations in New York unexpectedly offered me a job as the research director of a new study group that was to be set up there the following autumn. The salary was not substantially more attractive than my tax-free pay as an international civil servant, and the assignment was on the face of it a temporary one, good for a year or two at most, but I was not seeking either riches or security. Its chief appeal was that it promised to harness my politically activist instincts to a task that both served the cold war interests of my country and the broader ends of world development that had captured my interest at UNESCO; its aim was to discover how the United States through educational exchange programs, technical assistance, and other similar means might best strengthen or promote the emergence of what the project's sponsors termed "democratic leadership" throughout the world. The basic concept of the enterprise was a little hazy, I thought, but that was a condition to which my career at UNESCO had fairly well inured me, and in this case I could even see some advantage in it: Guiding the proposed inquiry out of the haze would offer a stimulating intellectual challenge.

I asked the Council's emissary for a few days to think over my answer, and on one of them, a Sunday, went for a long walk in the country with my wife to talk over such homely but relevant implications of an acceptance as moving our belongings across the Atlantic, finding a place to live in or near New York, and putting our children in school. We had not yet come to a formal decision— though our minds were virtually made up—when we got back to town to keep a dinner engagement with a French friend. He was sitting alone on the *terrasse* of the Deux Magots when we arrived, a little late, and his face looked so much like the French faces I remembered from August and September 1939 that instead of going straight to his table I stopped at the newspaper kiosk on the corner and bought the evening paper. A glance at the headlines explained my friend's dejection. The war that had just broken out this time was on the other side of the world, in Korea, but it was unmistakably a war, and one that directly challenged the interests, the prestige, and it seemed the honor of the United States. The case for going home was now complete.

22

Return to the Comanche

The three years, more or less, that I spent in the United States from September 1950 to August 1953 were outwardly uneventful ones for me, but they were full of occupation and learnings. It was not quite, perhaps, a happy time, but from the subjective viewpoint it was a relatively untroubled one. The day and more particularly the night of my arrival in New York, together with my wife and our children, stand out among my clearest memories of the period. I celebrated our homecoming by renting a far too costly suite, as high up as we could get in our hotel, and viewed from it the blazing, nocturnal skyline of Manhattan, like a crumpled or thrust-up firmament, was an unforgettable spectacle. I had never before seen the great city's lights look so beckoning and diamond-bright, and paraphrasing Rastignac's challenge in my mind, I felt like shouting *"A nous deux, New York,"* in the teeth of the interstellar gale that whistled past our tower window, above the remote dragon roar of the traffic. It was a queer feeling to have, perhaps, and a queerer one to remember so long, for in the end I conquered nothing, of course, and in my conscious thoughts I had not returned to America to conquer, but to share quite prosaically, unheroically, in what I felt must be an important American experience. Since my remembrance of the occasion still remains clear and good, like that of some youthful enthusiasm untarnished by any later bitterness, it is possible that my imagined hunger for sharing was not completely a romantic delusion, and that I managed to satisfy it in a measure.

All in all, my re-Americanization proved less painful than I had feared. Never a believer in half measures, I rented an old Colonial house under the elms in the distant Connecticut countryside and rode a commuters' train to my office in Manhattan for nearly three hours, back and forth, every day; I found it an excellent way to catch up on my reading. Later, when I worked in Washington, I led a similar exurban life in Maryland. I had always liked such activities as burning, or even raking, leaves and following a power mower over the lawn, and I have never had any objection to drinking with hospitable neighbors, though preferably not at a country club. Vreni found it harder to be a den mother, but learned in time to discharge her duties to the full satisfaction of her pack, if not that of their parents, who tended to deplore her Swiss nonchalance about poison ivy, thunderstorms, tree climbing, and similar hazards.

I continued to feel that the trivia of life in Europe were more agreeable—and, mainly, that there were more of them—but the rediscovered American ones were not without their charm. (I did not put such experiences as catching the dogwood in the ecstasy of bloom, or seeing the Blue Ridge Mountains spread out in their gaudiest plummage on a smoky October day, or strolling around Georgetown before anyone was up on a rainy morning in early spring in the category of trivia, but there were beauties in Europe, too, man-made or natural, that were not exactly trivial.) Whenever nostalgia for one or the other of my earlier lives—European, Asian, journalistic, or paleo-international—came over me I could find friends living in New York or Washington who had participated in them to help me slake it.

Winding up my affairs at UNESCO and getting ready for the move had taken the better part of three months. It was the reaction of Americans to the war in Korea that I had mainly worried about during that time, and for a short while afterward. My own feelings about it were complex enough. From one viewpoint it was a distant, dreary, semi-colonial expedition, clearly undertaken on behalf of an imperial interest, as well as for a moral principle. Our intervention served, moreover, to maintain in power a notoriously corrupt, at best dubiously democratic institution, the Republic of Korea, established after the war with Japan in South Korea when it was our zone of military occupation. There was a strong feeling, among both European and American liberals, that Washington had blundered into the present conflict through an accumulation of diplomatic and military imprudences.

Whatever follies on our part, however, or whatever provocations on that of our Korean protégés had led up to the conflict, it had actually started with a clear-cut, premeditated act of aggression committed by the Soviet-sponsored People's Republic of North Korea against the U.S.-supported southern state, a member of the United Nations. Without warning, the North Korean armed forces, trained and equipped by the Red Army and patently operating under the Kremlin's strategic direction, had launched a large-scale offensive, spearheaded by massed armor, across the 38th Parallel, the frontier between the two Korean states, on June 25. It was the news of this attack that had shattered my Sunday evening peace in Paris a little earlier and irreversibly tilted the scales of decision in favor of my return to the United States.

The Northerners' aim—and the Kremlin's—was to splinter the United States-trained Southern army, drive the Syngman Rhee government recognized by the United States out of the Southern capital, Seoul, and proclaim the unification of the two Koreas under Communist rule before the United Nations could adopt a firm position or Washington make up its mind to intervene effectively. It was a bold Soviet gamble and probably would have succeeded if President Truman had been the man that Stalin must have assumed him to be.

Mr. Truman, however, had reacted to the challenge in his usual uncomplicated, Missouri way. Some forty-eight hours after the Communist invasion of South Korea began, without waiting for Congressional approval or formal authorization from the UN, Truman announced that he had ordered U.S. naval and air forces in the area to support the troops of the Republic of Korea. Another two days later, after the UN Security Council—under American prodding and in the fateful absence of the Soviet representative—had recommended all necessary assistance to South Korea as the victim of an unprovoked aggression, the President ordered American ground units into action; he also authorized air attacks on selected targets in North Korea and proclaimed a naval blockade of the whole coast. Early in July he appointed Gen. Douglas MacArthur, the fiery, imperious proconsul of our East Asian sphere of influence, to head the United Nations Command in Korea just voted by the Security Council.

Though I had not been one of Truman's unqualified admirers I had gratefully applauded his courage in the June crisis. I still shared some of the European disquiet about the future trend of American policy in regard to the war, but I thought he had taken the right course. I was by no means prepared to endorse in advance every reckless act of violence to which we might be tempted in the course of the struggle.

I was not so sure about the attitudes of my fellow countrymen. War—any war—could hardly fail to accentuate the Comanche traits in the American personality, I reasoned, and a war against naked aggression, fought under the banners of the United Nations in defense of its charter, was psychologically the most dangerous kind. No delusion, I had learned during my own war, was so sinister as the delusion of absolute righteousness. Consequently, before my departure from France I had looked forward with some dread to the kind of talk I would have to listen to at home from friends, neighbors, taxi drivers, and radio commentators.

My apprehensions did not, of course, prove wholly groundless, but after my first few weeks in the United States I realized that they had been excessive. Lunatics and demagogues were ranting, as I had expected, but as yet fewer Americans than I had feared were taking them seriously. Occasionally, after the fourth martini in front of the fieldstone fireplace with its blazing logs, one caught a momentary glimpse of the homicidal primate under the sleek, suburban stockbroker's mask and detected an atavistic growl slurring the Ivy League inflections ("Maybe I'm too simpleminded, but I say, let's drop the bomb on them and get it over"), but at least as often one recognized a different kind of look, a different tone of voice, remembered from another war: a certain smug, almost arrogant acceptance of defeat, a strange, self-righteous embracement of dishonor ("Maybe we had better just pull out and wash our hands of the whole business").

A clear-cut and definitive victory in Korea, either for the United States or for our real adversaries, the Soviets, could prove as decisive as any of the great battles of the past; whoever lost might well be finished as a great power. I had witnessed the midsummer panic in Europe, reminiscent of August 1939, when the United States and Allied forces had been pushed back to the Pusan bridgehead; after the massive intervention of Chinese Communist troops officially termed "volunteers," and the debacle of MacArthur's march to the Yalu in November, one of my friends in Paris had written me asking for help in evacuating his family from France—he himself had decided as an honorable form of suicide to join a resistance network being set up by the writer Camus in advance of the expected occupation by the Red Army. In the face of such European reactions I failed to see how anyone could doubt that Europe's freedom was part of the stake in Korea; the fact that a number of Europeans apparently had no wish to preserve their freedom if it risked involving them in a war with the Soviet Union merely drove home my point. The Syngman Rhee regime might be as corrupt and repressive as American liberals believed, but in trying to shield it from overthrow by military invasion, the United States was thus once again trying to make the world safe for democracy, or at least a shade less dangerous.

Unfortunately, it was not always easy to reconcile such thoughts about the Korean War with the liberal ideology that shaped my outlook on most other contemporary political or social issues. It was if anything even harder to reconcile them with the sane, civilized, relatively open-minded American conservatism that most of my colleagues on the Study Group appeared to profess.

By the prudent standards of the Council on Foreign Relations, the very concept underlying the formation of our group was a bit heretical, but a fair sprinkling of our members were nonetheless representative of what it subsequently became fashionable to term the American establishment. They were in many respects—and on balance—an admirable type or class of Americans: un-self-conscious patriots of the old-fashioned sort who yet believed in international cooperation and sincerely wished to promote the welfare of the whole human race—men of goodwill if I ever met any. (Several of them—the outstanding example was probably John W. Gardner, who later became U.S. Secretary of Health, Education and Welfare —were likewise men of unusually broad, clear, and generous vision.)

I was unable to share the conviction many of them had that electing Gen. Eisenhower to the Presidency in 1952 was the best hope of the republic. I shared only within limits and up to a point their faith in both the practical and the moral virtues of the self-reforming, post-New Deal, free enterprise capitalism of America. I realized that I belonged to a different ideological family. The differences between us in political outlook were hardly great enough, however, to generate any emotional tension. Their position in the middle of the road was a little nearer to one side, mine to the other. The real gap between us—to the degree there was one—was more psychological: They were moderates because they instinctively recoiled from all extremes; I was one—most of the time—in the measure that I achieved a precarious balance of outlook between certain attitudes commonly associated with the revolutionary left and others identified with the radical right.

In the controversy over MacArthur's dismissal, for example, I felt that Truman had been right, not only on constitutional grounds, but because the United Nations commander through ideological fanaticism had become a threat and a discredit to the cause he was supposed to uphold. The proposal attributed to MacArthur of attacking a number of targets in Manchuria with atomic bombs seemed to me indefensible from the moral point of view, and I could place no further confidence in such a defender of world law. I could not help agreeing, however, with the old warrior's contention that in war—I would say in any basic power struggle—there is no substitute for victory.

I recognized that my intellectual funambulism was hazardous to perform and sometimes unnerving to witness, but I considered that the very effort to resolve contradiction favored growth. What sometimes depressed me in even the best American minds was a chronic underlying complacency or lethargy of the imagination which seemed to assume that history, too, invariably took the middle of the road. The need to meet its occasional and deplorable lapses into excess with equally extreme deployments of force or generosity —or of both together—was scarcely admitted by many civilized and educated Americans.

Fossils From a Private Collection

Have the rulers of the Kremlin passed into the shadowland of the mind that separates political paranoia from the clinical variety? Have subtle sociological and political changes caused the USSR to cross the thin line that divides a police state from a gangster state on the Hitlerian model?

. . . It may be that some invisible brake in Soviet society will halt the Communist revolution before its slide into total war and destruction gains irresistible momentum. There are no signs of any such mechanism, however, and many signs of an accelerating revolutionary spiral.

Perhaps our policy of containment will supply the saving brake from outside, as the originators of the policy appear to have hoped . . . Consequently there is a chance that the tornado which we see approaching will lose its rotary velocity and begin to dissipate itself before it is upon us, but it is certainly headed our way once more, and behind it, if we take the trouble to look, others are forming as far as the eye can see.

However close may be the ties between Moscow and Peking, it seems clear that the Chinese Communist revolution is not merely an extension eastward of the Russian one, but a distinct storm pattern of its own. In some ways it seems more menacing—though less immediately menacing—than the Soviet disturbance . . . Instead of one day seeing a Chinese Tito arise—as many people hope in the West—we may rather see a Chinese Tojo. The more immediate danger is that despite Stalin's seniority in the Communist world and his infinitely greater military strength, he may be forced psychologically into the position of Mussolini to Mao Tse-tung's Hitler— that is, pushed ahead against his better judgment on the road to world conquest by the ambivalent promise-threat of the new revolutionary dynamism unleashed in China.

It would be a fatal error, however, to think that communism, whether of the Russian or the Chinese variety, is our only enemy. The enemy is barbarism, which has many faces . . .

Even at home in America we have our barbarian problem. We have our lunatic fringe and our gangsters, and judging from the recurrent waves of popular hysteria and the systematic use of slander and defamation . . . we also have our homegrown apprentice-sorcerers.

Surely this is enough evidence at last to convince us that we are not near the end of our trials, that we are not living in a "normal" world, that we have not been living in one for many years, that neither our children nor our grandchildren are likely to live in one, that, in short, we are facing not a temporary emergency provoked by Stalin, but a deep, desperate, prolonged crisis of civilization, a tumultuous "time of troubles," a hundred years' war between the forces of human enlightenment and the forces of primeval night.

(UNPUBLISHED MSS. 1951)

History has so far neither wholly confirmed nor flatly belied the thesis of a permanent crisis in our civilization, linked with the menace of neo-barbarian inruptions, or eruptions, that captivated my imagination in 1951. One threat to our civilization, as I conceived it, lay in the regions where primitive, archaic, or semi-archaic civilizations were breaking down—sometimes because they were being culturally undermined by our own—releasing the pent-up barbarisms that they, like every other, had always contained. Demographic pressures, soil erosion, the menace of famine, the spoilage of natural resources, increasing illiteracy, and similar evils to which my stay at UNESCO had sensitized my mind were hastening the breakdown. The rapidly expanding city slums of the Far and Near East, of Africa and of Latin America—today, perhaps, one should include those of North America—were thus accumulating critical masses of newly or partly barbarized proletarians mixed with more primitive elements freshly uprooted from the tribal cultures of their backward hinterlands.

Barbarism is not a phenomenon peculiar to peoples of black, brown, or yellow skin, nor one confined to slum dwellers anywhere. The rot, I knew from my prewar contact with German and other European totalitarianisms, could start close to what was generally considered the top of society, and in the most advanced nations. Few men were civilized all the way through. Under disturbed conditions, individual or group lapses from civilization were ineluctable from time to time.

I was thinking of something graver and more chronic, however, than such lapses as mob outbreaks that turn reasonably civilized men into temporary savages. I suspected that the chief factor of crisis was simply what we called progress, in all its forms. Progress inevitably begot cultural lag, which left men trying to solve the problems of today with the understandings of yesterday, or futurism, which led them to neglect present reality for reckless surmise, or probably more often paralyzed response by the sheer volume, velocity, and complexity of challenge. It was the interaction of all the different causes that rendered crisis endemic in our age. On the other hand, because no single factor was wholly determinant, our doom was not irrevocably determined. Statistically the odds against our survival as a civilization—viewed in the perspective of the early 1950's—looked alarming, but nobody was entitled to say that our downfall was inevitable.

On the whole, I am glad that the paper in which I elaborated my analysis of the Western predicament as I saw it in 1951 had only a handful of readers. It was a personal project, on the margin of my work for the Study Group, but treated some of the more theoretical implications of the immediate problem that interested us: how the United States might effectively help other nations develop at all levels of society future leaders imbued with the ideals of democracy and trained in the skills necessary to uphold it. My colleagues, to whom I submitted the text for informal comment, had numerous criticisms, and merely to dispose of my own growing doubts or reservations would have called for more drastic rewriting than there seemed to be time for.

Looking back, however, I have no regrets for my lost labor, if it can be called lost. It is often enriching to the mind—if not to the pocketbook—to let one's thoughts grow almost to ripeness, then plow them back to compost for a season. The most useful by-product of this particular enterprise—and of my work for the Study Group generally—was the sharpened awareness they gave me of certain basic contradictions in contemporary American political attitudes, including my own.

The contradictions emerged at every level of the study. Perhaps the most fundamental one was between what might loosely be termed the Dewey and the Darwinian concepts (Darwinism in the popular sense) of social existence, between leadership in the endeavor of internal growth and leadership for survival in the never-ending competition with rival groups. My readings in history, and above all my personal exposure to the history of my own century, had reluctantly brought me to accept fitness for combat—whether physical or ideological—as an essential condition, though of course not the only one, of group survival. Hence, in one area of my mind I could not help feeling myself a disciple of those modern thinkers, from Pareto to Lenin and Trotsky, who tended to look upon elites of any kind primarily as the cadres of political warfare and to assess their social worth in terms of their effectiveness as political warriors.

Applied to the recruitment and training of democratic elites, however, this viewpoint, I recognized, could prove as dangerous to democracy as any external threat. In the nuclear age, indeed, it could easily become a recipe for group suicide rather than survival.

Some of the more immediate or practical dilemmas that confronted us seemed no easier to resolve. What position, for instance, should an American who was also a revolutionary democrat adopt in the face of such impediments to the development of grass-roots democratic leadership in the emerging nations as caste in India or peonage in Latin America? I thought that the best propaganda both for America and for the American interpretation of the democratic ideal would be, in the words of the unfinished paper, "the imprecations of feudal landlords or village usurers ringing round the world," but it was not always easy to reconcile the national policies—or even the acts of private American citizens—calculated to provoke these imprecations with our need for stable overseas bases and strong allies on every continent to contain the thrust of totalitarian expansionism.

The conflict between ideological and strategic imperatives was not a new one in American history, I realized, nor was it peculiar to the United States: The Communist world was no less bedeviled by it than ours, and Stalin's cynicism had not always proved more effective in dealing with it than had the mushy platitudes or symbolic gestures of American diplomacy.

The conclusion that I eventually drew from my unsuccessful wrestlings with the leadership problem was almost directly contrary to the premise on which I had originally based my paper. I believe as firmly today as I did in 1951 that neither democracy nor any civilized form of government can survive for long in a given society unless its leaders and elite groups of all kinds do in fact function effectively as combat cadres for the masses when the society meets a threat from without—including the threat of internal subversion instigated or supported from without. If, however, the leadership institutions of the society fail to produce the courageous and energetic leaders that the situation calls for, or to motivate and train them adequately to face it, I now question whether there is much that the United States can do by unilateral intervention, welcome or not, to remedy such basic defects. To pour American economic aid into a country where conditions of this sort prevail is to pour it down a rat hole; to commit American military forces to its defense is to deploy them on quicksand. Whatever the reach and mass of American power, it cannot hope to fill all the power vacuums of our planet.

Already, however, both the learnings and the intellectual frustrations stemming from my work with the Study Group were starting to provoke a conscious reaction from the Messianic Americanism that had inspired me. Though the evangelical urge was so deeply rooted in the American psyche that it could never be totally repressed without damage to the national morale, preaching the true gospel of democracy to the heathen and the heretic—or simply practicing it at home as an example to the universe—could no longer be considered the essential American mission. History had charged us with a new and more urgent one, less glorious, perhaps, and morally more hazardous, but also more responsible.

The duty of defending the citadels and policing the *limes* not merely of democracy but of civilization itself—Western civilization at least—had fallen on us because at this moment in history, and no doubt for a long time to come, no other Western nation, or possible coalition of nations, had the power to hold the new barbarians at bay. And however complex or subtle the factors of power might have become in our age, power remained what it had been in all the ages: the ultimate key to the rise and fall or survival of civilizations.

23

The Toils of Bureaucracy

The rather neo-classical trend of my historical outlook that developed while I was working at the Council on Foreign Relations or in Washington also owes something to the experience of several months I spent back in Europe during the summer lull of my Study Group in 1951. It involved both conformity to the almost hyper-American living patterns of a self-imposed bureaucratic ghetto in Germany—I could not help at moments thinking of the labored insularity of the British cantonments I had known in India—and the kind of total identification with an American group effort that I had not been called upon to practice since the war.

I had not revisited Germany since 1938, so when the State Department offered me a three months' job as a consultant in the Public Affairs division of the United States High Commission in Frankfurt I gladly accepted. Since my early assignments reporting for Col. McCormick on the doomed Weimer Republic and the nascent Third Reich, twentieth-century Germany history has always fascinated me as a particular and appalling illustration of the general crisis in contemporary civilization. The background reading I had recently been doing on the origins and fulfillment of the Nazi revolution had naturally whetted my curiosity to see what, besides wreckage, the twelve-year *Walpurgisnacht* had left behind it.

By the summer of 1951 the debris of war had been largely cleared away in West Germany, but to a newcomer who up to then had

416

seen nothing worse than the ravaged waterfront of Naples or the shattered towns of Normandy, the scale of the devastation that remained visible came as a shock. In Frankfurt, where the High Commission had its headquarters, whole neighborhoods, including most of the winding medieval streets and cobbled squares of the old city that had once charmed me by their unique blend of quaintness and grace, were buried beyond recognition under weedy moraines of rubble: mass graves that six years after the end of the war still gave off a charnel reek.

Yet Frankfurt had been less severely bombed than Dresden, Hamburg, Cologne, and several other large German centers. As for Berlin, its ruins—if the lunar noncity in the city's prewar heart could be called ruins—were so immense that they stultified any human feeling, except possibly a diffuse sense of ennui, the inevitably barbarian reaction to a barbarian masterwork of futile havoc.

Already, however, bulldozers and pile drivers were everywhere at work; a Gothic forest of cranes and scaffoldings laced the skyline in every West German community from the village level upward. Shiny, functional, somewhat trite structures of glass or metal or concrete—expressive of a resurrected, if perhaps lobotomized, German civilization—were rising from the cinder heaps of destroyed splendors and vulgarities. The newly reopened arteries of urban life pulsed with heavy traffic. What a little later was to achieve headlines as the "German miracle" was beginning to take form.

The daily, omnipresent contrast of ruin and renewal supplied both a philosophical context and a dramatic backdrop to my work at the High Commission. Its emotional implications were accentuated in my mind by another contrast which, directly or indirectly, was constantly being called to my attention: that between the two Germanies, the Western and the Eastern.

The glimpses of East Berlin I was able to get during my trips to the former capital were enough to supply me with valid human referents for the necessarily abstract intelligence reports or studies on economic, social, and political conditions that made up much of my official reading. The wall by which the Communist authorities later sealed off East Berlin from the Western sectors of the city had not yet been erected, and under the various wartime or postwar agreements between the Soviets and the Western Allies, some movement between the Communist and Allied sectors was still allowed, in theory, for Germans as well as for Allied or Soviet personnel. Relations between the Communist and the Western-controlled halves of the city were thus in a sense more "normal"—despite the current intensity of the cold war—than they subsequently became, but the differences in living standards and in the moral climate on the two sides of the boundary that separated them were far more striking.

Rubble clearance had hardly begun in large areas of East Berlin and reconstruction lagged badly, in comparison with the building surge in West Berlin. What had been built by the Communist regime looked drab and shoddy, except for the pretentious, heavy, tasteless facades, in the style of Socialist Realism—often with nothing but raw brick behind them—that lined the Stalinallee. The clothes that people wore were shabby and outmoded, their faces were lined and pale from overwork and undernourishment; the men almost without exception had ragged, uncut hair. The most expressive—and depressing—shibboleth of the East Berliner, however, was his characteristic gait, a kind of prison-yard shuffle, and the dejected sag of his shoulders; with a little practice one could pick out an East Berlin visitor or recent refugee in a West Berlin crowd from these signs alone.

I had been an active anti-Communist for more than two years, but in an abstract, intellectual way. Now, for the first time, I could see the enemy before my eyes, almost feel his presence in my own muscles: not the well-fed, usually good-natured Red Army soldier that one saw taking snapshots around the Hitler Bunker, nor even the equally well-fed if slightly too reminiscent East German militiaman in his jackboots; no human form, in fact, but an attitude imposed on human forms, the slouch of separate surrender.

The inhabitants of West Berlin, on the other hand, walked with a certain ideological swagger, considering themselves freemen living stoutly in a beleaguered outpost of freedom. Their talk and their minds were undoubtedly filled with the clichés of Western propaganda, but these clichés had been so recently hewn out of bed-reality that they still sounded fresh and convincing, even to a slightly skeptical newcomer who had not known the heroic period of the blockade. It was hard to spend as much as a week in the city without succumbing to its heady atmosphere and unconsciously adopting the somewhat romantic Berlin approach to the problems of cold war strategy. If the weight of the 175 Soviet divisions (probably an exaggerated estimate) which, according to Western intelligence officers, faced the fourteen NATO divisions in Europe seemed more palpable in Berlin than elsewhere, the political and psychological vulnerabilities in the Communist position likewise appeared more evident.

From my personal viewpoint the climactic event of the summer was the extraordinary debacle of the so-called World Youth Festival that the Kremlin's political warfare specialists had organized in East Berlin as part of the global propaganda campaign against United States intervention in Korea and West German rearmament. While there were to be delegations from many countries on both sides of the Iron Curtain, the chief mass of participants was to be drawn from East Germany, and HICOG's intelligence experts predicted that a number of them would take advantage of the occasion to visit West Berlin. The Communist authorities would naturally try to discourage such excursions, but with the eyes of the world upon them would probably avoid any measures drastic enough to be completely effective. There thus appeared to be an opening for some effective Western counter-political warfare, and I was ordered to Berlin to work with the *ad hoc* committee set up there to devise ways of exploiting the situation.

Our deliberations were laborious and at moments heated. One earnest young woman representing the powerful branch of HICOG concerned with "democratizing" the German educational system insisted that our expected visitors should be offered—by way of contrast—a total holiday from propaganda. Nothing more manipulative than the free distribution of bananas near the principal crossing points from the Eastern sector would be compatible with democratic ideals of encouraging youthful self-development and self-expression, she argued. While less concerned with self-development —or more sensitive to the logistic implications of the banana approach—the spokesman for the U.S. military commander in Berlin was almost equally opposed to any vigorous propaganda effort that might provoke the Communists into organizing retaliatory disorders. His British and French colleagues were even more reluctant to give the political warriors a free hand. Eventually agreement was reached on a fairly intensive program of radio and other propaganda that encouraged participants in the Youth Festival to visit West Berlin without explicitly urging them to do so, and also on arrangements assuring that they would be exposed to a certain number of discreetly anti-Communist themes during the visit.

Except as an educational experience, our planning proved magnificently futile. The appeals we had so cunningly drafted turned out to be unneeded, and the precautions with which we had so laboriously surrounded them almost alarmingly ineffectual. Intelligence had predicted that as many as 10,000 East German youths might find their way to West Berlin during the festival; the actual number was nearer to 100,000. While the lavishly stocked West Berlin shopwindows and the movies were probably the greatest attractions, the permanent or *ad hoc* propaganda displays of various kinds throughout the city elicited an interest—and often an enthusiastic response—far beyond our expectations. The politically conscious elements among the young visitors from the East found their way to the studios of RIAS—the American-sponsored but German-operated radio station which in those days waged unrelenting psychological warfare against the East German puppet regime— where they fearlessly took part in group interviews or forums on the air that they knew would be broadcast back to their home communities. (They were, of course, warned by the RIAS staff not to give their names or other identifying details.) To sit in on these sessions, as I did several times, was a deeply moving experience that strengthened or revived one's confidence in the ability of the human mind to resist both the tyranny of indoctrination and the invasion of nihilism.

Germany was a good antidote to the excessive pessimism with regard to the future of Western civilization that had occasionally tinged my thoughts in New York. Among other things, it converted me into a reasonably firm believer in the cause of European unity, which I had previously looked upon with some slight skepticism. The emotional dynamism that the United Europe ideal was unmistakably beginning to generate among young Europeans—including many on the other side of the Iron Curtain—convinced me that it was a force potentially capable of reinvigorating—perhaps even regenerating—European civilization, hence that of the West as a whole. Moreover, as several of the most thoughtful Eastern experts in HICOG pointed out, a developing federation or confederation of Western Europe would operate as an almost irresistible magnet to the oppressed peoples of Eastern Europe; sooner or later the Kremlin would be forced to relax its grip upon them.

My chief assignment at HICOG was to draft a master plan for the hitherto somewhat scattered U.S. information activities in Germany, and I soon came to the conclusion that the political unity of Europe should be its master theme. The promotion of democracy in the Federal Republic, the denunciation of communism, support for NATO and for United States policy, even our obsessive concern with the American "image" abroad, should all be subordinated to the task of strengthening the drive toward European political unity that had already started in Germany. The fact that the European movement—at least in the Federal Republic—had some traits of a political mystique should not worry us; that was precisely the most hopeful thing about it. If an undercurrent of rivalry with the United States, or a prickly concern for European independence, sometimes manifested themselves we should be tolerant—and take care to display our tolerance—of such inevitable, essentially healthy symptoms of a nascent European nationalism. The one qualification to our support of the movement was that it must continue to develop—as Secretary of State Dean Acheson had just put it—within the framework of a developing Atlantic Community.

The idea that instead of trying to "sell" America or Americanism to Europe we should use the considerable information and propaganda apparatus we then possessed in Germany primarily to help the Germans become more European—and therefore less dependent on the United States—scandalized certain of my HICOG colleagues. Some considered the proposal a betrayal of democracy, others a willful neglect of the national interest. (One middle-level member of the HICOG staff offered a counter-proposal—apparently in dead earnest—based on the assumption that if we simply promoted the sale of chewing gum in Europe, Europeans, by working their jaws like Americans, would come in time to think like them, and therefore support American policies.) A more serious objection was raised by a veteran Foreign Service officer who, rather to my amazement, informed me that I was proposing a radical innovation in United States foreign policy: We officially encouraged European economic integration, but fostering the political unity of Europe, or any part of it, was not as yet one of our national objectives. I retorted that it ought to be, and was upheld by the highest echelons of HICOG, then headed by John J. McCloy, where Europeanist sentiment was strong. The State Department itself eventually ratified my draft plan, with no more than the usual qualifications. Succumbing to *hubris,* I considered it a victory of reason over bureaucratic inertia and timidity.

For the first time since the closing phase of my OSS career in Southeast Asia, I enjoyed the heady feeling, always somewhat illusory, of being involved in history. It was also the first time since 1945 that I had felt wholly committed to an American national purpose I wholly approved of, one that in serving America served an even greater interest.

What I had just seen in Germany, after what I had earlier learned in France—and what I remembered from Asia—made the world role of the United States since the end of the war look not only more defensible but generally more rational and more constructive than I had yet realized. In the face of a spreading breakdown of civilization, East and West, with the barbarian or half-barbarian tyranny of the Kremlin seeming the only alternative to chaos, we had assumed the traditional responsibilities of an imperial power—on the world scale —without claiming the traditional privileges of empire. Our motives, of course, had never been wholly pure, nor our means wholly moral, nor even our policies wholly enlightened. We had made mistakes, and sometimes committed crimes, as all men do. The relationship between an imperial power and the civilization it has charged itself to uphold is inevitably worldly; it can never be innocent. What mattered in the light of history was whether the relationship was fruitful, and not degrading to either party.

From the subjective American viewpoint, it seemed to me there could be no serious doubt on that score. The enlargement of the American consciousness to a world horizon, the acceptance of a global responsibility, were developing a new, more complex, perhaps more tormented but unquestionably more mature American personality than we had ever before achieved. Its existence was what had made my return to America seem a repatriation rather than an interior exile.

In Asia, the benefits of our power presence—most evident in Japan—had to be weighed against the ruins of a new, though limited, war, brought on to some extent by the failures or errors of American policy. The balance, as far as I could judge, was positive.

The salvaging of Western Europe, and therefore of the core of Western civilization, had, however, been our masterwork, the necessary and sufficient justification of our self-appointed world mission. Without food relief in the immediate postwar era, without the Marshall Plan, without the Berlin airlift, without our political support of the German Federal Republic at its inception, without NATO, and without the United States nuclear umbrella over the skies of Western Europe, both the essential infra-structures of European civilization that had survived the war and its last, minimal shreds of self-confidence might well have collapsed, perhaps irreparably. Not only had we preserved and helped restore them, but in doing so we had made a civilized, sober, generally exemplary use of American power. We had managed, on the whole, to accomplish a morally valid end with means that had seldom been more than mildly blamable at worst (some probably unavoidable violence in Greece, some possibly unnecessary but relatively minor secret service skulduggery in Germany).

Three years earlier, I recalled, in one of my abortive book projects I had attempted to reconcile the laws of strategy and those of Gandhian morality as they applied to the cold war. I had eventually abandoned the undertaking because as the conflict became more bitter I ceased to believe that the reconciliation was possible.

Now, it seemed to me that the United States was successfully applying in Europe much the same strategy I had envisaged in 1948 —it is true that my own standards of cold war morality had become somewhat more flexible in the meantime—and that on this continent, at least, the victory without ruins—in other words without physical destruction of the adversary— that I had set as my aim was in sight, if still a long way off.

The new goals of American foreign policy that were beginning to crystallize out of the rosy vapors of official or semi-official eloquence—the politico-economic unification of Western Europe and the ultimate creation of a broader Atlantic commonwealth into which a united Europe would be integrated—seemed to me even more admirable than the results already achieved. Such a doubly articulated Eur-Atlantic community, if it was to be effective and durable, implied a sharing of America's leadership prerogatives to which we were not yet accustomed, and no doubt in some cases a subordination of purely national interest to that of the common cause. These sacrifices—if indeed they were sacrifices—were trivial compared with the benefits the American people, like all the other Western peoples, would derive from their participation in the grandiose undertaking. The mass of coordinated power that would be released would make the West invincible. It was a dream calculated to fire the American imagination; above all it was one whose realization promised to resolve some of the most basic conflicts of the contemporary American personality. As far as I was concerned, the only problem seemed how best to serve it.

A short time before I was due to leave Germany and return to my Study Group I happened to be in Bonn on some ritual HICOG consultation, and I decided to take the afternoon off. It was a raw, blowy day, edged with the steely gray of impending autumn: the kind of weather that airs one's soul. I walked for hours along the Rhine embankment, thinking about a decision I had to make, though I knew that in reality I had already made it. I had recently received a letter from Washington offering me what sounded like an interesting position heading the small plans unit in the servicing staff of a newly created organism for the coordination of all United States information and political warfare activities abroad: the Psychological Strategy Board, a somewhat oblique offshoot of the National Security Council. This was higher than I had ever thought of flying in the American bureaucracy—when I had thought about flying there at all—and my last 1947 qualms about political warfare as a weapon of defense and retaliation in the cold war had vanished during my summer at HICOG. Still, I felt I ought to give any voices of inner dissent a chance to make themselves heard. At moments during my walk I thought I detected a faint one asking about the book I had promised myself to write—the one I had started working on an UNESCO—but the wind was blustering too loudly and the river waves were slapping against the embankment, so I could not be sure.

There was another distraction, too: the almost unbroken procession of barges, flying the colors of every nation in the embryonic community of Europe, that kept passing in both directions before my eyes. The plumes of spray rising from their prows, the oily smoke streaks flattened by the wind, and the leaden color of the water gave the scene a certain dramatic intensity. One could scarcely imagine a more vivid visual metonymy of Europe's knitting.

The image produced a peculiar kind of inner glow, recalling the illogical exaltation of my first night in New York the year before. It would be absurd and vainglorious, I knew, to imagine that my summer's work at HICOG had contributed, however minutely, to strengthen or accelerate the trend toward European unity. A plan to coordinate American information programs in Germany did not mean necessarily that they would be coordinated, and even if they were, their impact on German thoughts and feelings could never be decisive. Yet I had accomplished something, perhaps something useful: I had succeeded in dramatizing the issue of European unity in the minds of a few American political or information officers, thereby making them a little more sensitive than they had been before to its promise and implications. That, if one wanted to feel boastful, was at least a small individual contribution to America's relationship with Europe. Modest as my role had been, I concluded that from my subjective viewpoint, if no other, it represented about as satisfying an expenditure of my thought and energy as any I might have achieved in a comparable lapse of time.

The job that was now offered me in Washington might or might not provide similar opportunities for underscoring the wider promise and implications of the Atlantic dream; if there was the slightest hope that it did, that was enough for me.

Viewed in the perspective of the present, the Eur-Atlantic mystique and the correlative dream of a bloodless crusade to liberate the captive peoples of Eastern Europe that took hold of my mind during my summer at HICOG seem wildly romantic. In reality, they were merely a little naïve. They took some account of both the law of struggle and the law of cooperation. What they underestimated was the force of social—and particularly institutional—inertia, whether in blocking endogenous reform or in resisting exogenous pressures. Working in Washington—I stayed there eighteen months—helped to make me more conscious of its formidable power.

If my aim had been consciously self-educational, I could not have picked a better observation post for studying the role of inertia in history, or at least in the development of American strategy and foreign policy, than the Psychological Strategy Board. Though a coordinating rather than an operating agency, and not primarily concerned with covert or para-military activities, PSB reminded me in some ways of OSS as I had known it in 1941. In administrative terms it was a bold experiment, whose success would have endangered entrenched and more traditional bureaucratic interests. (Consequently it was foredoomed to a brief and troubled existence.) The personnel, while professionally more qualified than Gen. Donovan's picturesque cohorts in the early days of OSS, were amateur by the standards of the permanent Washington bureaucracy. Their outlook was basically unbureaucratic; like the temporary officers or civil servants of the war period, they believed in the civilian virtues of enterprise and imagination. They were likewise apt to be casual about respecting jurisdictional frontiers.

Even the premises were vaguely reminiscent of OSS, though somewhat more chic in appearance, and geographically at least, much closer to the seat of authority. The Psychological Strategy Board was housed in a comfortably ramshackle brick dwelling of the Federal period overlooking Lafayette Square; it looked a little mysterious but not sordidly clandestine. During the long Washington summer I used to enjoy the torrid afternoons sitting shirt-sleeved in my old-fashioned, high-ceilinged office, with an electric fan blowing on me—I had stoically refused an air-conditioner—gazing out through the open French windows on the leafiness below; somehow I felt more intimately a part of the great machine of power and service than at other times. The faintly romantic tinge of this memory vignette may reflect some forgotten impression of my St. Louis childhood; perhaps the dedicated but easeful worker at his desk was not my actual self but a nameless figure symbolizing the privileged servitudes of the adult world, as seen through childish eyes. Possibly too, the image had its emotional roots in a slightly later stratum of remembrance: those scorched summer evenings in downtown St. Louis that seemed romantic to me when I was a cub reporter because they lay like a fever plague upon the city and I was one of the disaster elite entitled to slip through the quarantine lines.

A similar web of associations may account for the mild and mildly paradoxical pleasure with which I recall a chronic Washington affliction: the frenzied, crash planning sessions, usually after the event—who could have imagined that Stalin was mortal?—which periodically ravaged one's weekend or evening repose. Their rewards, insofar as they brought any, were a sense of initiation into the algebra of crisis and alarum akin to that which I had experienced in my City Hospital days, and the casual camaraderies of fellow Sabbathbreakers and night owls with whom I shared a lonely watchfulness in the sleeping or emptied capital.

Such satisfactions, I gradually came to realize, were puerile in more ways than one. Even the feeling that one had at last got behind the scenes of history was to a large extent illusory. The staff of PSB ranked fairly high in the Washington hierarchy of documentary security clearance, but, I soon discovered, above the nominal aristocracy of Top Secret, "Cosmic," or "Q-Clearance" holders there was an inner super-elite, contemptuous of all classificatory ritualism, whose thoughts were so arcane that they were seldom committed to paper at all, at least not in any official form. As one of these Great Initiates revealed to me in a rare moment of confidence —appropriately in front of the cold cuts table at the Metropolitan Club—the U.S., like many other nations, had two levels of national policy, the exoteric and the esoteric. The former found its typical expression in the papers of the National Security Council, available to the governmental plebe—PSB for example—to certain Washington columnists (usually in truncated or slightly garbled form), and to Soviet intelligence (it was hoped with a few weeks' delay). As to the esoteric policy, my informant's lips were naturally sealed. He could only imply that actions were louder than words, and silence or studied inaction often more significant than either. This revelation, of course, was made with ironic intent, but judging from my own experience and observations, it contained at least as much truth as irony.

If the subjective realities of national policy were thus concealed by veils of priestly secrecy, the objective realities on which policy decisions had to be based were often no less obscured or distorted by a special form of bureaucratic alienation that seemed inherent in the reporting and processing of data at every level of the governmental machine. Political and psychological intangibles naturally suffered the most from the dehumanization which, as Max Weber has pointed out, is a necessary feature—indeed one of the aims—of bureaucratic routine. The language of bureaucracy, for example, seemed to have no adequate means for indicating varying degrees of intensity in human reactions to United States policy; it was chronically unable to distinguish between fundamental changes in the climate of opinion in a given area or group and superficial squalls or clear spells.

An even more dangerous vice of our bureaucratic system, I thought, mirrored what is probably the worst failing of American journalism: its tendency to secrete unmanageable quantities of "facts"—which in reality are too often mere arbitrary generalizations—isolated from their contexts, or from any other pertinent information. The essential fact of structuralization almost never seemed to be included in the data available; either it could not be fitted into the approved form for reporting raw information, or it got lost in the overspecialized and compartmentalized organs that were supposed to digest it for the nourishment of the policy-making cells. Attempts to restore the missing holistic principle by specialist consensus at the level of the National Intelligence Estimates rarely produced anything better than a dubious *ersatz*.

The end product, that is, the image of strategic reality offered to policy-makers for their decisions, was excessively abstract at best, one that took little account of the human factor. Not infrequently it likewise embodied almost pathological errors of logic—or at least of mind process. The bureaucratic rationalism that Weber so admired seemed capable, at least in Washington, of annulling self-evident contradictions, of attributing magic virtues to ritual formulas, and of elaborating masterpieces of paranoid delusion from a mere scrap of verifiable fact. (The hysterical Washington witch-hunts of the McCarthy era were at least in part a bureaucratic phenomenon illustrating one form of institutional alienation; the self-deceptions of our war in Vietnam, which I later had occasion to study, illustrate others.)

No doubt, a certain degree of bureaucratic alienation had existed since bureaucracy first came into being; it was one of the factors that explained why the state had already become in Nietzsche's time the coldest of cold monsters, as he put it. In our age, owing to the parallel proliferation of bureaucracy and of information, the state, more and more closely identified with its bureaucracy, likewise behaved on many occasions like the blindest of blind monsters, the most deluded of self-deluded ones, the creature least capable of adaptation to environmental change.

From time to time, it was true, the coincidence of a great crisis and a great crisis leader—who in an increasingly bureaucratized civilization had 'to be, almost by definition, that supreme paradox, a charismatic bureaucrat—might temporarily infuse the state with the human qualities of energy, imagination, and generosity, along with the determination to overcome and the foresight to anticipate obstacles ahead. Roosevelt had achieved that in the United States—as Churchill had in Britain—and the administrative *élan* generated by him had lasted, with intermittent flagging, throughout the early postwar epoch; NATO and the Marshall Plan were among its fruits.

Now, in the last, tired year of the Truman Administration, Washington's reserves of virtue were running out, and the monster state was lapsing into its normal saurian lethargy of mind and soul. For a short while I hoped that the 1952 presidential elections—particularly if Adlai Stevenson should win—would bring about a resurgence of enthusiasm and idealism, but even before the campaign was over I realized that my hopes were vain.

Despite their real qualities, neither candidate, I reluctantly concluded, had the temper or stature of a great renovator. Moreover, the American people itself seemed emotionally exhausted after the tremendous struggles and accomplishments of the last decade, and the interminable sordid routine of war in Korea was helping to dull the national spirit. A return to the old-fashioned kind of isolationism appeared to be out of the question, but I was afraid we might be slowly retreating into a kind of moral isolationism that subtly estranged us from our partners in the Atlantic Community we were trying to found.

In my eyes, the most flagrant symptom of the trend was the insensitivity of the incoming Republican administration to the moral and psychological implications of an awkward problem that confronted President Eisenhower shortly after his inauguration: the fate of the two Communist spies, Ethel and Julius Rosenberg, who had been condemned to death two years earlier for betraying United States nuclear secrets to the USSR. An application for executive clemency on behalf of the condemned couple put the issue on the President's desk and after due consideration he publicly announced that he had decided not to commute the death sentences.

Communist propaganda had succeeded in creating doubt as to the couple's guilt in the minds of many Europeans, especially among liberal intellectuals, and even in circles where the fairness of the trial itself, or of the subsequent judicial reviews, was not disputed, people were shocked by the severity of the sentences. (The Rosenbergs were the first Americans to be condemned to death in peacetime for espionage.)

Appeals for reconsideration began pouring into Washington from responsible political, religious, and intellectual leaders throughout the free world. The bipartisan consensus among working-level government experts concerned in any way with foreign psychological reactions to United States policy or acts was that the political and propagandistic gains from commuting the sentences to life imprisonment would far outweigh any that might accrue from letting the two spies die in the electric chair. Though I usually took the militantly anti-Communist or "hawkish" side in the inter-office policy controversies of the day, I was wholeheartedly in the camp of those who argued for clemency. I had no doubts myself about the Rosenbergs' guilt, and therefore did not feel their execution would be a judicial crime, but in addition to all considerations of sheer expediency I thought it would signify a deplorable lapse of moral taste or style. Once the President had ruled, there was no possibility of PSB to intervene officially in the Rosenberg case, but I had a pleasant personal relationship with the newly installed presidential adviser on psychological matters, C. D. Jackson, and discreetly encouraged by colleagues and superiors, took it upon myself to approach him informally with a documented plea for last-minute reconsideration, based on the unexpected intensity of public reactions in the chief NATO countries.

Jackson was both a sophisticated and a humane man, and he appeared to welcome the arguments or factual evidence with which I supplied him. I believe that he made a courageous effort to put the case for clemency before the President, but it was foredoomed. I was present in his office during certain of his telephone conversations about the Rosenberg issue with other members of the White House staff, and it was evident that they shared little if any of our concern with what an earlier American conscience had termed the decent opinion of mankind. What seemingly mattered to them—when it was anything beyond the crudest political expediency—was exorcising the hobgoblins that McCarthy's demagogy had planted in the American public mind by the timely blood sacrifice of two ritual scapegoats.

I had already submitted my resignation from PSB several weeks earlier, having come to the conclusion that working inside the Washington bureaucracy at such a slack-water moment in history was probably the least fruitful and most frustrating way a political activist could contribute to the realization of his hopes. On the other hand, I had long since outgrown both the unworldly One-Worldism and the kind of personal isolationism that had tempted me earlier. The neurotic dread of power and its corruptions that had accompanied them had completely vanished from my thoughts, and I felt no private misgivings about the official aims of national policy. My present dissent, to the degree it could be called that, was not from any avowed American purpose or ideal but from a current American mood.

At first I had not altogether clearly understood the distinction, and had therefore been somewhat hazy about the exact social role I hoped to play once I was freed from bureaucratic trammels. My last few weeks in Washington, and particularly the upsurge of irrational and atavistic mental processes that I witnessed in connection with the Rosenberg case, helped to clarify the problem for me. The most dangerously subversive influences at work in America, it seemed plain, were precisely such unavowed or unconscious mechanisms of self-sabotage, whether in the public or the official mind, that contradicted and thus betrayed the conscious goals of the American people. To unmask these mental saboteurs seemed, therefore, one of the most useful ways that a loyally contrary Comanche might serve his tribe.

In practical terms that implied, for me, returning to journalism—some form of journalism—and most likely to Europe as well. Previously, whenever I had thought of going back to my old calling, I had been put off by the remembrance of either its trivialities or its servitudes. Now, whether because I felt stronger or because I had seen worse, I dreaded them less. Europe, of course, I dreaded not at all, though I had learned in the last three years to live in America with only a little of my former sense of exile—no more, I knew, than I would feel anywhere else on a planet that man had not yet learned to think of as his tribal home.

Book Seven

A
Late
Gathering

24

Paris Indian Summer

A Banquet of Ghosts (3)

An old Greek friend from my Paris years has been standing behind my chair as I write, for some time now, standing as
shades stand, dimly glimpsed in the corner of the mind's eye.
Was his profile as classically Athenian as I remember it, the bald skull
as elegantly modeled? What I recall most clearly was the implicit
paradox of childlike blue eyes and finely drawn lips, framed for irony.
There was something birdlike, too, it comes back to me, in the way
he held his head, but not a general bird: one small and particular
kind, quick, sharp-eyed and clear-voiced, whose name I forget, if I
ever knew it.

His own name was Apostoli, and he played a significant if indefinable role in my life—I am not sure whether as influence or as a
catalyst of influences—during part of the time that I have been writing about, and afterward, almost up to his death in 1967. In my
UNESCO days, for example, he was one of the left-wing European
friends who helped awaken me to the real nature of the new totalitarianism that menaced Europe; later, after my return to Paris in 1953,
the curves of our political evolution alternately converged and di-
verged throughout the French or international crises of the 1950's
and the early 1960's. Whether or not we thought alike at a particular moment, we always felt alike. Ours was the kind of friendship,

at once nourished by history and internally sheltered from it, that grows more easily in Paris than elsewhere.

Apostoli was already past seventy at the period I am chiefly thinking of, but still active and alert, practicing our common journalistic craft with a falsely cynical, slightly shamefaced zest. His shoptalk implied that he regarded journalism as a kind of banausic avocation, but I am not sure what his true profession was supposed to be, unless it was friendship. He was a poet, too, of course, though for the last half century or so, it appeared, a nonoperational one. In politics he professed a somewhat disembodied libertarian socialism, tinged with Gandhian pacifism.

I had only a limited respect for Apostoli's worldly intelligence—he was too much the poet to be a clinical observer of the world's disorder—but our talks together, usually at some long-frequented, Left Bank *bistro*, had enormous charm for me. His naïve political Platonism, all the more innocent for having the subtle grain of Mediterranean sophistication, was a good whetstone for my sense of irony.

Among the things I enjoyed in our conversations was Apostoli's innate talent for mythologizing event. Somehow he contrived to shed a kind of Homeric radiance—though it was usually in the name of a later bard- -upon the daily squalors of our epoch and calling, transmuting the synthetic tantrums of cold war diplomacy into the outbursts of wrathful Titans, the sordid machinations of French politicians into the wily strategems of Olympian rivalry. *"C'était du Shakespeare,"* he would exclaim of some tragic buffoonery witnessed from the press gallery of the National Assembly, and then proceed to recite a long, reasonably apt citation from the English poet's works, in French, of course, enriched by his Greek accent. Greek politics, in Apostoli's view, were too base to be fit table talk between friends, and he pretended to consider even the French or planetary varieties that furnished the most frequent themes of our intellectual communion as not quite worthy of such lofty employment.

There were occasions when my friend surprised me with flashes of something shrewder and deeper than mere good sense—he was normally just a little above, below, or simply beyond that—and made me wonder whether for all the value that I put upon his friendship I had ever valued him quite at his full worth. Once, for example, after my return from Washington to Paris, when I was going through a hyperideological phase that made me tiresome to everyone, including myself, he interrupted one of my salvationist harangues to remark, very gently, that after coffee he wanted to show me something.

We were dining at a small Italian restaurant near the Place St. Sulpice—Huysmans country—and Apostoli had only to lead me a few steps to an old house standing in the Rue des Cannettes, one of the narrow, winding streets that lead out of the square. In the dim lamplight he helped me decipher the marble tablet on its facade honoring the memory of a rather obscure but apparently estimable French poet, the friend of one of his dear friends:

The Poet Gabriel-Tristan Franconi
"Private Anonymous" of the French Army
Born in This House
May 17, 1887
Killed at the Wood of Sauvillers-sur-Somme
July 23, 1918
While Defending Against the Invader
His House, His Street, and the Place St. Sulpice.

Nonsense, I said, the poet had undoubtedly died for *liberté, égalité et fraternité*, like every other Frenchman, especially poets—for those abstractions and for getting in the way of a shell or bullet. But I never forgot the little incident.

Another time I had been expounding my theory about the permanent crisis of civilization and the new barbarians. We were lunching at Apostoli's apartment in Montparnasse on this occasion, and by way of comment he had only to take down a book from one of his shelves: the verse of Constantine Cavafy, whom he had known himself, and I gathered idolized, as a young exile journalist in Alexan-

dria, before the First World War. He soon found what he was looking for and while I continued to stuff myself with the orange tarts
for which his wife, Madeleine, was famous in a limited circle of
cognoscenti, he read aloud to me in his liquid Greek, then translated
the entire poem, "Expecting the Barbarians," into rhythmic French
prose that was all the more effective for being a little rough and
halting.

Just before the end, Apostoli paused and gave me a sly look.
Then, with deliberately exaggerated pathos, he recited the famous
last lines.

> *Because night is here but the barbarians have not come.*
> *And some people arrived from the frontiers*
> *and they said there are no longer any barbarians.*
> *And now what shall become of us without barbarians?*
> *Those people were some kind of solution.*

My old friend had no need to explain his point, though I am not
sure it was quite the same as his illustrious countryman's.

I have left Paris so many times in my life, and so many times come
back to her—in this context one naturally tends more than ever to
think of the city as a woman—have possessed her and been dispos-
sessed of her in so many ways, with such a wide gamut of emotions
and such a vast palette of sensory impressions, that all these ar-
rivals and farewells, all these ruptures or escapes and all these
melancholy or festival homecomings have become woven in memory into one seamless fabric, scarcely distinguishable from the
tapestry of life itself. As in a tapestry, however, there are back-
grounds no less than anecdotes that to the inward-looking eye stand
out more clearly than others. The wintry mood and vernal color of
my return in 1948 have always remained fresh in my mind but so
has the memory of a different and rather complementary visit which

took place in 1953. Except for a glimpse on the trip from Germany to the United States in 1951, I had not seen Paris in more than three years.

It was again a kind of parenthesis in my usual existence (if I had one), a moment of suspension and introspection, of accepted loneliness, but this time it was autumn, the season of hope, when the final evidence of summer's long decay brings with it the assurance of ultimate renewal. The leaves of the chestnut trees had turned brown but not yet fallen; the grass in the parks was still a hardy green. The crisp mornings were golden, the noon hours faintly blued around the edges. The Luxembourg Gardens had turned sumptuous and legendary like a canvas by Gustave Moreau; one kept expecting to come upon unicorns grazing at the feet of queens in stone.

Political and meteorological history appeared to be in tune for once, that year, along with my own life rhythms. Simply being back in Paris seemed in itself a kind of Indian summer. (I stayed there between trips to Germany or Switzerland from early November until the end of January, and no doubt the weather must have been rainy or cold part of the time, but memory has preserved only the impression of the first few days.) The city, of course, was no longer the movable feast of Hemingway's youth, but then, I had never truly known that feast myself; merely enjoyed its last scraps as it was breaking up. There was the brief, springtime moment of the Popular Front in 1936, but the dragon weeds of hate had soon choked out the buds of hope all over Europe. My personal memories of the last years before the war were relatively happy ones, but it was Vreni rather than Paris who had made them so. The Paris I rediscovered in 1948 was a ghost city welcoming a ghost.

Now, it seemed to me, Paris, from the viewpoint of an American of my generation, was almost its old self again, its old self a little older, warmed by the golden noon of St. Martin's summer. The invisible film of despair that had covered it earlier had nearly disappeared. The moral wounds of occupation and liberation were largely healed—those that were healable—and the hardly less cruel one that the Algerian war was soon to cause had not yet been inflicted. The

441

war in Indo-China was still going on, and going badly for France—
Dien Bien Phu lay only little more than half a year ahead—but it
was far away. The one in Korea was finished. Stalin was dead. The
French economy—and for that matter the European economy—
were on the upswing. Hope and confidence were reviving. The
crisis of the West that had opened with the Berlin blockade five
years before was unmistakably over at last.

The cold war continued, of course, but less obsessively than before. And increasingly, it appeared, to the West's advantage. (The
East Berlin riots of the previous summer had been the first unequivocal sign that the Soviet empire was entering its own crisis of de-
colonization.) In the relatively relaxed and mellow autumn air of the
French capital it seemed possible once more to turn one's thoughts
to things that had no connection with the struggle, to things of one's
own.

As on the former occasion I spent most of my days—one I had
carried out the professional errands that brought me to the city—
walking around its streets or sitting by myself in the sun. I stayed
at a small Left Bank hotel as before, but found myself often ranging
beyond my usual habitat, as if drawn by some newly awakened
migratory instinct, to quarters that as far as I remembered had no
emotional associations with any of my earlier Paris lives. (My mild
but enduring affection for the Jardin des Plantes with its staid
academies of chrysanthemums and its shade-haunting lovers, the
shyest in Paris, dates, for example, from this period, and so, I believe, does my appreciation of the faded, elegant Place des Vosges
across the river.) I shared some of my evening meals with Apostoli
and other old friends, and I read a little, but once again was more
frequently content to let my mind drift freely with its own invisible
currents.

Now and then they flowed back toward the past, but less compulsively than they once had, though there was more of it to draw
them. Even without conscious purpose they seemed to veer toward
a kind of purposeful though unconstrained reflection, rather than
toward simple reverie. I had had the same impression more than once

during the last few months but there had been numerous duties as well as pleasures to distract me, whereas now, for the few days I thought I could afford to give myself, I was deliberately avoiding both kinds of distraction, and Paris itself was a kind of focusing lens for the mind. There were no formal or urgent decisions that I had to make—some had already been made and the others could wait a little longer—but it was a good occasion for putting decisions out in the sun to ripen, and even better for becoming aware of one's own new awarenesses. Above all, I recall it as a time of gathering when old doubts were at last resolved, when recent choices, made half consciously, were consciously affirmed, when long unrelated strands of being were finally knitted into a coherent pattern.

Letter to V

. . . Went for a long walk around the Quarter this morning, the kind you would have loved: across Luxembourg Gardens, down Boul' Mich, to the Cité and the Île-St. Louis (I rounded the tip of the island just at the right instant to see Notre Dame cast loose and head downriver under full canvas) along quais to Jardin des Plantes, back along outer slopes of Montagne St. Geneviève, and finally lunch at a completely unknown little Moroccan restaurant behind the Pantheon (succulent couscous).

Along the way a memorable thought struck me: Here I am approaching my forty-sixth birthday and since 1940, for all practical purposes, crisis has been my only career. I have drifted from one world crisis—and crisis idealism—to another, the way the old-fashioned kind of itinerant copyreader or reporter in America used to drift across the continent from one newspaper to the next. I've had an interesting time on the whole and usually managed to keep us from starving, and occasionally perhaps accomplished something useful—or at least destructive in a high-minded way—but I don't really seem to have got anywhere, except back to Paris. Now that we've saved the world once more, for the moment at any rate, it does seem time to settle down, doesn't it?

In a narrow and practical sense, my self-critique was well founded. When I had decided to leave government service, nearly a year before, I had been sure that I wanted to return for good to my prewar profession—that of a foreign correspondent—and at the same time do a certain amount of less topical and perhaps more philosophical writing. My aim had been sensible enough as far as it went, but I had understimated the difficulties of such an enterprise for one of my age. The line between professional planning and mere hoping had been indistinct in essential areas. As a result, there had remained something a little amateurish in my whole attitude. Now, as the letter to my wife suggests, I was coming to grips with professional reality at last.

In the circumstances, things were going better for me than I had a right to expect. Instead of making the rounds of American editorial offices trying to line up an improbable job or long-term assignment abroad, I had decided to gamble my modest cash reserves on a return to Europe and on my ability to build up on a free-lance basis a dependable editorial market for my writings. As a starter I had an assignment for an article from *Harper's*, another from the liberal New York fortnightly *The Reporter*, and a conditional, but potentially more lucrative and important one for a series of newspaper pieces to be syndicated by the Washington *Post* and *Times-Herald*. The *Post* assignment, on which I was pinning my immediate hopes for a bravura relaunching of my journalistic career, stemmed from a slightly roundabout one-man crusade to make America safe from McCarthyism that seems a bit quixotic in retrospect.

The most effective way to destroy the Wisconsin demagogue as a political force, I had reasoned, was to discredit him in the eyes of his own followers, those who believed honestly and hysterically that the republic was threatened at home by a vast Communist conspiracy. And he would be discredited if he could be shown to be himself the unscrupulous accomplice, or simply dupe, of Communist *agents provocateurs*. Certain intelligence reports that had passed over my desk at PSB had made me suspect that McCarthy might, in fact, be getting some of the information on which he based his reckless pogroms of character assassination from highly suspect sources. The most interesting of these sources appeared to be in Germany—my summer at HICOG two years earlier had already given me an inkling of the extraordinary interpenetration of the reviving Nazi movement in Germany and of the clandestine Soviet or East German subversive networks operating in the Federal Republic—and it was in this ambiguous political demimonde that I hoped to find the evidence I was looking for. Naturally, the editors of the Washington *Post* had been interested, if not wholly convinced, when I outlined my plans to them. (I likewise mentioned them to one or two personal friends in the Eisenhower administration, who wished me luck, though not for attribution.)

Before coming to Paris, where there were some minor leads to run down, I had spent several fascinating weeks of search and research in Germany. They had proved neither completely successful nor wholly fruitless. My private conviction was stronger than ever that the Communist political warfare services in Europe, operating through neo-Nazi or other ultra-right-wing splinter groups, had from time to time deliberately furnished certain of Senator McCarthy's European informants with false information casting doubt on the integrity of loyal American government employees or public servants. (Their objective, of course, was to supply McCarthy with new, more incendiary ammunition for destroying America's national unity, and at the same time to further discredit the United States in the eyes of its European allies.) Unfortunately, while I was able to draw up a vast verbal spider web of interlocking conspiratorial contacts that by McCarthy's own standards more than sufficed to catalog him as the nation's No. 1 security risk, my case in final analysis had to rely too much on the dubious principle of guilt by association which was the very essence of McCarthyism.

"To achieve proper balance," I explained in an informal, revised outline for the articles I drew up in Paris, "I think [they] should also include a warning against the danger of encouraging Nazi-Communist conspirators by imitating their methods . . . It is important to note that the witches are tending more and more to disguise themselves as witch-hunters, but that is no justification for counter-witch-hunting. The fact that the Communists and Nazis are conspiring against democracy is dangerous, but the habit of conspiracy is still more so, and conspiracy can hardly become an obsession without also becoming a habit . . ."

By the time I wrote that (early January 1954) I had reluctantly come to the conclusion that the subject was too complex for satisfactory treatment in a daily newspaper series, and in agreement with the Washington *Post* had offered the article to *The Reporter*. The magazine had matched the *Post*'s original offer and promised me ample space to develop the material. The article—it finally appeared as a single long piece—by no means neglected McCarthy himself but substantially broadened my original focus. "Because the Communists' overall strategy now puts primary emphasis on splitting up the free world system of alliances," I concluded, "they concentrate their subversive propaganda and political warfare operations upon those groups in every country, whether left-wing intellectuals or right-wing terrorists, that are most strongly opposed to the theory and practice of democratic internationalism . . . the Kremlin is successfully developing in Europe, the United States, and elsewhere an 'internationale of haters' whose members foster treason in the name of super-patriotism and often conceal their own Communist connections by posing as the most extreme apostles of anti-communism." The same "internationale of haters," as I knew from friends in France, was at the time also campaigning—and all too effectively—against the project for a European army upon which many sincere internationalists on both sides of the Atlantic had pinned their hopes. A few months later I was to see the saboteurs achieve their aim.

I had learned a good deal from working on the assignment; and with some minor shifts of emphasis I believe that what I learned about the real threat of Communist subversion remains largely valid today.

What I discovered, or rediscovered, about the rewards and limitations of journalism, and about the unobserved contradictions in my own attitude toward them, was even more valuable. It was comforting to find that despite my long professional hibernation I had not lost all the tradecraft that as a foreign correspondent I had laboriously acquired during the 1930's. Nor, thank heaven, had I outgrown my old delight in the chase, the fox hunt after elusive truth which, along with the sense of wonder at the variety of human experience, counts among the most basic attributes of a true reporter.

All of my self-discoveries, however, were not so pleasant. When I settled down at last in my Paris hotel room to write the McCarthy article—rebaptized "The New Pattern of Conspiracy"—I found a number of unrealized gaps in the impressive-looking heap of notes and clippings I had accumulated during my weeks on the trail. What was missing was nothing vital from the viewpoint of my central theme—merely the little human touches that would have helped the reader feel he was reading one man's thoughts and observations concerning his fellow men.

True, the article was supposed to be a political exposé, not a human interest piece. But in trying to unravel the patterns of conspiracy I had sometimes forgotten they were woven by conspirators, that is, men. I had, perhaps, done a fairly good job of investigation as an amateur detective or public prosecutor, but not as a reporter. I had approached my task in the spirit of the man-hunter who only thinks of the game in his bag, instead of in that of the man-watcher to whom the sighting is its own reward. I had not been looking for the truth, merely for the facts. Thus I had succumbed to the same fact-fetishism, the same tendency to dehumanize and thereby distort human data, that I had deplored in Washington.

That familiar fiend, the *Zeitgeist*, was once more to blame: In a bureaucratic age, everyone—scholars, writers, and not least of all journalists—tended to think like bureaucrats, that is, machines. Yet it was not only the diffuse bureaucratic chill in the air of the century or the robot contagion of a technological civilization that made it hard for men to think and write like human beings. In my case, at least—and in many other cases that I knew of among my generation —there was a more direct factor.

Back in the anti-fascist era when I had come of age, journalistically speaking, I had uncritically accepted the currently fashionable dogma that no artist, writer, or intellectual of any sort, from journalist to biochemist, could hope to save his soul unless he was ideologically "engaged"—i.e. committed to the struggle against fascism, not merely as a citizen, but also in his professional capacity. In practice, engagement all too often turned into obsession; its justification was that it was an inevitably excessive reaction to an extreme crisis.

The trouble was that the extremity had disappeared with Hitler— or more accurately, the crisis of civilization in becoming chronic had simultaneously grown less acute—but our personal engagement to public cause—almost, it seemed, to any public cause—had remained as obsessive as when the Moors were at the gates of Madrid or the appeasers at those of Berchtesgaden. The result was a steadily widening inflationary gap between historical reality and our sense of history, reflected in a kind of cultural Gresham's Law: the conventionalized rhetoric of protest or alarm stifling the spontaneous utterance of concern, the forced idealism of humanity falsifying the sincere regard for human welfare, the synthetic guilt engorging the still embryonic social conscience of twentieth-century man.

Perhaps, I concluded, the time had come to reexamine the contemporary root myth that for twentieth-century man participation in history is at once the overriding social duty and the supreme personal experience. There were times when both propositions were probably valid; I had lived through several moments myself when they seemed to be. Such occasions were rare, however, perhaps no less rare than the romantic experience in private life—the wine that comes once a world, as Emily Dickinson had called it. But living for history was like living for love: It led in the end to a kind of ideological Byronism, or what was worse, Bovaryism.

At last, I thought I understood where and how I had gone wrong in a professional sense, why from 1939 on I had become a compulsive activist, making, as I had written my wife, a career of crisis. Tempted by a succession of intoxicating moments in history, I had let myself succumb to historicism, as many journalists succumbed to drink.

Well, my head was clearing at last, late, but not, perhaps, too late, and I knew what I wanted to do for the rest of my life, as long as my legs held out. I wanted to become an authentic reporter again, not solely a journalistic one, perhaps, but a reporter all the same.

Being a reporter, as I understood the term, did not imply ideological teetotalism; it merely required holding one's ideology like a gentleman. A reporter should have both convictions and sympathies, and if he were human he could scarcely help having some prejudices as well. If he had no distastes he could have no standards. He could write truculently or compassionately or warningly or even indignantly. He had to explain and interpret, and up to a point he could comment and argue and infer. He couldn't avoid living in history, but he didn't try to live for it.

There were as many levels as there were types and specialized fields of reporting. I felt most at home myself in the long, European-style reportage, like my conspiracy article, that combined research and interpretation with firsthand observation or interviewing, and preferably treated a moral or social as well as a political theme. Such a *reportage*, if the themes were significant enough and the documentation adequate, could sometimes be developed into a book.

The kind of reporting that I had in mind was easier for Europeans, whose cultural compartmentations were generally less rigid than our own, but it could be done even in America. In any event, there was no fundamental incompatibility, as I had sometimes imagined, between my natural bent for being a reporter and my intermittent enjoyment in being what I thought of as a "writer." On the contrary, they could be complementary phases of the same profession.

For several years I continued to stress the journalistic phase, though gradually turning to more unconventional forms of reporting. I wrote magazine articles from Europe and North Africa, and eventually became a staff correspondent of *The Reporter*. For a while I even tried writing a weekly syndicated newspaper column from Europe as well, and when my chief client, the Washington *Post*, offered me a regular job as a roving correspondent it needed all my strength of character to finally turn it down. Money, of course, was the main reason for devoting so much time to magazine and newspaper reporting, but it was not the only one.

I had always found journalistic writing easy—for a long time it had been much too easy—and even today I have not completely lost the naïve satisfaction that most journalists derive from reading their own copy, especially in print. I seldom, however, reread with the same complacency my attempts at other kinds of writing. In my early Left Bank days when I still thought of myself as a potential poet or novelist it had been my difficulty in mastering paramyth and hypnologue—in other words, futurism—which I assumed to be the idiom of the future, that depressed me. Later, I had discovered that the cultural predicament was even graver than I imagined: Most of our thoughts are at once futuristic and archaic, and not only our thoughts but our feelings; our hearts (arch.) are no less rent than our minds between lag (soc.) and skip (electron.). As to our tongues, the less said the better, for the more utterance the less speech: symbol leaping off the tower ledge of meaning; syntax strangling in its own vomit on the bathroom floor below; cliché and repeat swarming in from the sidewalks (repeat, you sinners, it's later than you think); jargon crawling up the service stairs from the engine room; popart and crimart, twin wombrats of the miscogenation between gutter barbarian and avant-garde decadent, playing chicken in the elevator shafts; demagogues electro-fornicating with masscom call girls on the living room carpets; bureaucrats trying to sodomize their computers in the library (keep your Kitchen-Latin clean, kitten); professors of mortuary linguistics lurking behind every drapery with their embalming needles at the ready (God Bless Our Happy Home); and we can no longer even say the rest is silence: The rest is entropy.

For a long time, everything I wrote merely served to remind me what a dark age for writing I was living in. Until man learned either to dike the flood of history he had let loose or to adapt himself better to the rush of its current, it did not seem to me that any writer—or for that matter any creative artist—could hope to rise much above the daily and the utilitarian. He was doing well if he managed to express them so that they sounded a little less drab and a little more human than they generally appeared.

It was not until my second return to Paris that I was struck by a somewhat more cheerful corollary to these conclusions: The same cultural factors that make good writing so difficult in our time, even for a good writer, are no less effective in safeguarding the less gifted one—so long as he is honest and tries to do his best—from committing completely futile writing.

It was reassuring, too, from one angle, that in a civilization based on universal specialization there could be no such thing as a reader of universal culture. That might deprive the potentially great writer of a needed spur to greatness, but it made the role of the ordinary writer more significant and less frustrating. Every reader was certain to be more knowing than the writer in some area, and likely to be less so in some other. What was cliché to one might therefore prove fresh insight to another: one man's jargon was another's lifework, that is, his mind's life blood.

This age had some good points, along with the others. One encouraging thing about it, from the writer's or artist's point of view, was that while today's anticipations became outdated almost as soon as they were put down on paper or canvas, the cultural discards of the day-before-yesterday were likely to turn up again as the latest finds of the day-after-tomorrow, and reputations were constantly being made reviving long-forgotten reputations, including many that had never existed.

At a deeper level of feeling, there was comfort in the possibility that between the death of any God symbol and its rebirth in some contemporary *ersatz* ideology, one might for a few moments perceive the undistorted realness of things, perhaps even attain a fleeting glimpse of cosmic reality as the awesome symbol of itself. The language, too, contained elements of hope. If it was being incessantly degraded, it was likewise being steadily renewed. The quick-frozen words might thaw out into mere Kitchenette-English, but at least it was utterance striving toward the communication of something as yet incommunicable, and if enough of us continued to strive hard enough, we might in the end rediscover speech, thus repeating at a higher level the process whereby, as certain contemporary scientists appear to believe, some ape-like creature in discovering its rudiments invented man.

In addition to all these cultural reasons for facing one's typewriter with a measure of optimism, a more personal, and in a sense more metaphysical, self-discovery that I made about the same time helped to liberate my mind from the despair that had so often hindered my efforts at serious writing in the past. Like most would-be writers in America I had been brought up in the puritan doctrine that one must sit down before the blank sheet of paper with the fear of God in one's heart (even if one didn't believe in God). There is an abiding truth in the injunction, but for some reason—perhaps because I had not been serious enough at first in my journalistic writing—I had carried it too far; I had unconsciously committed a sin graver than fearing God too little: the sin of fearing Him so much that I had come to doubt His mercy, to doubt Grace. As soon as I realized that, my writing started going better. By the end of my forty-fifth year I thought that I could claim to have achieved a reasonable measure of psychological maturity as a citizen of the century. I had learned to live with such harsh or confusing contemporary realities as historical indeterminacy, cultural flux, moral relativity, social revolution, bureaucratic inertia, the permanent crisis of civilization, the threat of nuclear annihilation, nationalism, science, progress, and monogamy. As an American—neither strictly conformist nor radically deviant—husband, father, householder—if rather nomadic one —and dog-owner, I measured my risks and assumed my responsibilities. I had found my second courage; my adult personality was formed.

452

Like everyone, I had my private dreams and nightmares, but now I rarely let them distort my public eyesight. I knew that the world of men I was engaged in watching was the home of paradox. Its iron law was the struggle for survival; but winning it implied cooperation. Justice, fraternity, compassion, and generosity were mere rhetoric in the absence of power, but in their absence power itself speedily degenerated into self-destroying violence. A great deal of what passed as news or history was nothing but ceremonial or make-believe—and nothing could be more important. Reason reigned in world affairs, but seldom ruled, and often that was just as well: Our highest aspirations are no less rooted in the irrational than our most sordid delusions. Under normal conditions human beings tend to be incorrigibly selfish, blind, lazy, cowardly, and dishonest; luckily, these failings make crisis inevitable, and crisis, when it does not destroy them, or turn them into monsters, transforms them for a while into seers and heroes, or at least men. Thus civilization advances—and thus a man grows.

From the narrow journalistic viewpoint, my development as a reporter had naturally lagged during the years when I was too busy with other concerns to do any reporting, but after I moved back to Europe in 1953 I caught up relatively fast. At a deeper professional level, that of a reporter trying to leave some record of his times whose relevance would not wholly vanish with them, I likewise began to make some progress—and here, too, I look back on my return to Paris as marking a decisive stage. Two complementary hormones of ripeness, minute and not easily identifiable but nonetheless essential—a certain sublimated form of hope, a sharpened sense of tragedy—were still deficient in me, as they seemed to be in most Americans of my generation. To achieve my full growth as a writer—such growth as I was capable of achieving—I needed the stimulus of further exposures to history, of new disillusionments and of new reassurances.

453

A Banquet of Ghosts (4)

I suppose this is the place to mention the contemporary writer who helped me the most to become a writer myself. He was a friend of mine in Paris named Leigh, though strictly speaking he hasn't been a contemporary for a long time, and he was never much of a writer, nor even exactly a friend, certainly not a close one.

I don't believe I had thought of him in nearly twenty years until one day soon after my arrival in Paris in November 1953 I had the kind of bleak and curious experience that often happened to me during my first return, in 1948, but which was now rare for me. I had wandered across the river and found myself somehow in the lower slopes of Montmartre, not very far from the old Chicago *Tribune* office in the Rue Lafayette where I had first worked in Paris, but not near enough to have sought it as an unconscious goal. There was a café with a small *terrasse* across the street from me and I saw a shabbily dressed man sitting by himself hunched over one of the tables. His face was turned away from me, but those high, narrow shoulders futilely braced against a world of terrors, the forlorn slump of the neck, that almost fetal position of refuge and despair seemed unmistakable, even after all these years.

I was about to cross over and say to him, why, Leigh, when did you get back? Then I remembered that I had myself delivered Leigh's brief funeral oration, and thrown the single sheet of copy-paper on which it was written into his grave in 1934 or '35. (He had committed suicide during the Great Depression when he found himself stranded without a job and unable to face the prospect of returning to America.) At the same moment the stranger lifted his head and I saw that of course he was not Leigh, not even an American, but some derelict from Eastern Europe.

Anywhere else in town the incident would have seemed a trivial coincidence, but this, I suddenly realized, was the street where Leigh had actually lived and I doubted that my legs had brought

454

me there by chance. His hotel room, as I remembered it, had high, narrow French windows, curtained with rather grimy lace, a table, a wardrobe, a couple of chairs, a washstand and a *bidet.* There had been a brass bed, too, where Leigh slept with his big, florid, Flemish mistress, Elvire, and a large commode whose drawers were stuffed with neatly typed and stapled manuscripts.

I had only been there once, and Leigh, as I have said, had never been a close friend, merely one of the rewrite men on the night shift with whom I occasionally had a *café-fine* and a hot *chausson aux pommes* during the 10:30 break when I was working on the ⹂aris Edition. I doubt, in fact, whether he had any close friends, though everyone liked him and covered up for him as far as possible; he was almost the only member of the staff who never passed out over his typewriter, but his deceptively neat copy was full of misspellings and general illiteracies, and it used to take him most of the evening to rewrite one or two little inside filler pieces from the cables or the French papers.

I might not even have remembered his name if it had not been for the time when he had invited me to come up to his room for a cup of Elvire's coffee and a nightcap, and had opened one of the drawers of the commode for me. I leafed through a number of the manuscripts, and Leigh read me excerpts from others. They were all short stories in a naturalistic vein dealing with the desolation of life in America.

"Jeez," Leigh would say in his high, cracked, old maniac's voice, after each excerpt, "that's pretty strong stuff, isn't it? You can see why no editor in the country would touch it, can't you?"

I said I could see, and I could; for that matter I had read enough of Leigh's copy at the office. I wondered a little at the shallowness and triteness of a caricature that seemed so obsessively repetitive; one would have expected more intensity, a kind of fixed glare. Leigh's multiple short story was merely a mechanical grimace. It was a rather long one, however, in each of its variants, and there were dozens or scores of them. That commode contained hundreds of thousands of words, many of them spelled correctly, because

Leigh had evidently edited his own copy with the help of a dictionary, more thoroughly than he usually did at the office, before painstakingly retyping each manuscript. One felt that every page had been written in the fear of God and in the hope of eternal life. In mental and physical labor, in care and conscience, in sheer courage, the contents of Leigh's commode represented a literary output that any professional writer might have been proud of. Unquestionably, Leigh had fought the good fight for civilization's sake; he was one of those futile but unavoidable casualties of the creative function, the unknown soldiers of literature, whose capacity for infinite, unrewarded pains, and masochistic willingness to suffer them, in some mysterious way made it possible for the survivors to struggle on. No man had ever been more entitled to take his rest.

25

The Renewal of Hope

S<small>CRAPS</small> F<small>ROM</small> <small>A</small> R<small>EPORTER'S</small> S<small>CRAPBOOK</small>

*A*lgiers—Diar-el-Mahçoul—the City of the Kept Promise—
where some 700 French families and a slightly larger number of Moslem ones live together as good neighbors in one
of the most adventurous achievements of modern urbanism is worth
seeing at any time. But it is particularly impressive to visit this hilltop oasis of human sanity soaring above the sparkling bay of Algiers
when you have just come from talking with the politician whose
respect for his campaign pledges brought it into being—Jacques
Chevalier, the dynamic liberal-minded Mayor of Algiers, a former
deputy and a minister in the Mendès-France government.

For to Chevalier, a slim, blond, youthful-looking, half-American
Frenchman, Diar-el-Mahçoul and half a dozen other almost equally
spectacular municipal housing projects that have provided new
lodgings for 15,000 persons in less than four years do not merely
symbolize the hope that Algeria's 1,000,000 Europeans and 8,500,000
Moslems may someday live together in peace. In his mind, they are
pilot projects demonstrating the feasibility of the policy of cohabitation between the two communities in which he sees the only hope
for solution of the Algerian problem.

(*Europe in Profile,* M<small>AY</small> 1956)

Hope, I wrote in one of the numerous drafts of my first chapter, has become such a precious commodity that its safekeeping can no longer be entrusted to professional, or simply habitual, optimists. Now, several years later, as I approach the end of this report on an American reporter's growing up, and try to think of the general conclusions, if any, that might usefully be drawn from it, the warning seems both more necessary than ever, and more pertinent here. I have never exactly been a chronic optimist, but much of my early life—well into middle age, to tell the truth—I was an incautious, and therefore rather sloppy, hoper. The failing has often hurt my work—and subjected me to the recurrent fits of gloom or cynicism that are the classic punishment of the too ready yea-sayer. A reporter needs hope as much as he needs whisky, but cut-rate brands of either will only turn him sour.

Over the decades, however, and particularly in the last ten or fifteen years, since I returned to reporting world affairs, I have gradually discovered that a small dose of skepticism, taken the evening before, may avert a major disillusionment the morning after. Above all, I have learned—or learned better—that a revolutionary age imposes on us the necessity of frequently reviewing, and when necessary revising, our goals, our dreams, and our expectations, whether for ourselves or for mankind. Being hard-minded is essential, but not enough; we must continually reharden our minds as they lose their temper in the fiery flux of contemporary history. Certain ideologies that were perhaps rational in the 1920's, on the basis of the facts as known, stand exposed as mere mythologies in the light of present knowledge. Certain doctrines that seemed—and were—idealistic ten or fifteen years ago have sometimes become crudely exploitative in the radically altered social or international contexts of today. Certain solutions to world problems that looked promising only five years back may have turned into woolly daydreams by now. Conversely, dangers that once were all too real have on occasion been transmuted no less rapidly into simple phantasms.

Judging from my own experience, the least painful aspects of my generation's never-ending cultural *aggiornamento* have been on the most metaphysical plane. For all the literary keening that we hear about the "Death of God" and the absurdity of existence, very few of my contemporaries, I suspect, have sustained any severe psychic damage as a result of the ontological revolutions, or fads, of our age. Perhaps our Victorian ancestors suffered more real anguish when they were first assailed by Doubts.

We survey the darkling plain with a somber, and what we trust is a suitably Existentialist eye, but the discovery that ignorant armies clash there by night generally causes no more spontaneous dejection than it does surprise. What else can one expect when men go prowling about the beaches past their bedtime, making war, not love?

Our most grievous emotional wounds have been essentially worldly ones. The stress and torment of our day has usually had some background of ideological conflict, but the main ideologies in question—capitalism, socialism, nationalism, liberalism, fascism, imperialism, and anti-colonialism—are identified with relatively down-to-earth group interests. The survival of civilizations, and even peoples, the safety or independence of nations, the power or material welfare of social classes, and the lives or freedoms of individual men have generally been at stake.

The problem of hope has therefore been both a highly concrete and very dramatic one for us. Most of the solutions that have occurred to us at one time or another have had to be, if not discarded, amended, not once, but over and over again. Realigning our world hopes with world change as it takes place has been an endless travail —but also a continuous liberation. Few things foster growth so much as casting away a superstitious dread—unless it be learning to live with a dangerous truth; nothing stunts it like clinging to an illusory hope—unless it be yielding to a groundless despair.

The hopes I once held for a united Europe, linked in a close and equal partnership with the United States, have fluctuated considerably since the blowy September afternoon in 1951 when I walked along the banks of the Rhine and dreamed of the reemergent Atlantis that would some day arise from the abyss of history. The nadir of this particular dream, as far as I was concerned, was probably reached in the summer of 1954 when the French National Assembly voted against ratifying the project for a European Defense Community, or European army, as it was generally called, an early brainchild of Jean Monnet never formally recognized by its parent.

I followed the emotional, if sometimes burlesque, debate from my old perch in the foreign press gallery of the Assembly and saw the internationale of haters—in this case the victorious coalition of Communists, Gaullists, and ex-Vichyite nationalists—take shape once again before my eyes. My cabled dispatch to *The Reporter* reflected my scorn for the caricature of democracy that the French parliamentary system had turned into, as well as my disquiet over the future of Europe. I spent several dollars in cable tolls—and no doubt spent them wisely—to relate a grotesque little incident that to my mind symbolized the irrationality of the whole debate: A shaggy religious fanatic, the disciple of a self-proclaimed Messiah from the *Midi*, the "Christ of Montfauvet," had contrived to slip past the ushers on to the floor of the Assembly, shouting to the startled deputies, "I bring you a substitute for EDC—love thy neighbor."

Considering how the dream of European unity had possessed my imagination during my summer at HICOG three years earlier, it is not surprising that seeing EDC gored to death in the parliamentary bullring of France was a somewhat trying experience for me. What may seem odd is that it was not more so. It was true that I had never shared the mystic enthusiasm for a European army felt by a number of Monnet's followers. The scheme seemed to me one of those slightly gimmicky institutional devices for trying to snare the future that rarely turn out to be practical substitutes for history. In all my correspondence with anti-Administration editors at home I had stressed Mr. Dulles's heavy-handed attempts to impose its ratification on the French government as one of the tactical errors of Republican foreign policy. "It is at least arguable," I wrote in February 1954, "that by putting brutal pressure on the French to ratify

EDC, while de-emphasizing the Atlantic framework in which it was supposed to fit, we have changed it into a time bomb which is eventually going to blow the whole Alliance to bits."

At the same time, I realized that the formal repudiation of EDC in the French National Assembly marked a black day for Europe. The first serious—and possibly irreparable—fissure had opened in the Western wall. I duly noted the ominous significance of the event in my report, but its tone was hardly that of a man who sees his world beginning to crumble.

Leafing through the magazine and newspaper reports I have written from Europe, Africa, and Asia during the last fifteen years —and particularly in reading over the usually more spontaneous and uninhibited, if sometimes emotional or hasty, comments on the course of events contained in my letters to various colleagues or employers—I am struck by a similar discordance on many occasions between the dramas of history I have personally witnessed and my emotional reactions to them. The crises of the fifties and sixties have been less spectacular than those of the thirties and, so far, less calamitous, but from the viewpoint of an American who feels himself deeply attached both to the national interest and to the national ideal, and who believes in the interdependence of all peoples and of all men, few of them have had what could be characterized as a happy ending.

The final curtain has not been rung down, and it is possible that I shall yet live to see some of my former, all-but-abandoned hopes eventually realized. Up to the present, however, I have been almost consistently obliged to discard, modify, or defer them, sometimes because they were not realistic to start with, sometimes because fundamental changes in the world situation have made them unrealizable. My files bear witness to innumerable intellectual and emotional readjustments of this sort, punctuated by frequent cries of indignation or alarm. On the whole, there are surprisingly few wails of despair.

My relative serenity in the face of such setbacks to hope as the chronic inadequacy—if not futility—of the United Nations system, the recurrent prenatal crises of Europe, and the apparently inexorable disintegration of the Atlantic Alliance has diverse roots, some more recently developed than others. The oldest one—it dates back to my League of Nations days, I think—is the skepticism I have already mentioned with regard to merely alphabetical solutions to humanity's problems. I mean by that the creation of international institutions, whether global or regional—UN, EDC, EEC, NATO, etc.—whose formal authority is not based on some real and deep consensus.

For a few years I let myself be misled by the widespread contemporary fallacy that if a given authority has been delegated supranational powers of decision or control it will automatically be effective. By the spring of 1955—when I started on a profile of Monnet—the EDC debacle and the history of the Coal and Steel Authority itself had already convinced me that the supranational principle was not the magic instrument for unifying peoples and purposes I had once believed. Whenever really vital national interests were at stake, national governments, as long as they remained that, would not relinquish their de facto veto power over the decisions of any multinational boards or commissions to which they might have theoretically delegated fragments of their sovereignty; and the boards in question would not venture in such cases to exercise their paper authority.

Some of my reservations about Monnet himself as the prophet of the New Europe stemmed from what I considered his overconfidence in virtues of merely formal supranationality; I likewise felt that he attached too much importance to the economic and technological elements in nation-buildings, and not enough to the political or psychological ones, especially to that deep, almost unconscious common sense of purpose that Renan calls the "daily plebiscite." When I finally interviewed Monnet at his office in the grimy, Graustarkian, Grand Ducal capital of Luxembourg, on the eve of his retirement as head of the Coal and Steel Community, Europe's first genuinely supranational institution since the disappearance of the Holy Roman Empire, I realized that the man was more impressive than his legend and made on the whole better sense. Much as I was captivated, however, by the indomitably youthful sexagenarian, with his remote, low-pitched, almost hypnotically precise way of speaking, his compelling, greenish eyes, his delicately twitching moustache—the visible antenna, it seemed, of some unique instinct of prevision—and his whole catlike self-possession, I remained skeptical in certain respects about the future of the European movement.

In the years that have elapsed since my talk with Monnet, I have watched his magnum opus, the Common Market, come into being and survive a series of violent crises. The European movement itself, though its validity has been challenged again and again, has so far never entirely lost its momentum; checked for a while in some direction, it soon starts moving in another. This vitality is encouraging.

Today, therefore, I think the chances are fairly good that a European polity of some sort—if nothing more, a loose confederation with a few specialized, quasi-federal institutions—will take form within a not too distant future, perhaps in my lifetime. All in all, the thought cheers me: The unification of Europe, even partial or proximate, would constitute an encouraging demonstration of man's capacity to modify his own destiny by acts of reason. I have become enough of a European myself to likewise feel that any authentic affirmation of the European personality is a good thing in itself—good for Europe and good for the world.

If, however, my expectations should prove too sanguine, it would not be a shattering blow to my morale. In recent years, I have seen both Europe and the world accumulate problems which European unification by itself cannot solve, which in some respects it may even aggravate. The creation of a new European superstate is not necessarily the ideal remedy for the overdeveloped statism that already afflicts most Western countries, including those of Europe, nor is it likely that the birth of another supernation will diminish the force of nationalism in the world. I suspect that if a united Europe does come into being it will be a rather Gaullist kind of Europe, even though General de Gaulle himself has often seemed the major obstacle to its unification. Unity might help Europe tackle the problem of its technological lag, which Monnet in 1968 warned would soon turn it into "an underdeveloped continent," but it is doubtful that even a united Europe can solve the problem alone. And whether or not Europe finally achieves its unity, the partnership between it and the United States that I once dreamed of is almost certainly going to remain less idyllic and more difficult than I imagined in 1951—or even in 1955.

I continue to believe that cooperation between the United States and its European allies, or former allies, in the historic heartland of Christendom is one of the essential bases of our general security; it is particularly vital to the preservation, even in a dilute form, of the capitalist system, to which, for all its faults, I remain attached. I am moderately hopeful that despite what seems to have become the more or less chronic state of tension or mutual misunderstanding in transatlantic relations, enough cooperation will continue to exist long enough to ward off major calamities. More positive and dynamic benefits than mere survival—though it is not a negligible one—may yet accrue from the once close alliance of the principal Western powers; it is perhaps too soon to bury the dream of a developing Atlantic community in our already overcrowded cemetery of lost hopes.

All the same, when I look back over the record of my professional activity since 1953, I am struck by the element of wishful thinking or other forms of self-deception that lingered for a long time in my view of the Western Alliance. The struggle to free myself from the addiction to such intellectual and moral narcotics has been one of the major themes of my post-adult education. It has also supplied the subjective background to what I believe has been the most useful endeavor of my career as a reporter, at least at the journalistic level: the identification and exposure of the unconscious contradictions in American official, and sometimes popular, thought that, as I noted earlier, repeatedly sabotage the conscious goals of national policy, especially of our European policies. The United States role in the EDC drama illustrated one type of national self-deception and self-sabotage. The Geneva Conference of 1954, which formalized France's withdrawal as a colonial power

464

from Southeast Asia, and laid the foundations of our own subsequent involvement in Vietnam, helped me to recognize others.

Several of the international conferences that I covered as a reporter before the war have remained vivid in my memory. It is perhaps curious that my recollections of the 1954 one are so dim, or at any rate trivial. The meeting opened on a note of high and tragic drama —the French garrison at Dien Bien Phu, which had heroically withstood a long siege, was overwhelmed by the revolutionary army of Gen. Vo Nguyen Giap ten days after it convened—and it closed almost three months later, after a government crisis in Paris had brought Pierre Mendès-France to power, with an East-West agreement apparently ending the bitter colonial war that had raged for nearly nineteen years in Indo-China. From the personal viewpoint, the occasion marked my professional homecoming to a place that was filled with emotional resonances for me, and it marshalled before my eyes a company of cheerful ghosts: the surviving friends or acquaintances of my prewar days as a Geneva correspondent. Indeed, one of my motives for covering the conference had been the hope that, in addition to any salable journalistic copy I managed to turn out, it might inspire a few autobiographical pages on the classic Proustian theme of time recovered, usable for my work-in-progress.

This hope, for some reason, was frustrated, or at least deferred to the Geneva Summit Meeting of the following year. My clearest memories of the Indo-China Conference are neither of interviews or press briefings—the actual sessions were held behind closed doors, of course, at the new United Nations building overlooking the lake—nor of talks with friends, but of the occasional evenings I spent dining alone at my hotel. Unable to find accommodations in the city, I had settled in a suburban lakeside resort for illicit honeymooners of modest means and sentimental disposition. The food was unexpectedly good, and it was pleasant to sit on the open-air *terrasse* in the mild spring night, looking at the lights across the lake on the Savoyard shore, selfishly relieved not to be sharing the superstitious expectations or secret torments of the couples at the surrounding tables, and listening to the jukebox play over and over a current French song-hit with its saccharine, endlessly repeated refrain, *Line, Line, Caroline chèrie, Méfiez-vous de la vie.* I had long since learned, though perhaps too late, to beware of life, so presumably it was the song's tune, or simply its repetition, rather than its philosophical message, that imprinted it so deeply on my mind. Of the work atmosphere of the Conference itself, I recall chiefly the smell of fresh paint, the coarse sisal carpeting, and the beaverboard partitions of the temporary international press center that the Geneva authorities had set up for the occasion. Though the building that housed the press center had formerly been a low-price department store, it at least supported the essential amenity of a journalists' bar. In the bar there was a warning bell that called us to the regular or special press conferences that were conducted in adjoining briefing rooms by spokesmen for the various national delegations. Whenever the bell sounded the ensuing stampede of my colleagues suggested a cohort of maddened housewives storming a bargain sale, where, as it seemed to me, the United States press spokesman usually appeared to be manning the remnants counter.

Perhaps my recollections of the Conference are not so frivolous, after all. It may be that my long holiday from the artificial conventions and unavowed complicities of diplomatic journalism had sensitized my mind to the propagandistic mirages and self-deceivings that constitute its basic raw material, thus enabling me to recognize for what they are the Potemkin's villages of fluorescent tinsel and beaverboard reality that furnish its habitual decor.

LETTERS TO AN EDITOR

The Geneva situation is rather baffling . . . Events are constantly demonstrating that the U.S. government is living in a dream world which bears only occasional resemblance to the world of hard

*political fact. Every time I attend one of the confidential briefings
for U.S. correspondents at the Delegation, I have the impression that
the most fundamental battle going on here is the battle in the minds
of our delegates between myth and reality . . . it is a gory fight, and
for every two myths that are exploded, at least one new one arises,
through the classic process of propagandistic auto-intoxication.*

*For instance, Dulles, on his arrival here last Sunday, told us—
apropos of Indo-China—that sometimes there is nothing the U.S.
government can do to prevent unpleasant things from happening,
thus, as it were, officially renouncing the "myth of American omnip-
otence" that has played such a big role in Republican thinking
about Asian affairs. On the other hand, Robertson [Walter Robertson, Assistant Secretary of State for Far Eastern Affairs] this
morning deplored the effect that Chou En-lai's propaganda was
having on the illiterate millions of Asia and wistfully remarked that
he wished he could hire some of those Communist psychological
warfare geniuses to work for our side . . . Thus, in Robertson's
mind Chou's success was not due to our obvious mistakes, but to the
more potent magic of Peking's witch doctors. When he mentioned
India specifically, several correspondents, including myself, suggested tactfully that one reason for Chou's good press there was
that he was plugging for India to be brought into the Conference,
while we were opposing it.*

*Robertson apparently thought that too materialistic an explana-
tion . . . The official reason for not wanting India, Indonesia, Burma,
etc., is that it would make the Conference unwieldy, and slow
down its work. On the other hand, the Delegation says that it does
not expect the Conference to accomplish anything constructive, but
wants it to drag on for a long time so as to smoke out the Communist intentions. Another U.S. reason for disliking India's presence is that the Indians have delusions of grandeur and want to
pose as the leaders of Asia. On the other hand there is much wring-
ing of hands because it is thought that Chou is posing successfully
as the leader of Asia . . . Similarly, the Delegation is now trying to
convince itself that we were all set to intervene militarily [to save*

the beleaguered French garrison at Dien Bien Phu] but were let down by our appeasement-minded allies. On the other hand reports from Washington make it increasingly clear that Congressional opposition to intervention in Indo-China did at least as much as British hostility or French unreasonableness to block it . . .

(GENEVA, APRIL 30, 1954)

In the light of subsequent history, I realize that my 1954 critique of Mr. Dulles's role at Geneva was only partly justified. As was to become clear even before the end of the conference, some of the apparent inconsistencies in the United States position were due less to the struggle between myth and reality in the mind of our delegation than to lack of candor in its relations with the press—an early manifestation of the "credibility gap" that has dogged the Vietnam policy of three administrations. If we seemed to cut a poor figure at Geneva it was because in a sense we were hardly there: Our perhaps unpremeditated policy, as it finally emerged, appears to have been to avoid responsibility for the kind of settlement of the Indo-China war that we knew was unavoidable, while preparing behind the scenes to scuttle it in favor of a more rigidly anti-Communist formula. This formulation, grossly oversimplified as all such condensed résumés of policy must be, sounds harsh. Yet in all that we have read since, including Eisenhower's own memoir, there is little if anything to disqualify it.

It was perhaps the only occasion during Mr. Dulles's career as Secretary of State when his diplomacy was characterized by a masterly lack of zeal that Talleyrand might have admired. He was rewarded by seeing his NATO colleagues, Premier Pierre Mendès-France and Britain's Sir Anthony Eden, assume the onus—at least in the American public eye—of negotiating a humiliating Western retreat in Southeast Asia, while the United States, unfettered by the terms of a treaty it had accepted without solemnly countersigning, stood forth as the high-principled, disinterested protector of the newly created South Vietnamese republic, which it was simultaneously saving from Communist tyranny and helping to free from French colonialism. Technically, and from the short-term viewpoint, it was a brilliant achievement.

What may seem to the present-day reader the most glaring flaw in Dulles's performance at Geneva, and in his whole Southeast Asia policy, was less evident at the time. The puppet regime of the Emperor Bao Dai in Vietnam had demonstrated its abject incapacity to mobilize mass support for the struggle against the Communist-dominated Vietminh. That, however, could be explained by the regime's colonialist taint. Now that Vietnam—even if reduced to South Vietnam—had an authentically independent national government, headed by that incorruptible patriot, Ngo Dinh Diem (who had, in fact, never compromised himself with the French), it was possible to hope that the country, bolstered by moderate American economic and military assistance, might become a dependable bulwark against further Communist expansion in Southeast Asia.

The hope, as I gradually came to realize over the next decade, particularly after I spent several weeks in Vietnam at the end of 1965, was based on the superficial analysis of inadequate data, but at the time of the Geneva Conference it was not, I think, a blatant example of self-deception on the part of United States policymakers. An analogous conclusion about another Asian country with somewhat similar problems, South Korea, seems to have been vindicated by history. I have seen, both before and since Geneva, more pathological examples of alienation from reality in the attitudes of U.S. policy-makers: for example, the mystic conviction in early 1954 that France could not fail to ratify EDC, and the equally mystic conviction of U.S. officials in Vietnam on various occasions that total military victory was just around the corner.

Mr. Dulles's cardinal error lay not so much in committing the United States to support an anti-Communist regime in South Vietnam as in the one-sided nature of the commitment. Not only did he deliberately avoid associating the neutral powers of Southern or Southeastern Asia—India, Indonesia—with an Indo-China settlement that might have given them a direct interest in maintaining the status quo, but he arrogantly disregarded the wishes of our European allies, who thought that what remained of their imperial interests in the area would be better served by a limited accommodation with Asian communism than by intransigent resistance.

Later that same year, in the view of France and England, Dulles aggravated the offense by bullying them into signing the Manila Pact, thus creating a paper analogue to NATO. In the eyes of these two chief NATO partners—especially, of course, France—United States Southeast Asia policy, as manifested immediately before, during, and after the Geneva Conference, aimed essentially at substituting American for European imperialism in that part of the world. That ours was a more benevolent, disinterested, and in a sense less "colonialist" imperialism than theirs naturally increased their resentment. A number of Europeans suspected that the aim reflected a lucid cynicism on the part of Secretary Dulles and President Eisenhower.

Those who knew both men and had a deeper understanding of the American soul realized that such suspicions simultaneously impugned the honor of two exceptionally high-minded American public servants, and gave them credit for a gift of self-awareness that neither they, nor many other Americans, possessed. The French, in their own lucidly cynical way, naturally inclined toward the first school of thought, while most of the British at Geneva, including Eden himself, belonged to the second, or mainly to the second. In either case they were appalled by what confronted them; and Mr. Dulles, by the manner in which he practiced the diplomatic arts of noncommunication with our Allies during the Conference, compromised the possibility of frank consultation with them in future crises. Thus, he can be fairly blamed for helping to sow the seeds not only of one war, but two: Vietnam and Suez.

The men who framed and carried out United States foreign policy—not only during the Dulles era, but often, alas, later—were so blind to their own contradictory motivations that at moments they seemed like sleepwalkers. On some occasions, at Geneva and elsewhere, they deliberately misled the press—not to mention their Allied colleagues—but on many more occasions they unwittingly deceived themselves. They preached the gospel of anti-colonialism to our European allies, and sometimes attempted to impose it on them; then as the repentant or defeated colonialists withdrew, the United States moved into their former possessions to take over their remaining political or commercial interests. They exalted internationalism, and practiced nationalism; they proclaimed a partnership of equals, but in the words of the London *Times* Washington correspondent that I cited at the time, wanted the United States "to be more equal than others."

For many years I regularly covered the chief NATO events of all sorts, and made a special point of listening to responsible European grievances against American policy, as it concerned the Alliance. The immediate issue varied—the war in Algeria, the Suez crisis, the United States monopoly of strategic weapons and of strategic decisions—but the underlying European complaint usually was that the United States claimed for itself a freedom of action it denied its allies. We defended our imperial interests in Latin America or the Far East by whatever means we judged suitable, without consulting our NATO partners and without heeding the cries of alarm or of moral indignation that our actions provoked among the European masses. When our allies similarly took the law into their own hands in the Near East or in the Congo, we forced them to desist in the name of world law.

Even Europeans who were most friendly toward the United States and who shared my own ideal of a true Atlantic Community felt that these attitudes on our part denoted elements of unconscious imperialism in our conception of the Alliance, and in a number of cases I could not help agreeing with them. I likewise sympathized with their repeated charge that our fetishistic concern with the collective military machinery of NATO tended to weaken its political and psychological bases.

"I had a long and very frank talk the other day with X——[the permanent delegate to the NATO Council from one of the smaller powers]" I reported in one of my letters at the end of March 1955. "His view is that NATO no longer has any military significance at all; its importance is purely political and economic, and he criticizes the U.S. government, among others, most harshly for continuing to harp on military problems while allowing the political situation throughout Europe to deteriorate . . . His formula is to stop worrying about a war that can't happen—and one which would destroy all the belligerents if it did happen—and concentrate instead on putting some teeth into Article 2 of the [NATO] Treaty.*

"To illustrate his point, or part of it, he told me a wonderful story . . . about his complicated negotiations with the security office at SHAPE over the destruction of outdated classified files. SHAPE insisted that he burn the files in his delegation's offices; X—— claimed it was too much of a fire hazard. Instead, he proposed that the documents be packed in a truck under the supervision of armed military guards and taken back to SHAPE for destruction there. To which X—— solemnly swears the SHAPE security officer replied, 'But suppose there was an enemy air attack while the truck was en route from Paris to Roquencourt and the guards were killed?' "

The magazine articles and syndicated columns in which I tried to make American readers with a certain degree of sophistication aware of how many American policies or acts looked when viewed through European eyes occasionally elicited an encouraging response of one sort or another from critics of the Eisenhower Administration, including some who worked for it. I was all the more inclined, therefore, to assume that what I regarded as the most disastrous traits of American foreign policy stemmed from the character and personal outlook of John Foster Dulles. I knew that Mr. Dulles was skeptical of his predecessor's "Atlanticism," if not

* Article 2 calls for the development of economic cooperation in particular among members of the Alliance.

472

actively opposed to it, though he was a sincere, almost fanatical partisan of European unification. The modest improvement in transatlantic relations under Dulles's successor, the gentle and gentlemanly Christian A. Herter, naturally bolstered this comforting illusion.

My disillusionment was all the greater when the Kennedy Administration, toward which I felt a good deal of ideological sympathy, began to reset the course of United States foreign and defense policies. Some of the innovations struck me as admirable and long overdue, others at least as bold and interesting experiments. I applauded the young President's eloquent dedication to the principle of Atlantic partnership and rejoiced at the favorable, often enthusiastic, response that his personality elicited both among the European elites and from the general public. On the fundamental issues of the Alliance, however, the new team in Washington seemed unaware of the basic contradiction lurking beneath its apparently minor internal divergences over "partnership" as against "interdependence." The latter term, favored by Defense Secretary Robert S. McNamara, was misleading, as Professor Arthur M. Schlesinger, Jr., has rather mildly put it, because "what McNamara meant at bottom was precisely the dependence of Western security on a nuclear deterrent under American control."*

To General de Gaulle—and to some other Europeans—the McNamara formula implied maintenance of an American colonial domination over Europe. The Secretary of Defense soon became the *bête noir* both of French nationalists and of the rising new breed of European Gaullists. He lacked the abrasive self-righteousness of Dulles, but his almost inhuman rationality was sometimes just as hard to bear, if not harder. Dulles could only imply that he was God's accredited representative in a conference or negotiation; McNamara could prove with a slide rule that his was the voice of reason.

As it gradually became apparent, however, McNamara was no more the sole mouthpiece of unconscious imperialism—or, at least,

* *A Thousand Days*, Arthur M. Schlesinger, Jr., Houghton Mifflin 1965.

nationalism—in the Kennedy Administration than Dulles had been in Eisenhower's; nor was our jealous insistence on our nuclear monopoly the only manifestation of it. Our disregard of European interests in the Congo, the "Skybolt" crisis with Britain, the unsuccessful struggle to force Britain's entry into the Common Market, and our offhand manner of keeping our allies informed, more or less, of our negotiations for a nuclear accord with the Soviet Union reflected the same tendency, which grew even more apparent during the Johnson Administration. It was also expressed, at least negatively, in Washington's contemptuous indifference to European fears, however exaggerated, of what some headline writers called the "dollar invasion" and the "brain drain" (both symptoms of the dangerous lag that was developing between European and American technological progress).

To me, as an American reporter in Europe following all these crises, or incipient crises, the most revelatory symptom was the fury with which American officials reacted to any European criticism, and even more, of course, to any European defiance of America's moral authority. It seemed to make no difference whether the official was a Democrat or a Republican, a liberal or a conservative. Private American citizens often reacted with equal violence. The reaction itself was almost never purely official, in the sense of being merely formal or ritual; it was an authentically personal one which reddened private jowls and hardened the timbre of private converse.

Obviously, the Americans who reacted in such ways identified themselves with their government (always a hazardous, but not necessarily irrational, procedure) and felt the blocking of a national policy as the frustration of a personal urge. The context, in the cases I recall, rendered unmistakable the nature of the urge: for power, or status, or both. The inference that the men who framed or carried out national policy had built some of their own power or status urges into it seemed logical, if not inescapable. A domineering exigency or attitude strongly suggested an underlying wish to dominate.

From what I knew both of American character and of how the American government works, I did not believe that dominating our allies, or abusively aggrandizing our prestige at the expense of theirs, or simply promoting selfish American interests to the detriment of Europe's were conscious aims of our European policy, even in the minds of our most Machievellian policy-makers. From one point of view, that was precisely the trouble. In my experience, Americans engaged in any joint undertaking often have a stronger feeling for the common good than Europeans do. But this relative altruism, by its very existence, blinds them—more than Europeans are usually blinded—to the residual selfishnesses and power lusts imbedded in their nobler motivations, as they are in all human striving. It is not the arrogance of power that we chiefly need to dread, but its cant, and above all, its blindspots.

Whether the American blindspots, moral and strategic, are those of every world power, or whether they are a specific product of American culture, is hard to determine. Perhaps they are both. I suspect, for example, that some of our diplomatic patterns of behavior mirror the present-day blandness of our free enterprise capitalism—particularly evident during the Long Complacency of the Eisenhower era—which though less rapacious than many another, seems more unaware of its vestigial rapacities. On the other hand, as I have already noted, they do not seem peculiarly linked with any political ideology.

No doubt, one of the hidden causes underlying the errors of American diplomacy in our relations with our allies has been the unavowed feeling that partly because of our immense strength, partly because of the seeming improvement in the world situation, we no longer really needed them. Without saying it, perhaps without consciously thinking it, our allies have sometimes behaved as if they, too, no longer looked on the Alliance as a vital necessity. For needless to say, the policies of many other nations, some of them much less powerful than the United States, show equally unmistakable traces of self-deception or self-ignorance in the minds of their framers.

475

During the early cold war years, I supposed that the political double standard—one measure for the son of the revolution, another for the imperialist—practiced by the Soviet government was the fruit of conscious cynicism. The more I see of world affairs, however, the readier I am to admit that the Communists may be as unconscious of the contradictions in their own minds as those Americans who believe that what is good for General Dynamics must automatically be good for European security and NATO solidarity.

Similarly, I used to admire General de Gaulle for, among other things, his supreme lucidity and his almost total freedom from cant. I continue to believe that in many respects he is less self-blinded and less self-deluded than most other statesmen of our day. Unlike his American counterparts and adversaries, De Gaulle, I imagine, has no unconscious urge to dominate; in a sense, domination is his explicit doctrine. (If there are elements in De Gaulle's pursuit of power and status for France of which he is himself unaware, they relate, most likely, to the completeness of the identification between his own personality and the nation's.) It is difficult, however, for an American reporter in France to escape the conclusion that along with some rational, if misguided, motives for opposing United States interests at times, the wartime leader of Free France has been more influenced than he realizes by a passionate thirst to seek revenge for past humiliations.

In an age when humanity is condemned to plod for an indefinite period along the narrow ledge of doom, it is not exactly reassuring to find that those who are leading us on the perilous march are sleepwalkers at least part of the time, as we are ourselves. To say that I have come to view contemporary political reality largely in such terms implies some fatalism, but is by no means a confession of despair.

The sleepers can be made to waken; perhaps they will eventually learn to wake themselves. Reason may be a thing we dimly see in sleep, as a contemporary poet says, but it is not a thing we can never see except in sleep. I do not believe that the men who rule the world are invariably fools or hypocrites, nor that they are constantly and completely self-deluded. Neither do I believe that power, by its essential nature, or nations, by the fact of their sovereignty, or social classes, by the law of history, are necessarily foredoomed to blind, conflicting, self-destroying greeds.

What I have learned, I think, from my years of watching human strife and striving, is that just as all men conceal from themselves and within themselves traces of cruelty or selfishness even in their most generous acts, so do the leaders of men, so do nations and peoples, so do social groups of every kind: the strong and the weak, the established and the disinherited; the bulwarks of every great tradition, and the champions of every noble reform.

It is not literally true that, as Oscar Wilde said, each man kills the thing he loves, but few men go through life without at some time cruelly wounding it. Similarly, every political movement tends on some occasion to betray its own ideals, and every political or military leader to nullify his own victories or destroy his own creations.

Life, as the great poets and moralists have always proclaimed, is essentially tragic; so, as the true historians have always known, is history. Always and everywhere, we are betrayed by what is false within; and always and everywhere, there is some hidden falseness to betray us. Hope itself is a kind of falsehood—except, precisely, when it is the hope that life and history, in uncovering us to ourselves, can sometimes save us from ourselves.

26

The Cool Peace

Among all the intellectual and emotional upheavals that my generation has gone through, I doubt that any have caused us so often to fluctuate between hope and despair as the successive changes in the relations between the Soviet Union and the West. Some of these changes—and their impact—have already been recorded. One of the most drastic was the Moscow-instigated *putsch* of 1948 that turned Czechoslovakia into a Soviet vassal state and wiped out its domestic freedoms. While Stalin lived, nothing, it seemed, could ever bridge the moral gulf that this brutal rape had opened between Soviet imperialism and the conscience of the West. Then Stalin died, and a new, seemingly more debonaire star began to rise in the Russian power firmament: that of Nikita Khrushchev. New words—thaw, coexistence, détente—gradually superseded the harsh vocabulary of the cold war. The subtle political reality that they stood for—to the degree there was one—proved scarcely less difficult to live with—and to adjust one's attitudes toward—than the unrepressed hostility of former years.

"Conference opened today in old Electoral Building," I noted somewhat elliptically in my log of the Four Power "Summit" Conference held in Geneva from July 18 to July 23, 1955. "Just where I came in, covering first League Assembly twenty-five years ago. Same decor; same faces often, though don't look quite the same . . . Eden drew good crowd on arrival—old Geneva star—but Ike even

478

larger one. Russians something of mystery—no change there—for new reason: experts not sure whether Bulganin or Khruschev is top man. Whoever is has evidently given Soviet correspondents their instructions: They stand large part of day around press bar radiating tight-lipped camaraderie like deceived wife who's decided to forgive all. Would like to talk to some of them, but can't stand kind of crowd hanging around. All this talk of thaw bringing things out of woodwork . . . Among things that have come out is A⸺ [a prewar British Communist] whom I used to see around press bar here with old Dell and other friends when Spanish Civil War was on agenda. Looked on him then as perfect Communist intellectual bureaucrat, archetype of faithful clerk. Understand A⸺ has had his troubles since, and looks it, poor devil. Never imagined he could have doubts, and perhaps it wasn't doubts that undid him but convictions, just being too faithful. Present Party position, if any, obscure but no question where his heart still lies. Basking in thaw, like few others. A⸺ sees me across hall and grins, impossible to resist that. Walk over to him and put out hand, carefully turning back on B⸺ and C⸺. Have drink together; private contribution to thaw. Nothing to talk about, of course, but no real need to talk. Enough to remember."

The Four Power Conference of 1955 was more than a reminder; it was also an illustration of the growth problem I had already had to face a number of times in my life and realized I would doubtless have to face again. I had just spent two and a half years forgetting the potentialities of "Education, Science, and Culture for International Understanding," and relearning the need for democratic cohesion in confronting the permanent "Threat to Our Civilization from Monolithic World Communism." One of the chief difficulties in maintaining the cohesion of the free world, I had been taught, was the tendency exhibited by some of its well-meaning but fuzzy-minded citizens to indulge in public daydreaming about peace on earth. President Eisenhower, the cold war experts felt, had come dangerously close to such fuzziness in Geneva.

Immediately after the close of the conference, however, when

479

I undertook to find out exactly how the cold war experts of the Communist world were exploiting Ike's regrettable lapse for purposes of thought control and mental subversion, I made several disturbing discoveries. For one thing, the diversity of themes and stress in both the domestic and the foreign broadcasts of the different people's republics sounded strangely unmonolithic. "No doubt the psychological strategists in the Kremlin still sit around pushing buttons," I wrote in a magazine article that never saw the light of day (by the time it reached the United States, the cold war seemed as cold as ever and the editors who read my manuscript felt, reasonably enough in the circumstances, that it was already outdated), "but crossed wires and blown fuses are increasingly frequent along the outer fringes of the one monolithic Soviet empire." Even in the USSR itself, I found that radio and press coverage of the conference had been handled "as if the Communist public mind were being lowered through successive locks from some inland reservoir of propagandistic fantasy to the waterline of world reality." Analysis of the Soviet-orbit radio programs monitored in Munich suggested that the Communist censorship and propaganda authorities had been forced into a greater liberalization of the news than they had originally contemplated by the widespread appeal of President Eisenhower's homely platitudes about international goodwill. Their impact likewise appeared to be a major factor in the unmistakable disarray among the Kremlin's European vassals. In short, Ike's old-fashioned, prairie optimism, psychologically akin to the even fuzzier UNESCO variety I had put behind me, had turned out to be one of the West's most effective weapons of political warfare. This finding came as something of a shock.

Had I been more of a realist, after all, when I had been an apostle of woolly-minded internationalism than when I had been a hard-minded specialist of power politics? Or had the nature of political reality changed—and changed again—while I was trying to apprehend it?

I could not say. What was self-evident was that at the age of forty-eight, for perhaps the fifth or sixth time in my adult life, I was faced—or at least threatened—with the need for once again drastically revising the ideological and emotional framework within which I had been operating as a reporter and as a human being. It was by no means for the last time.

Scraps From a Reporter's Scrapbook–Vienna

If he is still alive, Istvan B——, a 22-year-old expectant poet and member of the University Students' Committee that triggered the Budapest uprising, no doubt continues to take a pride in his country's tragically glorious "October Revolution" that neither the subsequent repression nor any future ordeal is ever likely to erase. When I talked with him, however, during a trip into Hungary on the eve of the brutal Soviet reoccupation, he had some refreshingly unorthodox views about the Hungarian freedom movement, and his own role in it.

"The first day of revolution I wrote an ode to freedom and published it in our underground newspaper," Istvan, a slim, eager, dark-eyed young intellectual of upper-middle-class background, told me as we jolted across the plains of western Hungary in a commandeered Budapest autobus with a delegation of his revolutionary comrades. "Later, I discovered all the poets in the other revolutionary groups were doing the same thing and every one of these poems was as bad as mine. This confirms my theory that revolution is the historic seedbed of dilettante poetry, and I hope that things settle down again before I am spoiled for good."

Istvan's worry was doubtless a rare one, even among Hungarian poets, and the little group of idealistic student revolutionaries to which he belongs, or belonged, was always a minority element in the national freedom movement. But judging from the carefree yet strangely uplifting day I spent in their company, unaware of the Soviet steel trap poised to spring shut upon us, Istvan and his com-

rades had contributed to the movement a kind of clear-headed though romantic moral enthusiasm which was one of the catalytic influences of the revolution. When I joined up with them they were trying to spread an appeal for moderation and unity among the nationalist extremists in western Hungary that the Soviet aggression was to render obsolete within a few hours. Even today the philosophic outlook upon which the group's appeal was based strikes me as having a valid and direct bearing upon the problem of eventually restoring democracy, not only in Hungary, but everywhere between the Elbe and the Urals. This bearing seemed apparent from my first encounter with Istvan in the drab little industrial town of Gyor (Raab), about halfway between Budapest and the Hungarian border, which had been one of the earliest of the revolutionary capitals in the provinces and was soon to be one of the most heroic centers of the Hungarian resistance.

In the course of a pulse-taking stroll through the town with another American reporter we had been waylaid in front of the implausibly grandiose city hall, where the local revolutionary council was sitting, by a large, heavy-jowled citizen in a gray wool cap who proudly proclaimed that he had been born in Gary, Indiana, and on the strength of that proceeded to scold American foreign policy with almost demential violence. As I was trying to escape from this sinister bore—not an easy thing because of the crowd gathered to gape at the fascinating Westerners—a young voice addressed me in cultured English.

"It's true as this man says that all Hungarians feel you owe us military aid, if we have need of it," the voice said, "but some of us believe that political and moral pressures will prove much more effective against the Russians than force."

I turned and saw Istvan, wearing a winter coat of Byronic cut that hung almost to his heels, a luxury few Hungarians can afford, with his left hand swathed in bloody gauze (he admitted to me later that his hand had slipped while he was trying to cut a loaf of bread in the bus).

482

"Was that true in Budapest?" I asked him.

"In a way, yes," he answered, "but it's a long and complicated story."

A few minutes later I was aboard the bus—piloted by a bewildered but philosophical employee of the Budapest transit company in the uniform of his calling—as the guest of Istvan and his friends, a half-dozen young men and women from the Budapest committee, plus a middle-aged woman doctor who had joined them in the vague belief that she might be able to pick up some medical supplies somewhere for the wounded.

"Most of us in the Revolutionary Committee of University Students are what you might call political agnostics," Istvan explained. "We believe in national independence and in the basic democratic freedoms. We think Imre Nagy, even though he is a Communist, has the best chance of keeping the country from falling to pieces and of negotiating successfully with the Russians for the withdrawal of their troops."

To spread this message of sanity as widely as possible Istvan proposed to visit all the important towns and villages between Gyor and the Austrian border, distributing his committee's newspaper and assorted leaflets and haranguing the local revolutionaries in the chief centers. Then, if the bus was allowed to cross the border, he hoped to continue to Vienna, making contact with Austrian students and returning the next day with a load of medical supplies.

"We'll spend the evening at Maxim's in Vienna," said Istvan with the exuberance of youth and the traditional Hungarian zest for leavening high thinking with high living, "and you can come back to Budapest with us, too, tomorrow if that strikes you as a good program."

(It struck me as a wonderful program but it was destined to remain tragically incomplete, for Istvan's group was not allowed to cross the Austrian frontier and a few hours after I reluctantly said goodby to them Soviet armored forces in a sudden pounce sealed off the border and threw up a roadblock between it and Gyor.)

All morning and most of the afternoon we rolled across the flat Hungarian countryside, curiously reminiscent of the American Midwest with its sluggish winding creeks and its fields of neatly shocked corn where golden pumpkins ripened on the vine. In the smaller villages with their flocks of cackling geese, their rutted, muddy lanes, and their thatched cottages shaped by the immemorial peasant culture of Eastern Europe, the bus would merely slow down while the girls scattered leaflets out of the open windows to be-mused rural militiamen of the revolution in their high leather boots and picturesque quilted or sheepskin jackets. In the larger villages and towns we would stop in the market square and hand out news-papers to the eager crowds that instantly surrounded us—soldiers of the regular army with their Soviet-style shoulderboards and their peaked Red Army caps with the stars replaced by red-white-green cocards with the traditional Kossuth crest; young workers and schoolboys in patched, threadbare civilian clothes, with tricolor armbands of the volunteer militia and Russian-style tommy guns carelessly slung over their shoulders; and arrogant-looking ex-officers in riding pants and leather jackets.

Sometimes Istvan or one of his comrades would talk to the crowd from the steps of the bus. On other occasions he invited the local revolutionary leaders to come aboard, the girls would spread slabs of dark bread with thick layers of butter and sausage paste from a relief parcel and pass them around, and a passionate discussion would get under way. From time to time Istvan would translate a bit of it for me or comment on the political attitudes of his guests.

"They're all very conservative, very clerical up here," he ex-plained. "Cardinal Mindszenty is their hero. But that doesn't matter —they are honest democrats in their way and wonderful, brave fighters. I only wish they had a more realistic idea of what they are up against."

Though he did not say so, Istvan made it clear that he and his friends would have been reluctant to start a putsch if they had known that was what they were doing. Few Hungarians, outside of the secret police and the high echelons of the Party, had less

484

reason to risk their lives in a revolution than students of Istvan's type. Though not himself a Communist—"You can't be a good Communist and a good poet"—he belonged to one of the pampered social groups of the regime.

At one time Istvan—or the teachers who had shaped his political thinking in high school and the university—had evidently believed that the ultimate goals of communism were close to their own humanitarian ideal. The judicial murder of Rajk, and even more the arrest of Imre Nagy, had convinced them that the moral pretensions of Stalinist communism were a monstrous fraud. Long before the recent Moscow ultimatum to Poland they had somehow come to the conclusion that post-Stalinist Soviet communism was also "a big lie."

"It was the workers who started the actual armed insurrection," he said. "They called us cowards and opportunists because we hesitated at first before joining them on the barricades. But it was our moral duty to reflect on whether we really had the right to use violence. As educated men we must be sure that we are guided by reason and not just emotion. When we satisfied ourselves that reason and justice were on the side of the revolution we got arms and joined up with the workers. It was magnificent, how they fought, but I think we students did all right too."

Istvan knows a little Russian and with the help of two friends who knew a little more they hastily printed a few hundred leaflets in Russian. Then during a lull in the fighting the three of them walked among the Soviet troops handing out their leaflets.

"The common soldiers just said, 'Nitchevo,' and motioned us to get moving," Istvan continued. "But many of the Soviet officers were very upset and tried to apologize for what they were doing saying they had been misled by reports about fascist counter-revolutionaries and so on. These fellows have a conscience. That's what you people in the West fail to understand. The Soviet conscience isn't the same as the Christian conscience or the democratic conscience. It's a Marxist conscience. But that makes it all the worse for them when they come up against something like the

Budapest uprising. It isn't only that they have to shoot down un-armed women and children. They have to fire into the masses. They have to shoot down the revolution. They have to stand against history. That breaks their spirit."

(REQUIEM FOR A YOUNG REVOLUTIONARY,

The Reporter, NOVEMBER 15, 1956)

The 1956 revolution in Hungary was the tragic denouement of the general crisis of decolonization that developed throughout the Soviet *imperium* after Stalin's death. It was likewise one of the most authentically, if irresponsibly, romantic episodes of our times; in the West, at least, it has generated a rich mythology. Traces—in fact, rather more than traces, I fear—of romanticism are evident not only in the substance of my conversation with the youthful poet and political commissar Istvan B——, but in the way I reported it.

Even today, rereading my copy some twelve years later, I am perhaps less contrite than I should be at this apparent example of middle-aged tough-mindedness surrendering to the contagious idealism of youth. The influence of mythologized ancestors like my Rebel grandfather does not cease merely because one has become a grandfather oneself. That picturesque revolutionary barnstorming with the students across the Hungarian plain, which was also a kind of cruise by time machine to the lost continents of democratic legend—the February Revolution in Russia, the victory of the Popular Front in France, the birth of the Republic in Spain, the Springtime of Peoples throughout Europe in 1848—was a further extenuating circumstance in my lapse; few adventures of my professional career, including those of my own youth, have left such a lasting freshness in my mind.

It is true that the Hungarian tragedy, like all human tragedies, had a core of self-deception and even of self-betrayal. As I dis-

486

covered during my bus trek, the nationalists, democrats, and left-wing idealists of diverse, often conflicting, allegiance who formed its cast had a common passion, but scarcely a common cause. They were not merely lacking in political and military realism; they were often willfully blind to the objective facts, as well as to their own contradictions. They lived in the intoxication of the moment, as romantics usually do, with no thought for those who would later have to clean up the mess, especially when it was the mess of their own dead bodies.

In reporting the revolution, I can see that I tended to idealize the failings of the revolutionaries almost as much as their virtues. Though not, perhaps, to quite the same extreme degree, I shared their reluctance to face the grim realities of the situation. I knew that in the strictly military sense the insurrection was doomed the moment the Kremlin opted for repression, but I believed that the underground resistance of the whole Hungarian nation would ulti-mately force its oppressors to withdraw. I underestimated both the ruthless tenacity of the Soviet oligarchs and the psychological vulnerability of romantics who have let their hopes run away with them. My errors of appreciation were by no means unique; I doubt whether there were many observers on either side of the Iron Cur-tain whose minds during those dramatic weeks were not, like mine, a battlefield where myth and reality continually clashed. The ex-ceptional directness and violence of the clash helped to make the Hungarian revolution a psychological turning point in the postwar history of my generation, and the political ambiguities of its out-come further contributed to upsetting existing ideological constel-lations. Pessimists and optimists alike were forced to reexamine a number of their basic premises.

The impact of the revolution on East-West—and particularly on Soviet-U.S.—relations was equally complex. The brutality and cynicism of the Soviet repression in Hungary opened the eyes of many overidealistic Western liberals to the element of wishful thinking in the hopes for bona fide cooperation between Moscow and Washington that they had founded on the Summit Conference of 1955. On the other hand, the Soviet leaders in crushing the insurrection demonstrated that if they were brutes, they were rational ones, capable of restraint as well as ruthlessness. Their restraint was specially noticeable whenever United States interests were in any way involved (as for example when Cardinal Mindszenty, one of the most irresponsible anti-Communist agitators in Hungary, took refuge in the United States Embassy). Washington reciprocated, not only by refusing military assistance to the Hungarian rebels—or for that matter succor of any kind—but by confining its denunciations of Communist "aggression" or "tyranny" to such a rarefied moral plane that there was little political sting in them. Indirectly, at least, the blood shed by the Hungarian freedom fighters thus helped the two world empires discover that they had more in common than either of them had previously realized; and so were laid or extended the foundations of the unedifying, precarious, but sometimes useful Soviet-American connivance in world affairs that has come to be known as coexistence.

I was naturally indignant at what I regarded as another of Mr. Dulles's betrayals, but my contact with the Hungarian Revolution, brief and peripheral as it had been, had opened my eyes to certain implications of the anti-Communist liberation myth I had earlier preferred to overlook. Like a number of other Western anti-Communists, I was eventually forced to admit to myself that victory without ruins had ceased to be a reasonable goal, if it had ever been one. The combination of military containment and political, economic, and moral pressures in a grand strategy of pacific liberation that I had formerly dreamed of would not suffice, I now saw, to "roll back communism"—Mr. Dulles's phrase—in Europe. Such a strategy could only accumulate new ruins. Though I did not yet fully realize it, by the end of 1956 the balance of terror had already superseded containment.

It took me some time, of course, to digest the harsh lessons of the Hungarian Revolution. It took some time for nearly everyone, including the rulers of the Soviet empire; indeed, I suspect it was precisely in their minds that there took place the most violent clash between myth and reality.

On the whole, despite the romantic distortions of perspective evident in some of my reporting on Hungary—perhaps even because of them—I believe that in viewing the Hungarian Revolution through the eyes of the young intellectuals I met in Gyor I caught a glimpse of its most essential reality, one that illuminates the whole modern paradox of hope. The Hungarian left-wing revolutionaries were naïve, of course, to imagine that the "Marxist conscience" of the Red Army—or of the Soviet bureaucracy in general—could produce the kind of immediate strategic effect that the Christian conscience has seldom, if ever, produced in Western history. They were profoundly right, however, to stress the survival of a Western moral tradition, not only among the nominally Marxist elites of the Russian satellites in Central or Eastern Europe, but in those of the master race itself, as one of the key elements in the situation that made their struggle meaningful for the future. As we have seen more recently, the existence of a conscience, Marxist or other, in the men who control and administer the huge Soviet power machine is no guarantee that it will never be put to criminal use, but it is an assurance that they will suffer, and therefore sometimes learn, from their crimes and self-betrayals—as they undoubtedly did in Hungary.

As we have suffered, and sometimes learned, from our own crimes and self-betrayals.

27

A Certain Note of Optimism

*C*onstantine, Algeria—Sundown transforms the lonely Carrère farm on the high, rolling plains some forty miles southwest of here into the unhappy North African version of a pioneer stockade.

To the men and women of the Carrère family who, arms in hand, continue to work the 3000 acres of wheat and pasture land wrested by their grandfather from the wilderness, the nightly ritual of barricading themselves to stand off a possible fellagha attack implies more than a heightening of the danger with which they have lived all day. It has a specially tragic significance that illustrates the complex human reality underlying the political catchwords on both sides in the Algerian conflict.

A glimpse of this recurrent tragedy was provided during an overnight visit to the farm. Henri Carrère checked out the Moslem farmhands after they had finished putting up the livestock and the valuable machinery in the heavy stone sheds. His left hand casually hooked into his belt a few inches from the butt of the .45 Colt automatic which is always tucked into his blue shorts, Carrère, a short, dark, wiry bachelor of fifty, who was born on the farm, gravely shook hands with each of his laborers and exchanged a few friendly words in Arabic with them.

"We've been warned not to let any Moslems get so close," he remarked. "But I have been shaking hands with these men all *my*

*life and I'm not going to stop now. It's bad enough to have to let
them see you are wearing a gun while you do it."*

The last Moslem to leave was the foreman, a dignified patriarch
with sad, gentle eyes.

"This is Noui," Carrère said, while the foreman touched his finger-
tips to his lips in the old, ceremonious style and then shook hands.
"We used to play together when we were children. Officially, he's
a homicidal lunatic, but he's the only one I trust completely."

As the heavy iron gates, surmounted with barbed wire, that convert the rectangle of farm buildings into a fairly efficient block-
house were slammed shut, Henri told Noui's story. Until a few
months ago the Carrères had had as their nearest neighbor a pious
old Moslem farmer who was a close friend of Henri's late father.
Possibly for that reason, or perhaps because he had refused a contribution to the war chest of the Nationalist Liberation Front, the
old Moslem had been found one morning outside his house with his
throat cut.

Noui had discovered the body and the shock had driven him
insane for a while. In his madness he had killed one of the other
farmhands. He had recovered his senses in prison and the authorities
had finally paroled him to the Carrère family.

"I'm not sure that even Noui would warn us if he heard the
fellagha were going to attack," Henri said. "But he would arrange
to die with us. As for the others, I don't think any of them would
willingly do us harm. My father was very kind to them. And we've
always been careful never to hurt their self-respect. But if the rebels
come and threaten to cut their children's throats unless they help
ambush us, what can they do?"

Three soldiers, armed with Sten guns, have been assigned to guard
the Carrère farm. At night they take turns keeping watch from an
armored tower on the roof of the farmhouse while the family sleeps.
The family consists of Henri, his elder brother Charles, Charles's
wife, and their three-month-old son. The three men are always
armed—Christian has been issued a Sten gun—and the two women
have revolvers handy as they do their housework.

491

The Carrères are the last Europeans in the region to remain on their farms. Most of the European farms are still worked, but the owners sleep at night in the nearest village.

Asked if they had ever thought of selling out, Henri replied:

"My grandfather planted those poplar trees you saw down by the creek. And they're the first trees ever grown on this plain. It wouldn't be easy to leave a place where we have such roots.

"But it's not the danger that you mind the most," Henri explained. "It's seeing a wall of hate and suspicion grow up between you and the people you've always looked on as friends. It's not being able to trust men you've worked with all your life."

(WASHINGTON *Post* AND *Times-Herald*
AUGUST 31, 1957)

A number of times in the years since I began work on this book I have had occasion—have in fact sought the occasion—to revisit the places associated with what I looked back on as some particularly dramatic, or at least decisive, experience. More often than not, these sentimental pilgrimages, insofar as they were that, have proved relatively fruitful, less, I suspect, because they have helped me to recall or relieve the past than because the contrasts or discrepancies between successive images of the same reality have introduced a truer perspective into my view of it.

The formula does not always work, however. For a considerable while my return to India and Southeast Asia in the fall of 1965, almost twenty years since my first visit, was one of the failures, and it puzzled me. As I remembered them, the two and a half years of my wartime service in Asia counted among the fullest of my adult life in terms of intellectual, and what I suppose one can call spiritual, development. It seemed strange, therefore, that I could detect in myself so little response to the physical and social landscape I had once found so moving and enriching to the mind.

My emotional reaction to India, for long the sovereign mistress of my imagination, baffled me particularly. There was no pathos in our reunion, hardly any constraint. Her face was much as I remembered it, certainly not ravaged, perhaps in some respects embellished. As far as I was aware there was no bitterness or sense of disenchantment in my feelings—at worst a mild and not wholly unexpected disappointment that the promise of twenty years ago had been so unevenly fulfilled—but there was no magic either, and hence no exorcism.

We were both preoccupied, of course, India with her war against Pakistan, even after it was nominally ended by a sporadically observed cease-fire under UN supervision, and I with reporting on the conflict or its aftermath for the magazine that was paying the expenses of my trip. I was not specially shocked by the somewhat brassy new Indian nationalism with militaristic overtones that appeared for the moment to have engulfed all but a surviving handful of Gandhian idealists—after all, my own views about war and peace and nonviolence as a tenable political philosophy had hardened considerably since the evening in Calcutta two decades earlier when I had sat cross-legged in the dust at one of Gandhi's prayer meetings and felt the pull of his gentle sorcery. What I did find a bit trying, though I knew it was inevitable, was that none of the Indians I met seemed able to talk of anything except the Pakistan affair in its various ramifications—especially the ramifications that concerned the fiercely-resented American position in regard to it—and the fact that I was not often in a position myself to talk about much else only made things worse.

Still, there were occasional quiet moments between assignments when I could forget that I was a reporter covering a confused politico-military dispute in a strategic hinterland of Asia, and I attempted to make the best use of them. During the time I spent in New Delhi, where I had been stationed for some months during the war—the other one, my war—and where I had first fallen under the spell of India, I conscientiously revisited whenever I could those scenes of my earlier avatar that I thought most likely to awaken

493

some resonance of their old effect. At first it seemed to no avail. I could find no magic mango (of course, it was not the mango season), no exotic equivalent of the classic Proustian madeleine to stir the dormant centers of remembrance. The vast web of participations, human and biological, that a humble army mosquito net had once cast over my mind as I lay in my tent listening to the scavenging chanty of the jackals—an unlovely Indian night sound I had come to love because it was so expressive of night and of India—could not be rewoven: There was no net in my air-conditioned hotel room—the mosquitoes in New Delhi, or at any rate the anopheles, having been too thoroughly decolonized—and the jackals, now considered a bit too native for a cosmopolitan Asian capital, had been banished, save for rare and fleeting incursions, to the new suburbs or to the still more distant outskirts of the Old City. Time remained lost.

A trip by car across the Punjab to the uneasy cease-fire line and over the mountain passes to the troubled vale of Kashmir brought back to me in some measure the hypnotic charm of the Indian countryside and the timeless poetry of the Indian highroad, as I had felt them before, but this was a merely touristic experience that did not much further my deeper quest. In the end it was a petty, typically Indian imbroglio—typical, that is, of a certain Western cultural predicament in India—that, as I might have expected, reopened my mind to the essential India it had known in my earlier existence.

I had a Sunday morning free of appointments or deadlines, and the idea came to me to employ it visiting the principal sites and monuments around Delhi associated with the Great Mutiny, about which I had recently been reading. I was already familiar with some of them—the Red Fort, where the last of the Moghuls, terrorized by his own officers, had proclaimed his senile revolt against British rule; the Kashmir Gate, through which a small punitive force had eventually stormed its way back into the city in one of the bravura episodes of the confused, ghastly upheaval—but I had never been up on the ridge overlooking Old Delhi from the northwest where the British had been encamped during the siege, and from which

Nicholson had launched his final assault. I was particularly curious to see the monument, described in my guidebook as lofty and impressive, that the victors had erected nearby in memory of their fallen comrades, of whom Nicholson himself was the most illustrious.

The expedition was uneventful enough up to the Kashimir Gate. What occurred from then on is best perhaps related in the account I jotted down in my diary on my return to the hotel a few hours later:

Stopped car near Kashmir Gate and walked over to interrogate stones, getting usual dusty answer. Told driver to go on through and continue to Mutiny Memorial. Surprised by his blank look: Have often driven around city with him before and usually found him fairly quick. Very Westernized, deturbanned young Sikh in blue jeans and open collar blue shirt; seems to understand every second or third word in English and apparently literate. Tried Hindi name for Memorial: Jit Garh. Same blank. Explained there was battle long ago with British and high tower built to mark battlefield. Blank look darkened; driver obviously bewildered and seemed to feel conversation somehow taking an indelicate turn. Told him never mind, just drive on through the Gate toward the Ridge. It was up there somewhere near Delhi University and we would probably see it, or else we could stop and ask. Chauffeur remained doubtful, kept muttering to himself something that sounded like "mitiny malament" and seemed very uneasy.

Familiar contrasts: smart-looking young Indians in white duck trousers playing cricket in park on our right despite air-raid trenches slashed in it; just across road on left incredible jumble of squatter hovels and tents. Worse than any Algerian bidonville. Refugees from 1947 that got overlooked somehow, I suppose. Reached top of Ridge but no tower visible, so started asking. Reaction generally same as driver's: bafflement mingled with vague disquiet. After pro-

longed introspection several Indians we stopped finally gave hesitant, confused directions, as if guiding us to some dimly remembered scene of their childhood, but obviously hadn't all grown up together, and their memories wildly divergent. Some suggestions appeared to have certain logic behind them: Thus after driving for some miles actually did find tower—several towers in fact, transmitters for All-India Radio. Another informant guided us to one bona fide English monument but it turned out to be Coronation Pillar, an unimpressive stone obelisk on a cracked cement base in middle of emptiness, commemorating great, greatly forgotten durbar organized by Curzon on occasion Edward VII's coronation. Thought we surely must be approaching goal now but next consultant sent us off on eccentric new tangent toward distant objective which turned out incomprehensibly to be Harijan's (Untouchable's) Institute. One self-important-looking, obviously Westernized and bureaucratic Indian near University grounds, undoubtedly Congress supporter who had done well, spoke English. Looked at me queerly when I explained I was trying to find Mutiny Memorial and said, "Why do you want to go there?" Seemed to suspect some link with Pakistan. Placated him ultimately, and he gave me clear, precise directions in English which he repeated to driver in Hindi. Directions turned out to be totally misleading, of course. Something somnambulistic about our progress, blundering but inexorable, across Indian Sundaymorningside, and eventually quite by accident did stumble on Memorial.

Monument much as expected: Tallish red sandstone spire in Victorian Moghul. Effect at once dingy and pompous, with slight necrophilous taint. Plunging view of Delhi slums and industrial suburbs. Ridge itself kind of semi-urban wasteland gradually returning to jungle, and weedy air of neglect about whole site as if memorial erected on some abandoned trash heap of empire. More than simple bad taste revealed: Triumph of second-rate and tacky in nineteenth-century Anglo-Indian society that V. S. Naipaul rightly stresses in his book.* Men who fell here deserved something

* *An Area of Darkness* by V. S. Naipaul, André Deutsch 1964.

*better, if more modest, than this forlorn, pretentious squalor, how-
ever dubious their combat seems to contemporary mind, however
anachronistic their whiskery heroism. Visitors understandably rare.
Dejected caretaker who finally crawled off* charpoy *on which he
had been sleeping in mausoleum-like chamber at base of monument
stared at me with dull resentment, like the old white cobra guarding
rajah's treasure in Kipling's* Jungle Book, *grudgingly pocketed coins
I gave him. Naturally Indians not interested in memorial—have not
even bothered to set off charge of plastic under it despite present
new wave of Anglophobia, as North African nationalists did with
similar monuments of French colonialism. Perhaps vaguely clerical
aspect makes them accept it as kind of shrine, one more among
thousands that litter Indian countryside, only little more alien than
the others. British on their side seem equally indifferent. Closed
chapter, and let dead past bury its dead. No doubt Mutiny as political phenomenon left significant mark on both Indian and British
history, but what was moment of high tragic drama in life of both
peoples now so dwindled in memory for both that cannot even be
exploited as tourist attraction. Not through this lamentable shaft, at
any rate; it commemorates less real drama of Mutiny or its denouement than mythology of triumphant self-righteousness in minds of
victors, which their descendants have long since repudiated. In this
sense the Memorial, like Coronation Pillar, is merely sham in stone-
work, celebrating kind of hole in history, renowned nonevent.*

*Walked for long time in reverberating heat slowly around and
around foot of nonmemorial with its sad-soaring spire, color of old
dried blood, meditating on great undramas and nonevents of past:
man's, my own. Midday glare like film of fine white dust on roof-
tops of city and surrounding waste. Lone vulture wheeling in empty
sky—his fellows still circling hopefully over cease-fire line no doubt
—and own thoughts similarly wheeling in emptiness. Reflected India
now as ever mother of shams and phantasms, but pitiless to them as
to all her other children, nurturing with absence. Only purest truth
and grossest delusions survive: how true. Candid self-deception, half-*

false hope, padded idealism ultimately wither in her dust. Denial of any durable intellectual comfort India's supreme hospitality to stranger whether pilgrim or invader.

A few days later, when I reread my notes, I was puzzled to account for the sense of exaltation that had evidently inspired them. I felt as one does when one wakes in the morning remembering that some great secret has been revealed in sleep but unable to recollect what the secret was. Something had undoubtedly come, or happened, to me at the foot of the Mutiny Memorial. But what? I had recovered something lost in my relationship with India, and perhaps acquired something new in my attitude toward life. But again, what? Why, for that matter, had the no doubt aggressive—but prosaically aggressive—mediocrity of the monument itself made such an impression on me?

My notes must offer some clue, I thought, but none was immediately apparent. From the objective viewpoint, several statements in them seem questionable. Was India really so catalytic of self-knowledge, so subversive of intellectual comfort? Not to judge from the political and social attitudes of the Indians themselves, especially those attitudes related to the conflict with Pakistan over the Kashmir question. Indeed, the thought had struck me more than once during my present trip that the age-old Indian quest for transcendental truth, for self-knowledge on the metaphysical plane, rendered them less self-critical in purely mundane affairs than many peoples with a less lofty spiritual tradition. The Indian patterns of self-deception reminded me at times of certain Western psychoanalysts and social scientists who in their preoccupation with the unconscious depths of the individual or collective mind are inclined to neglect the more superficial and relatively rational motivations that often underlie the apparent irrationality of human behavior.

If India had not helped the Indians to know themselves—in the human sense—had it, as my log implied, helped the British? The evidence was to say the least contradictory. British rule in India, from the early nineteenth century to the very end, had been marked by self-complacency, self-righteousness—or self-pity—and other forms of self-deception; the myth of the White Man's Burden was doubtless the supreme example. The Mutiny Memorial itself was a superb architectual expression of the most delusive and detestable elements, or a great many of them, in nineteenth-century British colonialism; it was almost impossible to imagine twentieth-century Englishmen perpetrating a comparable atrocity in stone today, even if they still held India; indeed, it was not easy to believe that their grandfathers had been capable of it, barely more than a century ago.

Ah, there was my clue; there was the reason, or one of them, why a sorry piece of Victorian bad taste had reopened a locked chamber of my heart to the Indian sky, the Indian earth, the Indian past that its very presence disparaged. The monument, once it was viewed in the right perspective, bore almost dramatic witness to the ultimate impermanence of illusion and to the relative shallowness of human self-concealments. Its own meretricious geometry demonstrated with Euclidian rigor that when the only alternative to truth is the grossest delusion, men will generally choose the truth. The numerous exceptions in Indian history merely showed that the choice was more tragic in India than elsewhere because the truth was likely to be more painful.

The British decision after the war to give India her independence had seemed so inescapable that its full significance as a paradigm of hope had not been appreciated at the time, even by those who like myself had some awareness of its more tragic implications. From my wartime exposure to the last phase of British colonialism in India, I would have expected not only a far slower and more grudging retreat from the rest of Asia and from Africa than actually took place, but a lingering, nostalgic twilight of empire in the British collective mind, bemusing it for half a century. Instead there had been one last, brief, delusive spasm—Suez—and then the whole anti-world of colonialist myth had disintegrated, leaving hardly a trace.

Even the Englishmen who had stayed on in India seemed so unlike the almost caricatural sahibs I had encountered there twenty years earlier that it was hard to realize they belonged to the same race— and were sometimes, indeed, the same men.

French colonialism had died harder, but even more quickly, once decolonization started. I had witnessed its death throes in Algeria. General de Gaulle's decision to accept Algerian independence had been in every sense more tragic than the British withdrawal from India. Strategically, it had been freer, less inescapable. From the military viewpoint, the French presence in Algeria could have been maintained almost indefinitely: It would merely have necessitated turning France permanently into a garrison state. De Gaulle had preferred to let nearly 1,000,000 *colons* and their native retainers be turned into refugees. The decision had almost cost De Gaulle his own life and had brought France for a few weeks to the brink of civil war. Yet seven years of not very costly war and three years of not particularly glorious peace in Algeria had sufficed, from the viewpoint of French public opinion at large, to close the book on 130 years of *présence française*.

What was even more encouraging in the Algerian example was the relatively inconsiderable heritage of racial hate left by one of the cruelest revolutionary struggles in modern history. If the majority of the French colonists in Algeria had permanently abandoned their homes after independence it had not been in most cases because their lives were in jeopardy, but because an inexperienced, politically immature Algerian government, misled by the currently fashionable catchwords of bush socialism, had wrecked the young nation's economy. That had been unfortunate, both for France and for Algeria, but it was a remarkably mild penalty to be exacted by history after seven years of massacre and torture, of terrorism and counter-terrorism.

When I had arrived in Algiers in 1962 on the eve of independence, bands of wildly excited Moslem youths, some of them brandishing revolvers, were roaming the streets in the predominantly European heart of the city to celebrate their triumph, but not a single *colon*,

as far as I could discover, was molested. Yet up to a few days earlier, the Secret Army Organization, a counter-terrorist movement
of die-hard settlers and mutinous army officers, had been systematically murdering Moslems suspected of Nationalist sympathies, and
blowing up public services or edifices to cripple the new republic
before it was even born. I had contrived, under rather dramatic
circumstances, to interview one of the group's minor clandestine
leaders, and to judge from his ravings, he and his fellow conspirators
belonged in an institution for the criminally insane.

It had been Jacques Chevalier, the liberal ex-mayor of Algiers—he
had been removed from office after the French Army *putsch* of
May 13, 1958, on suspicion of excessive "softness" toward the
fellaghas—who had finally averted a general interracial massacre.
At the hourly risk of his life, and with little support from Paris, he
had acted as mediator in the underground armistice negotiations
between the less demented Secret Army chiefs—it turned out there
were some—and the agents of the future Algerian government. Incredible as it seemed, the negotiations had succeeded; the sabotage
and killings had abruptly ended, the top Secret Army leaders were
quietly slipping out of the country, and when I interviewed M.
Chevalier at his villa overlooking the city, a few days after independence, he was full of colorful, off-the-record anecdotes of repentant European gunmen or dynamiteros swearing to become loyal
citizens of the Moslem commonwealth if only they were allowed to
stay. (Some of them have, in fact, returned to Algeria on occasional
visits, for old times' sake, and they usually report having been
warmly welcomed by the Moslem population.) Thus, while Chevalier's dream of a reconciled biracial community in Algeria had
been disappointed, like so many liberal dreams, it could not be said
that his efforts to bring it into being had been all in vain.

Though a good part of my postwar professional career had been
concerned, one way or another, with the problems raised by the
anti-colonial revolution throughout the world, until my present
visit to India I had more often than not thought of it in terms of my
own frustrated, wartime dreams of human unity. From that angle

the revolution was as ambiguous as most other developments in contemporary history. It had undoubtedly achieved some real gains, but they had been at least compromised by the excesses it had generated. If some of the former imperial powers had resisted the revolutionary surge too long, others had yielded to it much too soon or too suddenly. A number of peoples that by even the most easygoing standards were not prepared for self-government had almost overnight been given their total independence. Artificial, make-believe nations with no plausible basis in either history or geography had been recognized as sovereign states, and as such admitted into the United Nations, thereby helping to transform what was already the caricature of a world parliament into a microcosmic world mob. An unequal justice and a superficial order had given place in all too many regions of the globe to revolver law or undissimulated anarchy.

When, however, one looked at the anti-colonial revolution from the viewpoint of the history of morals in the West over the last century or so—as my visit to the Mutiny Memorial had accidentally caused me to do—one had a more cheering impression. There had no doubt been times when colonialism had been a school of virtues as well as of greeds for the Western peoples. But its moral evolution had not kept pace with that of political and social attitudes at home, and to fill the growing gap the colonialists had been obliged to pile lie on lie, sham on sham. It was the weight of all this falsehood that had constituted the real White Man's Burden. And in laying it down the West had recovered its own freedom, the most precious of all freedoms—that of the mind.

The thought was not startlingly original—I had myself written something similar in 1946—but in the intervening years the false hopes and fashionable cant of anti-colonialism, along with the real tragedies of America's internal decolonization, had led me to forget what an immense liberation had taken place, and was continuing, under my very eyes. My return to India, and that timely visit to a trash heap of empire on the ridge above Old Delhi, had served as useful reminders.

That Western man had succeeded in freeing himself so rapidly from so immense a heritage of myth and self-deception demonstrated an undeniable capacity for psychological and moral growth. It authorized a reasonable hope that he might learn in time to outgrow other errors, other delusions, other self-betrayals and self-contradictions. And unless one remained at heart a secret colonialist, there was no reason to suppose that the peoples of Asia, Africa, and Latin America were incapable of similar growth. They might be presently wandering, much of the time, in the Egyptian night of such ancient superstitions as nationalism, militarism, imperialism (camouflaged as self-determination), and racism (disguised as anticolonialism), but so, only a generation ago, were many people in the West (and some still are). May history humor them, as it has us (oh slowly!), toward the light.

Fragments From a Traveler's Log

Impressions of Calcutta: How to convey its incredible squalor? Appalling decay since my last visit 20 years ago, and it was already City of Dreadful Night to me then. Business and tourist area of town which used to be relative island of Western decency—and complacency—surrounded by sprawling Asian slum, now has Bowery look. Buildings grimy, plaster and paint flaking everywhere. Streets full of holes, sidewalks with loose slabs, gutters deep in filth.

Huge crowds of dirty, disheveled, hopeless-looking men and women drifting through streets without apparent aim, like waves of scummy water washing against banks of slough. Sidestreets littered with motionless, bare-legged bodies lying against walls of buildings; no telling whether sleeping or dead and nobody seems to care, like in famine of '43 that shocked me so. Betel nut spittle staining bodies, clothes, walls, sidewalks, everything, like tubercular sputum and no doubt it often is.

Pestilential swarms of beggars, and much evidence of undernourishment, as to be expected in famine year (naturally disruption of
war with Paks and all those Punjab grainfields flattened by tanks
aren't going to help). Worst thing, though, expressions on faces;
saw nothing like it in Delhi or in towns or refugee camps behind
Punjab front. Number of wild, quite frightening looks: must be
psychotics wandering around loose in streets—where else would
they go, after all? Most faces less dramatic: just sullen, dejected,
peevish, smouldering with dull hate of selves and fellows. Occasionally, especially on women, expression of gentle but incurable melancholy . . .

(NOVEMBER 1965)

One of the most vivid memory-images that I brought back with
me from my trip to Asia was imprinted on my mind—indelibly, I
think—as I was flying over the Mekong Delta on my way home
from Vietnam, after six weeks covering the war there. Seated in a
Thai International Airlines Caravelle headed for Bangkok, I was
savoring its coolness and luxury, after the sweaty hustle of my departure from Saigon, when I glanced down on the brown-green
quiltwork of paddy fields and coconut groves spread far below, and
noticed a column of thick, black smoke rising from the ground a
few miles on our right.

I had seen the smoke from air strikes or artillery bombardments
often enough during my travels around Vietnam, but never such a
huge, towering, comminatory pillar as this. Except for the pillar's
size, and the great height to which it rose—it was a little flattened
at the top, with the faint hint of a budding mushroom form—there
was nothing remarkable or dramatic about the sight, but somehow it
created an almost supernatural impression. The base of the column,
I thought, must be somewhere near the area of the Delta where only
two days earlier I had watched a rather lively amphibious operation

from the deck of a river patrol vessel in the Mekong, but as far as I had been able to tell there had been no villages or hamlets nearby sizable enough to produce that volume of smoke. Perhaps the South Vietnamese Rangers whose action I had been following had discovered and set on fire an enemy supply dump. Whatever had caused the phenomenon, I knew that I would never forget it.

I had once watched an American air strike with phosphorus and napalm bombs from the forward-air-control plane that was marking their target, but even the bellowing, red inferno they produced seemed less awesome in retrospect than this implicit reminder of war and doom. One expects to witness hellish destruction from the cockpit of a military plane, or from an observation post on a battlefield, but I was now in a civilian craft—a theoretically neutral one at that—on a routine flight between two friendly Asian capitals.

To my fellow passengers in the TAI plane—well-dressed civilians, all of them, and mostly I think, European businessmen—it obviously was a routine flight. None of them, as far as I could see, even glanced up from their books or magazines. It wasn't their war.

"Indecent to be flying over other men's deaths and torment in such comfort and safety," I jotted in my notebook. "Use of technolgy to disavow Donne: Everyman his own air-conditioned island, equipped with TV, of course, just to keep in touch. Callous brutality of warrior somehow much less blasphemous."

It was not the presumed ideological neutrality or non-engagement of the Caravelle's passengers that shocked me. It was their indifference; that had nothing to do with whether they supported or opposed American policy in Vietnam, or what they thought about the rights or wrongs of the war. I was none too sure what I thought about them myself. I had come during my stay in Vietnam to develop some definite ideas about the dangerous contradictions in our strategic concept of graduated violence, and about the seeming inability of the American official mind, whether military or diplomatic, to grasp the principles of revolutionary warfare; I had reservations about the human implications of certain counter-insurgency techniques that we were practicing; but on the basic moral issue of our continued intervention in Vietnam, I was as divided in my mind as most other Americans at the time probably were.

"Thoughts keep coming back obsessively," I noted in my log of the flight, "to problem of Vietnam, its moral and practical significance. Seemingly no escape from war without losing our national soul. Yet viewed from air in civilian plane, going away from it, war seems hopelessly anachronistic, irrelevant to anything that really matters. Temptation to rise above all this futile, beastly mess, to wash one's hands clean of it."

But it wasn't only the mess of war, I reflected, that one was tempted to put out of one's mind, to wash one's hands of. It was the whole mess of Asia. It was Kashmir, it was Korea. Above all, it was Calcutta. Vietnam was the nightmare of today. Calcutta—all the Calcuttas in Asia, all the Calcuttas in the world: the city-ghettos and the ghetto-cities, the country-ghettos and the ghetto-countries —those were the nightmares of today and of tomorrow, too, and of the day after.

It was the ghetto-world of Asia and Africa and Latin America, not Russia or China, that constituted the supreme challenge to Western, and particularly American, civilization. Not so much, as I had once believed, because of the famished, embittered, inevitably barbarized hordes whose poverty menaced our plenty—though that was a possible danger, too—but because their incoercible problems defied our shallow, immature, self-indulgent optimisms and put too heavy demands upon our too-long-uncultivated national sense of tragedy.

The dire expert predictions of relatively imminent world famine might or might not be founded, but the challenge—not merely of underdevelopment, nor even of poverty but of civilization-erosion —would continue for years, and almost certainly grow more acute. Science and technology might or might not succeed soon enough in creating the superabundance needed to solve the problem; war and revolution were sure—if only locally and momentarily—to squander it. The undeveloped areas of the human mind—the mind of the industrially advanced peoples, no less than that of the back-ward ones—grievously handicapped all our efforts to relieve misery and to promote civilization throughout the undeveloped regions of the earth.

Here and there, it was true, promising results had already been realized; others—especially if we made a greater effort—could un-questionably be achieved. For at least the life span of my genera-tion, however, and probably for that of the next, we would have to face the abominable truth that there will remain in many parts of the world vast, atrocious, irreductible pockets of unrelievable hu-man suffering. Against these residual bastions of poverty and deg-radation, all our science, all our energies, all our generosity—even if fully mobilized—were likely to prove unavailing—for a longer period, at least, than we had so far disciplined our hopes to sustain.

The temptation would grow enormous to concentrate all our developmental or humanitarian efforts—such efforts as we were willing to make—in the areas where we could expect to see relative fast, easy, and strategically or commercially profitable results (pre-ferably, too, where the beneficiaries would thank us nicely for our trouble), and to by-pass the pockets of despair, containing any po-tential revolutionary threat from them with military barriers, quar-antining both our minds and bodies against their plagues. The temptation was understandable—I had felt it more than once my-self—but we must at all costs resist it. Not only must we multiply many times over our present shamefully inadequate commitment of material and intellectual resource to the world war against poverty —and thus against barbarism—but we must intensify our efforts on every front.

We needed to have priorities, of course, and we were entitled to some preferences, but we couldn't allow ourselves to exclude any area, or any people—not even those who at a given moment might oppose us arms in hand, or threaten to do so in the future. We must continue trying to save those who we know cannot be saved, and even those who hate us for trying to save them. We musn't be afraid to stain our well-polished shoes with the spittle and excrement of their unsalvageable slums; we shouldn't even dread too much to stain our hands with blood, for the only way we could be sure that we should never have to kill or be killed by those we want to aid was to have no contact with them. The wounds of battle are healable in time; the alienations of withdrawal are apt to be incurable.

Short of the criminal madness of nuclear war, isolating ourselves from the dangers, the woes, and the problems of the blighted regions of our planet—starting, of course, with those in our own countries—was the one error among all the errors that we had committed and would commit—we, the West in general and America in particular—for which no reparation was possible: the one crime for which there could be no forgiveness. If we were tempted into committing it we would automatically cease to be Western— and probably to be civilized.

For our civilization had felt itself from the first to have a universal mission, and without this sense of mission it would not have become what it is. Our dream of universal dominion had proven delusive. Our hopes of promoting universal fraternity had been found premature. It was all the more essential not to betray our original and fundamental heritage of universal compassion. If we remained true to it, our new servitudes could become, from our own viewpoints, a new fulfillment.

That was the real and deepest meaning of the smoke-symbol. It was token no less than threat: a pillar of fiery wrath by night, a pillar of beckoning hope by day.

Several years have passed since my return from my second visit to Asia, and if the apprehensions and revulsions that it provoked have not yet faded from my mind, neither has the vision of hopeful challenge that I finally brought home with me. The political tumults and tragedies that I have covered as a reporter or lived through as a simple citizen during these years, in France, in Canada and in the United States—especially the United States—have sharpened the sense of challenge, but have not dimmed the element of hope.

What I find most hopeful in the vast and apparently deepening crisis of the age is precisely that it is so deep and so universal. Underlying all the conflicts between and within nations that keep the world in turmoil there is unmistakably a growing, if still inadequately recognized, interdependence of predicament. All civilized societies, whether fully industrial or developing, suffer to some extent from the same tensions and the same disorders; all are periodically shaken by the same upheavals. All are haunted—though not yet to the same degree—by the same nightmares of planetary holocaust and generalized famine. All are faced, whether they know it or not, by the common problem of environmental spoilage.

For the first time in recorded human experience, it is not a particular civilization that is challenged, but all civilization. And the main challenge comes not from a rival civilization, nor even from any identifiable tribe or class of barbarians, but from the barbarizing effect of complex, world-wide social and technical malajustments. More and more, therefore, our common and permanent crisis tends to take on an ecological, rather than an ideological, character; increasingly its resolution calls for a cooperative struggle on the part of civilized men everywhere to restore a planetary balance that man's very progress has upset. The day we achieve an adequate response to this immense and multiple challenge will no doubt mark a kind of mutational leap upward in man's cultural evolution.

That day, of course, still lies some distance ahead. In all probability, we are destined for a number of years or decades to go on living a split-level existence divided between tribal loyalties and global aspirations, between increasingly suicidal rivalries and growingly fruitful brotherhoods. Indeed, there can be no certainty that the world crisis through which we are now passing will ever be satisfactorily resolved; it may be that all civilization is ultimately doomed to perish from this earth.

What we can be reasonably sure of is that only an unprecedented challenge of the kind we face has any chance at all of spurring the principal tribes of man to the unprecedented effort of detribalization and reintegration required to found a world civilization worthy of the name. Conversely, if every kind of challenge were eliminated from our lives even the fragmentary and superficial civilizations that we know today would no doubt wither away and we would all revert to the state of pastoral savagery that is in fact the ideal of our more gentle contemporary neo-barbarians. Both my personal experience and what I have witnessed of the history of my generation convinces me—as the virile philosophers from Heraclitus onward have taught—that humanity never grows without challenge, nor even without struggle and conflict, and rarely achieves any great progress without first passing through some great crisis.

That philosophy is not a restful one to believe in at any time, but it holds up better than most in a time of troubles. I have come to regard it as one of the twin pillars of hope—or at least bastions against despair—in which an adult mind can reasonably place its trust under present-day conditions.

The other mature fundament of hope that still holds firms in my mind after many others have buckled under the stresses of the age is harder to substantiate than the first one, but no less solidly implanted. Essentially, it is the conviction—or perhaps I should say the faith—that man's latent capacity for self-correction and growth is virtually unlimited, and therefore equal to any demands that history as evolution is likely to put upon it. Undeniably there are elements of mystique in such a view, though it is not basically irrational. I cannot affirm that anything I have recorded here directly corroborates it.

As the reader has no doubt remarked, one of this book's central themes has been the gradual slowing down of the pendulum of illusion—swinging at first between extremes of unrealistic hope and unjustified despair—to a sane, consistent, and I like to think mature, arc of open-minded skepticism. This skepticism, however, concerns only the works and contrivances of man, not the mind or spirit that contrived them.

My confidence in the schemes for human betterment that I have seen my generation put forward tends with age to grow increasingly conditional and limited; my faith in man's potential for self-betterment grows steadily stronger and more absolute. That is why—paradoxical though it sounds—after forty odd years as a watcher of men in an age of crisis I believe more than ever that humanity and human civilization on this planet have the capacity to outgrow the crises that their own growth periodically generates, and will therefore keep on growing.

INDEX

513